Hollow Land

A.R.Barron '20

Hollow Land

Israel's Architecture of Occupation

New Edition

EYAL WEIZMAN

VERSO

London • New York

This paperback edition first published by Verso 2017
First published by Verso 2007
© Eyal Weizman 2007, 2012, 2017

1 3 5 7 9 10 8 6 4 2

Verso
UK: 6 Meard Street, London W1F 0EG
US: 20 Jay Street, Suite 1010, Brooklyn, NY 11201
versobooks.com

Verso is the imprint of New Left Books

ISBN-13: 978-1-78663-448-1
ISBN-13: 978-1-78168-436-8 (UK EBK)
ISBN-13: 978-1-84467-915-7 (US EBK)

British Library Cataloguing in Publication Data
A catalogue record for this book is available from the British Library

Library of Congress Cataloging-in-Publication Data
A catalog record for this book is available from the Library of Congress

Typeset in Garamond by Hewer Text UK Ltd, Edinburgh, Scotland
Printed in the UK by CPI Colour

'Cujus est solum, ejus est usque ad coelum et ad inferos'
(Whoever owns the ground, it is his from the depth of the earth to the height of the sky)

Contents

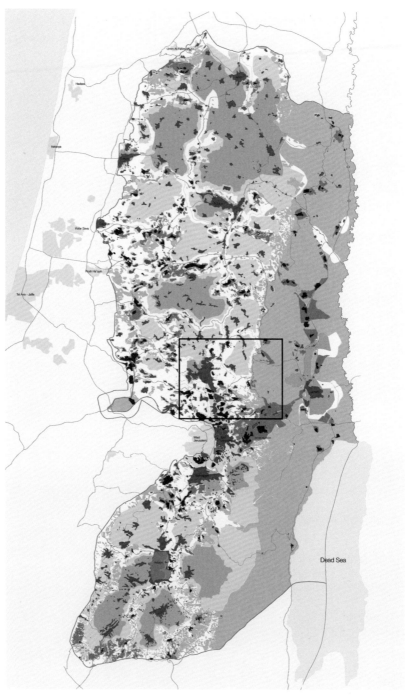

Map of Jewish settlements in the West Bank. B'Tselem and Eyal Weizman, 2002.

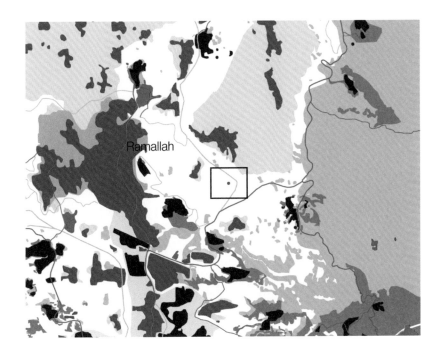

Ramallah

Built-up Area (Settlement)

Area within Municipal Boundary (Settlement)

Regional Council Jurisdictional Area (Settlement)

Military Base

Built-up Area (Palestinian)

Area A

Area B

Area C

Area H1 (Hebron)

Area H2 (Hebron)

Preface

The Vertical Apartheid

In the context of a recent, mildly critical interview about the political deadlock between Israel and the Palestinians, a former Israeli general, until recently the chief commander of the West Bank, claimed that the Israeli military has become 'world champions in occupation' and has managed to turn its control of millions of Palestinian into 'an art form', as if this two-generation-long degrading and lethal regime is some sort of sport or managerial challenge.[1] But bragging is not necessarily an exaggeration. This preface to the new edition of *Hollow Land* – published almost exactly fifty years after the beginning of the 1967 war (and ten years after the first edition) – charts the way Israel's system of control, which evolved in fits and starts throughout the occupation's first four decades, has, during its fifth decade, hardened into an exceptionally efficient and brutal form of territorial apartheid.

Indeed, on its fiftieth anniversary, the Israeli occupation seems to be in excellent form. Though the Gaza settlements have been removed, those in the West Bank and East Jerusalem prosper, and settler numbers have been growing at a rate of 15,000 people annually.[2] The domination of more than four million Palestinians has stopped being an economic burden and proven to be profitable. The people under occupation are a captive market (literally) for many surplus Israeli-manufactured goods. Private industries, including international companies working in the Jewish settlements, prosper thanks to tax breaks, low rents, government subsidies, and a Palestinian labour force that is rendered cheap and flexible because it enjoys no civil or labour rights.[3] Israel's international exports – many of them military and marketed as 'road tested in action' (on the Palestinians, that is) – are also steadily growing as more nations, including the United States and European states, adopt Israel-like xenophobic politics towards minorities, refugees, and migrants (especially Muslim ones).[4]

Within the Israeli political system there is currently no serious opposition to the settlement project. International diplomacy is largely inconsequential and there is no 'peace process' to threaten the settlements' further expansion. Representatives of the settler movement hold power in all major governmental offices, running not only the occupation, but also the business of the state.

Dissent is confronted with paranoid fervor and righteous rage. Activists are vilified as traitors, spied upon, threatened, and arrested. State officials, and even the prime minister, now openly refer to human rights groups as 'the third strategic threat' (after Iran and Hizbullah), treating them as foreign agents and spies, and the Israeli parliament has legislated laws to constrain their work. Civil society groups calling for boycott of and divestment from the Israeli economy and culture – one of the last peaceful means to challenge Israeli hegemony – are made illegal locally (and severely limited in some key countries such as Britain, France, Ireland, Germany, and the United States) and foreign activists promoting it are no longer allowed into the country,.[5]

Happy fiftieth birthday, indeed!

The durability and expansion of Israel's settler-colonial project in Palestine is no small achievement given the turns of recent history. In the ten years since the first edition of this book was published, the world was shaken by a series of transformative processes, none of which loosened Israel's grip on power over the Palestinians. In 2008, a global financial crisis overwhelmed the world economy and devastated real estate markets worldwide. At the same time, in the West Bank and occupied East Jerusalem the number of houses and settlers has nearly doubled: there were 400,000 settlers there when *Hollow Land* was first published and there are about 750,000 today. This number includes the residents of 131 official, state-sanctioned settlements and the twelve Jewish neighbourhoods in occupied East Jerusalem (this is what settlements there are called) as well as ninety-seven smaller outposts in the West Bank and the thirteen Jewish outposts inside Palestinian neighbourhoods in occupied East Jerusalem.[6] While the official settlements have expanded in terms of the extent of their built-up area and number of residents, the number of official settlements has not changed much. At the start of the Oslo process in the early 1990s there were already 120 settlements in place. It is the rogue outposts that have grown in number and expanded as their settlers torch fields and homes, harass and shoot Palestinians to take over their agricultural lands. The official settlements simply expand while relying on the military and the courts to do the same.

Another global process that Israel's regime of domination has been immune to is the so-called Arab Spring. Starting in 2011, a series of popular revolts, particularly within the Magreb and Middle East, toppled (or tried to) presidential regimes across the region, resulting in, not a series of popular democracies, but bloody civil wars and foreign military interventions. While these states were engulfed in revolutionary fervour, resistance remained relatively subdued in the West Bank and Jerusalem (though, as I will later show, it was fierce in Gaza). Civil protests and desperate, increasingly personally motivated armed actions (often with knives), were put down brutally with the help of the Palestinian Authority.

Despite popular protests, the wall and other physical barriers have expanded. Hundreds of miles of fencing systems and prefabricated concrete elements have been erected on Palestinian lands to protect Jewish settlements. These barriers are the physical manifestation of what Israeli officials call the 'segregation policy', a policy that seeks to separate Jews from Palestinians everywhere across the territory between the Jordan River and the Mediterranean Sea.

Separation, in space and by law, is the most fundamental component of Israel's system of colonization.[7] Even when settlers, Palestinians, and soldiers are brought together in the same incident, at the very same place, each group is still bound by different laws. The applicable law for the settlers is the Israeli civil law, by which settlers enjoy full Israeli civil rights including the right to vote. The reality for Palestinians is a military dictatorship in which civil and human rights rarely apply.[8] In military courts, where Palestinians are tried, the conviction rates for alleged violence against settlers or occupation forces are 99.74 per cent.[9] For soldiers the ratio is inversed. The mandate of the military legal system, inasmuch as it deals with Israeli military personnel, assigns criminal responsibility via the most narrow of frames and is oriented exclusively toward low-ranking soldiers: it investigates only harm caused by a breach of commands, never the legality of commands and the violence that underpins them. Less than one third of a single per cent of complaints brought against soldiers' violence lead to charges. This legal reality guarantees that violence is exercised with the full backing of the law. As a result, Israel's politics of separation has, in the past decade, surpassed South African apartheid, not only in the extent and sophistication of its architectural manifestations, but also in its duration: the South African version collapsed under international pressure after forty-three years.

Israeli domination of Palestinians is not confined to the spaces occupied in 1967. In its early decades, Israel's rule in the occupied territories used techniques of domination that were well-honed on those Palestinians who survived and remained in place during the expulsions of 1948. In recent decades, techniques of domination, land grab and separation, more intensely exercised in the 1967 occupied areas, inspired the further separation of Jews and Arabs within Israel itself. The occupation can thus not be thought of as an aberration of Israeli democracy, a 'cancerous tumour' that can be removed by dissecting more or less along the internationally recognized Green Line of 1949, as left-liberal apologists of Zionism propose. Rather, it is a local manifestation of Israel's regime of domination and separation that extends, in different forms, between the Jordan River and the Mediterranean Sea.

Examples of this policy within Israel are abundant. In recent decades the state-sanctioned 'battle for the Negev' has radically escalated, with Israel repeatedly, violently sending its demolition squads to destroy ramshackle homes and animal pens on lands that have been continuously inhabited by Bedouins for generations, and this to clear space for Jewish settlements and forests.[10] The Bedouins are amongst the only Palestinian refugees and internally displaced persons (those displaced within Israel) to enact, continuously, repeatedly, on the ground, their right of return, rebuilding again after every act of demolition.

In Galilee, Jewish outposts are designed to break apart the continuity of Palestinian space and limit the growth of villages. Elsewhere, Palestinian neighbourhoods in Jerusalem, Nazareth, Lydda, Ramle, and Jaffa are split into enclaves by roadways and barriers. An important aspect of Israel's overall domination of all the territorial fragments into which Palestine was shuttered is manifested in its control of the population registration. Every Palestinian birth in Gaza, death in the West Bank, marriage in Jerusalem, or change of address in Galilee must be entered into Israel's Interior Ministry database in order to exist. No one can travel, work, open a bank account, or even emigrate without it.

The Strangulation of Gaza

In the past decade, the focus of the armed struggle and the worst of Israel's policy of domination has shifted to Gaza. This took place against the backdrop of a punishing siege, which severely escalated after Hamas took power there in 2007. The siege replaced one system of control with another. As long as they were inside Gaza, several blocks of Jewish settlements and a string of military bases exercised a traditional form of territorial control – they controlled the roadways and surveyed the cities. In 2005 the Sharon government removed the settlements and relocated the military bases beyond Gaza's perimeter wall. Domination is now exercised from beyond the borders, from the sea and the air. Gunboats keep presence just off the coastline, shooting at fishermen that dare to venture more than a few hundred meters from the shore. The airforce controls things from above. Agreements with Egypt ensure Israel has some say over who can pass through Gaza's border crossing in Rafah.

The siege is a giant and unparalleled exercise in population control. It seeks to isolate the strip from the external world and gradually increase the collective hardship by reducing the incoming flow of all life-sustaining provisions. Israeli intelligence agencies monitor the effects of the siege and claim to be able to calibrate the privation to a level that is hard enough for the civilian population to reject Hamas but one that does not fall below some so-called 'red lines' that would 'bring the strip to a humanitarian crisis'.[11] The supply of food, calculated in calories, was gradually reduced to the UN humanitarian minimum of 2100 calories per adult (less for women and children). The inflow of electricity, petrol, and concrete was also gradually turned down to levels that ground life to an almost complete standstill, devastating infrastructural systems, hospitals, the economy, and civil institutions.

Unemployment shot up to 43 per cent (highest in the world), 72 per cent of the population fell below the poverty line, and the absolute majority of residents became dependent on international welfare, an important point of leverage when it is Israel that could decide to start and stop those welfare provisions. Electricity was reduced so radically that residents have power for only a few hours a day, hospitals are incapacitated, and there is not enough power to contain all sewage from flowing untreated. The shortage in basic medicines has become more severe, with people dying from easily preventable diseases and for lack of basic treatment. These deaths, unlike those from direct violence, are not statistically recorded. The United Nations has desperately repeated that a massive humanitarian crisis is already unfolding in Gaza and warned that if the current trend continues, the entire strip could become uninhabitable by 2020. Where does Israel want these two million Palestinians to go? The government does not feel it has to care. It claims that Gaza is 'no longer occupied' (the 'no longer' is strange because when the settlements were there, Israel never accepted it was an 'occupation') and thus its duties as an 'occupying force' under international law no longer apply (it never applied them anyway). Gaza is rather an 'enemy entity' – a designation that allows it to be attacked and starved as an enemy state but without the sovereign rights that come with statehood. This continues a double game that has been in place since 1967. Israel uses the rights afforded to a military occupier under international law, for example to build 'temporary military installations', while ignoring its duties by claiming that the situation isn't one of occupation at all. The UN, however, has never accepted this self-serving and paradoxical designation of Gaza and still regards Israel to be occupying Gaza because it has control over all aspects of life there.

Its interference extends into minute details. Decisions otherwise exercised at municipal levels are still undertaken by Israel – for example, by deciding how much concrete and steel are to be allowed in and how much should be allocated for which construction or reconstruction project, the Israeli military officers at the border act as the ultimate planning officers, determining what will be built and where.

Despite the siege, Hamas has not surrendered. Its hold of the strip and its influence over Gazans has only been strengthened. It has resisted the siege with continuous armed action. Constant skirmishes have escalated into three devastating Israeli attacks in 2008–9, 2012 and 2014. Israel's indiscriminate bombing of dense civilian neighbourhoods during these 'wars' has killed over 4,000 people, the overwhelming majority of them civilians. In addition, the constant bombardment has ruined most of the remaining infrastructure, destroyed or damaged close to 150,000 buildings, and driven half a million Gazans from their homes – a number only slightly exceeding that of the Jewish population the state helped house in the West Bank and Jerusalem over the same period.[12] The built environment – and its destruction and construction – is, as I have already written in *Hollow Land*, more than just a backdrop of this conflict. Rather, it is the means by which domination takes shape.

Stratigraphic Separation

The policy of separation does not only divide Jews and Palestinians but also creates divisions between Palestinians. Physical barriers now cut apart the three main districts occupied in 1967 – Gaza, Jerusalem, and the West Bank – and separate them from the Palestinians in Israel. The Gaza siege is enacted through a perimeter barrier composed of a system of roads, concrete walls and fencings similar to that of the more famous West Bank wall. It is built on the internationally recognized border of 1949, but extends inwards into a no-go area that extends up to 1500 metres from the border. Anyone entering this zone could be shot and killed.

The 708 kilometres of the West Bank wall cut between villages and their fields, effectively annexing 10 per cent of the territory for the use of the settlements. It also cuts Jerusalem apart from the West Bank. The eastern part of Jerusalem has been physically annexed to Israel but its Palestinian population was granted only 'permanent residency' – an oxymoronic term because this residency can be revoked at any time, and Israeli authorities use any excuse to revoke it whenever possible. Divided from all the rest are the million and a half Palestinians who live within Israel, where they have Israeli citizenship but not equal rights. Completely barred from entering Palestine are the four and a half million Palestinians, mainly refugees but also migrants, living outside the country.

In the West Bank, separation has grown increasingly complex. The Oslo Accords splintered the territory into areas A, B, and C, with areas A and B enjoying some degree of civilian administration, and area C (some 61 per cent of the total area, with about 200,000 to 300,000 Palestinians) remaining under the direct control the military's 'Civil Administration', which forbids all Palestinian construction and development.

Not only has architecture been weaponized in this conflict, but the system itself can be said to have an architectural form. What is this architecture of control and how does it work? In the early 2000s when I started my research into the formation of this territorial system, I approached the challenge as every architect might approach an analysis of a complex building: I drew a cross section through it. An architectural cross section cuts through the visible layers of a building – facades, internal walls, floors – to expose the structures, systems, and infrastructure that run through them – columns, beams, air ducts, plumbing, electricity or information systems – as well as the relation between floors and rooms.

The section revealed the depth of Israel's colonial project, because, like a building, the 'architectural project' of the occupation was arranged in layers. The Oslo Accords of the mid 1990s – which promised an incremental pathway to reconciliation but ended up providing the skeleton of the existing geographical system of domination and control – divided the territory into three principle political floors: the *surface*, landlocked pockets which were handed over to Palestinian control; the *subsoil*, including water and mineral resources; and the *airspace* above Palestinian areas, which was left in Israeli hands, primarily those of its air force.

But territorial stratifications get even more complicated. Israel's primary legal apparatus for land grab: an Ottoman land code from the mid-nineteenth century conceived to encourage agricultural cultivation after a great series of droughts and famines across the empire by promising farmers permanent tenure over any land they cultivated and threatening to take land away if they didn't. A contemporary reading of the logic of this law helped the state take legal control over all uncultivated lands, which were located primarily on the barren hilltops leaving only the lower cultivated valleys in Palestinian hands. In these hilltops, also important for territorial control, Israel could now 'legally' implant the settlement. This meant that the two national populations became intertwined and intermingled everywhere across the terrain.

This fragmentation into settlement hilltop islands over Palestinian valley enclaves necessitated a further degree of three-dimensional complexity: a mesh of separated roadways that could connect islands to islands and enclaves to enclaves. This completely divided the movements of Jews and Palestinians in three dimensions without the two ever crossing, or crossing only minimally.

A Jewish-only road network, the 'apartheid roads' started connecting the hilltop settlements with bridges that span over Palestinian fields and with tunnels that burrow underneath Palestinian towns. This type of infrastructure has in recent decades been greatly extended and currently comprises a full third of the total length of roadways in the West Bank.[13] In the last decade, as armed confrontations in the West Bank subsided, some military checkpoints were removed, allowing Palestinians freer movement between their villages and towns. But this movement was undertaken on a separate and tattered road network that, whenever crossing the Jewish network of highways, bows and bores underneath them. While the Jewish road network leads everywhere to Israel, the Palestinian road network is truncated on all sides by walls, checkpoints, and military zones.

Every Palestinian town and village has thus been fully enveloped by Israeli space in three dimensions. If Palestinians want to drive out of their enclaves, they encounter a fence, a wall, or an Israeli checkpoint. If they want to dig a well they need Israeli permission to pierce into its subterranean volumes, and face sanctions if they don't. If they want to fly – a question that is largely theoretical given that they are not permitted an air force nor a national airline – they need Israel's permission to enter into the airspace over their very roofs.

In Gaza, this three-dimensional partition organizes the frontlines of the armed struggle. Enclosed on the surface and unable to face the Israeli air force that continuously hovers above, Palestinian military efforts move in two directions along the vertical axis: they have retreated into the subsoil, where there are underground command centers, cross-border tunnels, and rocket-launching sites; and into the airspace through which these rockets travel.

If this system of volumetric separation were to be described in terms of a building, it would most closely resemble an airport with separate inbound and outbound corridors, splintering infrastructural ductworks, multiple passport control points, and security checks that direct some passengers on hustle-free paths through luxury shops to anywhere in the world, and others toward long queues, invasive security checks, and detention rooms that are sometimes separated from the luxury shops merely by a single floor or wall. Following this metaphor, Gaza would be the largest of the detention rooms. From it, those incarcerated might be able to see the people shopping on the other side, but are invisible to them (while being hypervisible to their security forces). The more these detainees try to resist or break out, the less provisions, water, and electricity these security people allow in.

I have previously called this layered political structure 'the politics of verticality'.[14] Throughout the last decade, this evolving and elastic territorial architecture has hardened into a permanent mechanism of separation and control. Verticality has become a form of apartheid. The word should in fact be synonymous with it.

Other layers of separation could be revealed by extending the section line downward across different geological layers. A section through these layers exposes the political logic of Israeli apartheid in the same way that seismological cracks help geologists examine hidden layers of rock. Recently, some scientists have proposed that our geological era should be referred to as the *Anthropocene*, a time in which humans have become the dominant force in shaping – destructively and dangerously – the very material composition of the planet. It is not only that the natural layers of the earth – deposits, minerals, and rocks – should be regarded as proper geological strata, but that the geology of the earth might also include artificial strata such as structures and buried infrastructures, asphalt, toxins, concrete, and mechanical transportation systems, including tens of thousands of satellites that form a permanent layer of aluminium forever circling the planet. If the concept of the Anthropocene helps us think about geology politically, we might also reverse its proposition and think about politics geologically.

The political geology of Palestine starts in the deep subterranean aquifers, buried under layers of aggregate soil and rock. The partition and use of the waters of this interconnected set of underground lakes, most of it under the West Bank, reflects the extent of inequality exercised on the surface. The Oslo Accords allocated 80 per cent of this resource for the benefit of Israel. As a result, average water consumption in Israel is more than four times that of the West Bank and Gaza. In recent decades, over-extraction of groundwater from Gaza's sole aquifer led to its permanent salinization, destroying the strip's single water source.[15]

Another geological stratum is archaeology. The buried remains of the land's historical occupants should be the subject of impartial scientific study. But the settler colonial logic of the Zionist project uses archaeology to construct an alibi for the Jewish 'return' and the claim that its indigenous rights are more fundamental and prior to those of all others. In this book, I have outlined the way ideologically motivated archaeology across Palestine, aimed at the remains of its biblical past, has discarded other archaeological strata (especially the long succession of Muslim periods from the seventh to the twentieth century) and organized the mode of occupation on the surface right above them. One excavation, which began in 2008, powerfully embodies this logic. It took place right under Silwan, a small Palestinian neighbourhood just outside Jerusalem's Old City walls. Promoted by settler associations and starting without proper permits, it searched for elements of 'King David's era' Jerusalem by boring tunnels through a hillside beneath homes in the neighbourhood, without informing the residents or securing their consent and refusing to stop despite their explicit protests and several attempts to halt it in court.

The underground works, a haphazard collection of improvised tunnels fortified with tonnes of steel and concrete, were recently inaugurated by dignitaries including the city's mayor, who ceremonially stated: 'When you stand in the City of David, you see layer after layer of foreign conquest, but when you come to the bedrock, there you find the Jewish layer.' His conflation of geology (bedrock) and archaeology (Iron Age ruins) – false for there being a millennia of earlier inhabitations in Jerusalem – was used to make a crude political point: 'after other countries' leaders visit here they will no longer have any doubts about who owns this city'.[16] But the excavation has also connected between the separate strata: cracks, originating inside the mountain, started moving up through geological and archaeological layers towards the surface, appearing and disappearing as they find their lines of least resistance, cutting through streets, homes, a school, and a mosque, some of which had to be abandoned. Digging for the ruins of ancient Jewish archaeology thus produced a layer of contemporary Palestinian ruin.

Indeed, in many places beneath the pavement of Israeli towns and universities, under the fields of Zionist villages and hillside forests, there is a layer made of the rubble of Palestine destroyed in 1948. The destruction has not ceased and Palestinian rubble is still piling up. It is made of homes, bulldozed for being built without permits in places where no permits are ever given to Palestinians. It is made of the bombed out buildings and greenhouses of Gaza and the improvised structures of the Bedouin villages of the Jordan Valley and the Negev. There is rubble across Palestine and everywhere people can be seen picking through its fresh top layers, where their homes stood, searching for something to salvage.

This layer of building rubble is directly related to the high-tech strata of the airspace and the electromagnetic spectrum occupied by the airforce. Since this book was first published, this layer has undergone a profound transformation. Domination from the air, which was largely exercised by manned jets and helicopters on short designated missions, is now increasingly enforced by overlapping swarms of unmanned drones on long missions. Hovering continuously over Palestinian towns and villages, they maintain a menacing, malevolent presence. The sound of their propellers' engines is the continuous backdrop of Palestinian daily lives.[17] These aerial platforms have rotated the geography of colonization by 90 degrees: the 'Orient' is no longer beyond the horizon, but now directly underneath it. 'Aerially enforced colonization', based on the drones' ability to maintain a perpetual 'surveillance and strike' capability, is an economically efficient alternative to the otherwise onerous and expensive tasks of colonial policing in the dense urban mazes of the Gaza strip. The availability of this form of control was central in convincing the Israeli leadership that territorial withdrawal from the strip could be possible without compromising Israel's overall domination. Hunter algorithms, programmed to follow patterns of behaviour, are programmed to learn the art of suspicion and violence in the same way that school children across our region currently do.

Cross sections through the layers of terrain reveal the politics of verticality to have an architecture composed of layers of radically different kinds – natural and artificial, material and immaterial, low- and high-tech – one equally composed of archaeology and drones. When something is said to have an 'architecture' it is tempting to imagine there is a single design team in charge, but the architecture of occupation was conceived at different periods by different people. That it has a layered structure laminated together into a unified and effective apparatus is because it was conceived under the ideology and practice of settler colonialism. The layering of democracy (for Israelis and Jews in the West Bank) and military dictatorship (in the areas between settlements) also makes this form of apartheid more resilient because it enables its apologists to deny its total nature and concentrates criticism on a different part of it every time. These different parts under criticism can then be compared to similar or equivalent practices in other places. Archaeology is politicized in other countries, drones are employed elsewhere, and other countries still divide their water unequally, etc. There is nothing inherently different, only that here these layers are woven into a complete system. However, this layered arrangement is rarely grasped in its totality; each layer is presented as a haphazard, often merely functional solution to a separate problem. A patch over patch, implemented stage by stage. One layer makes sure hilltops are seized by the state for the construction of settlements; another, annexes land along the roadways that connect these settlements (for their security); another, restricts building (only in and around Palestinian villages and neighbourhoods) in the name of environmental regulations for clean air, green areas, and natural reserves, or because the military needs live fire training areas (always next to Palestinian places), or because there are archaeological sites under these Palestinian areas, or, most effectively, to restrict access to underground water. It is the perceived separation between these layers that makes the politics of vertical apartheid so effective and resilient, and moreover an attractive model for other countries that seek form of population control

Delamination

Even the so-called 'peace plans', which still seemed 'in the cards' (and the subject of hopes or fears) until several years ago, relied on the overall logic of the politics of vertical separation. Whether in the framework of the one, two, or three state solutions (the latter refers to Gaza and the West Bank as two separate states), every Israeli proposal for a 'final status arrangement' demands that Israel retain control of airspace, borders, and subsoil. Even some versions of the 'single state solution', now experiencing an improbable revival, not with the domain of the 'radical left' but in some mainstream right-wing and settler circles, relies on the deepening of the politics of verticality. In this form, it expresses itself as the confederation of two unequal national systems, each with its own parliament, layered within an overall sovereign, monetary, and spatial envelope dominated by Israel.[18]

Given the architecture of Israel's settler colonialism, the decolonization of Palestine will require not ever more 'creative' volumetric arrangements and complicated lines of three-dimensional partition, but rather, the fundamental 'delamination' of Israel's vertical apartheid. Political delamination would need to pry apart and flatten the inflated structure – the overlapping jurisdictions, separate legal systems, and modes of topographic and architectural separation – as well as acknowledge a common (not a singular or unified) history that includes the Nakba. The only ethical future is for the 13 million people between the Jordan and the sea to have citizenship, freedom to move and live wherever they want, historical recognition, and modes of restitution. This could be achieved in the context of three, two or one state, certainly not one of an ongoing colonization and occupation.

A good place to start might be the equitable management of the fragile, finite, and common ecology and shared natural resources. The vulnerability of the politics of vertical apartheid lies in its totality and all-encompassing logic, and we might be able to find ways to delink the layers. All empires eventually collapse and few could grasp the internal or external causes that led to their demise, even when the agents of their destruction were right around the corner or already at the threshold of perception.

While Israel, and indeed the world, treats Palestine as a laboratory for military and political control, activists in Palestine continuously innovate new modes of civil society resistance. When agents of separation try to compartmentalize things vertically and horizontally, what is needed is the construction of collectivity between the people coming from the different zones into which Palestine has been fragmented, from the diaspora, from anti-apartheid Israeli activists, and with international solidarity. But in a situation of structural violence and inequality, mere cohabitation can become counterproductive, as it tends to support the status quo. Co-resistance – civil society actions that oppose and seek to terminate Israel's regime of domination – is small but kicking, and it manifests itself in inclusive, unarmed struggle: civil and human rights work, solidarity campaigns, exposures, and demonstrations. The lines of solidarity that are formed there around these small but committed communities of practice are the nuclei around which a new politics could one day be constructed. From previous anti-colonial struggles we have already learned that the society that will replace the colonial present will be defined by the sort of anti-colonial struggle it conducted.

One of the most effective forms of civil action to have emerged in recent years is articulated in the call by Palestinian civil society for economic and cultural boycott of Israel. The BDS (Boycott, Divestment and Sanctions) movement has already created widening circles of solidarity and is seen by the Israeli government, as noted above, as an existential threat to its economy, international standing, and ongoing domination.[19] That a movement calling for boycott is fundamental to engendering solidarity might seem a paradoxical proposition, but this form of activism should not be understood as one of negative agency, of blockage and separation. When it blocks non-democratic platforms, it opens (or should increasingly open) the possibility for new democratic ones to emerge, and it currently enjoys growing support from international Palestinian and Israeli activists. BDS activism also develops a global dimension because it must also oppose the very Western governments that offer unparalleled diplomatic, financial, and military support to Israel and try to criminalize this very act of civil solidarity and support.

Architecture also has a place in the struggle. Throughout the past decade, I have had the opportunity to participate in several initiatives that mobilize architecture as a means of civil co-resistance across the spectrum of actions that the disciple can offer, from analysis to proposition. One such attempt was undertaken with an architectural studio named *Decolonizing Architecture Art Residency* or DAAR, which I co-founded in Beit Sahour, Palestine together with my friends Sandi Hilal and Alessandro Petti. DAAR is affiliated with dozens of architects in Palestine and internationally and works on architectural propositions for the transformation and reuse of Israel's colonial infrastructure – settlements and military bases – for aims other than what they were built for: primarily for collective functions and public institutions. It also works on pedagogical initiatives and architectural proposals in refugee camps and in the sites, often marked by no more than a few old stones, that refugees were displaced from.[20]

Another project is *Forensic Architecture*. It mobilizes architectural tools and techniques to engage with the production of evidence of state violence in Palestine (and increasingly worldwide), and presents this evidence in political and judicial forums that include international courts and human rights and environmental reports.[21] Architectural investigations are urgent and essential given the role architecture plays in Israel's regime of domination – exposing the nature of the system in terms of both mapping the growth of Jewish settlements and demonstrating the ways in which Palestinian built-up areas have increasingly become the target for destruction.

Out of all those born in this land, Jewish Israelis like me are those most privileged by the regime. Unlike most Palestinians, we are able to travel through Palestine and outside it, and are afforded greater latitude of expression and access to information. Being Israeli in this space, we cannot avoid a degree of collusion, even when we confront the regime, even when we migrate away, as I did. Unable to escape our privileges, we can choose to use them against the regime that granted them to us with the ultimate aim to undo them. In any case, and in whatever form it might take, we engage in civil co-resistance not because we are certain of what might bring down this regime of domination, but because it is the only way to live here and there, in Palestine and the diaspora.

Migron. Milutin Labudovic for Peace Now, 2002.

Introduction: Frontier Architecture

Robinson believed that if he looked at it hard enough, he could cause the surface of the city to reveal to him the molecular basis of historical events, and in this way he hoped to see into the future. [1]

Patrick Keiller (London)

The duality of intelligence and stupidity has been part of the Zionist project from the beginning. [2]

Mourid Barghouti

'Nu'a nu'a sof.' [3]

Yeshayahu Gavish

('Move, move, out' – the order for the beginning of the assault of the 1967 war.)

A frontier scenario

In the years following the 1993 signing of the first Oslo Accord, which was intended to mark the beginning of the end of the conflict over Palestine, it became increasingly difficult for Israeli settlers to obtain official permits to establish new settlements in the West Bank. As a result, settlers resorted to increasingly sophisticated methods of piracy to help the government – which, unofficially, was keen to see settlements established but could not be seen to be helping in their foundation – bypass its own laws and international commitments.

In 1999 several settlers complained to the military of bad reception on their cellphones as they drove round a bend on the main highway, Road 60, leading from Jerusalem to the settlements in the northern West Bank. In response, the cellphone provider, Orange, agreed to erect an antenna in the area. The settlers pointed to an elevated hilltop overlooking the bend as a potential site for the mast. The same hilltop had been the site of previous – unsuccessful – settlement attempts: three years earlier settlers claimed that the summit was an archaeological mound under which the biblical town of Migron was buried. Sample excavations unearthed the remains of nothing older than a small Byzantine village, but the hilltop was named 'Migron' regardless. Two young settlers occupied the hill, living in converted shipping containers, but, with no prospect of being able to develop the site, left after a short time.

The hilltop, its slopes cultivated with figs and olives, was owned by Palestinian farmers from the villages of Ein Yabrud and Burka who were shepherds there. According to the emergency powers invested in the Israeli military, however, the construction of a cellphone antenna could be considered a security issue, and could therefore be undertaken on private lands without obtaining the owners' consent. Following a request by Orange, the Israel Electric Corporation connected the hilltop to the electricity grid and the national water provider connected the hilltop to the water system, purportedly to enable the construction work.

Because of delays in the mast's construction, in May 2001 settlers erected a fake antenna and received military permission to hire a 24-hour on-site private security guard to watch over it. The guard moved into a trailer at the foot of the mast, and fenced off the surrounding hilltop; soon afterwards, his wife and children moved in and connected their home to the water and electricity supplies already there. On 3 March 2002, five additional families joined them, and the outpost of Migron formally came into being. The outpost grew steadily. Since families were already living onsite, the Israeli Ministry for Construction and Housing built a nursery, while some donations from abroad paid for the construction of a synagogue.[4] Migron is currently the biggest of the 103 outposts scattered throughout the West Bank. By mid-2006 it comprised around 60 trailers and containers housing more than 42 families: approximately 150 people perched on the hilltop around a cellular antenna.[5]

The antenna became a focus of territorial intensity in the surrounding landscape. The infrastructure built for it allowed the outpost to emerge. The energy field of the antenna was not only electromagnetic, but also political, serving as a centre for the mobilizing, channelling, coalescing and organizing of political forces and processes of various kinds. Migron is not the only outpost established around a cellphone antenna. The logic of cellular communication seems oddly compatible with that of the civilian occupation of the West Bank: both expand into territories by establishing networks that triangulate base stations located on high ground along radiation- or sight-lines. Moreover, the cellular networks serve a military function. Using them for its own field communications, the military was able to replace its bulky military radios with smaller devices

The outpost of Antenna Hill. Note antenna at centre of the outpost. Milutin Labudovic for Peace Now, 2002.

capable of transmitting field imagery and GPS locations between soldiers and units.

An upsurge in the establishment of outposts has always been an indication of what settlers suspected to be 'impending territorial compromises'. Such activity is intended to sabotage prospects of political progress, and secure as much land as possible for the Israeli settlers in the Occupied Territories, in case partial withdrawals are to be carried out. After returning from negotiations with the Palestinian Authority and the Clinton administration at the Wye Plantation in Maryland in October 1998, Ariel Sharon, then Foreign Minister, rushed settlers 'to move, run and grab as many hilltops as they can . . . because everything we take now will stay ours. Everything we don't grab will go to them.'[6] In recent years, many outposts have been constructed in an attempt to influence the path of Israel's Separation Wall that, at the time of writing in 2006, is carving a circuitous route through the West Bank, the logic being that by seeding the terrain with 'anchor points' in strategic places, state planners would reroute the Wall around them in order to include them on the 'Israeli' side. Outposts thus mark some of the most contested frontiers of the Israel–Palestine conflict. Often, rarely beyond their teens, the so-called 'youth of the hill' reject their parents' settler–suburban culture for a sense of the wild frontier, one equally influenced by the myth of rough and rugged Western heroes as with the Israeli myth of the pioneering Zionist settlers of the early twentieth century. The armed outpost settlers often clash with local Palestinian farmers, violently drive them off their fields and steal their produce. In retaliation, armed Palestinian militants often attack outposts. Other outposts are then established as 'punitive measures' near locations where settlers have been killed.

Outposts have thus become the focus for political and diplomatic squabbles. Local and international peace organizations engage in direct actions against outpost expansion. In 2004 several Israeli peace activists managed to steal five trailers from Migron, provocatively placing them in front of the Ministry of Defence building in Tel Aviv, demonstrating that evacuation could be carried out if the will to do it exists.[7] Human rights lawyers petitioned the Israeli High Court of Justice with a string of legal challenges against the outposts, the most recent of which, against Migron, is still pending.[8] As international pressure mounts, Israeli governments announce (usually with great fanfare) their decision to enforce Israeli law and evacuate a number of outposts. Occasionally, clashes occur between government and settler forces: thousands of policemen battle with thousands of settlers, who travel for the televised fight from across the frontier. Often, however, a compromise is reached: the trailers are reattached to trucks, and relocated to another Palestinian hilltop.

Against the geography of stable, static places, and the balance across linear and fixed sovereign borders, frontiers are deep, shifting, fragmented and elastic territories. Temporary lines of engagement, marked by makeshift boundaries, are not limited to the edges of political space but exist throughout its depth. Distinctions between the 'inside' and 'outside' cannot be clearly marked. In fact, the straighter, more geometrical and more abstract official colonial borders across the 'New Worlds' tended to be, the more the territories of effective control were fragmented and dynamic and thus unchartable by any conventional mapping technique.[9] The Occupied Palestinian Territories could be seen as such a frontier zone. However, in relation to the dimensions of ancient empires – 'optimal', by several accounts, at forty days' horse travel from one end to the other – within the 5,655 square kilometres of the West Bank, the 2.5 million Palestinians and 500,000 Jewish settlers seem to inhabit the head of a pin. On it, as Sharon Rotbard mentioned, 'the most explosive ingredients of our time, all modern utopias and all ancient beliefs [are contained] simultaneously and instantaneously, bubbling side by side with no precautions'.[10] These territories have become the battlefield on which various agents of state power and independent actors confront each other, meeting local and international resistance. The mundane elements of planning and architecture have become tactical tools and the means of dispossession. Under Israel's regime of 'erratic occupation', Palestinian life, property and political rights are constantly violated not only by the frequent actions of the Israeli military, but by a process in which their environment is unpredictably and continuously refashioned, tightening around them like a noose.

Accounts of colonialism tend to concentrate on the way systems of governance and control are translated into the organization of space, according to underlying principles of rational organization, classification, procedure and rules of administration. What the above scenario demonstrates, however, is that in the Occupied Palestinian Territories, the organization of geographical space cannot simply be understood as the preserve of the Israeli government executive power alone, but rather one diffused among a multiplicity of – often non-state – actors. The spatial organization of the Occupied Territories is a reflection not only of an ordered process of planning and implementation, but, and increasingly so, of 'structured chaos', in which the – often deliberate – selective absence of government intervention promotes an unregulated process of violent dispossession. The actors operating within this frontier – young settlers, the Israeli military, the cellular network provider and other capitalist corporations, human rights and political activists, armed resistance, humanitarian and legal experts, government ministries, foreign governments, 'supportive' communities overseas, state planners, the media, the Israeli High Court of Justice – with the differences and contradictions of their aims, all play their part in the diffused and anarchic, albeit collective authorship of its spaces. Because elastic geographies respond to a multiple and diffused rather than a single source of power, their architecture cannot be understood as the material embodiment of a unified political will or as the product of a single ideology. Rather, the organization of the Occupied Territories should be seen as a kind of 'political plastic', or as a diagram of the relation between all the forces that shaped it. [11]

The architecture of the frontier could not be said to be simply 'political' but rather 'politics in matter'.

This book is an investigation of the transformation of the Occupied Palestinian Territories since 1967. It looks at the ways in which the different forms of Israeli rule inscribed themselves in space, analysing the geographical, territorial, urban and architectural conceptions and the interrelated practices that form and sustain them. In doing so, it provides an image of the very essence of Israeli occupation, its origin, evolution and the various ways by which it functions.

It does so not by offering a comprehensive history of the four decades of Israeli domination, nor by drawing a detailed portrait of its present spatiality, but by probing the various structures of territorial occupation. The following chapters form an 'archival probe',[12] investigating the history and *modus operandi* of the various spatial mechanisms that have sustained – and continue to sustain – the occupation's regime and practices of control. This forensic study of the spaces of occupation reveals how overt instruments of control, as well as seemingly mundane structures, are pregnant with intense historical, political meaning. Cladding and roofing details, stone quarries, street and highway illumination schemes, the ambiguous architecture of housing, the form of settlements, the construction of fortifications and means of enclosure, the spatial mechanisms of circulation control and flow management, mapping techniques and methods of observations, legal tactics for land annexation, the physical organization of crisis and disaster zones, highly developed weapons technologies and complex theories of military manoeuvres – all are invariably described as indexes for the political rationalities, institutional conflicts and range of expertise that formed them.

Architecture is employed in this book in two distinct ways. On the one hand, the book deals with the architecture of the structures that sustain the occupation and the complicity of architects in designing them. It seeks to read the *politics of Israeli architecture* in the way social, economic, national and strategic forces solidify into the organization, form and ornamentation of homes, infrastructure and settlements. On the other hand, architecture is employed as a conceptual way of understanding political issues as constructed realities. As the subtitle of this book – *Israel's Architecture of Occupation* – implies, the occupation is seen to have architectural properties, in that its territories are understood as an architectural 'construction', which outline the ways in which it is conceived, understood, organized and operated. The architects in this book are therefore military men, militants, politicians, political and other activists. I shall return to this latter meaning in the last section of this introduction.

Elastic geography

As the foundational narrative of Migron demonstrates, the frontiers of the Occupied Territories are not rigid and fixed at all; rather, they are elastic, and in constant transformation. The linear border, a cartographic imaginary inherited from the military and political spatiality of the nation state has splintered into a multitude of temporary, transportable, deployable and removable border-synonyms – 'separation walls', 'barriers', 'blockades', 'closures', 'road blocks', 'checkpoints', 'sterile areas', 'special security zones', 'closed military areas' and 'killing zones' – that shrink and expand the territory at will. These borders are dynamic, constantly shifting, ebbing and flowing; they creep along, stealthily surrounding Palestinian villages and roads. They may even errupt into Palestinian living rooms, bursting in through the house walls. The anarchic geography of the frontier is an evolving image of transformation, which is remade and rearranged with every political development or decision. Outposts and settlements might be evacuated and removed, yet new ones are founded and expand. The location of military check-points is constantly changing, blocking and modulating Palestinian traffic in ever-differing ways. Mobile military bases create the bridgeheads that maintain the logistics of ever-changing operations. The Israeli military makes incursions into Palestinian towns and refugee camps, occupies them and then withdraws. The Separation Wall, merely one of multiple barriers, is constantly rerouted, its path registering like a seismograph the political and legal battles surrounding it. Where territories appear to be hermetically sealed in by Israeli walls and fences, Palestinian tunnels are dug underneath them. Elastic territories could thus not be understood as benign environments: highly elastic political space is often more dangerous and deadly than a static, rigid one.

The dynamic morphology of the frontier resembles an incessant sea dotted with multiplying archipelagos of externally alienated and internally homogenous ethno-national enclaves – under a blanket of aerial Israeli surveillance. In this unique territorial ecosystem, various other zones – those of political piracy, of 'humanitarian' crisis, of barbaric violence, of full citizenship, 'weak citizenship', or no citizenship at all – exist adjacent to, within or over each other.

The elastic nature of the frontier does not imply that Israeli trailers, homes, roads or indeed the concrete wall are in themselves soft or yielding but that the continuous spatial reorganization of the political borders they mark out responds to and reflects political and military conflicts. The various inhabitants of this frontier do not operate within the fixed envelopes of space – space is not the background for their actions, an abstract grid on which events take place – but rather the medium that each of their actions seeks to challenge, transform or appropriate. Moreover, in this context the relation of space to action could not be understood as that of a rigid container to 'soft' performance. Political action is fully absorbed in the organization, transformation, erasure and subversion of space. Individual actions, geared by the effect of the media, can sometimes be more effective than Israeli government action.[13] Although it often appears as if the frontier's elastic nature is shaped by one side only – following the course of colonialist expansion – the agency of the colonized makes itself manifest in its success in holding steadfastly to its ground in the face of considerable odds, not only through political violence, but in the occasional piece of skilful diplomacy and the mobilization of international opinion. Indeed, the space of the colonizer may as well shrink as frontiers are decolonized.

In the meantime, the erratic and unpredictable nature of the frontier is exploited by the government. Chaos has its peculiar structural advantages. It supports one of Israel's foremost strategies of obfuscation: the promotion of complexity – geographical, legal or linguistic. Sometimes, following a terminology pioneered by Henry Kissinger, this strategy is openly referred to as 'constructive blurring'.[14] This strategy seeks simultaneously to obfuscate and naturalize the facts of domination. Across the frontiers of the West Bank it is undertaken by simultaneously unleashing processes that would create conditions too complex and illogical to make any territorial solution in the form of partition possible (many of the settlements were indeed constructed with the aim of creating an 'irresolvable geography'), while pretending that it is only the Israeli government that has the know-how to resolve the very complexity it created.

One of the most important strategies of obfuscation is terminological. The unique richness of settlement terminology in Hebrew was employed after 1967 in order to blur the border between Israel and the areas it occupied, and functioned as a kind of sophisticated semantic laundering. The controversial Hebrew term *hitnahlut* – a term with biblical roots describing the dwelling on national patrimony – is generally understood by the Israeli public to refer to those settlements of the national-messianic right, built in Gaza and the West Bank mountain range near Palestinian cities. In the popular grammar of occupation, settlements created by the centre-left Labor governments are referred to and seen more empathically as agrarian *Yeshuvim* (a generic Hebrew term for Jewish settlements within Israel) of the 'Kibbutz' and 'Moshav' type, as 'suburbs', 'towns' or, if within the boundaries of expanded Jerusalem, as 'neighbourhoods' (*Shhunot*). Semantic distinctions are also made between 'legal' settlements and 'illegal' outposts, although the latter are often the first stage in the development of the former in an enterprise that is illegal in its entirety. For the Israeli public, each of the above terms carries a different moral code. Large suburban settlements such as Ariel, Emanuel, Qiriat Arba and Ma'ale Adumim were officially declared 'towns' (*Arim*) in an exceptional process, long before their population had reached the demographical threshold of 20,000 required within the recognized borders of Israel 'proper'.[15] This was done in an attempt to naturalize these settlements in Israeli discourse, make their existence fact, their geographical location unclear, and keep them away from the negotiation table.[16] Indeed, accordingly, most Israelis still see the Jewish neighbourhoods of occupied Jerusalem and the large towns of the West Bank, not as settlements, but as 'legitimate' places of residence. Within this book all residential construction beyond the 1949 borders of the Green Line are referred to as 'settlements' – which in this context should be understood as 'colonies'.

In fact, despite the complexity of the legal, territorial and built realities that sustain the occupation, the conflict over Palestine has been a relatively straight-forward process of colonization, dispossession, resistance and suppression. The Israeli critical writer Ilan Pappe explains: 'generations of Israeli and pro-Israeli scholars, very much like their state's diplomats, have hidden behind the cloak of complexity in order to fend off any criticism of their quite obviously brutal treatment of the Palestinians . . . [repeating] the Israeli message: This is a complicated issue that would be better left to the Israelis to deal with . . .'[17] The attempt to place issues regarding conflict resolution in the domain of experts, beyond the reach of the general public, has been one of Israel's most important propaganda techniques. This book asks not only that we examine the complexity of the occupation and the sophisticated brutality of its mechanisms of control, but that we simultaneously see through them.

Laboratory

Although this book is largely framed between 1967 and the present, and primarily within the Occupied Territories of the West Bank and the Gaza Strip, it does not seek to claim that the spatial injustices of the conflict started only after the Six Day War of June 1967, and that the extent of the present injustices are confined to the 1967 occupied territories. Nor does it underestimate the century-old process of Zionist colonization, land-grab and dispossession that preceded it. It suggests though that any adequate address of the injustices and suffering of the conflict must begin by ending Israeli rule in the Occupied Territories and the daily suffering inflicted in its name. Focusing on the occupation itself, furthermore, allows Israel's spatial strategies to be investigated in their most brutal and intense manifestation, as within a 'laboratory of the extreme'. The technologies of control that enable Israel's continued colonization of the Palestinians in the West Bank and Gaza are located at the end of an evolutionary chain of techniques of colonization, occupation and governance developed throughout the history of Zionist settlement. Furthermore, every change in the geography of the occupation has been undertaken with the techniques and technologies of the time and in exchange with other developments worldwide. The main surge of the colonization of the West Bank in the 1980s coincided with the Reagan-era flight of the American middle classes and their fortification behind protective walls – both formations setting themselves against the poverty and violence they have themselves produced. Perfecting the politics of fear, separation, seclusion and visual control, the settlements, checkpoints, walls and other security measures are also the last gesture in the hardening of enclaves, and the physical and virtual extension of borders in the context of the more recent global 'war on terror'. The architecture of Israeli occupation could thus be seen as an accelerator and an acceleration of other global political processes, a worst-case scenario of capitalist globalization and its spatial fall-out. The extended significance of this 'laboratory' lies in the fact that the techniques of domination, as well as the techniques of resistance to them, have expanded and multiplied across what critical geographer Derek Gregory called the 'colonial present',[18] and beyond – into the metropolitan centres of global cities.

Indeed, beyond their physical reality, the territories of Israel/Palestine have constituted a schematic description of a conceptual system whose properties have been used to understand other geopolitical problems. The 'Intifada' unfolding in Iraq is a part of an imaginary geography that Makram Khoury-Machool called the 'Palestinization of Iraq'.[19] Yet, if the Iraqi resistance is perceived to have been 'Palestinized', the American military has been 'Israelized'. Furthermore, both the American and Israeli militaries have adopted counter-insurgency tactics that increasingly resemble the guerrilla methods of their enemies. When the wall around the American Green Zone in Baghdad looks as if it had been built from left-over components of the West Bank Wall; when 'temporary closures' are imposed on entire Iraqi towns and villages and reinforced with earth dykes and barbed wire; when larger regions are carved up by road blocks and checkpoints; when the homes of suspected terrorists are destroyed, and 'targeted assassinations' are introduced into a new global militarized geography – it is because the separate conflicts now generally collected under the heading of the 'war on terror' are the backdrop to the formation of complex 'institutional ecologies' that allow the exchange of technologies, mechanisms, doctrines, and spatial strategies between various militaries and the organizations that they confront, as well as between the civilian and the military domains.

The politics of separation

Each of the spatial technologies and practices to which the following chapters are dedicated is both a system of colonial control and a means of separation. Israeli domination in the West Bank and Gaza always shifted between selective physical presence and absence, the former dealing with Israel's territorial and the latter with its demographic strategy – aiming to gain land without the people living in it. It thus operated by imposing a complex compartmentalized system of spatial exclusion that at every scale is divided into two. The logic of 'separation' (or, to use the more familiar Afrikaans word, 'apartheid') between Israelis and Palestinians within the Occupied Territories has been extended, on the larger, national scale, to that of 'partition'. At times, the politics of separation/partition has been dressed up as a formula for a peaceful settlement, at others as a bureaucratic-territorial arrangement of governance, and most recently as a means of unilaterally imposed domination, oppression and fragmentation of the Palestinian people and their land.

The Oslo Accords of the 1990s left the Israeli military in control of the interstices of an archipelago of about two hundred separate zones of Palestinian restricted autonomy in the West Bank and Gaza. The military governed the area by modulating flows of different types between these enclaves (money, waste, water, traffic). During the second Intifada, the Oslo lines of partition further hardened into mechanisms of control. The military checkpoints and the Wall, slipping seamlessly into this geography, have become not only brutal means of segregation but active sensors within Israel's network of surveillance, registering all the Palestinians passing through them. The process of partial decolonization, which was recently embodied in the evacuation of the ground surface of Gaza and the building of the Wall in the West Bank, is indicative of an attempt to replace one system of domination with another. If the former system of domination relied upon Israeli territorial presence within Palestinian areas and the direct governing of the occupied populations, the latter seeks to control the Palestinians from beyond the envelopes of their walled-off spaces, by selectively opening and shutting the different enclosures, and by relying on the strike capacity of the Air Force over Palestinian areas. In this territorial 'arrangement' the principle of separation has turned ninety degrees as well, with Israelis and Palestinians separated vertically, occupying different spatial layers. This process of 'distanciation', which saw the reduction in Israeli direct territorial presence on Palestinian territories and with it a degree of responsibility for the Palestinian population, resulted in a radical increase in the level of violence, with the period since the withdrawal from the Gaza Strip being the most devastating to Palestinian life and welfare since the beginning of the occupation.[20]

This conflation of separation/partition with security, violence and control is not surprising when we realize that it was largely Israeli military officers, serving or retired, that conducted territorial negotiations during all the Israel/Palestine peace (or partition) processes. Israel's logic of 'peacemaking' throughout the conflict was the monopoly of its war-makers. In the hands of Israeli generals, the territorial discourse of partition blurred the distinctions between war and peace.[21] Partition plans were presented as peace plans, while settlement masterplans, prepared by or submitted to Israeli governments, were also partition plans (planners placed settlements in those parts of the territories they wanted the government to annex).

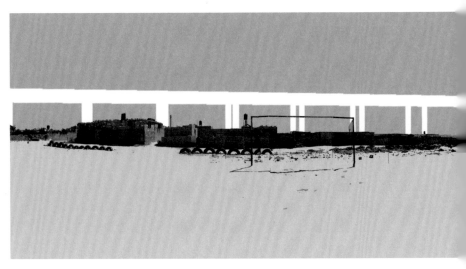

The proposed Palestinian link road leaving the Gaza Strip. Illustration: Eyal Weizman, 2002.

The politics of verticality

By 2006 the separation between Israeli and Palestinian areas in the Occupied Territories was not articulated on the surface of the terrain alone. Palestinians had been forced into a territorial patchwork of sealed islands around their cities, towns and villages, within a larger space controlled by Israel. Areas under Palestinian control included only the 200 fragments of land surface, but Israel controlled all the area around them, the vast water aquifer in the subterrain beneath them, as well as the militarized airspace above them. Revisioning the traditional geopolitical imagination, the horizon has been called upon to serve as one of the many boundaries raised up by the conflict, making the ground below and the air above separate and distinct from, rather than continuous with the surface of the earth.

The various borders of the conflict have accordingly manifested themselves as different topographical latitudes. Settlement master-planners aimed to achieve territorial control in the West Bank by constructing settlements on the high summits of the mountainous terrain. Across this fragmented geography the different Israeli settlements were woven together by lines of infrastructure routed through three-dimensional space: roads connecting Israeli settlements are raised on extended bridges spanning Palestinian routes and lands, or dive into tunnels beneath them, while narrow Palestinian underpasses are usually bored under Israeli multi-laned highways.

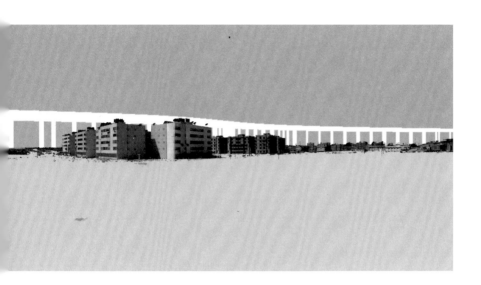

Palestinian militants have themselves discovered that Israeli walls and barriers can be easily bypassed in three dimensions. People and explosives are routinely smuggled in tunnels dug beneath the walls of Gaza, while home-made rockets are launched through the airspace above them. When the Wall's construction is complete, tunnels will no doubt be dug under it through the bedrock of the West Bank mountains.

In 2002, Ron Pundak, known as the 'architect' of the Oslo Process, explained to me that a three-dimensional matrix of roads and tunnels is the only practical way to divide and thereafter sustain the fragmented division of an otherwise 'indivisible territory'.[22] In the July 2000 negotiations in Camp David, President Clinton's outline for the partition of Jerusalem was based on the territorial/demographic status quo in declaring that whatever part of the city is inhabited by Jews will be Israeli and whatever part is inhabited by Palestinians will belong to the Palestinian state. According to Clinton's principles of partition, 64 kilometres of walls would have fragmented the city into two archipelago systems along national lines. Forty bridges and tunnels would have accordingly woven together these isolated neighbourhood-enclaves.[23] Clinton's principle of partition also meant that some buildings in the Old City would be vertically divided between the two states, with the ground floor and the basement being entered from the Muslim Quarter and used by Palestinian shop-owners belonging to the Palestinian state, and the upper floors being entered from the direction of the Jewish Quarter, used by Jews belonging to the Jewish state. Clinton also sincerely believed that three-dimensional borders could resolve the problem of partitioning the Temple Mount from Haram al-Sharif (for all others – the very same place). According to this plan Palestinians would control the surface of the Haram al-Sharif, the Dome of the Rock and Al-Aqsa mosque on top of it, while Israeli sovereignty would extend to the 'depth of the ground' underneath, where the temples were presumed to have lain. In an interview, Gilead Sher, Israel's chief negotiator at Camp David (and a divorce lawyer) explained it to me as a simple negotiation and 'bridging' technique: the swelling of the 'cake' to be partitioned (from a surface to a volume) will make each side feel that it has got more and done well out of the arrangement.[24]

Previously still, according to the Oslo Accords, the two main, estranged Palestinian territories of Gaza and the West Bank, 47 kilometres apart as the crow flies, should similarly have been connected into a single political unit.[25] In an interview given to the London *Daily Telegraph*, Prime Minister Benjamin Netanyahu explained the problem to his British interviewer by an analogy: 'You connected two states separated by water with a tunnel; we have the problem of connecting two entities separated by land . . .'[26] In the imagination of its engineers, the so-called 'safe passage' would become a Palestinian bridge in Palestinian jurisdiction spanning Israeli territory. This massive viaduct would support six lanes of motorway, two railway lines, high-voltage electricity cables and water and oil pipes. Over the past twelve years since the issue was first raised in the context of the Oslo process, thousands of hours of talks, dozens of professional committees and joint planning sessions, hundreds of plans, publications and declarations have been dedicated to the issue. Speculations included a bewildering variety of other possible solutions: sunken highways, tunnels and more elevated roads. At times, the political debate got entangled in the question of who should be on top: Israel preferred, naturally, that the Palestinian sovereign road should run under Israeli territory, in a tunnel or a ditch, while Palestinians preferred the alternative of an elevated bridge.[27] In 2005 the World Bank announced its support for plans drawn up by the RAND Corporation that adopted the model of an elevated Palestinian bridge spanning Israel between Gaza and the West Bank.[28]

In fact, similar territorial 'solutions' in three dimensions were a feature of each and every historical or contemporary partition plan for Palestine, and were outlined in the context of a series of partition plans prepared throughout the period of the British Mandate (1919–1948). Unable to carve out of Palestine a contiguous Jewish state, the map-makers of the 1947 United Nations Special Committee on Palestine (UNSCOP) presented an outline for two states, each of which was comprised of three elongated territorial bodies entangled with the other's three sections and connected at their corners. In these corners –

the 'kissing points' – where the border between the supposed territories of Israel and Palestine changed from a single-dimensional line to a non-dimensional point – planners proposed to embrace fully the third dimension, and maintain connections between the fragments of Israeli and Palestinian territories via tunnels or bridges.[29]

These massive infrastructural systems, drawing provisional borders through sovereign three-dimensional spaces, are the physical infrastructure of a unique type of political space, one desperately struggling to separate the inseparable, by attempting to multiply a single territorial reality and create two insular national geographies that occupy the same space, but crashing, as Israeli historian Meron Benvenisti remarkably put it, 'three dimensions into six: three Israeli and three Palestinian'.[30] Throughout this process the territory of Palestine emerged as a hologramatized 'hollow land' that seemed spawned of the imaginary world of seventeenth-century British astronomer Edmund Halley, or the nineteenth-century novels of Edgar Allan Poe and Jules Verne, who themselves foresaw a hollow earth inhabited in layers.[31] With it, the imaginary spaces of conflict have seemingly fully adopted the scale of a building, resembling a complex architectural construction, perhaps an airport, with its separate inbound and outbound levels, security corridors and many checkpoints. Cut apart and enclosed by its many barriers, gutted by underground tunnels, threaded together by over-passes and bombed from its militarized skies, the hollow land emerges as the physical embodiment of the many and varied attempts to partition it.

The organization of this book follows the different strata of this vertical construction of the Occupied Palestinian Territories. Starting in the deep aquifers of the West Bank, it progresses through its buried archaeology and then across its folded topographical surface to the militarized airspace above. Each chapter, describing different spatial practices and technologies of control and separation, focuses on a particular period in the history of the occupation. In this way, the succession of episodes following the development of Israel's technologies of domination and Palestinian resistance to them also charts a tragic process of cumulatively radicalizing violence.

However, with the technology and infrastructure deemed necessary for the physical segregation of Israelis from Palestinians, it appears that the vertical politics of separation and the logic of partition have been fully exhausted. The untenable territorial legal and sovereign knot created by the politics of separation/partition indicates a fundamental problem: although hundreds of proposals prepared by well-meaning cartographers from the period of the British mandate to the present have attempted to find a borderline and a geopolitical design along which Israel could be separated from Palestine, this path has repeatedly proven itself politically and geographically fleeting. The two political/geographic

The Tunnel Road, Daniel Bauer, 2002.

concepts of Israel and Palestine refer to and overlap across the very same place. The over-complex and clearly unsustainable practices and technologies that any designed territorial 'solution' for separation inexorably requires demonstrate this spatial paradox and beg us to consider whether the political road to partition is the right one to take.

Interlude – 1967

Israeli military strategy, conscious of the strategic limitations of Israel's pre-1967 borders, was defined by an oxymoron coined by former military general and then Knesset member Yigal Allon in 1959: 'pre-emptive counter-attack'.[1] According to a plan he drew up with Air Force Commander Ezer Weizman in the mid-1960s, Israel's Air Force would provide volumetric – that is, aerial – compensation for Israel's apparent inferiority on the ground.

In May 1967, after several clashes between Israeli and Syrian troops, originating in earlier dispute over water sources, Egyptian President Gamal Abd al-Nasser honoured his country's military pact with Syria and deployed ten divisions along the border to Israel, ordered UN observers to leave the Sinai and, on 23 May 1967, closed the Straits of Tiran to Israeli shipping. Israel formed a unity government, mobilized reserves and appointed, under popular pressure, the bellicose Moshe Dayan as Minister of Defence. In anxious anticipation of the war, sports grounds were consecrated as makeshift cemeteries and Israeli newspapers explicitly likened Nasser to Hitler. However, the Israeli Defence Force (IDF) under Chief of Staff Yitzhak Rabin, confident of its ability and seeing an opportunity to defeat the Arab armies, pressed – by some accounts even threatened – the hesitant government of Levy Eshkol into war. The 1967 war implemented Allon and Weizman's strategy to the letter. On 5 June 1967 the IDF launched an air strike that incapacitated the Egyptian and Jordanian Air Forces. This allowed Israel's ground forces to charge across the surface of the Sinai and the Gaza Strip. On 7 June the Old City of Jerusalem was surrounded and then occupied. The entire West Bank followed soon afterwards. On 9 June Israel attacked Syrian positions on the Golan Heights. By the end of the June 1967 war, Israeli soldiers were deployed behind clear territorial boundaries of mountain and water: the Suez Canal, the Jordan River on the Jordanian front and the line of volcanic mounts about 40 kilometres into the Syrian Golan Heights. The territory under Israeli control grew threefold, including the rest of former British Mandatory

Palestine – the 365 square kilometres of the Gaza Strip and the 5,655 square kilometres of the West Bank.[2] A period of economic prosperity began, due in no small part to the cheap labor drawn from the newly occupied Palestinian population of more than a million people, about a third of them refugees who had either fled or had been expelled to the region during the 1948 War.[3] On December 1967, the Israeli government decided to erase the internationally recognized 1949 Armistice Agreement's Green Line, which separated Israel from the West Bank and Gaza, from all atlases, maps and textbooks it published. However, except for the area around Jerusalem, Israel did not annex the territories, and according to international law, their status remained that of 'occupied territories'; in these territories, the Israeli military assumed legislative, executive and judicial powers.[4]

The area occupied had distinct topographical characteristics. The mountain ranges of Palestine were formed by the fissure of the Great Rift Valley, a 5,000 kilometre tectonic crack running north to south, from the Golan Heights to the eastern shores of Africa, on the Indian Ocean. The West Bank occupies the central portion of this mountain range. Marking its eastern edge is the Jordan River which meanders through the Jordan Valley where the weather is hot, dry and delusionary. The Palestinian population of the area is mainly located around the city of Jericho, a desert oasis on the Jerusalem–Amman road, in small villages and semi-nomadic Bedouin encampments. West of the Rift Valley the ridges rise fast and steep, scorched by wadies, deep canyons and cliffs. The mountain range itself is corrugated with a repetitive sequence of wrinkles and folds, whose elevation ranges from 500 to 1,000 metres above sea level. The summits are barren, rocky and windswept, while the valleys between are fertile and often cultivated with field crops. The six most populous Palestinian cities of the West Bank – Jenin, Nablus, Ramallah, Jerusalem, Bethlehem and Hebron – are strung from north to south along the mountain range's line-of-water-divide by the Mountain Road (now Road 60), the most important transport route in the West Bank. A few kilometres west of the line-of-water-divide are the western slopes of the West Bank – an area characterized by a benign landscape that slopes gently westwards, with fertile soil and plenty of water and a position close to and overlooking the main Israeli metropolitan centres on the coastal plain.

The hydrological cycle of the Jordan Valley basin, of which Israel/Palestine and the surrounding states form part, is a system of cyclical flows that cuts through the area's political and security borders. In winter the water evaporating off the surface of the Mediterranean Sea condenses into rain clouds. The clouds are blown eastwards over the Israeli coastal plains towards the West Bank mountains. There they break against their peaks in sudden bursts of violent rain.

The rainwater runs into gullies and streams that drain westwards through the western slopes of the West Bank mountains and back through the Israeli coastal plain into the sea. Some of this rainwater filters through the porous limestone and drains into the soil. Depending on the porosity of the rocks, it may take decades for the water to filter through and collect in underground 'storage areas', trapped by a 'floor' and 'ceiling' of impenetrable rock. There, within the western slopes of the West Bank mountains, on both sides of the 1949 Green Line, the water of the mountain aquifer, can be easily pumped out.

This hydrological condition asserts itself in the organization of habitation on the surface. The location of water-extraction points has determined the location of Palestinian towns and villages, later that of the Jewish settlements, and recently the meanderings of the path of the Wall in this region.[5] It is thus not surprising that, through specially constructed tunnels equipped with grills and drainage pipes, the Wall seeks to be as permeable to water as it seeks to be impermeable to people.

Indeed, one of the most crucial battlegrounds of the Israeli–Palestinian conflict is below the surface. About 80 per cent of the mountain aquifer is located under the West Bank. Israeli politicians generally believe, although this fact has recently been contested,[6] that Israel's future depends on these waters, and have therefore been unwilling to give control of it to the Palestinians, regardless of the question of who may control the surface terrain above. The erosion of the principles of Palestinian sovereignty in its subsoil is carried out by a process so bureaucratically complex that it is almost invisible.[7] Although the aquifer is the sole water source for residents of the West Bank, Israel uses 83 per cent of its annually available water for the benefit of Israeli cities and its settlements, while West Bank Palestinians use the remaining 17 per cent.[8] Hundreds of thousands of Palestinians in the West Bank and virtually all Palestinians in Gaza thus receive water irregularly and in limited amounts.[9] Israel's 'politics of verticality' is also manifested in the depth to which water pumps are allowed to reach. Israeli pumps may reach down to the waters of the common aquifers whilst Palestinian pumps are usually restricted to a considerably shorter reach, only as far down as seasonal wells trapped within shallow rock formations, which, from a hydrological perspective, are detached from the fundamental lower layers of 'ancient waters'.

Under the terms of what former Minister of National Infrastructure Ephi Eitam termed in 2005 'the Water Intifada', the Palestinians were accused of deliberate waste and sewage dumping in order to 'pollute Israel's ground water'.[10] In the imagination of the military general-cum-leader of the settlers, Palestinians were using the mountain topography as routes for a new kind of 'chemical-biological warfare'. His accusation did not acknowledge the fact that the Israeli authorities failed to provide the minimum necessary sewage infrastructure for Palestinians throughout the period of direct occupation although this is the legal duty of an occupying force.[11] The sanitary conditions of West Bank Palestinians were aggravated by Israel's segregation politics that isolated Palestinian towns and villages behind barriers of all kinds. This policy generated more than 300 pirate dumping sites where truckloads of waste were poured into the valleys beside towns and villages.[12] Paradoxically, the restrictions on the flow of people accelerated the trans-boundary flow of their refuse. Furthermore, Israeli companies have themselves used sites in the West Bank for their own waste disposal. Some tens of thousands of tonnes of household garbage from the Tel Aviv metropolitan area have been dumped, in one example, into the largest disused quarry in the West Bank near Nablus.[13] A total breakdown of sewerage systems has occurred throughout. The few existing treatment projects are overflowing, and unpiped sewage runs over-ground in most valleys. In the wild frontier of the West Bank, Israel's planning chaos means Jewish neighbourhoods and settlements are often constructed without permits, and populated before and regardless of sewerage systems being installed and connected. This sewage runs from the hills to the valleys, simply following the force of gravity and topography, through and across any of the boundaries that may be put in front of it. The topography of the West Bank guarantees that all raw sewage from hilltop settlements will pass down a valley next to a Palestinian town or village[14] and that, mixing with Palestinian sewage, travelling along the same open valleys, it will eventually end up in Israeli territory. Instead of fresh water flowing in the specially conceived water pipes installed under the Wall, Israel absorbs large quantities of raw sewage from all across the West Bank. The closures and barriers of the recent Intifada thus created the very condition against which they sought to fortify. The accumulated dirt within the walled-off Palestinian areas confirmed the hygienic phobia of Zionism. Blurring the literal with the metaphorical, the piles of dirt and sewage affirmed a common national-territorial imagination that sees the presence of Palestinians as a 'defiled' substance within the 'Israeli' landscape, or as 'matter out of place,' to use Mary Douglas's words, in whose book, *Purity and Danger*, dirt is defined and understood in terms of transgression of boundaries.[15] By inducing dirt and raw sewage, Israel could go on demanding the further application of its hygienic practices of separation and segregation. The legitimacy of these acts is defined as an immediate reaction to its own violation. The result is an ever-radicalizing feedback loop, by which sewage marks the point of collision between the two meanings – a metaphorical political notion concerned with the health of the state, and the literal physical sensation of abjection. The politics of separation has thus accelerated the emergence of a physiognomy of a carved up and compartmentalized landscape of discrete units, pulled apart by sharp contours, and woven together by the flow

Sewage flowing down Shiloh Valley in the West Bank.

of sewage. At points where the separation walls are so high that they create the illusion of complete separation, the thin path of foamy dark waters flowing across and under it, remains the last remnant of a shared ecosystem.

Sewage is also used as a tool in the hands of government agents. As part of the state effort to dislocate the Bedouin tribe of Jahalin, camped on the lower slopes of a mountain onto which the settlement-town of Ma'ale Adumim is now expanding, the military civil administration disconnected one of the settlement's sewage pipes, flooding large areas within and around the Bedouin camp with streams and ponds of polluted matter, forcing it to relocate.[16]

Only half of Gaza Strip residents are actually connected to the central functioning sewerage system. Raw sewage flows overground the length of some Palestinian refugee camps, pouring out onto the sand dunes that surround them or directly onto Gaza's beaches. When sewage overflows and 'private shit', from under the ground, invades the public realm, it becomes a private hazard but also a political asset.[17] In some places, efforts by UN departments to replace existing systems of infrastructure with permanent underground plumbing have been rejected. The raw sewage affirms the refugee camp's state of temporariness and with it the urgency of claim for return.

For Israel, the same sewage continuously affirms another preconception – the connection between pollution and terror. At the beginning of 2005, Avi Dichter, then head of the GSS – Israel's General Security Service (Shin Bet) – and now a government minister explained to the Knesset (Israeli Parliament) Security and Foreign Relations Committee: 'From the level of the satellites' the rectangular grid of streets in the Gaza refugee camp of Jebalia 'looks like that of Manhattan, only when you get nearer to it, one notices that the large pool at its centre is not the lake in Central Park, but a huge pool of sewage.'[18] Indeed, in the eyes of generations of Israeli security officials, the refugee camps are seen not only as the locus of resistance, but the very condition responsible for its perpetuation. Accordingly, if sewage breeds terrorism, these Palestinian spaces must be disinfected.

Indeed, in his only commitment to release Palestinian money held by Israel to fund Palestinian public services since the outbreak of the Intifada, in 2003 Finance Minister Benjamin Netanyahu allocated funds in order to pre-empt a hygiene crisis, hoping the money would be used to construct a few sewage treatment facilities near Palestinian cities. His actions echo the confession of Jerusalem's long-standing mayor Teddy Kollek: 'For Jewish Jerusalem I did something in the past twenty-five years. For East Jerusalem? Zilch! . . . Yes, we installed a sewage system for them and improved the water supply. Do you know why? Do you think it was for their good, for their welfare? Forget it! There were some cases of cholera there, and the Jews were afraid that they would catch it, so we installed sewerage and a water system.'[19] He further remembered: 'When modern sewage and drainage systems were finally installed the unbearable stench that was prevalent in east Jerusalem before the [1967] war was finally eliminated . . .'[20]

The Jewish neighbourhood of Shmuel Hanavi, early 1970s. Image courtesy of the archive of the Israeli Project (IP), Zvi Efrat and Zvi Elhyani.

1.

Jerusalem: Petrifying the Holy City

On 27 June 1967, twenty days after the Israeli Army completed the occupation of the eastern part of Jerusalem, the unity government of Levi Eshkol annexed almost 70 square kilometres of land and incorporated approximately 69,000 Palestinians within the newly expanded boundaries of the previously western Israeli municipality of Jerusalem.[1] The new delimitations were designed by a military committee with the aim of redrawing the state's 1949 borders, prior to any evacuation of occupied territories that might have been forced on Israel by international agreement. The outline attempted to include empty areas for the city's expansion and to exclude, as far as it was possible, areas densely populated with Palestinians.[2] The new boundaries sought to 'unite' within a single metropolitan area the western Israeli city, the Old City, the rest of the previously Jordanian-administered city, 28 Palestinian villages, their fields, orchards, and tracts of desert, into a single 'holy', 'eternal' and 'indivisible' Jewish capital. Years later, Mayor of Jerusalem Teddy Kollek (who served in this post on behalf of the Labor party between 1965 and 1993) would say of the incongruousness captured within these borders: 'Jerusalem is, most likely, the only contemporary capital that pays drought compensation to farmers in villages within its boundaries . . .'[3]

The following year a new urban masterplan for the city outlined in drawings and verbal instructions the guiding principles of development and 'unification' of the urban ensemble now called Jerusalem. The 'first and cardinal principle [of the 1968 masterplan] was to ensure [Jerusalem's] unification . . . to build the city in a manner that would prevent the possibility of its being repartitioned'.[4] Following this masterplan and a series of subsequent masterplans, amendments and updates during the forty years of Israeli occupation, twelve remote and homogenous Jewish 'neighbourhoods' were established in the occupied areas incorporated into the city. They were laid out to complete a belt of built fabric that enveloped and bisected the Palestinian neighbourhoods and villages annexed to the city. Industrial zones were located beyond the new neighbourhoods on the fringes of the municipal area, keeping West Bank Palestinians who provided the city with a cheap and 'flexible' labor force (until Palestinian labor was almost completely barred from the beginning of the second Intifada in the autumn of 2000) out of the city itself. An outer, second circle of settlements – termed by Israeli planners the 'organic' or 'second wall', composed of a string of dormitory suburbs – was established beyond the municipal boundaries, extending the city's metropolitan reach even further. It is around this 'second, organic wall' that the concrete Separation Wall now meanders. An ever-expanding network of roads and infrastructure was constructed to weave together the disparate shards of this dispersed urban geography. 'Greater Jerusalem' became thus a sprawling metropolis reaching the outskirts of Ramallah in the north, Bethlehem in the south, and Jericho in the east – a massive section of the middle of the West Bank – isolating Palestinians from their cultural centres in Jerusalem and cutting off the north of the West Bank from the south. At present the new Jewish neighbourhoods within the municipal boundaries is home to about 200,000 settlers – almost the same number as all the other settlers in the West Bank combined. Together with the inhabitants of the dormitory settlements of the 'second wall' around the city, the total Jewish population of 'Greater Jerusalem' represents about three-quarters of all Israelis settled on areas occupied in 1967. Israeli activist Jeff Halper was therefore not exaggerating when he stated that 'metropolitan Jerusalem *is* the occupation'.[5]

This project could not have been undertaken without massive government investments in infrastructure and subsidized housing for Jews, but an additional major factor in this colonization was a cultural one – the attempt to 'domesticate' the occupied and annexed territories – to transform, in the eyes of Israeli Jews, the unfamiliar occupied territories into familiar home ground. The problem of planners and architects was not only how to build fast on this 'politically strategic' ground, but how to naturalize the new construction projects, make them appear as organic parts of the Israeli capital and the holy city. Architecture – the organization, form and style by which these neighbourhoods were built, the way they were mediated, communicated and understood – formed a visual language that was used to blur the facts of occupation and sustain territorial claims of expansion. This project was thus an attempt to sustain national narratives of belonging while short-circuiting and even blocking other narratives.

This role invested in architecture has been written into the 1968 masterplan. Although the planning principles that guided this masterplan were largely based on modernist town planning principles, apparent in the plan's promotion of massive traffic networks and the separation of the city into mono-functional zones (housing, shopping, service, industry), the 1968 masterplan also professed its 'commitment' to the orientalist aesthetics and urban development principles

The Wall in the Jerusalem region. The red line includes the authorized and built sections of the Wall within and around the Jerusalem area. The dotted red line is the planned extension of the barrier eastwards around the settlement of Ma'ale adumim. The shaded area is the extent of Jerusalem's municipal boundaries. The neighbourhoods/settlements are marked blue. Palestinian towns and village are marked brown.

of 'colonial regionalism', a sensibility characteristic of the period of British rule over Palestine (1917–48), especially in its earlier years.[6] The manifestation of this sensibility, promoted across the British Empire by followers and members of the 'Arts and Crafts' movement, was an attempt to preserve and incorporate local building traditions, materials and crafts within contemporary buildings. On the urban scale it was expressed in attempts to dissolve 'old' with new, archaeology with living fabric.

A special section of the 1968 masterplan was dedicated to a discussion of a British Mandate-era municipal ordinance, a bylaw enacted in 1918 by the first military governor of the city, Ronald Storrs, which mandated a variety of different kinds of limestone, collectively and colloquially known as 'Jerusalem Stone', as the only material allowed on exterior walls in the city.[7] During the early years of the Israeli state leading to the occupation (1948–67), the bylaw has remained officially in place, mainly at the centre of the western part of Jerusalem. However, as it became increasingly controversial in the eyes of architects and planners, it was not always rigorously enforced, especially not in the peripheries of the municipal areas. The 1968 masterplan supported the tightening of the stone bylaw and the use of stone cladding within the entire area annexed to the city. By emphasizing and reinforcing the power of the bylaw, stone cladding was used to authenticate

new construction on sites remote from the historical centre, giving the disparate new urban shards a unified character, helping them appear as organic parts of the city. 'The value of the visual impression that is projected by the stone', stated the 1968 masterplan, is that it carries 'emotional messages that stimulate other sensations embedded in our collective memory, producing [within the context of new construction] strong associations to the ancient holy city of Jerusalem'.[8]

Storrs' 'stare of Medusa'

On 9 December 1917, surrounded and with their supply lines cut, the Jerusalem divisions of the Ottoman army surrendered to the Allied forces under General Sir Edmund Allenby in a battle celebrated in the British press as a modern crusade.[9] Three weeks later, Colonel Ronald Storrs, a political attaché to the British military, was appointed military governor of Jerusalem. Storrs considered the return of Jews to their land as an act of salvation and historic justice. He later wrote that the Zionist enterprise was 'forming for England "a little loyal Jewish Ulster" in a sea of potentially hostile Arabism'.[10] Storrs saw Jerusalem through the religious-orientalist perspective of a European purview, and his role in Herodian terms, as a link in the long line of the city's builders. Although Jerusalem of the late Ottoman era was a rather cosmopolitan city, with large, often lavish, compounds belonging to different nations and faiths, the war had transformed it quite radically. Mud, wood and tin constructions proliferated as Jerusalem became a destination for war refugees. For the British administration the urgent urban problem was the city's 'parasitic population . . . priests, caretakers, monks, missionaries, pious women, clerks, lawyers, and a crowd of riffraff'. The Jewish Quarter was referred to as a ghetto possessing 'the squalid ugliness and disharmony of the cities

Building in Jerusalem, 1967–72: Film stills, Ministry of Construction and Housing.

of south-eastern Europe'.[11] An artificial topography had been created outside the city walls by generations of refuse deposited there.

Determined to find a solution to the city's 'overcrowding and unsightliness', Storrs invited Alexandria's British city engineer, William H. McLean, to draw up a redevelopment plan. McLean arrived in Jerusalem in March 1918 and took two weeks to submit an initial report to the military administration recommending that all new structures within the Old City, including those rooftops that were visible from higher ground, were 'to be constructed of and covered with stone'.[12] Furthermore, according to McLean, the municipality should have removed all rubbish and 'ramshackle buildings' abutting the external perimeter of the Old City wall in order to make way for a ring-shaped park where thousands of trees were to be planted. Set in the centre of this green parkland, the Old City was to be presented as a precious rock, an exhibition-piece of living biblical archaeology. On 8 April 1918, a week after McLean's departure, Storrs declared a freeze on all construction within and around the Old City. He went on to ban the use of plaster, mud, tents or corrugated iron as construction materials, stating that only local limestone was to be used in the construction of new buildings, extensions and rooftops within the perimeter around the Old City.[13] Storrs then invited an architect of the British Arts and Crafts movement, Charles Robert Ashbee, one of the main promoters of 'colonial regionalism', whom he had met during his service in Cairo, to become director of a newly founded Pro-Jerusalem Society, which was conceived in 1919 to oversee the preservation and reconstruction of the city according to the McLean plan.

For Storrs, stone embodied biblical tradition. 'Jerusalem is literally a city built upon rock. From that rock, cutting soft but drying hard, has for three thousand years been quarried the clear white stone, weathering blue-grey or amber-yellow with time, whose solid walls, barrel vaulting and pointed arches have preserved through the centuries a hallowed and immemorial tradition.'[14] Although the stone regulation attempted to reinforce an image of orientalized locality, it had also made the cost of new construction prohibitive to all but the rich, the British authorities, and large overseas organizations; paradoxically, therefore, by pricing out the local population of Jerusalem, it delocalized the city with its own supposed vernacular crafts and architecture.

Although the aim of the McLean plan and Storrs' stone regulation had been to isolate and differentiate the Old City from its surroundings, ten years after Storrs' departure from Jerusalem, in the 1936 Town Planning Ordinance, the stone regulation was extended to apply to the entire municipal area and, significantly, to the new neighbourhoods that were rapidly sprawling beyond the Old City walls. By requiring the same architectural rigour outside the walls, this amendment allowed the outer neighbourhoods to share in the city's particular visual character.[15] The spread of Jerusalem had been accelerated by the relative prosperity of the 1920s and by improvements in building technology. As concrete technology developed and concrete structures became cheaper, more available and more efficient, the Arts and Crafts tradition promoted by Ashbee and Storrs through the Pro-Jerusalem Society, with its emphasis on traditional stone *construction*, came under attack from developers and builders. Towards the end of World War II and the period of the British Mandate, the pressure to develop led to a compromise that was represented by a seemingly minor textual modification of the stone regulation. While the previous Ordinance of 1936 demanded that 'the external walls of all buildings shall be *constructed* of stone', the masterplan of 1944 confirmed practices that were already in effect when it demanded only that 'the external walls and columns of houses and the face of any wall abutting on a road shall be *faced* with natural, square dressed stone'[16] [my emphasis]. This amendment reduced the role of stone from a construction material to a cladding material. Stone became a stick-on signifying element for creating visual unity between new construction and the Old City, thus visually confirming the municipal boundaries – as whatever building appeared to be built in stone was perceived part of the city of Jerusalem.

With the years, the layer of stone has thinned. At the beginning of the Mandate period, and following the principles of the 'Arts and Crafts' movement, stone was primarily used as a construction material, and walls were made of large blocks of solid stone. Since the 1930s a mixed concrete and stone construction technique became more common and a thinner layer of stone – 20cm thick – became part of the structural logic of the building, and together with reinforced concrete, took some of the building load. As mere cladding, the stone has become thinner still and no longer formed a structural part of the building. Today, Israeli building standards allow layers of sawn stone just 6cm thick.

In the 1948 war, Jerusalem was divided between the Kingdom of Jordan and the state of Israel, with the former securing total control over the Old City and its eastern neighbourhoods. In the Jordanian city, whose size under Jordanian administration was deliberately restricted to prevent it competing with the Jordanian capital, Amman, the 1944 masterplan still remained in full effect. The plan was updated in 1964 by its original architect, Henry Kendall, a Briton who continued to enforce the stone cladding bylaw throughout the entire though compact Jordanian city. On the other side of the partition lines, until the 1967 war, Jerusalem's 1955 planning codes separated the Israeli part of the city into rings in which the use of stone was required to varying degrees.[17] At the centre, comprehensive use of stone cladding on all visible planes of the building was still required. In the second ring out from the centre, the requirement became more lenient, allowing the use of other materials to varying degrees, while the outermost circle, which included the industrial areas, was entirely liberated from the requirement to use stone. In the post-1967 period, this logic was effectively inverted. The demand for a varied application of stone was replaced by a unifying regulation that demanded the most rigorous application of stone cladding throughout the entire expanded municipal area. Since most new construction now took place on the periphery of the city, remote West Bank hilltops, never historically part of Jerusalem and now gerrymandered into it as sites for new construction, fell within the legal boundaries of the most rigorous application of the stone bylaw.

This time, the demand to stone clad the housing projects in the new Jewish neighbourhoods met with the resistance of Israeli developers. Indeed, two political considerations seemed to meet head on over this issue. The Ministry of Housing, implementing government policy, wanted to promote new construction as fast and as far away as possible from the city centre in order to buttress Israeli claims to the entire annexed area. Fast construction meant doing it cheaply and there was no place in such a scheme for the rigorous use of expensive stone cladding. The alternative, political-aesthetic consideration was presented by Mayor Kollek and his Deputy Mayor for Physical Planning, the historian Meron Benvenisti, who wanted a smaller, denser city, and to make new neighbourhoods appear as parts of an organic whole by demanding the use of stone cladding.[18] Facing intense government pressure, the municipality has been unable to determine the location and size of the new neighbourhoods. Furthermore, although the Jerusalem planning department and even Mayor Kollek personally insisted that the extra investment in stone cladding would repay itself in little over a decade through savings on repainting and other maintenance costs, developers were under pressure to reduce their immediate expenses, and so insisted on a relaxing of the bylaw.[19] Under the jurisdiction of the municipality, the bylaw was not relaxed, but developers were granted a bizarre but revealing concession: the stone cladding was allowed to project beyond the building's envelope. Where this jutted out into a public thoroughfare, the layer of stone performing a 'public' service could occupy a thin sliver of public space.

There were other grounds for resistance to the requirement for stone cladding. For Israeli architects raised on modernist traditions, stone cladding countered their belief in the 'honesty of materials', and the received wisdom that the function and structure should dictate a building's organizational logic and visual appearance. These architects saw stone cladding as decadent veneer. Debates between municipal planners and architects regarding the use of stone cladding also engaged with other formal and technical questions, centring at different periods on the relation of stone cladding to raw concrete, on the logic of applying stone cladding to the upper floors of high-rise buildings, and on the correct relation between stone and glass in office buildings. Various cladding details and construction methods were developed in response to these debates. Some cladding elements sought to emulate the appearance of solid stone construction. Cladding exposes its thickness, and thus its nature, at the corners of buildings, and it is usually enough for an architect to study the corner to verify whether a building is clad or built of solid construction. The architecture of the corner has thus quickly become an obsession in Jerusalem and a particular architectural detail – the 'Dastor Stone,' a hollowed-out stone with a 90-degree 'L' section – can now be placed on the corners of buildings thereby rendering cladding indistinguishable from solid construction. While some cladding details were designed to simulate authentic stone construction, others were developed in order to make sure the observer understood that the stone is anything but structural.[20] The 1968 Jerusalem masterplan referred to these architectural details and alluded to the debates regarding the use of stone cladding, siding firmly with those seeking to preserve its rigid application. 'The function and value of the masonry construction must be measured not only according to an architectural value that seeks to reveal a building's construction method in its appearance, but according to a cultural value that sees buildings as conveyors of emotional messages referring to the image of the city. It is against this cultural value that we must weigh the [extra] price of construction . . . this justifies, even today, the requirement to maintain the continuity of stone facing as the material which embodies the appearance of the city.'[21] That a simple limestone cladding could be imbued with this quasi-religious mysticism is hardly surprising in a climate in which 'Jerusalem Stone' is presented in the sales brochure of one of its local manufacturers as 'a precious stone, carved from the holy mountains of Jerusalem . . . a wonderful masterpiece of nature', or by an Israeli architectural critic as an element 'in whose texture, the signature of the twentieth century is not yet engraved, sensually reminding us that man is but a small detail in a large and timeless life-cycle'.[22]

Indeed, for a succession of the city's builders, from Ronald Storrs to the Israeli planners of post-1967 Jerusalem, the stone has embodied not only the earthly nature of place, but also a sense of spirituality and even holiness. Indeed, by the various religious traditions that inhabit it, Jerusalem is perceived to be much more than a city that contains a number of holy places, or the location of historical holy events; instead, it is perceived to be a holy-city in its entirety.[23] When the city itself is perceived to be holy, and when its boundaries are flexibly redrawn to suit ever-changing political aims, holiness inevitably becomes a planning issue. Since the extent of the municipal area is also the border of a zone that is understood to be holy, wherever the stone façades were applied, so the holiness of Jerusalem sprawled. And holiness, as Meron Benvenisti explained, is an extremely potent political definition, for 'all of the territory within its municipal boundaries is regarded as the "Holy City" by the religious establishment [that forms part of the Israeli state]. And this is no trivial matter, since from the moment a particular area is designated as part of the Holy City, it comes under Jerusalem's religious laws, whose sole objective is to strengthen the spiritual ties between Jews and their sacred city.'[24] Like the stare of Medusa, Storrs' bylaw has been used by Jerusalem's planners to petrify all construction in the new neighbourhoods – shopping malls and kindergartens, community centres and synagogues, office buildings, electrical relay stations and sports halls and, above all, housing – into stone. Suburban neighbourhoods placed on remote sites outside the historical boundaries of the city were thus imbued with the city's overall sacred identity.

But these architectural/optical manipulations were not always convincing. Azmi Bishara, the notable Palestinian member of Israeli parliament, sarcastically observed: 'only in Jerusalem the natural stone that was quarried from these very rocks could look as a foreign element within these same mountains . . .'[25] Furthermore, the stone itself is often foreign to Jerusalem. Contrary to perceptions, before the 1967 war, 'Jerusalem Stone' also came from outside the city, from quarries adjacent to Palestinian villages and towns in Galilee in the north of Israel. When the environmental hazard of stone dust restricted the quarrying industry in Israel 'proper', the stone quarries mushroomed in the West Bank to cater for Jerusalem's endless appetite for stone. It is a paradox that the very material used for cladding the expanding Jewish Jerusalem has become one of the most important branches of the Palestinian economy, quarried mainly from the bedrock around Hebron and Ramallah. The largest of these quarries, located just outside the northern limit of the Jerusalem municipality, leaving a layer of dust on the clothes and skin of anyone travelling past it, is referred to by Palestinians as 'Tora-Bora' because the monochromatic tone of its artificial topography is reminiscent of images of the landscape of Afghanistan.

Above: The Jewish neighbourhood of French Hill. Below: East Talpiyot neighbourhood, early 1970s. Images courtesy of IP.

Housing Cluster in Gilo, 1972 (Architect: Salo Hershman), IP.

Architectural transformations

Throughout its ninety-year history, the Jerusalem stone bylaw has been applied within the context of different architectural periods, styles and fashions. Not being an exclusive feature of any of these, it has been applied and understood differently within these various contexts. Stone has been demanded and applied in the 'traditional' context of colonial regionalism, it has clad buildings of the modern movement's 'international style', it was used to clad hotels and tall office buildings, government buildings, theatres, shopping malls and community centres. It has been also a central element in the production of the historicist context of post-modern architecture that fully emerged in the city to coincide with the housing boom of the post-1967 war period.

Two Israeli critical architectural historians of the new generation – Zvi Efrat[26] and Alona Nitzan-Shiftan[27] – have each showed that 1967 marked the culmination of a process of stylistic transition within Israeli architecture. It was primarily the state housing projects in and around Jerusalem that helped redefine Israeli architectural practice. Although the emergent style has been a continuation of previous attempts by Israeli architects to 'orientalize' architecture, the post-1967 war period coincided with a time of uncertainty and turmoil in the development of architecture worldwide. As the 1960s were drawing to an end, the tenets of the modern movement were being challenged. The vanguard of planning and architecture attempted to escape the 'simple' utilitarian logic of the modern movement, reinvigorate design with a reawakened obsession with urban history and charge the language of architecture with symbolic, communicative and semiotic content. The architecture of the period started to be infatuated with 'place', 'region' and the 'historic city', with a passion that pitched the idea of 'dwelling' against that of 'housing', and 'home' as a remedy for an increasingly alienating modern world.[28] These emergent sensibilities went worldwide under the general terms of 'post-modernism'. Within this context it is not surprising that Jerusalem became an international *cause célèbre*.

In 1968, to help deal with the complex implications of planning and building in Jerusalem, Mayor Kollek inaugurated the biennial Jerusalem Committee which was set up to review and advise on municipal plans for the city's restoration and development. Kollek, the Viennese liberal who loved to surround himself with intellectuals who would portray him as an enlightened ruler, recalled that 'immediately when the city was united, I invited 30 or 40 people here, the best minds of the world, to consult on what we should do . . .'[29] The Advisory Committee included prominent international architects, urban planners, theologians, historians and academics, amongst them the architects Louis Kahn, Isamu Noguchi and Christopher Alexander, the architectural critic Bruno Zevi, the American historian of technology and cities Lewis Mumford, and the philosopher Isaiah Berlin. The 1968 plan was presented to the Jerusalem Committee on its second meeting in December 1970. The passionate academic discussion of the Jerusalem Committee never challenged the political dimension of the municipal plan and Israel's right or wisdom in colonizing and 'uniting' the city under its rule, nor did it discuss the dispossession of Palestinians that it brought about. Rather, it argued about the formal and architectural dimension of this colonization.[30] The history of the occupation is full of liberal 'men of peace' who are responsible for, or who at least sweeten, the injustice committed by the occupation. The occupation would not have been possible without them.

Although members of the committee supported the use of stone cladding, as was already outlined in the masterplan, they were unanimous in their rejection of the plan's overall modernist premise, especially in its lack of regard for the historical nature of the city. Upon being presented with the masterplan some of the committee members were enraged and others brought literally to tears, lamenting the impending 'destruction' of the city by a modernist development plan of yesterday, and demanding that Jerusalem's planners instead 'translate [Jerusalem's] special quality into generative principles which would guide the city's future growth'.[31] The committee finally managed to convince the municipality to cancel a dense system of flyovers proposed in the 1968 masterplan to be contructed near the Old City. The main concern of the committee, however, was with the Old City itself, but before further engaging with its advice on plans for its restoration, a few words must be expended on its war-time destruction, and what was revealed under its ruins.

Destruction by design

On the evening of 10 June 1967, before the cease-fire was reached and while still under the fog of war, the Israeli military performed the first significant urban transformation in the Occupied Territories, flattening the entire Maghariba (north African) Quarter, which was located immediately in front of the Wailing Wall on the southeastern edge of the Old City. This destruction was undertaken in order to make way for an enormous plaza extending between the Jewish Quarter and the Wailing Wall. This urban transformation, undertaken by the military without explicit government order, demonstrates more than anything else that the military had no intention of retreating from this occupied area. Chaim Hertzog, the Irish-born first military governor of the Occupied Territories, and later the sixth president of Israel, took much of the credit for the destruction of this densely populated neighbourhood, home to several thousand people living in 125 houses. 'When we visited the Wailing Wall we found a toilet attached to it . . . we decided to remove it, and from this we came to the conclusion that we could evacuate the entire area in front of the Wailing Wall . . . a historical opportunity that will never return . . . We knew that the following Saturday, June 14, would be the Shavuot Holiday and that many will want to come to pray . . . it all had to be completed by then.'[32] In 1917 Chaim Weizmann, president of the World Zionist Organization, pleaded futilely with the British military to do the same several months after they had occupied Jerusalem. With the Maghariba Quarter intact, access to the Wailing Wall was by means of a small winding alley, which became the focus of much conflict between Jews travelling to pray at the Wailing Wall and residents.

After the complete destruction of the Maghariba Quarter, the military set about evacuating the 3,000 Palestinian refugees from the 1948 war, who had settled in the Jewish Quarter, which was adjacent to the Maghariba Quarter in the west, and now overlooked the huge destruction site between it and the Wailing Wall. In 1948 the Jewish Quarter was besieged by the Jordan Legion, and its population of about 2,000 was forced to flee. Thereafter the Quarter became the destination of Palestinian refugees fleeing from areas that had come under Israeli rule. After the 1967 war the government wanted to restore Jewish life in the Jewish Quarter. First to be forcibly removed were eighty families of the Palestinian refugees who lived in buildings that had formerly been synagogues.[33] The rest of the inhabitants of the Quarter – Muslims and Christians, Palestinians as well as Armenians – were gradually expelled after an Israeli High Court of Justice ruling allowed it. Prior to the 1948 war, the borders of the Quarter had been porous and its dimensions could not be precisely defined. After the 1967 war, the government cleansed an area of approximately 9 hectares, larger than all previous accounts of the area of the Quarter. Two months after the war, on 31 August, the entire Old City was declared a site of antiquity, and no building was permitted until an archaeological survey had been conducted. The enlarged Quarter, now brutally emptied of its life, became the site of intense archaeological surveys. Three years later, in 1971, a company for the restoration and development of the Jewish Quarter was set up, supported the by German-born British architectural historian and critic Nikolaus Pevsner.[34]

Archaeology provided not only a pretext for an Israeli 'return' to occupy Palestinian lands, but, as Palestinian writer Nadia Abu El-Haj claimed, also the 'footprint' of historical authenticity that could be developed into built form by Israeli architects. Biblical archaeology was used to validate the claim that Palestinian

The clearing of the Western Wall Plaza, 1967, IP.

vernacular architecture was in fact Jewish at source, and allowed, as Nitzan-Shiftan showed, 'Israeliness' to define itself as a local 'native' culture, appropriated and altered by the latecomer Palestinians.[35]

Biblical archaeology

Archaeology has been central to the formation of Israeli identity since the establishment of the state. When Israel's first prime minister, David Ben-Gurion, claimed in his memoirs that the Jewish right over Palestine is 'based . . . on digging the soil with our own hands',[36] he was referring to the two practices that would establish and demonstrate Zionist rights to the land – agriculture and archaeology. Having established itself on much of the surface of an unfamiliar Palestine, Zionism continued its vertical quest for the Promised Land downwards. The existing landscapes of Palestine were seen as a contemporary veil under which historic biblical landscapes, battlegrounds, Israelite settlements and sites of worship could be revealed by digging. The national role assigned to archaeology was to remove the visible layer and expose the ancient Israelite landscape and with it the proof of Jewish ownership. The subterranean strata was thus perceived as a parallel geography akin to a national monument, providing an alibi for new colonization that could be argued as a return to sacred patrimony. Archaeology further influenced the reorganization of the surface terrain. Throughout Zionist history, new villages, towns and settlements had been established adjacent to or

literally over sites suspected of having a Hebraic past, adopting their biblical names.[37] Indeed, only a few metres below the surface, a palimpsest of 5,000-year-old debris, a vertical chronological stack of cultures and lives, narratives of wars and destruction, has been compressed by soil and stone. Israeli biblical archaeologists were interested in the deeper levels of the Bronze and Iron Ages,[38] which generally cover the period of time mentioned in the Bible, and the first four centuries AD, referring to the period mentioned in the more recent interpretative religious studies of the Mishna. The upper layers of the Muslim and Ottoman periods were marginalized in digs and museums, often dismissed as representations of a stagnant period, discarded as 'too new', or simply left alone to rot and crumble.[39] This reflected the tendency of Israeli biblical archaeologists to short-circuit history. In this, Israeli archaeology was not politicized in a substantially different manner to these employed in the service of other national movements.[40] Moreover, the practices of Israeli biblical archaeology were largely inherited from British and American archaeologists who had been excavating the area since the nineteenth century.[41] However, in contrast to their predecessors, Israeli biblical archaeologists had national rather than religious aspirations. Excavations were often carried out by secularists, men who, like Ben Gurion, saw the Bible as a historical national text that could fuse the relationship of a national identity to its state.[42] The archaeological digs were themselves often reminiscent of military operations, with the work organized by retired military officers.[43] On 27 June 1967, the same day that Arab Jerusalem and the area around it was annexed to Israel, the Israeli government declared the archaeological and historical sites in the West Bank, primarily those of Jewish or Israelite cultural relevance, to be the state's 'national and cultural property',[44] amounting to a de facto annexation of the ground beneath the Occupied Territories, making it the first zone to be colonized. The centre of attention for Israeli biblical archaeologists was the Jerusalem area and, in particular, the Jewish Quarter of the Old City.

Louis Kahn, The Hurva Synagogue (left), IP.

After the war, archaeological data became more easily available, with the most organized archives of archaeology and antiquity – the East Jerusalem-based Rockefeller Museum, the American School for Oriental Research, the French École Biblique et Archéologique – together with their collections and libraries, coming under Israeli control and thereby providing Israeli biblical archaeologists with a treasure trove of sources.[45]

Archaeology into architecture

In the Old City archaeological finds were incorporated into the overall urban design scheme. Louis Kahn, who was the leading voice in the early meetings of the Jerusalem Committee, envisioned the reconstruction of the evacuated quarter as 'an archaeological grid in which [new] architectural, urban forms are shaped after and in juxtaposition to their ruins'.[46] One of Louis Kahn's most significant proposals for the reconstruction of the Old City, privately undertaken, was his plan for the restoration of the *Hurva* [Ruin] Synagogue, an eighteenth-century building that stood at the centre of the Jewish Quarter before it was demolished by the Jordan Legion after the 1948 war. The proportions and outline of Khan's design for a monumental and archaic-looking synagogue-fortress, growing out of its ruins, were such that, if built, it would have competed on the city's skyline with the Al Aqsa mosque and the Holy Sepulchre. Although never realized, the plan had considerable influence on Israeli architecture in the Quarter and beyond. Ram Karmi, one of the most promising young Israeli architects of the second generation of state builders, was Kahn's foremost follower and promoter in Israel in the 1970s. For Karmi, writing in 1970, Kahn's design for the *Hurva* Synagogue

The reconstruction of Kikar Batei Machase, the main square in the Jewish Quarter early 1970s, IP.

marked the end of Israeli modernism that was closely associated with the architecture of Israel's founding generation and that of his father, Dov Karmi. 'Israeli architecture . . . did not manage to artistically and properly express the desires of a nation returning to its routes . . . the new *Hurva* building provides an opportunity to fill this absence.'[47] The call was for the disciplines of archaeology and architecture to merge. Indeed, throughout the restoration work in the Quarter, Israeli archaeologists and architects collaborated, carrying out, often simultaneously, excavation, restoration and reconstruction.[48] Archaeology was vertically extended into a new building style that Zvi Efrat called 'archaeologism'.[49] In some cases, the upper storeys of new homes would become literal extensions of their archaeological footprints, while other buildings would be built using older stones for the lower floors and newer stones at higher levels: others still were simply built to appear old.

In 1974 Karmi became chief architect at the Ministry of Construction and Housing, which at the time still oversaw most residential construction in Israel and which had gained a reputation for promoting fast and cheap housing solutions in rows of housing blocks. Karmi was the most visible of a group of Israeli architects attuned to the historicist tendencies of the Jerusalem Committee and to worldwide developments in architecture. These architects were mostly young, returning from study periods in elite architectural schools worldwide, and in particular from the hot-house of new architectural ideas, the Architectural Association School of Architecture in London, from which Karmi himself had graduated. Like many in Israel's professional class, most of them were supporters of the Labor Party, which between 1967 and 1977 was the executive force behind the colonization of Jerusalem and the rest of the occupied territories.

For these young practitioners, the architecture of the 1950s and 1960s – epitomized by the state-sponsored socialist housing blocks of European modernism – was sterile, heartless and lacking an important component, 'meaning'. These architects had not for the most part returned to Israel out of nationalist conviction but rather because, as young architects, they were happy to be given the opportunity to build, and to engage with issues that were then at the centre of architectural discourse. They may have been aware that their projects were built on expropriated Palestinian lands, and precipitated personal and national tragedies, but they suppressed such thoughts, pretending to engage with these projects in a 'purely' professional way.

Upon taking up his role, in a move echoing that of Storrs, Karmi halted all projects in Jerusalem and set a team of experts to oversee a new citywide planning programme. For Karmi, 'the search for national identity must be conducted through architecture.'[50] In the introduction to 'Israel Builds' the 1977 official publication of the Ministry of Housing, he explained the shift in the focus of architectural production: 'We live under the pressure of a shortage of housing . . . We make every effort to build as much as our budget permits . . . Still I feel that in all those efforts there is a lack of one component, the component around which Israel came into existence: the establishment of a "national home" . . . Home means more than just the narrow confines of one's apartment; it also implies a sense of belonging to the immediate surroundings . . .'[51] Architecture was to become a central player, no less, in the redesign of territory as a home.

But where was such 'meaning' to be found? According to Karmi, it was located in the particular nature of the nation's terrain itself: 'Just as we did not create the Hebrew language ex-nihilo, but built it up on the foundations of the language that was spoken 2000 years ago . . . so we are not starting [to construct buildings] on a blank sheet of paper.'[52] Inspiration was sought and found, as Alona Nitzan-Shiftan forcefully demonstrated, both above and below the surface: 'While architects were seeking locality on the ground, archaeologists sought Jewish history underneath its surface.'[53] Above the ground, the fabric of Palestinian vernacular architecture – found in the hillside villages and Jerusalem neighbourhoods – was deemed by Israeli architects to retain not the social-physical typologies that have undergone complex historical development, but fossilized forms of biblical authenticity.[54] Israeli-built culture has always been locked between the contradictory desires to either imitate or even inhabit the stereotypical Arab vernacular, and to define itself sharply and contrastingly against it. Zionists saw the Palestinians either as late-comers to the land, devoid of thousand-year-old roots or, paradoxically, as the very custodians of the ancient Hebrew culture and language of this land – all this without any sense of contradiction.[55]

Israeli architects' attraction to local Palestinian architecture was also inspired by another theoretical framework prominent at the time: the 1964 MoMA exhibition 'Architecture without Architects'. Its extended catalogue became influential in promoting the integration of principles derived from vernacular buildings into the context of international modern architecture. However, in focusing its attention on the formal dimension of vernacular domestic architecture, the exhibition ignored the political and social developments of the communities that constructed them, being somewhat more inclined to see them as atemporal embodiments of 'the noble savage'.[56] In a similarly romantic and orientalist vein, Israeli architects' fascination with the Palestinian vernacular was blind to the complex socio-economic development of the Palestinian villages and towns they now studied; instead, they assumed that such housing forms had developed organically, without planning. It was a view encapsulated in an observation by Thomas Leitersdorf, another graduate of the Architectural Association in London, who had returned to Israel from a period of work abroad to plan Ma'ale Adumim, the largest settlements in the West Bank, a few kilometres east of Jerusalem: 'in terms of beauty they [the Palestinians] are way ahead of us! "Architecture without Architects" – this is the Arab village, and this is its beauty . . . I look upon the morphology of the Arab villages with envy. The beauty of the Arab village lies in its accumulative and somewhat irrational nature . . . it is always better than when an architect comes in, the architect only spoils things because the architect has to work logically, and they do not . . .'[57] The modernization of the Palestinian village – its development as a complex socio-political entity, the conversion of its agrarian economy into a semi-urban one, the abandonment of traditional stone construction, and even, more ironically, the influence of Israeli culture, economy, architecture and construction techniques – remained largely invisible to Leitersdorf and his contemporaries. But beyond his orientalist perspective, which doomed the Palestinian village to a permanent romantic backwardness, an island of 'tradition' within an ocean of 'progress',[58] Leitersdorf has missed the contradiction in his own work: the buildings he designed to overlook the Palestinian villages are what irrevocably damaged them.

At the end of the 'reconstruction' of the Jewish Quarter of Jerusalem only about 20 per cent of the original buildings were actually conserved. The rest were rebuilt, with more storeys in order to accommodate government targets for larger numbers of residents. At present, more than 4,500 people, a third of them *yeshiva* students from all over the world live in the Jewish Quarter. Most of these inhabitants are national-religious Jews, many of them from the United States, but several artists and architects, influenced by the culture of 'return to the city centre' have also made it their home. An example for the latter type of settlers

Model of the Yeshiva of Porat Yosef, the Jewish Quarter, overlooking the Wailing Wall 1970 (Architect: Moshe Safdie), IP.

are the architects Moshe Safdie and Elinoar Barzacchi, later the Chief Architect of the District of Jerusalem, who returned to Israel in 1977 after a period of study and work in Paris and Rome. She recently explained her decision to settle there: 'I came from Europe and I thought the most wonderful place to live in Jerusalem is in the Old City. In Rome I lived in the Old City. In Paris I lived in Montmartre. Here in the [Jewish] Quarter it looked to me like the most Jerusalemite thing there is, the most authentic, the most multicultural it can be.'[59]

Rather than a multicultural city centre the Jewish Quarter might be better described as an artificial, ethnically homogenous, gated neighbourhood, whose construction was made possible by the forced displacements of its inhabitants. It is a 'biblical' theme park, sending out further tentacles of Jewish housing enclaves and religious study-centres into the Muslim Quarter to which it is connected above street level via protected and exclusive roof paths. The separation of this enclave from its surroundings is further enforced by the fact that all entrances and exits to the Jewish Quarter are guarded by the border police, providing access, after body and bag scans, only to Jewish residents/settlers, tourists, and the Israeli army and police.

Reproducing the Old City

The expropriations of Palestinian property that enabled the 'reconstruction' of the Jewish Quarter went in tandem with the beginning of a wave of expropriations at the peripheries of the municipal area. Over a third of the land annexed to by the state was expropriated from its Palestinian owners for the establishment and expansion of the Jewish neighbourhoods, under the pretext of catering for 'public needs'. The use of the term 'public' reveals more than anything else the government's political bias: the 'public' on whom expropriations were imposed always comprised Palestinians; the 'public' who enjoyed the fruits of the expropriation always exclusively comprised Jews.[60]

Notwithstanding the reconstruction of the Jewish Quarter, Jerusalem's city centre was torn apart by centrifugal forces. In 1977, ten years after the war, when the right-wing Likud replaced Labor in power, the Jewish Quarter was home to almost 4,000 people, while about 50,000 Israeli Jews were already settled in the new Jewish neighbourhoods established on the peripheries of the occupied areas annexed to Jerusalem.[61] The Jewish inhabitants of the city, wary of the congested, multi-ethnic and disputed older neighbourhoods of the western part of the city, opted for the ethnic, cultural and social homogeneity of the suburbs. These suburban developments were referred to as 'urban neighbourhoods' rather than 'settlements', not because of their nature, economy or distance from the centre, but because they were still located within the much-expanded boundaries of the Jerusalem municipality.

However, the significance of the Quarter's 'reconstruction' lay not just in the number of people who inhabited it, but in the establishment of a foothold in the Old City and the creation of a laboratory for an emergent sensibility in architecture, one later exported and implemented in the construction of the city's outer neighbourhoods. The neighbourhood of Gilo, located on the southernmost edge of Jerusalem, on a hilltop overlooking Bethlehem and the refugee camps surrounding it, offers one of the best examples of the attempt to reproduce something of the feel of the Old City within Jerusalem's periphery. Marking the southern edge of the extended city, Gilo is, according to its planner, the architect Avraham Yaski, writing in 1977, both 'part of the wall enclosing Jerusalem' as well as 'a well defined, enclosed city'. 'Though Gilo is a suburban quarter', Yaski admits, 'an effort has been made to create the feeling that it is an organic part of Jerusalem and not a dormitory town.'[62] With the reclusive nature of Gilo's urban form, Yaski echoes yet another emerging ideal of the time – the American 'New Urbanism', which promoted a type of development (inspired by the writing of Jane Jacobs and Lewis Mumford) that sought to replicate city-centre-like, human-scaled walkable communities most often on the fringes of American cities. In Jerusalem, city-centre-like developments meant the reproduction of the Old City. One of the best examples of this phenomenon is the 'Housing Cluster' designed by the architect Salo Hershman in Gilo in the early 1970s. The housing is laid out as several walled-city-like ensembles. They are entered via large gates leading into a series of internal courtyards and squares. The latter are woven together by arched walkways, alleyways and colonnades, and are overlooked by balconies. The entire concrete-built cluster is clad with slated 'Jerusalem Stone'. Indeed, Gilo has been the most distinct of the new neighbourhoods in demonstrating the transformation of Israeli architecture. The modernist, standard, cheap, prefabricated apartment block, formerly the basic unit of state-sponsored housing, was replaced, according to Efrat, by other typologies of 'formless, borderless clusters composed of a multitude of small terraced houses that morphed onto the existing topography of the Jerusalem hills . . . "contextual" architecture, sentimental buildings, influenced by alleged "regional" connections . . . pseudo historical creations of oriental and Mediterranean mimicry . . . embodying an association with antiquity and national roots'.[63] This architecture would thereafter provide, through an eclectic agglomeration of episodes and a museum-like arrangement of elements, the fantasy deemed necessary for the consolidation of a new national identity and the domestication of the expanded city. It placed every remote and newly built suburb well within the boundaries of 'the eternally unified capital of the Jewish people', and thus, as far as most Israelis are concerned, away from the negotiating table. Whatever is called Jerusalem, by name, by architecture and by the use of stone, is placed at the heart of the Israeli consensus. Indeed, although in July 2000 the Israeli negotiation team in Camp David agreed in principle to Clinton's proposal that asked for Israel to hand back the archipelago of Palestinian neighbourhoods and urban-villages in Jerusalem, they have insisted on maintaining sovereignty over the remote, stone-clad suburban neighbourhoods of Jerusalem, referred to in Israel as 'Jewish Jerusalem'. Borders designed by a military committee have been visually domesticated and culturally naturalized to such a degree that returning or removing state housing projects built within them has become a politically controversial act of 'partitioning Jerusalem'. Any act of decolonization in the area now called Jerusalem must thus start with a process of secularizing and denaturalizing the Jewish neighbourhoods/settlements of greater Jerusalem.

Demographic architecture

Like many colonial cities, Jerusalem has its dark enclaves for its native inhabitants, ruled by the border police, with surprise checkpoints between neighbourhoods. For the Palestinian inhabitants of Jerusalem, unlike the Jewish residents, hardly anything was ever planned but their departure. Within the municipal borders of the city, architects and planners were given the task not only of constructing homes and developing a new 'national style' but also of maintaining the 'demographic balance', which at the time of occupation in 1967, and within Jerusalem's gerrymandered borders, stood at about three Jewish inhabitants to every

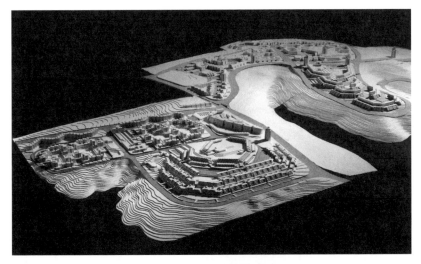

*Top: Model of the neighbourhood of Gilo (Architects: Arvraham Yaski, Yaakov Gil, Yosef Sivan).
Bottom: Design session on Gilo in the early 1970s. In the centre, pointing, is team leader Avraham
Yaski, who later received the Israel Prize for this design. Ram Karmi (with sunglasses and sideburns)
is sitting at the centre.*

Palestinian. The faster growth rate of the Palestinian population was seen by
Israel as a 'demographic time-bomb'. In 1993 City Engineer Elinoar Barzacchi
echoed an ongoing state policy when she outlined how the municipality intends
to deal with this problem: 'There is a government decision to maintain the proportion between the Arab and Jewish populations in the city at 28 per cent Arab
and 72 per cent Jew. The only way to cope with that ratio is through the housing
potential.'[64] This policy of maintaining 'demographic balance' has informed the
underlying logic of almost every masterplan prepared for the city's development.[65]

By trying to achieve the demographic and geographic guidelines of the political masterplans, the planners and architects of the municipality of Jerusalem and those working for them have effectively taken part in a national policy of forced migration, unofficially referred to in Israeli circles as the 'silent transfer', a crime according to international law.[66] The evidence for these crimes is not only to be found in protocols or in the wording of political masterplans, but in the drawings of architects and planners. They can be seen as lines in their plans.[67] Yet, remarkably, in spite of all Israel's efforts to keep the 28 per cent Palestinian to 72 per cent Jewish ratio, its planning policy is falling short of its target. Out of the 650,000 registered residents of Jerusalem in 2005, about a third were Palestinians. This has obviously increased the frustration that further accelerates Israel's draconian measures.

Whereas demographic policies are clearly outlined in political masterplans, which are seen as guidelines only, in town-building schemes and local plans – which are statutory documents having the force of law – these intentions are camouflaged within the techno-professional language of planning. Since the government guidelines are in blatant violation of both Israeli and international law, a deliberate discrepancy in language has opened up between political and architectural documents. The illegal policy was implemented by manipulating seemingly mundane planning categories. Maintaining the 'demographic balance' through the 'housing potential', when Palestinian demographic growth is so much faster, implied the use of one or both of two planning policies: one promoting the construction of housing in Jewish neighbourhoods and the other limiting the expansion of Palestinian ones. While issuing an annual average of 1,500 building permits to Jewish Israelis and constructing 90,000 housing units for Jews in all parts of East Jerusalem since 1967, the municipality has issued an annual average of only 100 building permits to Palestinians in the city, thus creating a Palestinian housing crisis with a shortfall of more than 25,000 housing units.[68] Without the possibility of obtaining planning permissions, many Palestinian families have built homes 'illegally' and exposed themselves to the random actions of municipal demolition squads. These demolitions are undertaken mainly in the most disadvantaged Palestinian neighbourhoods, where residents cannot afford legal defence.[69]

Other spatial manipulations were similarly undertaken to try to maintain the 'demographic balance'. The construction of the new Jewish neighbourhood/ settlements were also seen as antidotes to Palestinian urbanization and were planned in such a way as to create wedges between Palestinian neighbourhoods and villages, limiting their possible expansion and splintering Palestinian urban contiguity. For example, the neighbourhoods of Ramat Eshkol and the French Hill north of the Old City were laid out to form an elongated arc that cut the Palestinian neighbourhood of Shuafat from the Palestinian Old City and the neighbourhood of Seikh Jarah, which previously comprised a continuous urban area. Indeed, the location and layout of the new neighbourhoods were conceived not only as a utilitarian receptacle for the Jewish population, but also as a means of preventing Jerusalem from functioning as a Palestinian city and making it harder to be a Palestinian in Jerusalem.

The massive overcrowding in Palestinian neighbourhoods, and the rapid increase in property prices that ensued, ultimately forced many Palestinian families to leave Jerusalem for nearby towns and villages in the West Bank, where housing is considerably cheaper. This was precisely what the government planners intended. By leaving the city, Palestinians also lost the status of 'Israeli residency', which differentiates those Palestinians included within Jerusalem's post-1967 borders from those in the rest of the West Bank, and which, among other things, allowed the former access to state services and healthcare, and freedom to enter and work in Israel. In the past forty years more than 50,000 Palestinians have lost their residency status in this manner. Tens of thousands of others have moved outside the municipal boundaries but have kept an address in the city in order to keep these rights and often travel to work there. One of the factors in the routing of the Separation Wall around Jerusalem was to cut these Palestinians out of the city, and close this loophole. The Palestinian residents of Jerusalem now face having to choose which side of the Wall to live on – a crowded and expensive Jerusalem, where they cannot build, or give up the rights they previously had and live in the surrounding towns and villages of the West Bank.[70]

Throughout the years of Israeli domination in Jerusalem, about 40 per cent of the land that would have been available for Palestinians in the occupied part of the city was marked up on municipal plans as open, public space. This was presented, for legal reasons, as an amenity for the improvement of the quality of life and air of the residents of the Palestinian neighbourhoods, but it effectively framed them within zones into which expansion was forbidden. Whenever the status of these 'green areas' was 'unfrozen' and earmarked for construction, they were allocated for the expansion of Jewish neighbourhoods. This was openly admitted by Mayor Kollek: 'the primary purpose of defining Shuafat Ridge [then still an empty hill in the occupied part to the north of the city next to the Palestinian neighbourhood of Shuafat mentioned above] as a green area was to prevent Arab building [there] until the time was ripe to build a new Jewish neighbourhood'.[71]

Yet another planning strategy used to limit Palestinian residential construction and demographic growth is the pretext of preservation. Professing to protect the traditional rural character of Palestinian villages within the municipal area, and the historic nature of Palestinian neighbourhoods, the municipality insisted that the floor area ratio (FAR) – a planning ratio that defines the relation between the size of a plot and the size of the building – is kept low. So, while the building

Jerusalem (north). 1. Hebrew University on Mount Scopus; 2. Jewish neighbourhood of French Hill; 3. Government district; 4. Jewish neighbourhood of Shuafat Ridge; 5. Jewish neighbourhood of Ramot; 6. Shuafat refugee camp; 7. Palestinian neighbourhood of Anata; 8. Palestinian neighbourhood of Beit Hanina; 9. Jewish neighbourhood of Pisgat Ze'ev; 10. Palestinian neighbourhood of Issawa; 11. 'Green Open Space' zone forbidden of Palestinian construction; 12. Erich Mendelsohn's Hadassah-Hebrew University medical complex; 13. Tunnel mouth of the Jerusalem ring road; 14 'Vertical intersection'; 15. Palestinian neighbourhood of Shuafat; 16. The old Jerusalem-Ramallah road.

rights in the Jewish neighbourhood of Talpiot-Mizrah permit the construction of buildings of five storeys, in the adjacent Palestinian neighbourhood of Jabal al-Mukaber, buildings may occupy only 25 per cent of the building plot, resulting in a small house within a large plot.[72]

Horizontally limited by the green zones around them, and vertically by a 'preservation' policy, the Palestinian neighbourhoods of Jerusalem were transformed into an archipelago of small islands of conjured 'authenticity', within an ocean of Jewish construction, their architecture functioning as an object of aesthetic contemplation to be seen from the concrete-built but stone-clad Jewish neighbourhoods. These 'preservation zones' surrounded by parks, multiply the principle of the 1918 McLean plan, and reproduce, on the urban scale, the image of the Palestinian 'Bantustans' of the West Bank.

Moreover, Palestinian villages and neighbourhoods in Jerusalem very often exhibit anything but the ostensible 'oriental authenticity' which they are meant to embody. Contrasting sharply with the Jewish neighbourhoods of Jerusalem's periphery, the Palestinians often do not abide by the Jerusalem stone bylaw and the architectural styles that attempt to give Israel's colonial architecture an image of authenticity. Many buildings constructed without permits and facing prospective demolition are built cheaply, with their structural walls of raw concrete and cinder blocks left bare. The utilitarian modernist silhouette of their slab construction, supported over the hilly landscape by columns, was influenced by the modernist ethos of early Zionist architecture. Appearing as a local adaptation of modernist villas, they testify to a complete reversal, which the policies of Israeli domination have brought on the building culture of Israelis and Palestinians alike.

The vertical schizophrenia of the Temple Mount/Haram al-Sharif. Illustration: Walter Boettger, Eyal Weizman 2003.

The Temple Mount is the site of the First and Second Temples. Haram al-Sharif is where the Al-Aqsa Mosque and the Dome of the Rock are located. Both sites share the same location – a flattened-out, filled-in summit supported by giant retaining walls located by the eastern edge of the Old City of Jerusalem. The western retaining wall of the compound is believed to be the last remnant of the Second Temple. The Wailing Wall is the southern part of this retaining wall.

The issue of the Temple Mount/Haram al-Sharif was the most contentious one in the Israeli-Palestinian negotiations at Camp David in July 2000. Although most Israeli archaeologists would agree that the Second Temple stood on a platform at the same height of today's mosques, US mediators seemed to have believed in another, more politically convenient archaeological-architectural explanation. They argued that the upper parts of the Wailing Wall were originally built as a free-standing wall, behind which (and not over which) the Second Temple was located at a depth of about sixteen meters below the level of the water fountain between Al-Aqsa Mosque and the Dome of the Rock. The theory originated with Tuvia Sagiv, a Tel Aviv based architect and amateur archaeologist. Sagiv spent much of his time (and money) surveying the site, and even overflew it several times with helicopters carrying ground-penetrating radar and thermal sensors. Sagiv's report determining that the remains of the Temple are located under the mosques were submitted in 1995 to Ariel Sharon, then an opposition Knesset member, together with an architectural proposal that aimed to resolve the problems of Jews and Moslems praying on the same site by dividing it vertically, in different floors. According to Sagiv's architectural proposal, a giant gate would be opened in the Wailing Wall through which Jews could reach a subterranean hall at the level of the Temple, under the level of the mosque. Via Sharon, Sagiv's proposal reached the attention of the American administration which asked the U.S. Embassy in Tel Aviv to obtain a copy. Clinton thought that if remains of the Temple are indeed, to be found *under* the present level of the mosques, the issue of sovereignty could be resolved along the outline of Sagiv's architectural proposal. Clinton delivered his proposal – geopolitics performed on an architectural scale – orally so that it could be withdrawn at any point. In a daring and radical manifesta-

tion of the region's vertical schizophrenia he proposed a stack of horizontal sovereign borders. The first would have passed under the paving stones of the compound. There the border between Arab Al-Quds and Israeli Jerusalem would, at the most contested point on earth, flip from the horizontal to the vertical. Palestinians would gain sovereignty over the platform of the Haram al-Sharif, the mosque of Al-Aqsa and the Dome of the Rock. Under the paving of this platform would be a layer of 150 centimeter deep UN zone. This zone will be uninhabited but will function to separate the parties. Israeli sovereignty would comprise the volume below this layer to include the Wailing Wall and the sacred 'depth of the mount', where the Temple is presumed to have existed, extending further down to the centre of the earth. Furthermore, the airspace over the site, just like that over the entire heavenly city would remain in Israeli sovereignty. This startling proposal of stacking sovereign volumes in layers, earned it, as Gilead Sher lightheartedly told me, its nickname – the Arkansas 'Big Mac'. Since Israeli sovereignty would extend over the entire area around the compound, Barak, who claimed, for the purposes of negotiation, that he was only *'willing to consider the proposal'* but in effect fully embraced it, suggested *'a bridge or a tunnel, through which whoever wants to pray in Al-Aqsa could access the compound'*. This special pedestrian bridge would have connected the Palestinian areas east of the Old City with the religious compound, otherwise isolated in a three-dimensional 'wrap' of Israeli sovereignty in all directions. The bridge, on which Palestinians would have received full sovereignty, was to have itself spanned a section of the Mount of Olives and the ancient Jewish cemetery there on which Israeli sovereignty would be internationally recognized. The Palestinians, long suspicious of Israel's presence under their mosques, wary of Israel's presence in the airspace over them and unreceptive to the idea of their capital woven together with bridges, flatly rejected the plan. Arafat, somewhat bemused, asked Clinton whether he would have accepted *'a foreign sovereignty under the paving of Washington DC'*. Saeb Erekat, a Palestinian minister and chief negotiator in Camp David dryly summed up Palestinian demands that *'Haram al-Sharif … must be handed over to the Palestinians – over, under and to the sides, geographically and topographically'*.

Israeli Defence Force outpost at the Rafah Salient, circa 1969, IP.

2.

Fortifications:
The Architecture of Ariel Sharon

Although the 1949 cease-fire lines became the internationally recognized political borders of Israel, they were seen by many in the Israeli military as indefensible.[1] Since neither Israel nor the Arab states which signed the 1949 cease-fire
agreements believed that the new lines would mark a permanent international
border and since both had territorial ambitions and military plans beyond them,
these lines never hardened into physically fortified borders of substance; in some
places they were marked by a shallow ditch, in others by a flimsy fence. After
the 1967 war, the new cease-fire lines – marked by the Suez Canal, the Jordan
River and the Syrian Golan Heights – were perceived as a completion of sorts: the
creation of a territorial form that resonated with the phantasmagorical Zionist
dream of the 'complete land of Israel'.[2] These new boundaries were also thought
to form the strategic enclosure that would buttress the defence of the state. Yet
the Occupied Territories, twice the size of pre-war Israel, grew large in the
national imagination. A creeping agoraphobia led to frenzied and varied attempts
at studying and domesticating these territories from within and efforts to fortify
their edges against counter-attack from the outside. The debates around these
issues within the Israeli military and government were the first to define the
terms, form and the practices of the occupation thereafter. This chapter will
follow the debate around the construction (1967–73) and fall (1973) of Israel's
fortification along the Suez Canal. Following military debates and battle analysis,
it attempts to trace a process of 'civilianization' whereby ideas and organizational
systems were transferred from a military to a civilian domain, resulting, in the
late 1970s, in the translation of a military occupation into a civilian one.

Shortly after the 1967 war, two Israeli generals of the Labor movement
started engaging in attempts to fortify different fronts of the 1967 Occupied
Territories. The systems conceived by Yigal Allon (Minister of Agriculture and
Director of the government Settlements Committee) and Chief of Staff Chaim
Bar Lev, were products of a similar territorial doctrine – one that sought to estab-

lish a line of defence along the outermost edge of the territories. The Allon
plan, the first draft of which was presented to the government a few weeks after
the end of the war, advocated the redrawing of state borders along the main
topographical feature of the region, the Great Rift Valley, the deep tectonic crack
that formed the eastern edge of the territories occupied by Israel. Allon proposed
to annex a strip following the length of the rift, which extended from the Golan
Heights in the north, through the Jordan Valley down to the southernmost tip
of the Sinai Peninsula at the Egyptian coastal town of Sharm el-Sheikh. This strip
would generate, according to Allon, 'maximum security and maximum territory for
Israel with a minimum number of Arabs'.[3] The fact that this strip was sparsely
populated was due to the fact that during the war, wanting to secure its new
borderlines, the Israeli military evacuated and destroyed the Palestinian villages of
the Jordan Valley (except the city of Jericho), the Syrian towns and villages of
the Golan Heights and all Egyptian citizens but the Bedouin in the Sinai. On
this generally arid and now sparsely populated strip, remote from Israeli population centres, Allon proposed to establish a string of agricultural Kibbutz and
Moshav settlements, as well as several paramilitary outposts of the NAHAL
Corps – the settlements arm of the Israeli Defence Force (IDF).[4] Although never
officially endorsed by the government, the Allon plan was gradually put into
effect during the first decade of the Israeli occupation under Labor administrations. The settlements in the Jordan Valley in the far eastern edge of the West
Bank were to fortify this border along the Jordan River. Their establishment was
perceived as the regeneration of Labor Zionism and the revival of its agricul-

Construction of the Bar Lev Line, circa 1971. Film stills, IDF film unit, IP.

tural pioneering spirit. Agriculture in this arid landscape, sustained by over-extraction of water from the mountain aquifer, was seen, according to the common Zionist slogan, as an attempt to 'make the desert bloom'.[5] The Jordan Valley was conceived as a hybrid military/civilian defensive zone, split by four parallel roads that strung together military bases and agricultural settlements. In the event of an armoured invasion from the east, the valley's cultivated fields would be flooded, and the settlements hardened into fortified positions that would allow the military to organize and channel invading forces into designated zones of Israeli fire. Moreover, the inhabitation of the area by a civilian population, rather than military bases, was to demonstrate, according to Allon, Israel's political resolve to annex this frontier zone.

The Bar Lev Line was the military counterpart of the Allon plan, attempting to achieve with military strongholds what the Allon plan sought to achieve with a combination of civilian and military ones. Fearing international pressure and a possible replay of the 1956 Suez Crisis, when the US administration forced Israel (as well as France and Britain) to retreat from the areas they had occupied in Egypt, Minister of Defence Moshe Dayan did not want the IDF to reach the Suez Canal at all during the 1967 war. The IDF gained the canal regardless during the third day of the war, out of its own tactical inertia. Immediately after the war, Dayan advocated a retreat from the canal. Following the advice of Allon, however, Dayan's chief political rival, Prime Minister Levy Eshkol, and later Golda Meir, wanted to keep the canal under Israeli control, and close it to all shipping, in order to pressure the Egyptian government into signing a peace treaty on

Ariel Sharon, Chief of Southern Command (last in line, on left); Chaim Bar Lev, Chief of Staff (centre, on left); and David Ben-Gurion, on the Bar Lev Line, Suez Canal, 1971.

Israel's terms. Dayan, on the other hand, did not want an agreement at all, and thought that a tactical retreat from the canal would allow Israel to permanently hold onto the rest of the Sinai Peninsula. Bar Lev was asked to provide a technical solution for fortifying the Canal against Egyptian attack. He set up a team, headed by his loyal divisional commander, Avraham Adan, to design the system of fortifications. Adan approached the design with the enthusiasm of a young architect on his first commission, researching historical examples and building scale models. His main influence, he later claimed in his autobiography, was the architecture of the fortifications of Kibbutz Nirim in the Negev desert, one of the settlements that had become the focus of a Zionist myth after it had successfully resisted the Egyptian army in the war of 1948.[6] Adan took a month to design the fortification system, after which construction work immediately began.

However, the Bar Lev Line was not so much a product of planned construction as the result of incremental evolution – a series of 'solutions' based upon Adan's system to protect military forces under constant artillery fire. During the intense skirmishes of 1968–71, later known as the 'War of Attrition', the Line gradually became an immense infrastructural undertaking. Huge quantities of sand were shifted across the desert and piled along the eastern bank of the canal to form an artificial landscape 20 metres high, with a 45-degree incline on the side facing the Canal, and 200 kilometres long. Thirty-five Ma'ozim (strongholds), named after the fortification system in Adan's Kibbutz, each designed for twenty-five to thirty soldiers, were situated on the sand dyke at 10-kilometre intervals, overlooking the Egyptian line a mere 200 metres away. The strongholds had deep underground bunkers, fortified by crushed rocks in nets and a fencing system made from steel lifted from the Cairo–El-Arish railway and other abandoned Egyptian agricultural equipment, and were surrounded by minefields. The entire length of the line contained emplacements for tanks, artillery pieces, mortars and machine guns. Unlike other systems of fortifications that used concrete and so could always be destroyed with enough explosive, the sand ramparts of the Bar Lev Line were designed to absorb and dissipate the impact of bombardment. The fortification thus seemed complete, and the Israeli government consequently did not feel it had to rush to the negotiating table. Since the balance of power was apparently tilted in Israel's favour, it was generally thought that Egypt would not risk attacking. This assessment was known in the Israeli security circles as 'the concept'.

Meanwhile, in 1971, on the other side of the Suez Canal, Egyptian President Anwar Sadat appointed Lieutenant-General Sa'ad El Shazly as Chief of the Egyptian Military Staff. Shazly's task was to mastermind the storming of the Bar Lev Line. In his book, *The Crossing of the Canal*,[7] Shazly illustrated the Bar-Lev Line with the pride of a person describing an obstacle successfully breached: 'the Suez canal was unique. Unique in the difficulties its construction presented to an amphibious assault force. Unique in its scale of defences the enemy had erected on top of those natural obstacles . . . To all that saw it, the Suez Canal seemed an impassable barrier . . .' The first and most difficult obstacle was the water in the canal, 'the second obstacle was a gigantic sand dune built by the enemy along the length of the eastern bank. For six years, Israeli bulldozers had laboriously piled the sand ever higher – their most sustained effort coming, naturally, at likely crossing points . . . Above this formidable barrier rose the third obstacle: the 35 forts of the Bar Lev line . . . Hidden from our view, the enemy could manoeuvre its armour to reinforce any sudden weak point . . .'[8]

Shazly contended that one of the major aims of the giant earth rampart of the Bar Lev Line was to deny the Egyptian armies a view of Israeli positions in the Sinai, while simultaneously creating the artificial topographical conditions that would allow Israelis to observe Egyptian territory. The rare advantage gained by Soviet anti-aircraft missile technology over Western fighter jets in the early 1970s, led to aerial photography missions becoming precarious, and had the effect of flattening the battlefield into a horizontal, two-dimensional surface in which the ground, eye-level perspective was reinvested with strategic significance. From the Egyptian army's point of view, the Bar Lev Line was a visual barrier. The dyke created an immediate limit to their observational field, making a 'blind zone' that denied them the view of their occupied territories.

From the moment that construction started on the Bar Lev Line, barely three months after the 1967 war, Ariel Sharon, then director of military training, began challenging the strategy of defence it embodied. This initiated the first major debate within the Israeli General Staff concerning Israel's concept of defence. It was seen as a crucial issue over which Sharon, together with a handful of other officers – Israel Tal, Rafael Eitan and Matitiyahu Peled – were to clash repeatedly with the rest of the General Staff. The argument was polarized in increasingly geometrical terms, until the defence proposals became fully embodied within two spatial models, both derived from existing military vocabulary: linear fortification and a dynamic defence nested in a network of strongpoints in depth.[9] Sharon publicly accused his superiors of ignorance and stupidity, blaming them for the mounting war casualties along the construction site of the Line, and demanded that the static defence embodied in what he called 'the Israeli Maginot Line' be abandoned and replaced with a flexible system of 'defence in depth' comprising independent strongpoints located on hilltops in an area stretching far back from the frontline, in a way that would allow military units to travel between these strongpoints, and, in case of invasion, attack the enemy's flank and surround it.

This debate, and Sharon's role in it, corroborated in later accounts of the 1973 war, was to become one of the most controversial chapters in Israeli military history, so much so that the IDF has not yet published an official account of the war – partly because Sharon mobilized all his political weight to suppress it. Among the other reasons for the ambiguous and incomplete historical record is that most of the war's leading protagonists, Israeli and Egyptian, who physically and politically survived it, continued in political life. Their military autobiographies, as well as other oral and written accounts, contain widely differing interpretations of events that were mobilized in support for or in resistance to the dramatic political transformations of the post-1973 war period. During these processes the military achievements of the various generals as well as the performance of different units acquired immense political significance, with the constantly changing historiographies of the 1973 war tied to the political fates and fortunes of its main players. In the Israeli popular imagination, the linear, static, Bar Lev Line embodied the failing Labor Party, whereas the dynamic, flexible network promoted by Sharon, and especially the concept of 'depth' on which it relied, was later associated with a rejuvenated Israeli right and with the opening of Israel's state frontiers. Accounts that foregrounded Sharon's role in the war were generally associated with political attacks on the Labour government. After 1973, the decline of the Labour administration and the rise to power four years later of the right-wing Likud retrospectively gave more prominence to Sharon's military role in 1973, projecting him as a national hero. The US military has itself contributed to the creation of the myth of Sharon as a 'military genius', finding in him a model of command according to which they could inspire military transformation after the failures of their armies in Vietnam. Ariel Sharon's rapid, albeit not untypical, transformation from a popular military general to minister in charge of settlement activity in the first Likud government of 1977 allowed him to translate military doctrine and the principles of a dynamic battlefield into planning practices of civilian settlements and the creation of political 'facts on the ground'.

Transgressive unit

Throughout his military career, Sharon has become the personification of the Israeli 'myth of the frontier',[10] which celebrated the transgression of lines and borders of all kinds. Like its American predecessor, the Israeli frontier was understood as a mythical space that shaped the character and institutions of the nation. It was also a laboratory for the emergence of and experimentation with new spatial strategies and territorial forms. According to the Israeli sociologist Adriana Kemp, between 1948 and 1967 the Israeli state created a series of 'rhetorical and institutional mechanisms' that presented the frontier region as the symbolic centre of the nation, 'a laboratory for the creation of a "new Jew"'.[11]

The establishment of Special Commando Unit 101 for the purpose of frontier raids, under the command of Ariel Sharon, became central to the blurring of state borders and for the distinction it created between the idea of what constituted 'inside' and 'outside' the political state. Throughout its several-month independent lifespan in the second half of 1953, the unit transgressed, breached and distorted borders of different kinds: geopolitical – its operations crossed the borders of the state; hierarchical – its members did not fully obey orders and operational outlines and often acted on their own initiatives; disciplinary – they wore no uniforms, and expressed an arrogant intolerance, encouraged by and embodied in Sharon himself, of all formalities perceived as urbane and outmoded 'military procedures and bureaucracy'; and legal – the nature of their operations and their flagrant disregard for civilian life broke both the law of the Israeli state as well as international law. Although Unit 101's activities mostly constituted the slaughter of unarmed Palestinian civilians in villages and refugee camps, and its most infamous 'attack' was the killing of 60 unprotected civilians in the West Bank village of Qibia, it quickly cultivated a mythic status that greatly appealed to the imagination of Israeli youth. According to Moshe Dayan, who acted as a mentor to both the unit and Sharon personally, Unit 101 was 'a workshop for the creation of a new generation of [Hebrew] warriors'. Dayan also believed that it served a national purpose beyond the narrow military one. By turning the frontier into a mythical space and 'border transgression . . . into a symbolic practice and a spatial ritual', it signified the fact that the borders of the Israeli state were liquid and permeable, presenting its territoriality as a still incomplete project.[12]

Unit 101 also short-circuited hierarchies within the IDF and between it and the political system, connecting Sharon, then still in his twenties, in a close strategic triangle with Dayan and Prime Minister David Ben-Gurion. Although this triumvirate made many of the strategic decisions during 1953, Dayan and Sharon often conspired together to mislead the 'old man', while Sharon himself became accustomed to misleading Dayan as to the real extent of Unit 101's operations. But these lies were in fact a central facet of the triumvirate's relationship. Sharon was selected for his post because, from the outset, he never asked for written orders, thereby giving Dayan and Ben-Gurion the option to deny responsibility for or knowledge of operations whenever they chose. The command style of the two men was oblique, implicit; they were accustomed to giving orders in a tangential manner: 'would it not be good if [this or that] had taken place . . .'[13] Dayan's orders were always oral and ambiguous: Shlomo Gazit, one of his deputies, once observed of his commander that 'he doesn't know how to write'.[14] This tendency for the need to interpret Dayan's speech rather than follow his orders gradually became common knowledge in the military to the degree that it could help explain how Israeli soldiers got to the canal despite Dayan's orders. During the 1967 war, when Dayan ordered forces to stop short of reaching the Suez Canal, his subordinate officers were wondering 'what does he mean when he says "stop"?' According to Sharon's biographer, Uzi Benziman, throughout his career Sharon was continuously promoted by Dayan because he understood the logic and potential in Dayan's ambiguity and because he was willing to perform 'every bad thing that Israel needed to carry out but didn't want to be associated with – there were no orders needed, only a wink . . . and Sharon would carry out the dirty job'.[15] Dayan, however, never stopped seeing Sharon as a political rival. At the end of December 1953, upon Dayan becoming chief of staff, he adopted 101 as the model for the transformation of the rest of the IDF, merging the unit with the paratroopers, and placing Sharon in charge of both. In the following twenty years, until the 1973 war, the IDF was central to the formation of Israeli identity. Most Israelis accordingly saw 'patriotism' in military terms. Sharon had a central role in this process.

The military matrix

Sharon's view of the static linear fortification of the Bar Lev Line after the 1967 war was typically forthright. As he later wrote: 'from the beginning I felt that such a line of fortifications would be a disastrous error . . . we would be committing ourselves to static defence. We would be making fixed targets of ourselves

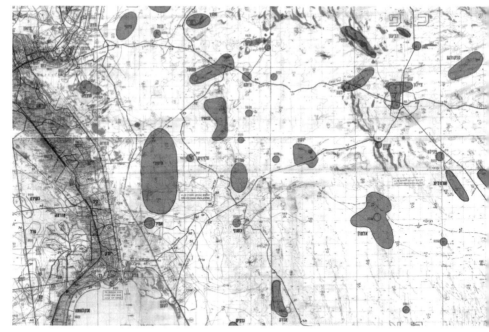

'Plan Sirius', marking Israeli fortifications in the Suez Canal zone before October 1973. The strongpoints, organized in depth, are marked as brown 'eggs'.

. . . our positions and movements would be under constant surveillance. Our procedures would become common knowledge. Our patrols and supply convoys would be vulnerable to ambushes, mining, and shelling.' The IDF, Sharon claimed, 'cannot win a defensive battle on an outer [canal] line . . .' He proposed instead that it should 'fight a defensive battle the way it should be fought – not on a forward line but in depth . . .'[16] Sharon's alternative military strategy had the advantage of providing weight to Dayan's politically sensitive argument that the Suez Canal be abandoned; in developing it, Sharon was most likely encouraged by Dayan off the record – but officially, Dayan chose not to intervene.

Militarily speaking, Sharon's system was a flexible adaptation of the traditional doctrine of defence in depth. It was based upon a series of strongpoints, which Sharon called Ta'ozim to differentiate them from Adan's Ma'ozim (strongholds), spread out on a series of hilltops at tactically important locations, overlooking the canal from a distance of about a dozen kilometres. Between these strongpoints, Sharon proposed to run unscheduled and unpredictable mobile patrols. The rationale behind this arrangement was to deny the Egyptian army an obvious target, a fixed layout against which they could plan their attack. Unlike Bar Lev, Sharon believed an attack on the Israeli defensive line on the Suez Canal was unavoidable and inevitable; accordingly, he sought to disguise the IDF's defensive organization.

Sharon's defensive plan aimed to maximize visual synergy, lines of fire and movement across the terrain. The isolated, semi-autonomous strongpoints were to be located so that each could be seen from those adjacent to it, and spaced apart at the distance of artillery fire so that they could cover each other. The strongholds were essentially command and logistic centres from where what Sharon called 'armoured fists' – tank battalions – could be mobilized against the enemy's main effort in crossing the canal. Moreover, equipped with command, control and long-range surveillance facilities, underground bunkers, anti-aircraft positions and emplacements for tanks and artillery, each strongpoint had a semi-independent battle capacity.[17] An expanding network of roads and signal stations was to weave the strongpoints together. Towards the rear, the emplacements gave way to military training bases, airfields, camps, depots, maintenance facilities and headquarters.

While unable to convince the IDF General Staff of his plans for the Sinai, Sharon, in his role as director of training, dispersed the various training schools under his command throughout the depth of the West Bank. Moreover, Sharon saw military installations as a first stage in the domestication and naturalization of the vast Occupied Territories: the layout and infrastructure of the camps were to become the blueprint for their civilian colonization by settlements.[18] Beyond that, it was an innovative geographical time/space arrangement with the system of defence in depth requiring a different form of military organization.[19] Linear fortifications rely on the ability of central command to control all areas of the extended linear battlefield equally; in contrast, defence in depth seeks the relative dispersal of military authority and the increased autonomy of each semi-independent battle unit.[20]

Although nested in traditional military hierarchies, the system's diffusion of the command structure allows independent units to develop what the military calls 'flexible responsiveness', according to which local commanders can act independently, on their own initiative, and in response to emergent necessities and opportunities without referring to central command. Diffused command has been a standard component part of a military response to the chaotic nature of battles in which chains of command and communication are often severed and the overall picture of battle is often blurred. Sharon's command style was well suited to such a situation. It was encapsulated in his oft-repeated statement 'tell me what to do but don't tell me how to do it'. Although this was indicative of the command style of the IDF, Sharon took it further, seeking to break as much as possible with standard command structures and organizational forms. Equally, he often avoided – or pretended to avoid – intervening in his subordinates' actions, providing them only with general guidelines and making them believe that they themselves had planned their own missions.

If the principle of linear defence is to prohibit (or inhibit) the enemy from gaining a foothold beyond it, when the line is breached at a single location – much like a leaking bucket of water – it is rendered useless. A network defence, on the other hand, is flexible. If one or more of its stongpoints are attacked and captured, the system can adapt itself by forming new connections across its depth. The category of 'depth' is thus not only spatial but conceptual, and is used to describe the level of synergy between various elements that compose a military system. The degree of a system's depth lies in its distributed capacity to reorganize connections, and the degree to which these connections can permit, regulate and respond to information flow from strongpoints positioned in other areas in the battlefield. The relation between the system's components is a relative figure defined by the speed and security of travel across its depth, between the different strongpoints.[21]

While the rationale of the Bar Lev Line was to stop the Egyptians from disturbing the geopolitical status quo that the line delineated, Sharon's plan conversely encouraged an Egyptian attack; Israeli forces would then counterattack the moment the enemy's supply lines became overextended:[22] 'If the Egyptians did try to cross [the canal], we could afford to let them get a mile or two inside the Sinai. Then we would be able to harass them and probe for their weak points at our convenience . . . [after which] we would be in a position to launch the kind of free-flowing mobile attack we were really good at.'[23]

Therefore, while the line is a military-geometrical instrument that seeks to separate two distinct hostile realms, the spatial–organizational model of the network creates a more diffused and dynamic geography. Following this logic, the system of defence in depth has the capacity to exchange space and time alternately. At the beginning of an attack it trades space for time – the attacker is allowed to gain space while the defender gains organizational time; later, it exchanges time for space as the trapping of the attacker within the web of the network enables the defender later to progress into and attack the latter's unprotected rear.

The Israeli public was exposed to the classified disputes between Sharon, Bar Lev, and the other members of the General Staff that reached their peak in 1969. Sharon was leaking them to the press, which in turn used his anonymously delivered comments to portray the military and political elites as reactionary 'slow thinkers', a tactic that had particular impact on Bar Lev, whom the Israeli public loved to mock for his slow, ponderous manner of speaking. The disagreement was also presented as a conflict between the tank officers with their heavy-handed, technical way of thinking and the pioneering maverick frontiersman/commando-soldier embodied by Sharon.[24]

By the summer of 1969, when Bar Lev realized he could no longer contain Sharon's ability to mobilize the media against the rest of the General Staff, he dismissed him from military service on a technicality: Sharon had forgotten to sign routine documents for the renewal of his military contract. Bar Lev's action was supported by Prime Minister Golda Meir who, remembering the days of Unit 101 and Sharon's rumoured threats to lock the entire Israeli government in a room and force it to order the start of the 1967 war, saw Sharon as a liar and a 'threat to Israel's democracy', a man 'capable of surrounding the Knesset with tanks'.[25] In response, Sharon revoked his membership of the Labor Party, which all officers over the rank of colonel were expected to hold at the time. He scheduled a meeting with Menachem Begin, then head of the right-wing opposition, at Jerusalem's King David Hotel, whose lobby was generally well frequented by journalists, ensuring that the meeting was widely noted and reported. The meeting was a political masterstroke. The Labor Party was apprehensive of the possible swing in public opinion that Sharon could provoke before a general election scheduled for October 1969. Party officials forced Bar Lev to reinstate Sharon – landing him where Bar Lev needed him least and feared him most, on the banks of the Suez Canal as Chief of Southern Command. There, between 1969 and July 1973, Sharon immediately set about implementing his defensive network behind the Bar Lev Line, which was by then almost complete. After the end of the War of Attrition in 1970, Sharon started evacuating parts of the line, cutting the number of strongholds from thirty-five to twenty-two.

The canal zone was enveloped in a frenzy of construction. Hundreds of trucks and bulldozers were assembled, and hundreds of thousands of cubic metres of crushed stone were again hauled into the desert. Mountain outposts were constructed and fortified, and a network of high-volume military roads were paved to connect them. The western Sinai Desert was fashioned by Sharon into a future battlefield, and the desert seemed to Sharon to be perfect for this; it contained only military installations, bases, roads and minefields, with no civilians to disturb the wargame. However, Sharon's sphere of operations was soon shifted elsewhere: shortly after entering into his new post received orders from Dayan to crush Palestinian resistance entrenched within the densely populated urban areas of Gaza, where IDF units were losing control. This was the real reason Sharon was given the Southern Command: it was another of the dirty jobs no other officer wanted to – and at the time very probably could not – undertake.

The 'Haussmanization' of Gaza

Since his time with Unit 101, Sharon had grown to view the armed conflict with the Palestinians as an urban problem, and the rapid expansion of the refugee camps as something that Israeli occupation forces would later call the 'Jihad of

New roads carved through the Jebalya refugee camp, Gaza Strip. Israeli Defence Force, 1972.

Building'. The IDF sought to address this problem by physically transforming and redesigning the very 'habitat of terror' whose centre was in the refugee camps.[26] In the years to follow, regional and urban planning was to merge into a militarized campaign against the Gaza-based resistance.

After the 1967 occupation of the West Bank and Gaza, Palestinian groups began to establish armed cells around a loose network of local command head-quarters. Without the thick jungles of Vietnam, the Fatah, PFLP (Popular Front for the Liberation of Palestine) and other armed groups that belonged to or splintered from the PLO, based their command within the dense, winding fabric of the refugee camps, which they themselves developed into an extra-territorial network of armed enclaves. From there they engaged in military operations against the occupying forces, as well as in terror attacks against Israeli civilians and against Palestinians suspected of collaboration. The grid of roads along which UN agencies laid out prefabricated sheds to house the 1948 refugees grew into a chaotic agglomeration of structures and ad hoc extensions, forming a shifting maze of alleyways, no more than a metre or so wide. Although they came under Israeli control, the occupation forces could rarely enter the camps, make arrests, collect taxes or impose regulations.

The counter-insurgency campaign in Gaza started in July 1971 and lasted until resistance was suppressed in February the following year. Sharon ordered extended curfews and a shoot-to-kill policy of suspected insurgents, and established assassination squads who worked their way through lists of names. Sharon was trying to break the resistance by killing anyone involved in its organization. Over a thousand Palestinians were killed. The campaign also acquired a different dimension: that of design undertaken by destruction. Writing the latest and most brutal chapter in the urban history of the grid, Sharon ordered military bulldozers to carve wide roads through the fabric of three of Gaza's largest refugee camps – Jabalya, Rafah and Shati. The new routes divided these camps into smaller neighbourhoods, each of which could be accessed or isolated by infantry units. Sharon also ordered the clearing of all buildings and groves in an area he defined as a 'security perimeter' around the camps, effectively isolating the built-up area from its surroundings and making it impossible for anyone to enter or leave the camps without being noticed. Other activities such as the paving of roads and the introduction of street lighting, were meant to enable the occupation forces to drive into the camps rapidly and without fear of land mines.[27] Together, these actions caused the destruction or the damaging of about 6,000 homes in a seven-month period.[28] It was not the first – nor the last – time that the single-mindedness of Sharon's military planning was transferred to the ground without mediation, adaptation or friction, giving the execution of his plans the functional clarity of a diagram.

The urban destruction of the Gaza camps was complemented by proposals for two types of construction; both demonstrated Sharon's ability to mobilize planning as a tactical tool. The first was for Jewish settlements to be built along what he called 'the five-finger plan', which positioned settlements as deep wedges into Gaza in order to separate its towns and break the area into manageable sections. The southernmost 'finger' was to be built in the Rafah Salient, beyond the southern edge of the Gaza Strip on occupied Egyptian Sinai, and was meant to sever Gaza from the arms-smuggling routes in the Sinai Desert. The other project that Sharon enthusiastically promoted was considered more 'experimental' and involved the construction of new neighbourhoods for the refugees. It was designed to bring about the undoing of the refugee camps altogether, and so remove the reasons for dissent that Israel believed was bred there through the immizeration of their Palestinian populations. When, in February 1972, Palestinian resistance appeared to have been suppressed, Dayan, reacting to home-grown and international outrage at Sharon's excessive military measures, transferred responsibility of the Gaza Strip from Southern to Central Command, taking it out of Sharon's hands. Sharon had done his job and now Dayan wanted to dissociate him from it. In the summer of 1973 Sharon finally resigned from the military when he realized he had no chance of being awarded the top job.

Egyptian military engineers making openings in the Bar Lev Line and moving across it, October 1973.

Breaking the Line

In 1973 the Bar Lev Line looked so firm that it seemed to justify Dayan's boast, probably for propaganda purposes, that it 'would take the American and Soviet engineer corps together to break through [it]'.[29] The Egyptian daily *Al-Ahram* claimed, some thirty years after the war, that some Soviet military experts, themselves wanting to make a point, had argued in 1973 that nothing less than a tactical nuclear explosion would breach it. But, on 6 October 1973, on the Jewish holiday of Yom Kippur, in a surprise Syrian–Egyptian two-front attack, it took only a few hours to break through Israeli fortifications using conventional military strategy. General Shazly recounted the clockwork operation that led to the breaching of Israeli lines on the Egyptian front:

> At precisely 1400 hours 200 of our aircraft skimmed low over the canal, their shadows flickering across enemy lines as they headed deep into the Sinai . . . their overflight was the signal our artillery had been waiting for . . . The 4,000 men of the first assault group poured over [the Egyptian] ramparts and slithered in disciplined lines down to the water's edge . . . a few minutes after 1420 hours, as the canisters began to belch clouds of covering smoke, our first assault wave was paddling furiously across the canal.[30]

The breached Bar Lev Line, circa 1974. Film stills, IDF film unit (Images courtesy of IP).

Because the attack started with an artillery barrage, the 450 Israeli soldiers manning the strongholds on the canal at the time of the attack were forced to dive into bunkers beneath the surface of the artificial landscape, thereby losing eye-contact with the Egyptian soldiers who were scaling the ramparts. By the time the bombardment stopped and the Israelis were able to resume their battle positions, the line had already been stormed and its strongholds encircled. The ramparts of sand, which had withstood two years of Egyptian artillery fire during the War of Attrition, succumbed to water. Using the Suez Canal, special units of the Egyptian engineering corps used high-pressure water cannons to dissolve the hardened packed sand and open more than seventy breaches within the artificial landscape.[31] The water cannons were similar to those that, throughout the late 1960s, had helped clear the banks of the upper Nile in preparation for the Aswan Dam whose construction was inaugurated in 1970; indeed, the idea for breaching the Bar Lev Line came from an Egyptian engineer employed on the Aswan Dam project.[32]

Once the Bar Lev Line had been breached, two Egyptian armies, about 100,000 soldiers, were transported over pontoon bridges and through the breaches in the earth dyke and onto the eastern, Asian, previously Israeli-controlled bank.[33] They advanced through the ravaged landscape a few kilometres into the Sinai. Then, wary of the fortified depth of Israeli defences and at the limit of their anti-aircraft umbrella, they halted and dug themselves in, facing east.[34]

The dawning of 8 October 1973, two days after the Egyptian army had breached the Israeli line, heralded the most bitter military defeat in IDF history, when, in a counter-offensive, waves of bewildered Israeli tank units broke against an entrenched Egyptian army equipped with the previously little-known Sager anti-tank missiles. The Israeli counter-attack was defeated, and with it Israeli military and civilian moral. The perception that the breaching of the Bar Lev Line was akin to breaching the city walls and storming the homeland was more imaginary than real, considering the hundreds of kilometres Egyptian troops would have had to cross before reaching any Israeli settlement. But this sensation was nevertheless evoked in Dayan's famous hysterical statement that the 'Third Temple was falling'. The trauma of the breached line, resonant with a sense of divine punishment, began a shift in national consciousness that helped liberate Israeli religious and messianic sentiment and in four years was to force Labor out of government.

In Israel the political significance of the 1973 war was amplified by the fact that it had started only weeks before the general elections scheduled for 31 October 1973, and a few months after both Sharon and Bar Lev had retired from military service. Both were busy campaigning for opposing political parties but when war broke out they were both called back to service. Since all senior positions were manned, each had to accept a single step down the command ladder. Sharon received command of the 143 armoured division (later known as the Likud Division) and Bar Lev the overall command of the entire southern front. As the war unfolded over the following weeks, old rivalries resurfaced when the glory-hungry generals used the military campaign as an extension of their electoral one. Sharon realized that whoever first crossed the canal to its African side would be crowned the war's hero. Bar Lev and the other generals associated with Labor understood that if Sharon was allowed to achieve personal success he would 'turn into a major political headache' after the war. Sharon himself undoubtedly turned the war to personal political advantage. He used open radio communications so that many of his division's soldiers could hear him, and he continued to leak secret military information to his large embedded entourage of admiring reporters.[35] The battles of 1973 demonstrated that war could be more than simply the continuation of politics by other means; it could itself become electoral politics, conducted within the resonating chamber of mediatized military manoeuvre. It also established different military officers as independent political players.

In his relentless drive towards the canal, Sharon allowed himself a large measure of autonomy, ignoring the desperate restraining orders of Bar Lev, again his direct military superior. The latter complained to Chief of Staff David Elazar that Sharon was 'out of control', and was disrupting the entire command hierarchy at the front: 'I have a divisional commander here who is a politician . . . who wants to [get the political credit for] crossing the canal.' Elazar asked Dayan for his opinion on dismissing Sharon. Dayan agreed that 'Arik can only think "how will this war make [him] look, what can [he] gain from all this" . . . He is trying to do a Rommel-type breakthrough – if it works, good; if not, the People of Israel lose 200 tanks . . .'[36] Fearful of the impact on army morale that Sharon's removal might have, they decided for the meantime to leave him in command of his division.

Sharon was indeed deliberately out of control – and out of communication. At times he switched off his radio altogether. When he was available on the radio, it was hard to talk to him because of his wilful misunderstanding of orders; at other times, he was heard snoring into the microphone. Sharon's attitude to military communications both concealed and emphasized his scramble to achieve those ends that he deemed politically important.

The following is a transcript of one of the rare occasions when contact was made successfully with Sharon. On the night of 17 October Sharon was called to the radio to take orders from Southern Command. The communications officer tried to remind Sharon of a plan for which he had received orders the previous day. Because it was a non-encoded radio connection, the officer dropped hints – which Sharon resolutely refused to take:

> *Southern Command*: A second thing, you were asked to carry out a manoeuvre in the manner of Wingate – do you understand what this is?
> *Sharon*: No . . .
> *SC*: It is what the 'chopped-finger' did in Burma in the manner of Wingate.
> *Sharon*: I don't understand what he [Bar Lev] wants . . .
> *SC*: You remember a wooden structure, a line of soldiers?
> *Sharon*: Listen, I can't remember . . . yesterday I was woken up at 23:00 to be asked if I could remember Anthony Quinn in a movie – I couldn't remember. What can I say . . . If there are ideas, tell me in the morning, now I cannot [do anything].[37]

Three days earlier, on 14 October, during the second week of the war the Egyptian army, holding a narrow bridgehead a few kilometres east of the canal, tried to progress deeper into the Sinai.[38] The four Egyptian brigades that entered IDF defences in depth were destroyed by nightfall. The Egyptian military had to transfer more forces to hold the eastern side of the canal. Because of the new numerical balance, Sharon finally got permission to prepare for a counter-attack and cross to the western side of the canal. This was to be done according to plan 'Stout Heart', which Sharon had conceived, planned and prepared during his tenure as Chief of Southern Command. In the last stages of the war he led the attack through an unprotected gap in Egyptian lines, separated the second

Egyptian Army from the third, reached the canal, broke through the Bar Lev Line and constructed two bridges across the water into a small enclave on the western bank of the canal that the IDF dubbed 'Africa'. Over these bridgeheads rolled most of the IDF armour, led by Adan and his deputy Dov Tamari, smashing into the rear of the third Egyptian army; it was now within striking distance of Cairo.[39] It was a perfect demonstration of what British war theoretician Basil Liddell Hart called the 'indirect approach'.[40] According to this doctrine, to defeat an army it is enough to direct an attack against its weak points and unprotected rear, throwing its organizational logic off balance. The Israeli counter-crossing of the canal had created a bizarre stalemate, with the two armies exchanging sides – and continents – across the canal. Such was the power (or lack thereof) of linear defence that it was crossed twice in both directions during a war that lasted less than three weeks.

On the international stage it was clear, however, that victory was Egypt's and Sadat's. Although much of their military was surrounded, the Egyptians held on to their territorial gains. When the war ended, the knotted-together positions of the two armies necessitated direct negotiations, which Sadat used to lead to the diplomatic process that would win him back the entire Sinai peninsula.

In Israel the military blow handed out by previously little-respected Arab armies was seen as proof of the fact that the military elites and ruling Labor Party were completely out of touch. As gloom descended, Sharon's popularity increased: he was perceived as the only rebel against the government and its crony generals. After the fighting, banners were hung on his division's vehicles, carrying the slogans that would later feature in so many political campaigns and carry the right-wing coalition to power in 1977 – 'Arik King of Israel!' A photograph of Sharon driving a military jeep with a blood-stained bandage around his forehead, his hair blowing in the wind, featured on the posters of his party-political campaign. In contrast to the ageing Meir and Dayan, he seemed to offer a youthful, energetic and anti-institutional alternative to Labor.

The debate surrounding Sharon's conduct during the 1973 war is still ongoing today. The significance of his military undertakings were exaggerated by all those who had a political stake in showing up Labor's incompetence. They pitched him as a military genius, an unparalleled tactician who had 'saved the nation'. Sharon indeed demonstrated he could successfully improvise amid scenes of chaos. However, what the war best demonstrated was Sharon's understanding of conflict as a means of communication; throughout the war, his decisions were governed by his desire that his actions resonate through the media with an anxious public consciousness. It was primarily Sharon's personality, the criticism he levelled at his superiors and his access to the media that made him the focus of attention.[41] His appeal stemmed from the popular perception that he was an undisciplined rebel, a radical, a violent transgressor. Sometimes he was seen as a 'hippie', a Kurtz-type lone-rider and the only alternative to a tired and failing political system.

Reinforcing the narrative that placed Sharon at the centre of a new military paradigm was TRADOC, the US military Training and Doctrine Command, which was established a few months before the 1973 war. TRADOC started its activities with a comprehensive study of this conflict, examining the performance of different Western and Soviet weapons systems; it also studied IDF organizational and command structures, especially Sharon's 'generalship'. Tracing his military career backwards, TRADOC researchers examined Sharon's strategies in previous battles, retelling their histories in a way that demonstrated their doctrinal aims, which engaged then with a 'system' approach to warfare and early engagement with network theories.[42] In particular, US military researchers examined Sharon's command of an IDF divisional raid on the main Egyptian line in the northern Sinai at Abu-Ageila, on the first night of the 1967 war. This raid, suggested the researchers, was unique by the standards of the time. It was conducted as a simultaneous attack by a multiplicity of small forces, each attacking a different unit in the synergetic Egyptian defence system – so that, instead of covering and supporting each other, as they were designed to, each of the Egyptian units was fighting for its own life. This battle exemplified for TRADOC the very approach it sought to promote. It was via the TRADOC researchers that this battle, otherwise played down in the Israeli historiography of the 1967 war – a story more concerned with emotional images of weeping soldiers at the Wailing Wall, of armoured columns storming through the desert landscape and of Egyptian casualties and abandoned military equipment – later became a central component of military education in the United States and the IDF.[43]

For the US military, the battlefields of the 1973 war, one of the last 'symmetrical conflicts' pitching fully mobilized state militaries against each other, provided a laboratory for a possible European ground war with the Warsaw Pact, and had profound effects on NATO's European geography. The military doctrine of 'active defence,' based upon a study of the war, was introduced in the 1976 edition of the US military field manual. Although this doctrine has since become extremely controversial, and was replaced, it emphasized the concept of 'depth', introducing it into the military discourse of the late 1970s and 1980s.[44] The doctrine of 'active defence' translated the paradigm of US military operations into a territorial model that led to the construction of an expanded network of American military bases within potential battlefields in West Germany.[45]

The IDF's crossing of the Suez Canal also triggered a series of global reactions. On 16 October 1973, incidentally the day Israeli forces established a foothold on the western (African) bank of the Canal, the Arab states announced a blanket 70 per cent increase in oil prices and a progressive monthly 5 per cent reduction in output, which would continue until Israel withdrew completely from the Occupied Territories and 'restored the legal rights of the Palestinians'. On 23 December, OPEC members decided to double the already inflated oil prices – in fact, the price of a barrel of oil quadrupled from $2.50 before the war to $10 at the beginning of 1974. The world was plunged into recession and an inflationary spiral that lasted a decade. It precipitated a shift in the global economy from the socio-political unity that the Keynesian, welfare, state-centric model sought to create and maintain towards the network economies of neo-liberalism. Indeed, the 1973 war coincided with major transformations worldwide – industrial production retreated in favour of an 'immaterial' service sectors that gradually shifted its production from analogue to digital technology, and one increasingly interested in flexible and dynamic networks.

In the Middle East, an arms race in conventional weapons ensued, partially supported by the increased oil revenues of the Arab states.[46] Total Israeli spending on security itself grew to a monstrous 23 per cent of the state's GDP, almost 30 per cent of the state budget, which in the years 1974–85 led to a massive economic crisis that further increased Israel's reliance on financial and political aid from the United States.[47]

Political fragmentation

The debate between the two different military doctrines of territorial organization – linear fortifications and a network of strongholds laid out throughout their depth – recalls comparisons suggested by Antonio Gramsci between the 'war of position' and 'war of manoeuvre', with similar political patterns.[48] For Gramsci, the shift from the former to the latter implies an erosion in political hegemony. He noted (allegorically perhaps) that since linear defence 'demands enormous sacrifices by an infinite mass of people . . . an unprecedented concentration of hegemony is necessary, and hence a more "interventionist" government . . . [that will] organize permanently the "impossibility" of internal disintegration – with control of every kind, political, administrative, etc'.[49] The political 'war of manoeuvre', by contrast, exists according to Gramsci as a multiplicity of non-centralized and loosely coordinated actions that aggressively compete with the power of the state.

In local terms, the breaking of the Bar Lev Line seemed to have turned the former model into the latter. The war and the breaching of the line fragmented more than military geography. It dislocated the cohesive structures that seemed to have held Israeli society together, and set in motion a general process of social and political upheaval that shattered the unity and hegemony of the state. Indeed, in the post-1973 period, processes of fragmentation took place in the social, economic, political and geographic arenas. The political hegemony of the Labor movement started to cede power to a variety of micro-political, non-govern-mental, extra-parliamentary organizations and pressure groups that began to comprise a larger, more complex and multipolar political landscape. These organizations challenged the state centralized power structure, a structure best described by the term 'Statism' – in Hebrew *Mamlahtiyut*, literally 'kingdomhood'.

Throughout the autumn and winter of 1973–74, the Labor government was confronted by a nationwide wave of demonstrations, which ended up bringing down the Meir–Dayan government. The protests were the first public expressions of dissent in Israel concerning issues of security. Other movements were already emerging before the war[50] – for example the Israeli 'Black Panthers', a protest movement of Mizrahi Jews that came to public attention in Jerusalem in 1971[51] (and of whom Golda Meir famously remarked that they were 'not nice'). The difference was that the postwar protesters were coming from the affluent layers of Israeli society and from soldiers returning from battle. That the polit-ical dissent was closely associated with the breaching of the Bar Lev Line is evidenced by the fact that Moti Ashkenazi, who established one of the protest movements and soon became its symbol, was a reserve officer who, during the war, commanded the only stronghold on the Bar Lev Line – stronghold Budapest – which did not fall to the Egyptians. Whether they were promoting left- or right-wing agendas, expansionist or partitionist politics, the protesters did so with the attitude and some of the style of the US anti-Vietnam War movement, which paradoxically found in Sharon, again, the very image of the anti-institutional rebel.[52]

In the following year in Cairo, Palestinian delegates at the 12th Palestinian National Council interpreted the wave of protest in Israel as heralding the possible beginning of civil war and Israel's imminent collapse. The delegates passed a resolution stating that the PLO would form a Palestinian government in every area of Palestine that might be liberated. Although the political implications of this position were clearly articulated and officially adopted only in 1988, the 1974 resolution was effectively the first time that the PLO accepted a two-state solu-tion, even if this acceptance was seen only as a temporary stage in the complete liberation of Palestine.[53] In fact, at the same time, the 1973 oil crisis kick-started a process that gave birth to a multiplicity of 'sovereignty-free actors' worldwide.

These were independent organizations as varied as protest and revolutionary movements, religious groups, humanitarian organizations, new businesses and guerrilla groups who positioned themselves on the international stage, conducting 'private sphere diplomacy' and engaging in actions previously reserved for states only.[54]

In Israel this process was best exemplified by the consolidation as an extra-parliamentary organization of a powerful new brand of national-religious Zionism, one that knitted together disparate and contradictory threads already existing within Zionism – pioneering and militarism, religion, nationalism and messianism. The core of the religious-messianic right-wing Gush Emunim (Block of Faithful), which was founded to promote the Jewish settlement of the 1967 occupied territories, was formed by demobilized soldiers and officers who had served together during the 1973 war. Its ideas were consolidated by soldiers stationed on the Suez Canal before the IDF completed its withdrawal from the area in March 1974. For these activists the 1973 war was a part of a messianic process that started with the conquests of 1967, and was a test for the nation of Israel. They viewed any conflict as a war over Jerusalem, and thus a war against God, a point seemingly underscored by the timing of the Arab armies' attack on Yom Kippur. The Israeli victory to come, through their combined effort, would thus be the victory of the 'rule of God', a conquest of light over darkness. For them, the moment of national regeneration – a revival that could only come through belief – must emerge from below, from the people themselves, because earthly governments failed them. Indeed, once the messianic process of settlement was under way, no withdrawal ordered by the government from any part of the holy land was to be countenanced.

The emergence of Gush Emunim could also be seen as part of a general revival of political religion around the globe from Iran to the United States, loosely collected under the term 'fundamentalism'. Gush Emunim attempted to liberate some of the previously repressed messianic sentiments within Zionism, and to invert the social hierarchies and cultural values within Israeli society.[55] In particular, the organization sought to replace the secular, and therefore temporary, 'state of Israel' with the transcendental power of the complete and permanent 'land of Israel'.[56] For the settlers of Gush Emunim, the frontiers of the West Bank and the Sinai were a zone liberated from the stifling 'statism' of government, the conceptual terrain for the formation of yet a new Israeliness, one that sought to combine some of the rough and rugged characteristics of frontier individuality, intolerance to the law and central government, with a devotional and pious way of life.[57]

Demobilized soldiers from the 1973 war also formed the basis of an organization that in 1978 evolved into Peace Now, which had an entirely opposite aim to that of Gush Emunim: to promote peace treaties with Arab governments based on security arrangements and the formula of 'land for peace'. Within a weakened centralized state, these two non-governmental organizations were the key protagonists in the reshaping of an extended political field. It was Gush Emunim, however, that best managed to exploit government weaknesses and organizational chaos, and build for itself a small settlement empire within an expanding (mini) state empire.

The suburban matrix

The febrile postwar political climate brought Likud's combination of right-wing foreign policy and hands-off economic policy to power under Menachem Begin in May 1977. In this election Sharon did not run on the Likud ticket but at the head of a small party that he had formed called 'Shlomzion'. After gaining only two seats he joined his party with Likud. Sharon demanded the Defence Ministry, but was instead appointed Minister of Agriculture; he also took over the Ministerial Committee for Settlement. He made the latter position into an influential and powerful portfolio in an administration of politicians who, with the exception of Dayan – who had also crossed political lines and joined Likud – were accustomed to permanent roles in political opposition, lacking any experience in government.

By the time Likud came to power, almost thirty settlements inhabited by some 4,500 Israelis had already been established in the West Bank, mostly within the borders of the Allon plan, but also in Hebron and in Gush Etzion southwest of Jerusalem.[58] Having publicly demonstrated the shortcomings of the Bar Lev Line, and having used the war to prove his point to the Israeli public, Sharon now turned against the second of the Labor defence lines. Seeking to implement the lessons learned from the 1973 Sinai campaign, Sharon claimed that: '. . . a thin line of settlements along the Jordan [i.e. the linear Allon plan] would not provide a viable defence unless the high terrain behind it was also fortified . . . the vital strategic issue was how to give depth to the coastal plain . . . the answer was to build a [network] of urban, industrial settlements on the ridges overlooking the plain'.[59]

Forty days after assuming ministerial office, Sharon announced the first proposal in a series of plans for the creation of Jewish settlements throughout the West Bank. The plan was prepared in collaboration with the architect Avraham Wachman, a professor at the Technion Institute of Technology in Haifa. Wachman was by then already world renowned for his role in the development of the Eshkol-Wachman Movement Notation, designed in 1958 to enable choreographers to 'write' a dance down on paper like composers write notes. And so

Sharon's plan for the colonization of the depth of the West Bank emerged out of the meeting of the architect of dance notation with the architect of manoeuvre-warfare.[60] The plan projected a network of more than a hundred points to be inhabited by suburban, urban and industrial settlements on the mountain ridges across the depth of the West Bank.[61] According to the plan, settlements were to be organized in sustainable 'blocks', in which a number of smaller rural and suburban settlements would receive services from larger urban, industrial ones.[62] Each block of settlements was to be connected along major highways to other such conurbations, and to the main metropolitan centres in Israel proper. The high-volume traffic network that would connect the settlement blocks was itself to be protected by other settlements along the routes.

According to the Sharon–Wachman plan, the settlements would also function as barriers, enveloping the Palestinian-populated mountain region from both east and west, and fragmenting it internally with Israeli east–west traffic corridors and by settlements located on the Palestinian road network. The Sharon–Wachman plan was not therefore a network of fortifications placed in an empty abstract space; rather, it was a network superimposed upon another, the pre-existing living Palestinian spaces. The aim of the Israeli settlement and roads was to splice and paralyze the Palestinian one. The result would be several isolated Palestinian cantons, each around a major city, with the connections controlled by Israel. Years later, the Israeli activist Jeff Halper called the interlocking series of settle-ments, roads, barriers, and military bases built throughout the West Bank, the 'matrix of control', and likened it to a game of 'Go' – inadvertently referencing Deleuze and Guattari:[63] 'The Matrix, an intricate and an interlocking series of control mechanisms, resembles the Japanese game of "Go". Instead of defeating your opponent as in chess, in "Go" you win by immobilizing the other side, by gaining control of key points of a matrix, so that every time your opponent moves he or she encounters another obstacle.'[64] The nodes of the West Bank's matrix of control act as on/off valves regulating movement, replacing the neces-sity for the physical presence of Israeli forces within Palestinian cities. This distrib-uted logic would later allow Israelis to pull out of densely inhabited Palestinian areas under the terms of the Oslo Accord while still dominating the Palestinians physically, collectively and politically by remotely controlling their movements.

On the smaller, tactical scale of the Sharon–Wachman plan, individual settle-ments were located on strategic summits, thereby allowing them to function as observation points: maintaining visual connection with each other and over-looking their surroundings, main traffic arteries, strategic road junctions and Pales-tinian cities, towns and villages. Sharon claimed that 'there was no place [settlement] that was built without a reason'.[65] The logic of visibility – to both see and be seen – dictated the overall mode of design. Visual domination was important

IDF defence in depth throught the West Bank, late 1970s. The 'eggs' represent military strongpoints. Jaffee Centre for Strategic Studies 1982.

not only in order to exercise domination, but to demonstrate the presence of the occupation's power. Sharon, flying over the Occupied Territories once remarked: 'Arabs should see Jewish lights every night from 500 metres.'[66] Tactical consideration engaged simultaneously thus with both seeing and being seen. The sense of always being under the gaze was intended to make the colonized internalize the facts of their domination.

Sharon's plan was not officially accepted by the first Begin government – indeed it was unintelligible to most of its members – but the government did authorize some settlements, and more were built without official permission through Sharon's private initiative. By the late 1970s and early 1980s there began the frenzy of construction that was indicative of Sharon's proximity to executive power. A growing spider's web of installations was being spun throughout the West Bank. Like the Sinai a few years previously, the land was being inscribed

Ariel Sharon as minister of Agricultur and Head of the Government's settlement committee, 1979.
Photograph: Arnold Newman, Getty Images.

by two symbiotic and synergetic instruments of territorial expansion: the settlement point and the road network. The latter served the former, the former overlooked and protected the latter.

Without full government backing, and fearing the reversal of his project, Sharon was reluctant to implement his plans sequentially, one settlement after the other, but adopted a simultaneous approach. He believed that it was important 'to secure a presence first [in all points] and only then build the settlements up'.[67] He wanted to establish the entire skeleton for the geography of occupation, present it as an ineradicable fact on the ground and later allow it to evolve and consolidate. He accordingly started scattering the West Bank with small outposts, some hardly more than footholds, composed of tents or mobile homes, knowing that each of these places, once established on the ground, could later grow into a settlement. Journalists writing in this period described the outposts as akin to frontier towns in the wild American West: caravans organized in a circle around a windswept hilltop, inhabited by rugged but enthusiastic settlers slinging the straps of their guns around their shoulders. To complete the analogy, even their religious Tzitziot (the tassels attached to garments worn by observant Jews) resembled those of ponchos.

The outposts had a potential for immediacy, mobility and flexibility; they were the perfect instruments of colonization. Tents and prefabricated homes could be deployed quickly and under cover of night on the back of trucks or, in cases where a road was not available, by helicopter. Named after their topographical latitude – 'hill 777', 'hill 851' – settlement outposts are often referred to in Hebrew as 'points on the ground', and a single settlement sometimes simply as *Nekuda* – 'point' in Hebrew (*Nekuda* is also the title of the official journal of the settlers' movement). This is indicative of a planning culture that conceived the settlements in essence more in terms of their strategic location than as places of residence. Strategy is the choice of points where force is to be applied, and points themselves are nothing but coordinates, abstract positioning. The rigidity of the prefabricated caravans and mobile homes allowed for the quick multiplication and flexible distribution of settlements: an instant urbanism. The outpost-seed could then evolve into a 'mature' settlement when conditions permitted. This is the reason why contemporary outposts (numbering 103 at present, according to 'Peace Now') should not be seen differently to settlements, but rather as a stage in their evolution.

The network of roadways that was purportedly built for the purpose of facilitating military manoeuvres became effective instruments of development – not only for the ideological core of Gush Emunim, but for Israeli suburb-dwellers. The settlements project was explained to an Israeli public traumatized by the 1973 war as a defensive system designed to help protect the state from invasion, a precaution against another surprise conventional war, this time not in the 'endless' open deserts of the Sinai but much closer to home – in the West Bank. Sharon, expert in manipulating and profiting from public fear, warned: 'If we don't begin settling in Judea and Samaria [the West Bank], Jordanian artillery will come to us.' He later explained in military terms the logic of defence embodied in the project: 'In any attack our lines had to be held by limited regular forces in conjunction with the civilian communities whose role is to guard our borders, secure roads, insure communications, and so on . . . [the West Bank settlements] would be organized for defence, with their own weapons and ammunition, their contingency plans and their integration into the overall defensive system.'[68] Battlefield terms such as strongpoint, advance, penetration, encirclement, envelopment, surveillance, control and supply lines migrated, from the military to the civilian sphere. For Sharon the architect/general, politics was war as much as war was politics and both were exercised in space making. The concept of 'depth' was also civilianized. Flexibility became the hallmark of Sharon's work as an architect across the Israeli frontier. The mobile home and later the small red-roofed single family house replaced the tank as a basic battle unit; homes, like armoured divisions, were deployed in formation across a theatre of operations to occupy hills, to encircle an enemy, or to cut its communication lines. Sharon 'trekked from place to place, climbing with map in hand to decide where settlements would be located, looking for high, important terrain and vital road junctions'.[69] In the hands of Sharon, his followers and colleagues, architecture and planning were presented as a continuation of war by other means. The civilianization of military terms was to lead in turn to the militarization of all other spheres of life. War was only over because it was now everywhere.

The 'ascent' of the Elon Moreh Settlement core to Sebastia, West Bank, December 1975.

3.

Settlements: Battle for the Hilltops

Although he played a central role in the settlement of the mountain region of the West Bank, and his visions were partially implemented, Sharon cannot be said to be the master-planner of the settlement project there. The 'authorship' of this project was diffused rather amongst a multiplicity of agents and organizations and embodied more contradictions than a set of coherent strategies. Far from being a result of an ordered government-led master-planning process – the translation of a single governance or defence rationality to a process of territorial organization – the colonization of the mountain district of the West Bank has in fact emerged out of a series of fundamental crises and conflicts that took place between various ministers and ministries within a series of Israeli governments, and between these governments, the settler organization of Gush Emunim, other non-government organizations and the High Court of Justice from 1967 to 1981. These conflicts, a feature of both the Labor governments of the first decade of occupation (1967–77) as well as the first Likud government of Menachem Begin (1977–81), were physically acted out on the hilltops of the West Bank, but also within the halls of the Israeli High Court of Justice in a number of landmark legal cases. During these years the High Court was transformed into an arena in which government agents, military officers, settlers, Palestinian landowners and Israeli peace and rights groups battled over land expropriation and the establishment of settlements. In the process of these legal battles, terms such as 'defence', 'security', 'temporariness' and 'divine right' were argued and defined in a way that continues to inform the practices and strategies of the occupation to this day.

The organizational chaos and improvisation that characterized the settlement project in these years could be contrasted with what Israeli architectural historian Zvi Efrat called the 'Israeli Project' – the top-down planning and construction of the physical environment of the Israeli state in the first two decades of its existence prior to 1967. According to Efrat, during the 1950s and 1960s the

'Israeli Project' was based on state-centric master-planning that he described as 'one of the most comprehensive, controlled and efficient architectural experiments in the modern era', echoing 'Stalin's Five Year Plan for the Soviet Union . . . the American New Deal infrastructural projects and public works of the 1930s . . . and the post-World War II British schemes of New Towns'.[1] This project was subjected to centralized political control, it was governed by rational principles of organization and standardization, a clear division of labor and the distribution of the population according to a single plan and a book of instructions that were prepared in 1949 by the Bauhaus school graduate, architect Arie Sharon. Whereas in the 1950s and early 1960s state planning was undertaken by professional architects and planners, after the 1967 war it was mainly undertaken by politicians, generals and ideological activists. While the Arie Sharon plan regarded the borders of the state as fixed, post-1967 settlement efforts, in which Ariel Sharon played a major role, saw the territoriality of the Occupied Territories as 'elastic' and up for grabs.

Shortly after the end of the 1973 war, a group of young women, led by Daniella Weiss, who would later become secretary-general of the settler organization Gush Emunim, met with Prime Minister Golda Meir. They came to ask for government permission and assistance in establishing a small settlement in the mountain region of the West Bank. The location, recommended by Ariel Sharon, who had recently left military service to begin his political career, was a disused Ottoman-era railway station located near the Palestinian village of Sebastia, northwest of the town of Nablus. The site was well outside the borders of the Allon plan, which sought to colonize mainly the Jordan Valley and the areas around Jerusalem, and thus in contradiction to its principal goal of only settling areas sparsely populated by Palestinians. Meir was personal and supportive, but politely declined the request. Her refusal led to eight consecutive attempts in the following three years to settle the location without government permission.

The 'ascents', as the settlement-establishing expeditions were called, were led by a group of would-be settlers who comprised the 'settlement-core' of Elon Moreh, logistically supported by the Israeli National-Religious Party. On occasion they were accompanied by a large entourage of rabbis, university professors, writers and Knesset members. The ascents were often confronted by demonstrators of the Zionist left and were disbanded by the military. Sharon himself had a role in organizing some of the ascents, and in evading military attempts to break them up. Leading a group of settlers in July 1974, Sharon broke through military roadblocks, leading soldiers on a wild goose chase through the surrounding hills, only to let another group quietly arrive on site from another direction. When the settlers arrived at the railway station they chained themselves together, so that Arie Shalev, the then military governor of the West Bank, had 'to bring a large hammer from the prison house in Nablus to break apart the steel chains that held together a settlement constructed of living bodies'.[2] In February 1974 the members of the Elon Moreh core and various other national-religious groups joined together to form Gush Emunim. In the winter of 1976, during the holiday of Hanukkah, after another ascent, a compromise was reached between the settlers and the government in the main hall of the Sebastia railway station. In one of his famous 'creative solutions', Shimon Peres – serving as Minister of Defence in the Labor government of Yitzhak Rabin, formed after Golda Meir's forced resignation in April 1974 – allowed the settlers to remain within a specially allocated section of the military base of Qadum, southwest of Nablus. Over the next two years, the settlers' enclave grew larger than the entire base, and was officially civilianized into the settlement of Qedumim.[3]

This *modus operandi* exemplified the power and capabilities of Gush Emunim. The group's function was twofold: to act as an extra-parliamentary activist pressure group in the halls of power, and to serve as a settlement organization in the hills of the West Bank. By these means, it tried to fashion itself as the true heir to the pre-1948 Labor pioneering movement. In its 'ascents' to the hilltops of the West Bank, Gush Emunim also attempted to resolve the paradox inherent in the territorial approach of Zionism: while seeking a return to the 'promised land', early Zionists settled in the coastal plains and northern valleys that had good agricultural soil but relatively little in the way of Israelite history. The later 'ascents' were seen as the 'regeneration of the soul' and the achievement of 'personal and national renewal', infused with the mystical quality of the heights. For these settlers, the 1967 occupation was not understood as a mere progression along the horizontal axis of expansion. It was primarily an uphill assault from the Israeli coastal plains to the mountains of the West Bank, the Syrian Golan Heights and the Sinai mountains. For them the mountains were seen both as strategic ground as well as the cradle of the nation. Years later Ephi Eitam, the retired general who further radicalized the National-Religious Party, opposed any dismantling of the mountain settlements of the West Bank in these terms: 'Whoever proposes that we return to the plains, to our basest part, to the sands, the secular, and that we leave in foreign hands the sacred summits, proposes a senseless thing.'[4]

According to Gush Emunim, the state's 'weak governments', those administrations responsible for the catastrophe of the 1973 war, were to be suppressed by the group's outpouring of religious energies and mystical power. The settlements became a tool in the modern struggle between the people and the sovereignty of the state of Israel.

That the government could be pressured into authorizing and establishing settlements had become evident only three months after the 1967 war when, in

September of that year, Kfar Etzion became the first settlement to be established in the West Bank southwest of Jerusalem. It was established contrary to general government guidelines in response to insistent pressure by a group of settlers, some of whom were relatives of the residents of the original community of Kfar Etzion, one of several Jewish communities that fell to Palestinian militias and the Jordan Legion at the beginning of the 1948 war.

Gush Emunim's most effective tactic was to settle sites without government permission with the intention of forcing it to give retrospective legitimacy to settlements whose existence was already established in fact. The strategy was to build many settlements in areas that the government may have otherwise evacuated under international pressure, thereby forcing it to hold onto as much of the territory occupied in 1967 as possible.

The methods of Gush Emunim demonstrate the difference between the top-down master-planning logic of governments and the bottom-up operational logic of independent political organizations. While a masterplan generally seeks to mobilize resources and organize the landscape and the built environment in a manner that embodies a political strategic vision, Gush Emunim sought to identify cracks and fissures within the organization of executive power, and exploit conflicts between government members, political opportunities and ad hoc alliances.[5]

In 1977, shortly after the handover of power from Labor to Likud, Egyptian President Anwar Sadat made a visit to Jerusalem and the peace process began. Although Menachem Begin's government was engaged in peace talks with Egypt, it was not yet inclined to acquiesce fully to the impatient demands of Gush Emunim, although it did authorize some settlements and continued building around Jerusalem. However, the organization again found an ally in Sharon, then head of the government's Settlement Committee, seeing in him a champion in their battle against the 'defeatism' of the other members of the government, who seemed all to have fallen under Sadat's charm. Angry at having been excluded from the peace negotiations by Begin, who feared his impulsive nature, Sharon timed the launch of new settlements to coincide with impending diplomatic breakthroughs, or to clash with the trips to Egypt of his main political rival, Minister of Defence Ezer Weizman, whose job he coveted – and four years later got.

Together with Gush members, Sharon even initiated some 'Potemkin settlements' – empty decoys and ship containers that could be mistaken for settlements in order to convince the Americans, who were monitoring the area from the air, that new settlements were being constructed under their noses in areas of the Sinai that Israel had already agreed to hand back – thereby causing the Egyptians to suspend negotiations.[6] Settlement construction therefore provided

Sharon with the means to intervene in, or interfere with, Israel's foreign policy. A hilltop scattered with several mobile homes and manned by a group of young zealots was the kind of micro-tactics, replete with geopolitical implications, that was his particular forte.

Settlement chaos

One of the characteristics of Sharon's military command and civilian ministy was his reluctance to outline precise operational plans. 'I settle where I can,' he often said. What Sharon said, what he did, what he proposed, was based on general improvisations, which he decided upon only at the moment he needed to act, had an opportunity to act or felt compelled to act. His advantage was that if he did not know what he was going to do the following day, neither would his enemies and rivals. One of Sharon's other obvious talents was the use of maps and cartography. In photographs of various periods, both as soldier and as politician, he is often seen pointing to details on maps, or marching with a rolled-up map tucked under his arm. Taking advantage of the limited experience among his colleagues in the government, he drew complex maps of new settlements that could not be easily understood or, in total contempt for his colleagues' abilities, presented maps of areas other than those in discussion, and still forced through decisions in his favour.[7] At other times he helped disguise new settlements from his fellow ministers by claiming they were actually only ad hoc 'workers camps', 'military bases' or 'archaeological sites'.

In early 1978, Sharon persuaded the rest of the government to award a group of Gush Emunim members a permit to establish a 'work camp' for the purpose of archaeological excavation at the presumed site of the biblical town of Shiloh. There, on the foothills of a ridge separating the present-day districts of Ramallah and Nablus, during the time of the biblical 'occupation and settlement' of Canaan by Yehoshua Bin-Nun, the Tabernacle was believed to have temporarily rested on its way to Jerusalem. Although the 'archaeologists' were more engaged in prayer and dance than in digging, the deeper the excavation went, the more established the encampment became. Soon after, the 'site accommodation' of the 'archaeological expedition' was expanded and family members of the 'archaeologists' arrived to live with them on site. Mobile homes replaced tents, water towers were built, and electricity was provided courtesy of a nearby military base. When the excavation camp was finally exposed as an act of optical-political camouflage, the modern settlement of Shiloh was already a fact on the ground.

Until the end of 1981, when the second Begin government fully adopted Gush Emunim's ideology, and was so acquiescent to its demands that the organization

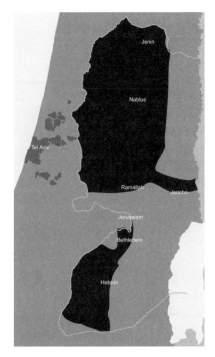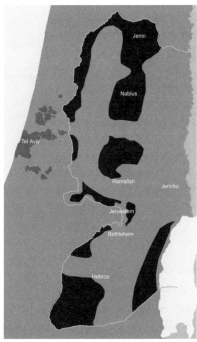

Left: Allon Plan, 1967–77. The dark sections mark the areas to be handed back to Jordan (58 per cent of the West Bank). Right: Sharon Plan (the H Plan), 1977–82. The separate areas of Palestinian autonomy would extend over 40 per cent of the West Bank. In both plans the separate parts of the West Bank are to be linked by extra-territorial roads.

considered disbanding itself,[8] the settlement project in the mountain district of the West Bank could be described as an 'anti-government' project conducted by Gush Emunim with support from allies within the government.

The number of settlers and settlements in the West Bank rose, no doubt, after Likud was elected to power in May 1977. At this time there were about 4,500 settlers living in twenty-eight settlements throughout the West Bank (a further 50,000 settlers were already living in Jerusalem), most of them in the Jordan Valley according to the Allon plan, but also in several Gush Emunim settlements in the mountain region as well. At the end of the Likud government's first term of office, in June 1981, the number of settlements had more than doubled to sixty-eight and the number of settlers almost quadrupled to 16,200.[9] In these years, however, the geography of the occupation did not emerge out of clear government decisions and planning guidelines, but mostly evolved out of confused interaction between different, mostly inconsistent, and often opposing political agents and ideological interests. In fact, although many people

HOLLOW LAND

– including Sharon himself – would have liked recognition as the master-planner of the settlement project, the colonization of the occupied territories did not grow out of any masterplan; rather, it evolved as a 'strategy without a strategist'.[10] Because the settlement project was founded through ad hoc improvisation, opportunist actions and conflicts between different politicians, its imprint on the ground cannot be read as the material embodiment of a single coherent ideology. Despite there being countless government masterplans for settlements, in its early years the project deliberately fostered an 'anti-planning' ethos. 'Operators' on the ground, and the facts they managed to establish, rather than the master-planners, dictated the larger political priorities and agendas, intentionally limiting some political options of the government, and opening others.

The indecisive nature of the post-1967 war Eshkol government, the paralysis that has plagued the traumatized post-1973 Meir government, the power struggles between Rabin and his Minister of Defence Shimon Peres during the first Rabin government, and the contradictions between the desire to settle and the peace process with Egypt during the first Begin government, meant that most often executive political power in these years did not fully mobilize for the settlement effort but swung behind the makers of 'facts on the ground'. The indecision of these governments was often in fact structural; successive Israeli governments decided not to risk splitting public opinion by outlining a clearly defined policy on this deeply divisive issue; instead, they let events take their course.

There were, however, several colonization plans prepared; indeed, during this period, planning became something of an obsession. Israeli technocrats, ideologues and generals all put forward their own plans, each proposing different areas to be carved out of the West Bank and annexed to Israel. Throughout the 1970s each of these colonization plans tried to outdo the others in its territorial ambition, thereby unleashing a process of ever-increasing territorial radicalization. Immediately after the 1967 war, the Eshkol government believed it would have to return the West Bank to Jordan, but sought to annex only Arab Jerusalem and the areas around it.[11] The first settlement plan debated by the government after the 1967 war was, as previously mentioned, the Allon plan,[12] according to which the strategic prerequisite was to separate the West Bank from the Arab countries on its eastern border. Consequently, the plan primarily envisioned settlement along the Jordan Valley that runs between the West Bank and Jordan, on the river's western bank. Allon, the main political rival of Minister of Defence Moshe Dayan, was at the time seen as the most likely candidate to succeed Eshkol as prime minister. In 1968, in response to Allon's plan – and no doubt in order to refute it with a completely different vision – Dayan suggested a diametrically opposed solution in which the most important strategic requirement was in fact to settle the mountain strip of the West Bank, the high terrain that dominates the Israeli cities on the coastal plains. To this end Dayan proposed building five large military bases along the central mountain range of the West Bank, and surrounding them with what he called 'fists of Jewish settlements' that would 'dismember [Palestinian] territorial continuity'.[13] Unlike Allon's settlements, these were to be not agricultural but industrial, turning the local Palestinian population into a source of cheap labor. Around the same time, Chief of Central Command Rehavam Ze'evi submitted yet another strategic plan. This positioned settlements according to a military logic, near all tactically important crossroads throughout the entire depth of the West Bank. Sharon's plan of a few years later incorporated elements of previous plans: it sought to settle the Jordan Valley along the outline of the Allon plan, the mountain range along that of Dayan's, and, adding his own unique contribution, settlement blocks on the western slopes of the West Bank mountains that were meant to completely envelop Palestinian habitable areas, physically separating them from the villages and towns of nearby Palestinian citizens of Israel.[14] Although it never followed formal plans – even those of its own devising – Gush Emunim presented to the government a series of provocative masterplans that further radicalized Sharon's proposal. Gush Emunim suggested locations for settlements not only according to military-strategic or economic-suburban logic, but also according to a national-religious one, near 'historical [that is, Arab] towns . . . in order to naturalise the Jewish people as a healthy nation sitting safely in all its land'.[15]

Most settlement masterplans, drawn up by people either within or outside the government, were also partition plans: planners placed settlements in the areas they wanted the government to annex. The logic of partition of the Occupied Territories has always swung between selective presence and absence, addressing two contradictory Israeli strategies: territorial (attempting to annex as much empty land as possible) and demographic (attempting to exclude the areas most heavily populated by Palestinians). Moreover, as has been seen, each successive plan aimed to undermine politically the plans that preceded it. In these years it seems that Israeli politics was acting out its internal and external conflicts on the hill-tops of the West Bank. None of the plans provided the basis for a coherent settlement policy, and none was officially adopted by the government, although certain elements of each of the different plans were followed in the construction of settlements.

Governments gradually learned to benefit from the settlement chaos; indeed, they sometimes promoted or even agitated it, creating the atmosphere that allows certain crimes to take place.[16] Although the trajectory of political initiative has swung from the institutions of the centre to the organizations of the frontier, when the settlement activity seemed to degenerate into complete chaos it was because this chaos was often promoted from the centre. Actual or claimed loss of control in the Occupied Territories thus itself became an effective government strategy. The appearance of being out of control allowed the state to achieve its ideological objectives without accepting responsibility for them.[17] When criticized internationally, the state was always able to absolve itself of responsibility, claiming that what was taking place were illegal actions, local initiatives of non-governmental organizations or exceptional excesses undertaken by 'rogue citizens' – when, in fact, these exceptions were the norm. In the late 1970s, the fact that settlement activity could be presented as 'rogue' allowed the Begin government to negotiate with the Americans and Egyptians in seemingly good faith, while settlement activity was still going on. The fact that settlements were illegally established helped Begin explain to the Americans the significance of the West Bank to Israeli public opinion and argue that this area could not simply be handed back as the Sinai Peninsula had been. Speaking to the 'outside', the government did not own the settlements; but when speaking 'inside' it boasted about them.

Adding to the organizational chaos was the 1977 change in power which also led to wholesale changes in state bureaucracy. The largely well-tested functionaries of the Labor movement, accustomed to running state matters, were replaced with inexperienced new political functionaries, resulting in increasing institutional chaos.[18] The geography of the West Bank settlements became the territorial result of pressure by Gush Emunim and other settler organizations, the willing suspension of government control, irregularly imposed 'facts on the ground', Sharon's haphazard improvisation, military 'emergency solutions', and conflicts between different Zionist agencies and ideologies. This incoherent, conflictual process and the involvement of independent activist agencies seem to have increased motivation and efficiency and was, paradoxically, one of the reasons for the success of the settlement project – both in terms of politically dictating national priorities from this point onwards, and in terms of its burgeoning population and economic sustainability. Significantly, all of this was achieved against the backdrop of the general economic and social failures of the state-centric 'Israeli Project' of the 1950s and 1960s.

Legal tactics

Throughout the 1970s the Israeli High Court of Justice (HCJ) became the central arena where conflicts regarding settlement activity were played out between Palestinian landowners, settler organizations, the military and relevant government ministries. These took place in three consecutive landmark cases debated in

Outposts, the West Bank. Daniel Bauer, 2001.

response to petitions of Palestinian landowners and Israeli human rights groups against land requisition for the purpose of establishing the settlements of the Rafah Salient in north Sinai (1972); the Bet-El settlement near Ramallah (1978); and the Elon Moreh settlement (1979) near Nablus in the West Bank. In these cases the High Court determined the legal rationality that helped define the political, ideological and military nature of the occupation.

Access to land was essential for the establishment of settlements. However, according to the principles of the Hague Convention on the laws and customs of war on land, and the accompanying Hague Regulations of 1907, which define the rights of civilians and the duties of armed forces in situations of belligerent occupation, and were accepted by Israeli courts as binding, an occupying power may only requisition land and undertake physical transformation in occupied territory if such acts serve one or both of two purposes: 'urgent military necessity' or 'benefit to the local population'.[19] An occupying power could, for example, erect temporary barriers on private fields or temporarily take possession of buildings in strategic locations in order to house its military forces and administrative units.[20] Requisition is distinct from land expropriation or seizure in that it does not change the title of ownership over the land, but rather constitutes only the *temporary* right to its use. Therefore, when the reasons for requisition no longer exist, the land is to be returned to its owner. The lawmakers' emphasis on this category of 'temporariness' reflects the perception that belligerent occupation was understood to be a transient state, one to be quickly resolved by agreements on annexation or return after wars are won or lost. In the imagination of its European lawmakers, war was a temporary aberration in a general history of peace.[21] Suspension of rights was therefore defined by this vague concept of 'temporariness' – to which, however, no prescribed time limits applied.

'Temporariness' and 'security' have thus become the two central categories around which the aforementioned three High Court of Justice cases revolved. The tactical-legal manipulation of the term 'temporary security necessities', testified to whenever needed by the military, has turned into a government charade in attempts to deny the HCJ the possibility of blocking government access to private Palestinian land.

Strategic settlements

The first High Court of Justice petition challenging the legality of land requisition for settlement took place in 1972 in response to actions undertaken by Ariel Sharon, then still Chief of the IDF's Southern Command. As part of his counter-insurgency campaign in Gaza, Sharon wanted to sever the strip from the Sinai

Desert and thereby from the PLO guerrilla supply lines that supposedly traversed it. The area south of Gaza, known as the Rafah Salient, was settled by a 5,000-strong Bedouin tribe. 'Between the dunes, in places where the meagre rainfall collected, Bedouin farmers tended almond, peach, olive, and castor-oil trees and patches of wheat. Near the coastline, where groundwater rose almost to the surface, they farmed a strip a few hundred meters wide that yielded richer crops. Herds of sheep and goats added to their livelihood . . . they were settled tribes; some lived in tents, but more in tin shacks and concrete houses.'[22] In the winter of 1972, acting without an explicit government order, but very likely in response to an indirect oral suggestion from Dayan, Sharon ordered the destruction of the orchards, the blocking up of the water wells and the deportation of the villagers. He drew a line on the map where the encampment was located and ordered bulldozers to drive along it, carving a swathe several dozen metres wide that crushed all obstacles in its path.

The eviction of the Bedouin from their lands provoked outrage in a nearby Kibbutz, whose members commissioned a human rights lawyer to represent the villagers via their tribal elder, Suleiman Hussein Uda Abu Hilo, in an HCJ petition against the state of Israel in general and against Ariel Sharon as the military commander in particular. This is how the eviction was described in court: 'In the early morning hours of the 14th of January, 1972, Petitioner no.1 [Abu Hilo] was urgently alerted by members of his tribe that soldiers of the Israel Defence Forces had ordered them, orally, to leave their homes and their community. Petitioner no. 1 proceeded to those IDF soldiers, addressed their commander, a second lieutenant, and asked that he explain the actions of his soldiers. The officer answered Petitioner no.1 that, "This is a government order to expel you from here."'[23]

Although Sharon appeared personally in court, bringing with him maps and documents that apparently demonstrated existing, urgent 'security concerns', the petitioners claimed that the evacuation was undertaken for no other reason than to make way for the construction of a town and several smaller agricultural settlements, which they further argued should not be considered a 'temporary security matter' at all. Indeed, while the case was still pending in court, the Tel Aviv-based architects Yehuda Drexler and Ze'ev Drukman, together with a group of planning experts, were secretly commissioned by Minister of Defence Dayan (who had known Drexler when he was an officer in the military) to prepare the blueprint for the development of the small port town of Yamit in the Rafah Salient. After the planners had – rather naively – produced a design brochure for distribution, soldiers arrived in their office and confiscated all copies in case they should come to the attention of the court. Their design replicated existing moulds of Israeli development towns with rows of block housing. In its ruling,

Yamit, circa 1980. Yehuda Drexler and Ze'ev Drukman.

however, the HCJ was prepare to accept that these settlements, if indeed constructed there, might in themselves be considered as a legitimate security measure, in creating a wedge of loyal Israeli residents between the Gaza Strip and Sinai. In ruling this and in most other petitions, Justice Vitkon represented the general spirit and tone of the court. He stated that although 'the area [or part thereof, may be] designated for settlement of Jews [these settlements] . . . are in themselves, in this case, a security measure'.[24]

A similar use of the 'security value' of settlements was again tested in 1978, when Suleiman Tawfik Ayub and Gamil Arsam Mataua petitioned the HCJ on behalf of themselves and five other Palestinian landowners against the requisition of their land for the establishment of the settlement of Bet-El near Ramallah. In this verdict, Justice Vitkon explained in further detail his decision to allow the land requisition for the sake of settlement:

In terms of purely security-based considerations, there can be no doubt that the presence in the administered territory [the occupied territories, according to the terminology of the time] of settlements – even 'civilian' ones – of the citizens of the administering power makes a significant contribution to the security situation in that territory, and facilitates the army's performance of its tasks. One need not be an expert in military and defence matters to appreciate that terrorist elements operate more easily in territory occupied exclusively by a population that is indifferent or sympathetic to the enemy than in a territory in which there are also persons liable to monitor them and inform the authorities of any suspicious movement. With such people the terrorists will find no shelter, assistance and equipment. These are simple matters and there is no need to elaborate.[25]

That a High Court Judge imagined that this matter needed no elaboration testifies to how far the idea of settlement was coextensive with that of security throughout Zionist history. From the perspective of international law, the problem with Vitkon's rulings was that, under these conditions, the reverse must also be correct: if settlements are used for security purposes, they may also become legitimate targets for attack.[26]

Curtain of sand

In June 1979, in an operation again directed by Ariel Sharon, the settlement-core of the Elon Moreh settler group once again made an 'ascent' on a site near Nablus. The Palestinian owners of the land on which the provisory encampment was set, Azat Muhamed and Mustafa Dweikat, representing sixteen others, petitioned the HCJ against the requisition of their land by the state of Israel.[27] In an affidavit presented to the court in support of the government's position, IDF Chief of Staff Refael Eitan, then still a protégé of Ariel Sharon (the relationship between them soured during the Lebanon war of 1982 and over responsibility for the massacre in the Palestinian refugee camps of Sabra and Shatila), provided a historical account of the military function of Zionist settlements. This was undertaken in order to demonstrate that the settlement of Elon Moreh was, like its historical predecessors, of the highest military necessity. This account could help explain how Zionist mythologies, which celebrated the significance of early agrarian frontier settlements in setting and buttressing the borders of the areas under Jewish control, eventually evolved into a set of legal arguments, used for the establishment and post factum justification of contemporary suburban settlements.

For a man notorious for being economical with words (and with a bizarre tendency to speak in basic rhyme), Eitan's account was rather surprising in its extent. His narrative began in the pre-state years of Zionism, during the years of the 'Arab Revolt' of 1936, with the story of the paramilitary 'Tower and

Stockade' – a prefabricated, fortified settlement system designed to be assembled in one night across the frontier zones of pre-state Palestine, and be strong enough to withstand counter-attacks in the morning after its establishment.[28] Eitan's narrative also took in other periods of Zionist expansion. According to him, the architecture of the Zionist rural settlement was shaped not only by the methods of agricultural production and in response to its socio-ideological organization, but also according to tactical considerations dictated by a militarized logic. In his account Eitan was nourished by generations of military generals involved in physically planning Zionist frontier settlements.

Foremost amongst those was Yigal Allon. In his role as the commander of the Palmach, the Haganah's (the Labor movement's pre-state armed group) elite guerrilla battalion – Allon, himself a Kibbutz member (Kibbutz Ginnosar on the Sea of Galilee) was instrumental in locating and planning new frontier settlements. Allon later dedicated an entire chapter to settlements in his 1959 strategic and political manifesto *Curtain of Sand*, observing that,

> The integration of the civilian settlement in the military regional defence, and especially in frontier areas . . . will provide the state with forward observation posts, saving on military men. These settlements are capable not only of informing the military in advance about a surprise enemy attack, but of trying to halt it, or at least delaying the progress of the enemy until the military reinforcements arrive to control the situation . . .[29]

'Regional defence' was a military doctrine that sought to integrate civilian settlements with military units in the protection of the borders of the state. For Allon the organized layout of the Kibbutz – a cooperative settlement sharing its means of production with separate areas demarcated for housing, public functions, fields and farms – was superior to all other forms of Zionist settlements. Moreover, the Kibbutz 'is no less valuable than a military unit, and may even surpass it'.[30] Indeed, as he himself remarked, some Kibbutzim in the Negev, Adan's Kibbutz Nirim being one,[31] played a role in holding back regular military units of the Arab armies during the 1948 war.

Strategic and tactical considerations also informed the design of other settlement types, and led to the formulation in 1948 of a military document entitled 'Security Principles in the Planning of Agricultural Settlements and Workers' Villages', by the Settlement Department of the IDF General Staff's Operation Branch.[32] The fact that such a department existed at all testifies to the strategic importance that the military attributed to rural settlements. The 'Security Principles' provided some guidelines on the organization of Moshav – a type of settlement, which unlike the Kibbutz, combines private property with joint owner-

Moshav Settlements in Lahish region, Israel, 1953, IP.

ship of some means of production.[33] To prevent infiltration or the return of Palestinians to their lands, the 'Security Principles' instructed planners to devise a compact and dense layout, in which homes were located no more than 30 metres apart, and laid out concentrically so that, when under attack, settlers could gradually withdraw to a more secure core. Following the principle of military perimeter fortifications, the report also advised that the roads of the Moshav, along which homes and farms were organized, should form 'star shapes' so that 'flanking fire could be maximised'.[34]

In his affidavit to the HCJ, Eitan, himself a Moshav member (Moshav Tel Adashim in the Jezre'el Valley), criticized his predecessors' neglect of the principle of 'regional defence'. Eitan claimed that this neglect was one of the main reasons for the initial setbacks suffered by the Israeli Army during the 1973 war,[35] and he had already taken it upon himself to reverse this trend. 'Today the settlements of regional defence are armed, fortified and trained for their task, which is to defend their area. Their location was dictated after consideration of their contribution to the control of the region, and in assisting the IDF in its various tasks.'[36] Eitan further explained the primary advantage of civilian settlements over military positions:

> In times of war, the military forces exit their bases in order to undertake dynamic and offensive tasks [whereas] civilian settlements [whose population] remains in its place, are essential in controlling their immediate surroundings by observation, and would resist enemy's attempts to take control of them. In the early stages of a war, it is important to keep the roads open, in order to ensure fast movement towards the enemy.[37]

Eitan was one of the officers who, supporting Sharon, clashed with Bar Lev on the issue of fortifying the Suez Canal, and who supported 'defence in depth'. Eitan believed that the frontline of the Allon plan would quickly fall under attack just as the Bar Lev Line had fallen, and that a network of settlements throughout the depth of the terrain would serve military purposes to far better effect.

Permanent temporariness

To obtain a legal ruling in favour of land requisition the government had to convince the court that the settlement in question was designed to meet 'pressing security needs',[38] and also that it was a 'temporary intervention', and not a 'permanent transformation of the occupied area'. If the role of settlement in defence was well established in Zionist culture, Palestinian petitioners wondered how settlements built on land requisitioned from them could possibly be considered as 'temporary'. Commenting on the ruling of the 1978 Bet-El case, Justice Landau addressed the issue:

> to answer . . . how is it possible to establish a permanent settlement on land that was requisitioned only for temporary purposes? This is a serious question. The civilian settlement will be able to exist only as long as the IDF holds the land on the strength of a requisition order. This possession itself may one day come to an end as a result of international negotiations which could end in a new arrangement that will gain force under international law and will determine the fate of the settlement, like all other settlements in the Occupied Territories.[39]

Settlements could be understood by the judges of the HCJ as 'temporary' in the context of contemporary developments. The Bet-El case was argued in court in the winter of 1978–79, when the terms of the peace process with Egypt had to start to be fulfilled. In the Camp David peace talks, Menachem Begin agreed to evacuate all Israeli settlements from Sinai, including the town of Yamit and the smaller agricultural settlements of the Rafah Salient. This was enough to convince the court that all homes, public institutions, roads and industrial zones that had been built in the West Bank and Gaza since 1967 had a purely temporary presence on the ground. Indeed, in the same Bet-El ruling, Justice Miriam Ben-Porat recorded the judgment that the term 'permanent community' was a 'purely relative concept'.[40] Indeed, the nature of property title deeds in the settlements reflects their temporary nature. They consist of the standard Israeli renewable 49-year leases, but include a clause that emphasizes that the deeds are valid only as long as the Israeli military maintains a presence on the ground. The title explicitly leaves with the military commander the authority to regain immediate possession of the property.[41]

Two seemingly contradictory conditions thus maintained the 'temporary' state of Israel's military regime: the persistence of violence, on the one hand, and initiatives for political resolution, on the other. The fact that some degree of violence persisted justified the continual application of what the military understands as 'urgent, temporary security measures'. Violence allows 'security' to be invoked as a legal argument to justify the undertaking of transformations that could otherwise not be accepted. For security to go on fulfilling its role, a condition of insecurity and instability must therefore be continually present. Security measures should thus not bring about absolute security, because that would mean the loss of the rationale for the further application of such measures.[42]

Secondly, the constant presence of political initiatives on the diplomatic table – and there have been proposals for conflict resolution from day one of the post-1967 war era, right through to the present day – helps create and maintain the perception that the conflict is always just on the brink of being resolved, and that therefore the 'temporary' measures and violations of rights will no longer be relevant. Indeed, throughout the occupation, arguments based on 'temporary' security needs have not been confined to court cases, but have been deployed in order to create political facts of various kinds.[43] Israeli writers Adi Ophir and Ariella Azoulay claim that the entire logic of military rule in the West Bank and Gaza relies on the principle of 'temporariness', and that it is the very definition of the 'temporariness' of the state of conflict that allows it to continue indefinitely:

> Temporariness is now the law of the occupation . . . temporary encirclement and temporary closures, temporary transit permits, temporary revocation of transit permits, temporary enforcement of an elimination policy, temporary change in the open-fire orders . . . This occupier is an unrestrained, almost boundless sovereign, because when everything is temporary almost anything, any crime, any form of violence is acceptable, because the temporariness seemingly grants it a license, the license of the state of emergency.[43]

The position of the HCJ demonstrates the extreme tautology embodied in the term 'occupation'. Because the occupation is 'temporary' – and an occupation is 'temporary' by its very legal definition – any project carried out across the Occupied Territories could also be 'legalized' as 'temporary'. The use of the term 'occupation' for the forty-year-old Israeli military control and administration of the West Bank and Gaza Strip may thus itself be complicit with the legal charade on which its entire system rests. An 'occupation' is understood as a transitional state, in process of being resolved or terminated politically or militarily.

There is another anomaly in the legal use of the category of 'temporariness' in the context of this conflict. In international law the definition of 'temporariness' is predicated on the states of 'war' and 'peace' being clearly distinguishable. Wars between states may be long, but they tend to have clearly delineated beginnings and ends. By contrast, the Israeli–Palestinian conflict, like many other colonial conflicts, is an ever-present asymmetrical, low-intensity conflict between a state and quasi-state actors. It is a conflict that persists throughout time rather than one which disrupts its flow. Throughout the occupation, 'war' and 'peace' are no longer simple dialectical opposites, but merge into a single extended continuum. Resistance is violent, constant, but sporadic; pacification missions are sometimes brutal and at other times bureaucratic. Peace is not possible but war has no end.

Between 1967 and 1979, on the basis of the exceptions of 'temporariness' and 'security' the government issued dozens of orders for the requisition of private land in the West Bank. When called upon to do so, the government and the military demonstrated their claim for the pressing security needs by inviting expert witnesses, usually high-ranking military officers or the Chief of Staff himself, to testify that a particular settlement dominated a major artery, or another strategic location, that it could participate in the general effort of 'regional defence', or in the supervision and control of a hostile population. As long as this claim was maintained, the High Court of Justice rejected all petitions of Palestinian landowners and accepted the government's interpretation of the term 'temporary military necessity'.

Security vs. defence

In its rulings the High Court of Justice tends to place a good deal of weight on the professional evaluation of the security forces. Military officers appearing before the court presented 'security' as a specialized discipline and implied that the court should simply accept its logic as objective and final, rather than trying to question it. However, the trust placed by the court in the military ability to evaluate security issues was eroded after the setbacks suffered by the Israeli military during the 1973 war.[44] High Court Justices gradually started insisting on the necessity of comprehending, evaluating and ruling on issues of security. The court started examining military and settlement plans, and defining its own position in relation to them.[45]

In his affidavit to the 1979 Elon Moreh case, Chief of Staff Eitan claimed that the settlement was strategically necessary, as its location – dominating a major crossroads – served urgent security needs in taking part in the military effort of 'regional defence'. However, in this case the petitioners invited several former Israeli military generals to testify to the opposing view. Two of the generals were Sharon's political rivals – Minister of Defence Ezer Weizman and the then general-secretary of the opposition Labor Party, Chaim Bar Lev. Both intended to give their professional opinions – but they were also eager to disrupt any plans associated with Sharon. Bar Lev challenged the arguments of military necessity in establishing the settlement. In his own affidavit on behalf of the petitioners he stated that in a time of war the settlement would not contribute at all to defence of the state: 'Elon Moreh, to the best of my professional evaluation, does not contribute to Israel's security.'[46] To expect a suburban settlement to withstand an attack by a regular Arab army with artillery and tanks seemed to him nothing but preposterous. Moreover, Bar Lev claimed, the settlement would present a drain on military resources because the IDF would have to allocate forces to protect it. Instead of guarding, the settlement would itself have to be placed under guard.

Referring to his former rulings, Justice Vitkon made an important distinction that raised another considerable objection to Eitan's testimony:

> In my ruling concerning the Rafah salient and in my ruling on Bet-El, I assumed that the Jewish settlements are located to help the quotidian struggle with the terrorists . . . but this time the Chief of Staff Eitan explained to us that the most important security value of the settlements is in their integration to the system of regional defence in a case of a 'total' war . . . I must say that this [argument] is not clear of doubt.[47]

For an HCJ judge to directly criticize the military judgement of the Chief of Staff was no light matter. But with it Vitkon insisted on a distinction between two military concepts: 'defence' and 'security'. Of the two, he was willing to accept only that of 'security' as an acceptable legal basis for settlement, questioning that of 'defence'.

The difference between the terms is spatial as much as it is conceptual. The logic of defence deals with wars and seeks to constitute with borders, barriers and fortifications clear distinctions between 'inside' and 'outside' – the territory that falls within the state and that which is exterior to it. The danger that is perceived to exist outside borders generally comes in the form of a regular army threatening full-scale war. In the logic of defence, settlements were seen as components in a fortification system to keep this threat at bay. The logic of 'security', on the other hand, presupposes that the danger is already inside, presented by a population in which subversive elements exist. The relation that 'security' implies between 'inside' and 'outside', as well as between military and police action, is ambiguous. Although the logic of security tends to be ever-present and formless, covert and ghostly, its practices engage with an active and constant reconfiguration of the built environment. If defence engages directly with the concept of war, security engages with the temporarily ill-defined and spatially amorphous 'conflict' not only between societies, but within them as well. 'Security' conceives new spatial practices and arrangements. It erects barriers and channels and rechannels the flow of people and resources through space. According to the logic of security, only a constantly configured and reconfigured environment is a safe environment. The logic of security conceives of the settlements not as fortification systems, but as components in a project of pacification, as places from which observation and control can be generated and the circulation of people can be managed.

Interpreting the order and intensity of danger – deciding which threats are more serious than others – is a political-ideological process that reflects more than objective professional valuations. The umbrella term 'security' includes a variety of concepts, many differing from the common uses of the term (usually in referring to protection from bodily harm or damage to property) and morphing into political and ideological uses directed at the preservation of political hegemonies. In Israel, 'security' has always been associated with the ability of the state to remain sovereign and Jewish. This is the very reason why the demographic growth of one category of its citizens – Arab Palestinians – can always be presented as a 'security problem'.

'Security' replaced 'defence' as the legitimate consideration in the High Court of Justice's ruling because, given the nature of the political situation, judges viewed the Palestinian problem as more crucial than the problem Israel had with the Arab states. Indeed, as the 1970s drew to a close, with the terms of the peace agreement with Egypt finalized and Soviet military assistance to Arab states declining, the danger Israel faced from an armoured invasion was considerably reduced. The Israeli military apparatus, which had grown so monstrously large in the years immediately following the 1973 war, accumulating excessive armament and technology designed to defend the state's borders from another war like the last, would gradually begin to focus on the Palestinian problem both in Lebanon and the Occupied Territories. In the latter instance, Israel has turned its back on the cease-fire lines to concentrate on regulating and controlling the population already inside.

Other differences in the perception of settlements emerged during the 1979 Elon Moreh court case. Several Gush Emunim settlers of the new Elon Moreh core, called as witnesses for the state, sowed even more confusion when they claimed that their right to settle the 'land of Israel' was based neither on 'security' nor on 'defence' but on biblical commands, and is thus 'permanent' and not 'temporary'. Encouraged by the 1977 handover of power from Labor to Likud, which seemed to share some of their ideology, settlers decided to challenge the security concept which, thus far, had done them a service. Their right to the land, they claimed, was not 'temporary' at all – rather, it was ineffably 'permanent'. Menachem Felix, one of the Gush Emunim settlers called to testify in the trial, explained the difference between Gush Emunim's view, and that of the state and military, in the following way: 'Basing the requisition orders on security grounds in their narrow, technical meaning . . . can be construed only in one way: the settlement is temporary and replaceable. We reject this frightening conclusion outright, and see Elon Moreh to be a permanent Jewish settlement . . .'[48]

Given its own criticism of the military position based upon settlers' testimony, the HCJ had no option but to order the settlement dismantled and the land returned to its owners. However, the previous requisition orders undertaken for the purpose of constructing settlements were not reversed. The Elon Moreh case was the first in which contradictions in the Israeli discourse of settlement and security were publicly exposed. No land requisition for the purpose of settlement construction based on security considerations has since been permitted by the HCJ. Land requisition for 'security' purposes, based on a similar justification of 'urgent and temporary military needs', has, however, continued to allow the establishment of 'sterile security zones' around the settlements, for the construction of settlers' bypass highways, as well as, years later, for the construction of the Separation Wall. Use of private Palestinian land went on after 1979 regardless of the ruling mainly because private landowners had not the means, the physical access or the political inclination to address the Israeli High Court of Justice.[49]

Although the liberal press celebrated the Elon Moreh ruling as a victory over the Likud government, it later became clear that this ruling was nothing but a Pyrrhic victory. Not only was Elon Moreh established on an alternative site; indeed, for whoever wished to read it, the ruling's wording itself indicated alternative methods of access to land. The court confirmed that future access to land in the Occupied Territories for the construction of settlements would be permitted on public land entrusted to the custodianship of the military power, and added that if the state adheres to this principle, the court would no longer interfere in its future settlement efforts.[50] The government thus managed to make the best of this ruling, transforming the High Court's prohibition concerning the expropriation of private land into a potential for seizure of huge quantities of public land in the Occupied Territories.

Indeed, with the possibility of gaining regular access to land opening up before it, and with a more solid right-wing coalition, the second Begin government embarked on an ordered, national and master-planned process that sought to turn an improvised, 'temporary', occupation into a permanent one, and with it to domesticate and close the open frontiers of Palestine.

Ma'ale Adumim. Adam Broomberg and Oliver Chanarin, 2005.

4.

Settlements: Optical Urbanism

The first morning in Ramallah. I wake up and hasten to open the window. 'What are these elegant houses, Abu Hazim?' I asked pointing at Jabal al-Tawil, which overlooks Ramallah and Bireh. 'A settlement . . .'[1]

Mourid Barghouti

I look out of the window and see my death getting near.[2]

Unnamed Palestinian

In 1978, a year after it came to power, the Likud government made an early attempt to transform the settlement project from an improvised undertaking into an elaborate state project. It decided to establish a city on the upper slopes of the Judean Desert of the West Bank, a few kilometres east of Jerusalem, at a place where a makeshift 'workers camp' of twenty-three families had been established some three years previously without formal government authorization but with the active support of former Defence Minister Shimon Peres.[3] The government's decision to award the project of designing the city to Thomas Leitersdorf, an architect and planner associated with the Liberal Party – then part of Likud – was meant to set a new architectural benchmark for the settlement project in the West Bank's mountain regions. Leitersdorf was an international architect. He had been educated at the Architectural Association in London and began his career working with the Southern California 'glamour' architect Bill Pereira on suburban projects in places such as Orlando, Florida, on US military bases worldwide, and, among other things, on a city extension for Europeans in the Ivory Coast capital of Abidjan.

In order to determine the settlement's location, Leitersdorf's team set up climate-measuring stations and conducted detailed topographical surveys of several hilltops. The hilltop finally chosen, 500 metres above sea level, was selected for its location near Jerusalem, so that the settlement could function as a dormitory suburb, and for its overlooking of a strategic traffic route, Road Number 1, which connected Jerusalem with Jericho and with the Jordanian capital, Amman, across the border Leitersdorf described his presentation of the project to government representatives as follows:

> When we put the alternatives to the Ministerial Committee for Settlement, headed at the time by Ariel Sharon, the only questions asked were: 'Which of the alternative locations has better control over the main routes?' I replied that according to these criteria the ideal location would be location A . . . At that moment Sharon rose up and declared, without consulting the Committee that 'the State of Israel decides on location A.'[4]

Proximity to power taught Leitersdorf what one needs to say in order to get a settlement approved by Sharon and his proxies.

Directing a team of twelve architectural practices, economists, transport specialists and climate experts, Leitersdorf planned and oversaw the construction of an entire city in less than three years. This undertaking, according to him, was nothing less than 'revolutionary, compared to what had previously gone on [in the West Bank]'; indeed Ma'ale Adumim ('Red Ascent', after the colour of the desert earth into which its foundations were sunk) was designed and built for a first phase comprising more than 2,600 housing units at a time when other settlements in the West Bank consisted typically of a dozen or so mobile homes scattered on a hilltop, usually before infrastructure was even provided. Because the work took place against a tight time schedule, and for reasons of secrecy (there was a fear such a large-scale undertaking would create diplomatic problems for Israel) the contracts were not put out to public tender, Leitersdorf simply commissioned the companies he chose to work with. He later boasted of his achievement in the official publication of the Ministry of Construction and Housing:

> The need for rapid development made it necessary to abandon the conventional approach to planning, which proceeds in stages from the general to the specific (regional plan, town building plan, site plan, block plan, building plan, etc.). Instead, it was decided to engage a multi-disciplinary team [to work] on all levels simultaneously. Consequently work on the infrastructure systems was started within less than 4 months from the approval of the town's location. The allocation of all required resources, made it possible . . . four years later, with the combined efforts of 10 construction companies and 80 consultants and experts in all fields to construct 2,600 dwelling units – a unique rate of development in Israel.

Ma'ale Adumim. Milutin Labudovic for Peace Now, 2002.

This rate could be achieved by establishing a 'rapid feedback process' between his office and all other teams to enable them to work in parallel, so that, at 'the time the town building plan was complete all the neighbourhoods were already designed . . . and all construction companies could start working at once'.[5]

The process revealed some of the contradictions and confusions that beset Israel's relations with the United States at the time. At the start of the peace process with Egypt in the autumn of 1977, the US administration demanded that Israel freeze all settlement activity. Since it did not trust the Begin government, and was acutely aware of Sharon's tactics of misleading the Israeli government, the US embassy sent observers to make periodic visits to various parts of the West Bank to check that no building works were in progress. At the same time the United States was funding several massive construction projects in the Negev Desert in southern Israel, including two new Israeli Air Force bases to replace those that Israel was evacuating in the Sinai, for which purpose much new construction equipment was brought to Israel. The situation was described by Leitersdorf: 'The State of Israel wanted a city; true, there was a fear of the Americans, but there was a lot of construction equipment standing motionless in the desert. One day someone said that the observers are gone and ten construction companies with six big infrastructure companies went up the mountain and in one go erected a city.'[6]

*   *   *

Film Stills, 'A City in the Desert: Ma'ale Adumim', 1983 (Film by Israeli Ministry of Construction and Housing). Standing on left: Thomas Leitersdorf.

Leitersdorf described his scheme for Ma'ale Adumim as a 'Garden City'.[7] This combination of city and country, conceived as a utopia by the British architect Ebenezer Howard at the end of the nineteenth century, aimed to provide a healthy and hygienic alternative to the 'material filth and grime, unparalleled in history' of the congested slums of industrial urban England; it gave rise to an evolutionary chain of urban forms that similarly attempted to merge city and countryside, leading to the modern suburb.[8] The concept arrived in Palestine with the British in the early years of the Mandate, one of its earliest examples being built outside the predominantly Arab port town of Haifa. The Zionists who originally lived within the town's Arab neighbourhoods sought to move out to a modern 'European suburb' on the ridges of Mount Carmel, above the Arab city.

Patrick Geddes, a Scotsman and one of the most eminent British town planners of the time, first visited Palestine in September 1919, while en route to India, in response to an invitation from Chaim Weizmann, the then president of the World Zionist Organization.[9] Geddes stayed in Palestine for less then three months, producing town planning schemes for Tel Aviv and Haifa that subsequently had a considerable impact on the development of these and other Israeli cities. Returning to Palestine in May 1920, Geddes spent the summer months completing his plans before returning home to Scotland. Although Geddes promoted Ebenezer Howard's utopian vision, which he called a 'neotechnic order, characterised by electricity, hygiene, and art, by efficient and beautiful town planning and associated rural development[10]', he also drew on his first vocation, biology, in order to devise organic layouts that distorted Howard's machine-like

Film Stills, 'Emanuel: A City that is a Home', 1984 (Film by Israeli Ministry of Construction and Housing). By plans: Thomas Leitersdorf.

circular diagram. Geddes saw urban design as an instrument with which a new social order could be invented – something that resonated well with Weizmann's idea of national regeneration, as well as with his admiration for all things British. Unlike his well-known urban plans for Tel Aviv, Geddes produced no drawings for Haifa, but only conducted a single site-visit and helped formulate a written report. In their studied account of the history of modern architecture on the Carmel, Gilbert Werbert and Silvina Sosonovsky described some of the principles of this project: 'For Geddes, respect for topography was a cardinal principle . . . he deplored the over simplicity of regular gridiron planning [as he said, "to rule lines on paper plan is easy office work"] and instead of the desk-bound indoor draughtsmanship, called for "design on the spot."'[11] Establishing a direct relation between city form and human body, the urban design was undertaken while walking the landscape of the proposed development site. Disembarking at Haifa, Geddes, then sixty-five years old, spent the next days walking the upper slopes of the Carmel, dictating his plans orally to his Zionist companions who struggled to keep up, and in particular to his son-in-law, later renowned architect, Captain Frank Mears, who jotted notes and produced sketches as they trekked along. The hikers' principle of walking along a fixed altitude line following the curves of the topography, a habit Geddes must have acquired during his treks in the Scottish highlands, was well suited to the principles of modern planning, in which roads and infrastructure are themselves constructed along topographical lines. According to Geddes' 'walked plan', the city's neighbourhoods were to be located on the ridges, following the natural form of the mountain, leaving the valleys between them as green open spaces.[12]

In his design for Ma'ale Adumim, Leitersdorf followed similar principles, often walking the desert hilltops that formed the site of the settlement's construction.[13] He later wrote that his 'planning concept reflects the morphological structure of the mountain'. He placed the neighbourhoods on the ridges 'which because of the morphology are integrally connected to the centre, with the valleys between left open and untouched, leading directly to the heart of the town . . .'[14] In his next design for a settlement – a private commission to plan the ultra-Orthodox religious city of Emanuel, west of Nablus – Leitersdorf's confidence had grown considerably: 'instead of sending surveyors to the site we took large-scale [topographic] maps and enlarged them up to the scale of 1:1,000. We decided, as we were not road engineers, that we would simply lay the roads on the natural morphology, that we would not change the mountains at all. It was as if you were to take a topographic line from the map and make a road on it – this is how it was built.'[15]

Strategies of planting

Regularizing access to land was another component in the Begin government's attempt to formalize the settlement project under state control. In 1979, in the wake of the Elon Moreh case, which ruled that access to land for the construction of settlements for 'security reasons' could no longer be permitted, the government embarked upon a new method of gaining access to land, one that would be immune to further petitions to the High Court of Justice.

Government agencies started a large-scale project of mapping and land registration in order to discover public lands to which Israel could lay claim. Any piece of land that Palestinians could not prove was privately owned, and any privately owned land that Palestinians could not prove was actually in use at the time of survey, i.e. public Palestinian land, was declared 'state land' and seized by the state. This 'state land' could then be leased out to a variety of Israeli and Jewish organizations for the purpose of settlement construction. The legal playing-field was thus transferred from the late nineteenth- and early twentieth-century international laws of belligerent occupation to the agrarian land laws of the Ottoman Empire.[16] Whereas previous legal battles had been argued on the basis of different conceptions of 'security', and lawyers and judges had had to become experts in the ins and outs of military fortification and security, they now had to do so (literally) in the field of agriculture, with lawyers having to become experts in different cultivation techniques and crop types.

The Israeli government's main legal resource was the Ottoman Land Law of 1858. This law was the result of an agrarian reform across the Ottoman Empire, of which Palestine was part until 1917. The 1858 law continued to exist in the West Bank as a reflection of local tradition during the successive periods of British and Jordanian rule, and was designed to regulate traditional agrarian economies by means of a new tax system. It recognized a plot of land as 'miri' (privately owned) land, if it had been continuously cultivated for at least ten years. If a landowner failed to farm the land for three consecutive years, the land changed its status to 'makhlul', which came then under the possession of the sovereign.[17] The rationale behind this provision was to create an incentive for cultivation – which in turn increased taxation. Farmers, on the other hand, did not want to pay tax for land that could not be used for cultivation, and therefore gave up ownership over uncultivated areas, even if these were only small patches of rocky ground that actually existed within their fields. Uncultivated 'state land' therefore existed in widely differing scales, some large tracts of desert – as in the southern and eastern parts of the West Bank, mainly along the Jordan Valley and the Dead Sea – others smaller islands of rocky land, punctuating and puncturing the private fields of farmers. The borders between cultivated and uncultivated lands often followed a clear topographical logic. The mountain range of the West Bank is corrugated by a repeating sequence of wrinkles and folds. The agriculturally suitable alluvial soils erode down from the summits to the slopes and the valleys. These summits are thus rocky and windswept, while the slopes and valleys are fertile and cultivated with orchards and arable crops.

The 'makhlul' land seized by the state of Israel in areas suitable for settlement was therefore primarily the high ground of the West Bank.[18] In total, by the early 1990s, more than 38 per cent of the land area of the West Bank, comprising this patchwork quilt of isolated plots and non-contiguous pockets of land, as well as tracts of desert, were registered under Israeli ownership.[19] If, by this time, one were to slice the terrain of the West Bank along an invisible horizontal datum line a few hundred metres above sea level, almost all the land over this line was settler territory annexed by the Israeli state; the valleys below it remained 'occupied territories'. The topographical folds, summits, slopes, irrigation basins, valleys, rifts, cracks and streams, were no longer seen simply as naïve topographical features, but as signifiers to a series of legal manipulations. Many of the complex borderlines of the present-day West Bank were thus generated by the application of the principles of a nineteenth-century land law to the particular nature of mountain topography. Latitude became more than a mere relative position on the contoured surface of the terrain. The colonization of the mountain regions created a vertical separation between two parallel, overlapping and self-referential ethno-national geographies, held together in startling and horrifying proximity.

Sometimes irregularities in the patterns of land cultivation left 'islands' of small privately owned orchards within an area of uncultivated 'state land'. This gave rise to a situation in which some private Palestinian land could be left between the homes of a Jewish settlement. In such cases accommodation was sometimes reached whereby the settlement council in question permitted access to Palestinian farmers to cultivate their orchards. But after the start of the second Intifada in 2000, Palestinian farmers were no longer allowed to enter settlements. And so, after three years of non-cultivation, these orchards themselves became 'state land', according to the 1858 Ottoman Land Law, and ownership was duly handed to the settlement council.

The Likud government lived to present the new legal technique for land seizure as evidence of its commitment to liberal values of 'private property', which it compared to Labor's aggressive security logic. In fact, during the Likud years, large tracts of private Palestinian land were still being secretly grabbed for the use of Israeli settlements – this without official requisition orders, and without being challenged in court. The public land, which Israel claimed so easily on the grounds that it was 'uncultivated', very often had other legitimate uses for the Palestinians, such as grazing. More fundamentally, all peoples have the right to open space and common land. In this light, the Likud claim that these lands were unusable for cultivation, and thus that their appropriation by Israeli settlers could hardly be seen as 'dispossession', is tantamount to claiming that any public land of one nation can be claimed and used for the settling of another. In fact, here, as in other incidents throughout the occupation, the law did not prevent violations, it simply became a tactical tool for regulating them and giving them a cloak of legitimacy.

Beginning in December 1979, the government launched a systematic, large-scale project of topographical and land-use mapping across the West Bank in order to define all those areas that were not under active cultivation. Mapping the West Bank was primarily undertaken from the air.[20] The advantage of aerial photometry lies in its rapid collection of data. It saves map-makers the trouble of moving through a hostile terrain and undertaking slow triangulations using visible land-marks. An area of a few thousand square kilometres takes only four hours to photograph. Photometrical land surveying from aerial photography, reproduced at variable scales and with breathtaking clarity, has now replaced the conventional land-surveyed maps as the most rapid and practical way of studying a territory. Every two years since 1967, a thorough aerial survey has been undertaken.

The mapping project was run by the director of the civil department of the State Prosecutor's Office, Plia Albek, an ultra-Orthodox woman who entered Israeli settlement folklore by touring the West Bank mountains by helicopter and driving through areas under dispute in jeeps, determining land ownership

Fragments of 'state land', Regional Council of Binyamin, Hebron region.

by cutting the trunks of olive trees to count the number of rings (since every year makes a visible ring, she could thus establish the age of an orchard), and walking the sites intended for expropriation with Palestinian village elders to register any possible objections and obstacles to her policy. Her survey sought to identify private 'miri' land that had not been farmed for at least three consecutive years, thus becoming 'makhlul', and 'miri' land that had been farmed for less than ten years, and which had therefore not yet come under the farmer's private ownership.

Prior to this system of land grab coming into general practice, the Israeli military government had focused on the improvement and expansion of Palestinian agricultural production. Throughout the first decade of the occupation, Israeli agencies conducted a survey of 30,000 farms in about half of all West Bank villages, examining the utilization of farm areas and their yields. They offered Palestinian farmers development loans to purchase agricultural equipment and machinery, introduced fertilizers and pesticides, improved varieties of seeds for arable crops and devised about 400 model plots where almost 20,000 Palestinian farmers were trained to use modern equipment and technology.[21] According to Israeli political theorist and activist Neve Gordon, this policy was part of a governing rationale initially devised by the Ministry of Defence under Moshe Dayan, which sought to pacify the territories under occupation by reducing poverty and increasing the dependency of the Palestinians on Israel by improving the general quality of life. Dayan wanted to be remembered as an enlightened sovereign. According to one of Dayan's speeches at a government meeting, Israel should follow the model of enlightened colonialism. In the Togolese Republic in West Africa, he claimed, 'people still had good memories of German colonial rule before WW1 . . . the Germans "left orchards and culture". Israel . . . should follow the example of benevolent colonialism.'[22] Dayan's policy had the effect of increasing agricultural productivity throughout the first five years of the occupation by 16 per cent annually; it also allowed Palestinians to cultivate areas that had previously gone uncultivated.[23] In 1976, the policy was scaled down. By 1979, when the government realized that the expansion of the Palestinian agrarian economy was counter productive to its aim of annexing uncultivated lands, it stopped the policy that actively encouraged cultivation altogether. Thereafter, Israel's gradual reduction of water quotas to Palestinian farmers forcibly reduced the scope of the West Bank's agricultural sector, forcing more Palestinian farmers to seek jobs as day laborers in Israel.[24] By 1985 the cultivated land in the West Bank had decreased by 40 per cent. The decrease in the Palestinians' ability to cultivate land enabled the confiscation of more land.[25] As if this was not enough, the government also invaded private fields that settlements needed for their expansion. For this purpose another category of land was established. 'Survey land' refers to land whose ownership is in dispute, generally in cases where a Palestinian's title to the land is being challenged by the state. Under Israeli law, such land cannot be developed legally, either by the state or by the Palestinian claiming ownership. But in reality, settlement construction has been taking place on such land too.[26]

This direct relation established between land use and land ownership led to the widespread and strategic use of planting throughout the Occupied Territories. Understanding the logic of Israeli land seizure, Palestinians intensified their agricultural land use, planting as a pre-emptive strategy in areas they felt were threatened with impending expropriation; such planting was often subsidized by Palestinian and international solidarity organizations.[27] On the other hand, the Jewish National Fund (JNF), an organization dedicated to the development of Israeli state land for the benefit of its Jewish population, was planting pine forests in areas declared as 'state land', mainly around greater Jerusalem in what it called 'the green belt'. These planting programmes were undertaken to prevent Palestinian planting, and to maintain land reserves for new settlements or for the future expansion of existing ones. Pine trees were chosen both because of their fast growth and because of the acidic deposit of pine needles they leave on the ground, which eradicates most smaller plants and undergrowth between the trees. 'Pine deserts' were meant to make the land unusable for Palestinian shepherds by depriving their flocks of pasture. In many places across the West Bank where there has been large-scale forestation by Israel, there has also been small-scale planting by Palestinians; the lines separating pines and olives are among the many boundaries produced by the colonization of the West Bank.[28]

A complex fabric of laws, regulations and military orders thereafter combined to turn Israel's land seizure into a de facto project of annexation. All the separate tracts of 'state land' throughout the West Bank – a non-contiguous archipelago of thousands of separate 'islands' – were imbued with Israeli law. The military, which is the actual sovereign in these areas, simply stamped Israeli law books with military insignia, turning Israeli law into military orders.[29] The seized highland thus acquired an effective extraterritorial status.[30] This divided the West Bank into two zones in which different laws separately applied to Jews and Arabs. The laws of the state were applied to the mountain summits whereas military rules were still in effect within the cultivated valleys below and between them.[31] To almost all intents and purposes, the lives of settlers resemble the lives of Israeli citizens within Israel.

In 1981, a year before he took Israel to war in Lebanon, Ariel Sharon, now Minister of Defence in the second Begin government, set up the Civil Administration, a subsidiary of the military designed to deal with the government of the Palestinian population in the West Bank and Gaza. The separation of the Civil Administration from the regional territorial command made a clear distinction between the two roles with which the military was then engaged in the Occupied Territories: the protection of Israeli civilians (through the suppression of the Palestinians) and sovereignty over the Palestinian population. Through its latter role the Civil Administration demonstrated Israel's intention of making the occupation permanent and underscored its desire to continue normalizing it.[32]

Under the Civil Administration, development plans for the Occupied Territories similarly operated along two parallel, complementary lines: one promoting the construction of Jewish settlements, the other working to limit the expansion of Palestinian towns and villages. On the one hand, the Civil Administration granted the Jewish regional councils the status of 'special planning committees', empowering them to prepare and submit detailed outline plans and to grant building permits to settlements within their municipal boundaries,[33] effectively fast-tracking the planning and development process. Meanwhile in Palestinian areas, every conceivable obstacle was placed in front of Palestinians attempting to plan and develop their lands. In regulating the planning system in the West Bank and Gaza, the Civil Administration rarely updated the regional plans prepared in the 1940s by British Mandatory planning offices for a Palestinian population that was a fraction of its current size. This has severely limited the areas available in which to modernize and expand.[34] The Civil Administration

The settlement of Efrat – note the Palestinian fields around and within the settlement, and the small pine-planted areas on the left. Milutin Labudovic for Peace Now, 2002.

planning office has in many cases used aerial photographs to draw schematic 'blue lines' as close to the Palestinian built-up area as their felt-tip pens permitted. Construction outside these perimeters was prohibited. Whatever housing or other buildings were subsequently 'illegally' constructed there were, sooner or later, demolished.

Suburban colonization

Although before 1979 the case for Israel's settlement policy was argued on the basis of strategic and security considerations, the settlement process was also driven by other impetuses: religious-ideological (seeking to settle the higher summits close to sites of biblical history), political (trying to pre-empt the possibility of territorial compromise by settling areas in and around the major Palestinian towns and cities) and economic (the search for cheap land for the construction of suburbs and urban sprawl close to the metropolitan centres). Each of these approaches saw the mountains of the West Bank as a different kind of resource, finding in the contours of its terrain different locations to suit its requirements. Israeli policy towards the settlements in the West Bank has undergone various changes over the years, reflecting the divergent political views of decision-makers, the relative weight of various interest groups active in this field, and developments in the international arena. While these divergent approaches have been manifested in changes in the scope of resources allocated to the settlements, and in the areas in which it was decided to establish them, all Israeli governments, Labor, Likud or Unity governments, have actively contributed to the strengthening, development and expansion of the settlement enterprise.

The centrifugal forces that led the Israeli middle classes to flee the city centres for suburbia started to gather momentum in the early 1980s. They reflected a global phenomenon of metropolitan sprawl and segregation into ethnically and religiously homogenous communities that mirrored the American and South African gated communities. With the exception of the national-religious Gush Emunim, which inhabited the mountain ridges of the West Bank, the majority of settlers moved into suburban settlements located close to Tel Aviv and Jerusalem, only a few kilometres beyond the 1967 Green Line. They were drawn there by the promise of high living standards – a better quality of life at a very affordable price.

Since the inhabitants of suburban settlements have to seek work outside them, they rely on a road system to connect them with the employment centres in the metropolitan areas around Tel Aviv and Jerusalem. The population mostly consists of secular, middle-class Israelis, but includes two other groups encouraged by the government to move into the area: new immigrants from the former Soviet republics and the ultra-Orthodox non-Zionist communities. The latter, large families of limited economic means, were concentrated in dense, custom-built settlements, such as Modi'in Ilit, Beitar Ilit and Kiyat Sefer, close to the Green Line and on the road between Tel Aviv and Jerusalem. These settlements have been designed to cater for their particular way of life, and have also been a magnet for large corporations establishing factories where ultra-Orthodox women are employed as cheap manual labor in the high-tech industries.[35]

However, settlement growth has been fuelled not so much by economic forces of supply and demand, but by a sophisticated government programme designed to encourage Israeli citizens to migrate there from the urban centres of Tel Aviv and Jerusalem. The government keeps as one of its most closely guarded secrets the precise amount of money allotted for the benefit of settlements in the West Bank and Gaza Strip. The state budget was deliberately constructed so as to make this information opaque, with the money allocated to support settlements divided between general categories without mentioning whether the communities in question are within Israel or the Occupied Territories. In the most comprehensive audit of this issue, conducted at the end of 2003, the Israeli newspaper

The settlement of Giveat Ze'ev, circa 1983 (ZE).

Ha'aretz claimed that the additional cost of the settlement project since 1967 had already passed the $10 billion mark.[36]

However, the geography of economic incentives was already outlined in a masterplan prepared by the rural settlement division of the World Zionist Organization (WZO) at the beginning of 1983. The *Masterplan for Settlements in the West Bank through the Year 2010* was prepared by Likud party member Matityahu Drobless, who worked in collaboration with Sharon's Settlement Committee. This plan was also known as *The Hundred Thousand Plan*, a reference to its main objective to bring the total Jewish population in the West Bank to 100,000 by 1986.[37] In the accompanying text, the masterplan admitted that 'the settlement process as a whole includes "natural" motivations for settlement guided by economic demand, as well as "artificial" motivations for settlement based on ideological commitments'.[38] It went on to suggest the principles of the geography of economic incentives: the amount of government subsidy was to be inversely proportional to the level of economic demand. Thus, areas of low demand were highly subsidized, with the government covering most development expenses, and effectively offering almost free housing to whoever agreed to settle there, while high demand areas in the West Bank received less (but still considerable) financial aid. High demand areas were defined as those within a 'travel time of 30 minutes from the outer ring of Tel Aviv metropolitan region, and about 20 minutes' drive from that of Jerusalem', and were marked on the map as a strip of 15–20 kilometres wide, immediately east of the Green Line, and as a band 10 kilometres wide around Jerusalem. Other factors defining high demand areas included 'local elements with positive attraction, such as the view', while low demand areas included elements possessing 'negative attraction value, such as proximity to Arab population'. Areas of medium and low demand were generally defined as those located 'in the mountain range . . . fifty minutes drive from Tel Aviv and thirty-five minutes drive from Jerusalem'. There, 'ideological population with high human potential and social quality is to be located in small groups within small settlements . . .'[39] In general, the government's subsidy policy followed a simple rule: the more settlers were willing to undertake personal hardship and danger, the further they were from Israeli employment centres, the higher the government subsidy.

The policy of financial incentives was successful in continuously channelling increasing number of Israelis into the West Bank. This could be demonstrated by the following statistics. In May 1984, at the end of the Likud government's second term in office, 35,000 settlers were living in 102 settlements in the West Bank. By 1992, when Likud lost power to Labor and the Oslo process began, about 100,000 people occupied 123 settlements. In the following decade, under the Oslo process, although the number of settlements did not increase, each settlement became much more densely populated, with the population doubling to about 200,000.[40] Despite the violence of the second Intifada, the growth in the number of settlers continued, especially in the ultra-Orthodox settlements, increasing the total number of settlers by 15.3 per cent in the first four years of the conflict, so that the total number of West Bank settlers (excluding Jerusalem) had reached 268,000 inhabitants in 2006.[41]

The community settlement

The settlements established in the West Bank fall into a range of different types. Cooperative agricultural settlements of the Kibbutz and Moshav types are the historical settlement forms of the Labor Zionist movement.[42] There are currently nine settlements of the Kibbutz type and twenty-two of the Moshav type in the West Bank, most of them established during the 1970s under the Labor governments and situated in areas within the Allon plan. The remaining settlements established throughout the 1970s were *urban* or *rural settlements*.[43]

Since the method of land seizure restricted settlement construction to uncultivated land annexed by the Israeli state, and since the Israeli-Jewish settlers (both the national-religious Gush Emunim as well as secular city-dwellers seeking an improvement in their quality of life) had no experience in agriculture nor any wish to start engaging in it, a new settlement typology had to be conceived. In the early 1980s the 'community settlement' was developed by the settlement division of the WZO together with Amanah, the settlement arm of Gush Emunim, for the purpose of settling the mountain areas under Israel's control, both within Israel in the Galilee, and in the occupied areas of the West Bank. In both regions this was part of the national effort to create a 'demographic balance' between Jews and Arabs.[44]

The 'community settlement' is legally defined as a cooperative association registered with the Israeli Registrar of Associations; in essence, it is a private, members-only, suburban village. Each 'community settlement' has an independent admission process and a monitoring mechanism that regulates all aspects of community life, from religious observance and ideological rigour to the very form and outdoor use of homes. Members can be expelled after ignoring warnings, if they refuse to conform to community regulations, or if they do not integrate socially, religiously or ideologically. The 'community settlement' was conceived in this way to avoid the possibility that Palestinian citizens of Israel might make their homes in these settlements.

The system developed other mechanisms of exclusion against Palestinian citizens of Israel that were designed to bypass Israeli laws prohibiting the allocation of resources according to preferential criteria. 'State land' within Israel or the Occupied Territories was transferred to the custody of either the Jewish Agency (JA) or the WZO, both non-governmental associations registered in the United States. Their registration outside Israel enabled the state to circumvent its own laws.[45] The WZO and the JA represent not the citizens of Israel but 'world Jewry', and their stated mission is to direct resources exclusively to the state's Jewish population. Both organizations are sustained by donations from Jews abroad and, as US-registered charities, benefit from special tax exemption.[46] When a 'suitable' settlement core is formed, the WZO and the JA pass the lands on to it and the cooperative association of the settlement is thereafter entrusted with the further screening of members.[47]

Residential construction in these settlements might be undertaken by government development companies, by a commercial developer, or on a private basis. Uniformity of architectural taste is often imposed through the repetition of a small variety of single and double, family house-and-garden designs. Another option that exists within some settlements is the 'build your home' scheme, in which people are encouraged to design and build the 'house of their dreams' on a small plot of land.[48] Within all these types, the red pitched roof became the emblem, the ubiquitous symbol of Jewish settlements. In an interview, a young architect based in the West Bank explained this issue to me:

Left: A house in a Jewish settlement in the 1980s. Right. A house in a Palestinian village.

A lot of ink was spilled [in critical discussion] over the issue of the red roofs . . .
I personally think that there is something interesting about it though . . . since it
was inaugurated as the common practice some twenty years ago . . . you can easily
recognize, even as you are coming from the distance a Jewish settlement! . . . maybe
it really does not blend in with the surrounding, but it makes a strong statement
and marks an orientation point – this settlement is Jewish![49]

Beyond responding to typical middle-class suburban aesthetics, the adorning of
settlement homes with red roofs also serves a security function: the sites can be
identified from afar as Israeli. This common architectural practice was formal-
ized when, in the 1980s, the military recommended that settlement councils
impose the construction of red-tiled roofs as part of the settlement planning
bylaw. Besides allowing the settlers to orient themselves within the landscape, the
roofs aid the military to better navigate and identify 'friend from foe', from both
ground and air.

The red roof has also become a common sight in Palestinian cities and
villages, with red roofs being constructed over what is otherwise a perfectly
serviceable flat roof common to Palestinian single-family homesteads. During
the urban euphoria of the Oslo years (1995–2000) a real-estate boom in Palestinian cities was fuelled by wealthy returnee elites, and new neighbourhoods were
built on the peripheries of Palestinian cities and towns. As French theorist Sylvain
Bulle observed, the architecture of these housing schemes resembled the suburban
and semi-urban nature of the settlements, reproducing many of its urban and
architectural typologies – and similarly responding to the anxieties that drive the

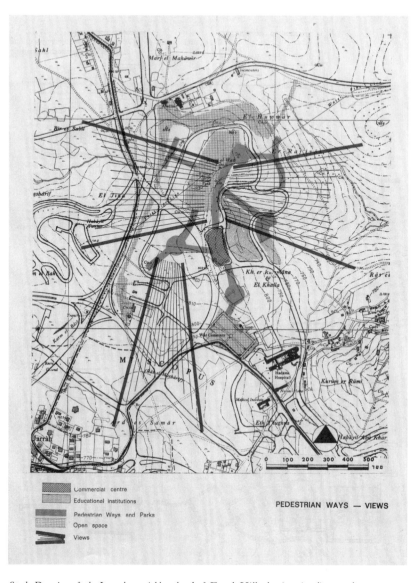

Study Drawing of the Jerusalem neighbourhood of French Hill, showing view lines as the generator of the urban layout. Source: Israel Builds, Ministry of Construction and Housing, 1972.

Facing page: Above, the settlement of Geva'ot (road plan); below, the settlement of Har Shmuel (outline plan).

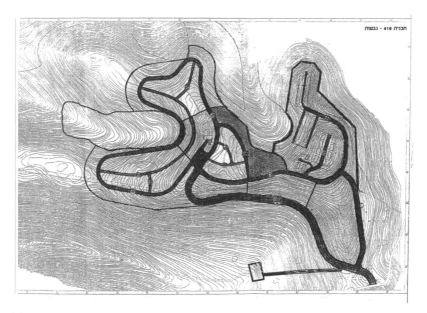

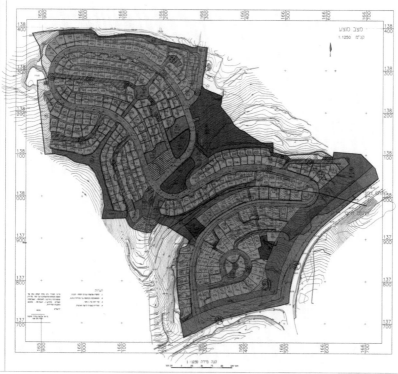

SETTLEMENTS: OPTICAL URBANISM 129

The settlement of Eli. Eyal Weizman, 2002.

middle class everywhere to seek privacy and security away from the congested and potentially dangerous city centres. New Palestinian housing, built on hilltops with concrete domes, arches and other oriental paraphernalia, sometimes followed romantic inclinations similar to those of the Jewish neighbourhoods of occupied Jerusalem.[50] Such mimicry, or perhaps – considering the military directive mentioned above – camouflage, sustains a discourse of mirrors which destabilizes the decisive visual boundaries, creating two types of architectural hybrids that challenge the visual binary opposition of 'settler' and 'native' architecture.[51]

Optical urbanism

In 1984 the Ministry for Construction and Housing published a guidebook entitled *Building and Development in the Mountain Regions*.[52] Its author, the Israeli architect Michael Boneh, aimed to provide what would in effect become the first official advisory guideline for architects engaged in the design of settlements in the mountain regions under Israeli control. These were primarily areas inhabited by Palestinians: the Galilee (inside Israel proper), and the mountain district of the West Bank. Summarizing the experience gained in the construction of settlements and Jerusalem suburbs, the publication testifies to the shift in the focus of Zionist planning, from the coastal plains and agricultural valleys to the mountains. It stated that: 'the continual growth of settlements in the Jerusalem, Galilee, Judea and Samaria Mountains [the West Bank] is dependent on the development of difficult mountainous areas' and concedes that 'the expertise in building on mountain regions is not yet fully established'.[53]

The construction of the mountain settlements necessitated building in areas with steep slopes. Boneh divided up the mountain area according to various topographical conditions, allocating a distinct settlement typology to each.[54] In these formal codifications, which base the design of mountain settlements on distinct topographical conditions, the laws of erosion have seemingly been absorbed into the practice of urban design. The specific morphology of the hilltops on which settlements were to be designed became the blueprint for the layout of the settlement. According to this guideline, and following the principles tested by Leitersdorf in Ma'ale Adumim, the suburban layout of a mountain settlement typically follows a principle of 'concentric organization', in which the topographical contours of the map are retraced as lines of infrastructure. The roads are laid out in rings following the shape of the mountain to create a complete circuit around the summit, with the water, sewage, electricity and telephone lines buried under them. The division of lots is equal and repetitive, providing small, private red-roofed houses positioned along the roads, against the backdrop of the landscape.

Most often, settlement layouts aspire to create an 'ideal' circle around an elevated civic centre positioned on the summit (generally, it is the synagogue that stands at the centre of the settlement at the hilltop's highest point). But in reality, a settlement's contours are distorted by specific topographical morphology and by the constraints of land ownership, as well as in response to a generally accepted rule – first defined in Leitersdorf's planning of Ma'ale Adumim – that sought to limit to 250 metres the distance pedestrians have to walk from their homes to access civic services and amenities, preferably without having to cross a main road.

However, a major issue arose in the Ministry's guidelines of views and sightlines as outlined in Boneh's text. His guidelines advise that: 'Positioning openings [windows] in the direction of the view is usually identical with positioning them in the direction of the slope . . . [the optimal view depends on] the positioning of the buildings and on the distances between them, on the [built] density, the gradient of the slope and the vegetation.'[55] The publication further advises that in order to maximize visibility, the inner circle of homes should be positioned in front of the gaps left between the buildings along the outermost ring. Vision dictated the discipline and mode of design in all aspects, down to the positioning of windows in houses. Discussing the organization of the buildings themselves, the text recommended that sleeping quarters be oriented towards the inner public spaces and living rooms oriented towards the distant view.

This geometric order seeks to produce what can in effect be understood as optical devices on a suburban scale. The type of mountain settlement in the Galilee – akin to that in the West Bank – is referred to in Hebrew as *Mitzpe*

(Lookout) settlement, a term that itself indicates the primary function of settlements in the mountain regions. The arrangement of homes and roads as rings around summits imposes on the dwellers an axial visibility oriented in two directions: out and down, towards the surrounding landscapes; and in and upwards, a gaze folded in on itself, overlooking the common public spaces and homes of the other members of the community. Each of these constructed gazes, inwards and outwards, embodies complexities and contradictions of different kinds. The inward-looking gaze aims to reinforce a sense of community, facilitating the intimate management of the inhabitants' lives, and with it, regulating 'acceptable' public behaviour. The disciplinary power of this urban layout conforms the subject under a common gaze which is diffused amongst all other community members. The fact that the circular layout is closely oriented inwards towards the common public areas, promotes an 'unconscious policing' with controls on acceptable public behaviour.[56] With the social and physical cohesion of its cul-de-sac environment, closed off to its surroundings, the 'community settlement' promotes a communal coherence in a shared formal identity. Indeed, many inhabitants of West Bank 'community settlements', initially coming in search of an improved quality of life, have been gradually drawn into a more nationalist ideology, and will no doubt struggle against any policy initiatives to remove them from their homes. It is in everyday life and its small rituals, travel, work and spare time that the ideology of settlers is transformed and sustained.[57]

The outward-facing arrangement of homes orients the view of the inhabitants towards the surrounding landscape. In this context the wording of the verdict of High Court Justice Vitkon on the security function of the settlements of Bet-El should be revisited.[58] It attests to the perceived role of visual control in the state project of pacification: 'terrorist elements operate more easily in territory occupied exclusively by a population that is indifferent or sympathetic to the enemy than in a territory in which there are also persons liable to *monitor* them and *inform* the authorities of any suspicious movement' [my emphasis].[59] Implicit in this statement is the Israeli government's enlisting of its civilian population to act as its agents alongside the agencies of state power, and the fact that the settlers' presence is being used to serve the state's security aims.[60] The task of civilian settlers – men, women and children – is to investigate and report Palestinian movements in the West Bank, to help turn the occupied territory into an optical matrix radiating out from a proliferation of lookout points/settlements scattered across the landscape.

In a further affirmation of the power of observation, until the recent Intifada made the life of settlers extremely precarious, only few settlement councils accepted the advice of the security establishment to fence themselves in from the surrounding landscape. The thinking behind their refusal to do so combined the metaphorical with the practical. Fencing themselves in might signify that settlements have no further territorial claims beyond their outer fences. Confirming this argument, in one of his documentary films, Israeli film-maker Avi Mugrabi recorded Sharon bragging off record while sitting down to a meal in one West Bank settlement: 'I told [them]: don't build fences around your settlements. If you put up a fence, you put a limit to your expansion . . . we should place the fences around the Palestinians and not around our places.'[61] On the other hand, some settlers believed that the self-protection afforded by visual supervision rendered the material protection of a fortified wall or of a fence redundant and even obstructive. The security officer of the settlement of Qdumim, Shlomi Hazoni, stated this in a manner that confirms the prejudices which Israeli security officials are thought to harbour against Palestinians and Arabs: 'Fences project fear that the Arabs can sense . . . When they can sense our fear they will attack . . . fences are definitely not working as a security measure.' Instead, Hazoni proposed that 'the layout of the settlement and the design of its houses should be part of a single security concept'.[62]

Seeking safety in vision, Jewish settlements are intensely illuminated. At night, across the landscape, they are visible as brilliant white streaks of light that contrast with the yellowish tint of the light in the Arab villages and towns. Seeking their safety in invisibility, Palestinian neighbourhoods, on the other hand, employ blackouts to protect themselves against impending aerial attacks. During the Intifada, the military finally ruled that settlements be surrounded by several layers of fencing systems, cameras equipped with night-vision capability and even motion detectors placed on the perimeter fence, further extending the function of the naked eye. Reinforcing this one-way hierarchy of vision, according to rules of engagement issued by the occupying forces at the end of 2003, soldiers may shoot to kill any Palestinian caught observing settlements with binoculars or in any other 'suspicious manner'.[63] Palestinians should presumably avoid looking at settlements at all.

But it is hard not to see a settlement from wherever one is in the contemporary West Bank. The Israeli journalist Gideon Levy writes:

> You can hardly find a window in a Palestinian house that does not open onto some red-tiled roof of the neighbouring settlement . . . From the window of a burnt clothing store in re-occupied Bethlehem, from a bathroom window in Kafr Beit-Dajan, from a living room window in the village of Sinjel, from the mouth of a cave belonging to the cave-dwellers in southern Mount Hebron, from an office in Nablus, from a store in Ramallah – from everywhere you can spot the settlement

The settlement of Nili (left) and the Palestinian village of Shabtin. Eyal Weizman, 2002.

on the hilltop, looming, dreadfully colonial . . . alienated, threatening, conquering houses, lusting for more.[64]

The paradox of double vision

Most Israeli architects building in the West Bank do not see the panorama as constituting a strategic or defensive category. They have simply internalized the security discourse of the state and have learned to use it when discussing matters with state agents in order to get their projects approved. When they have designed neighbourhoods and settlements overlooking the surrounding landscape, they have generally done so in order to provide residents with views of the landscape – as any architect would do in a hilltop environment. The value of the landscape visible from windows in the settlement of Ma'ale Adumim, was summed up succinctly by Leitersdorf: 'We were selling something that did not cost us a penny.'[65] Similarly, the majority of settlers did not migrate to the West Bank in order to act as security agents of the Israeli state. Settlers have migrated to the West Bank for a variety of other reasons. Beyond ideology, these included a subsidized, high level of services and amenities, a cheaper life close to nature – and of course, great views.

The sales brochure for homes in the ultra-Orthodox settlement of Emanuel, the second settlement designed by Leitersdorf, published for member recruitment in the United States, evoked the picturesque: 'The city of Emanuel, situated 440 metres above sea level has a magnificent view of the coastal plain and the Judean Mountains. The hilly landscape is dotted with green olive orchards and enjoys a pastoral calm.'[66] In the image of the pastoral landscape, integral to

the perspective of colonial traditions, the admiration of the rustic panorama is viewed through the window-frames of modernity. The retreat from the city to the country reasserts the virtues of a simpler life close to nature. It draws on the opposition between luxury and simplicity, the spontaneous and the planned – themselves the opposite poles of the axis of vision that stretches between the settlements and their surrounding landscape. In the settlement of Emanuel, Leitersdorf's plan aimed to provide 'panoramic landscape views for all homes'.[67] For most settlers, the landscape was not initially much more than a pastoral view, but for the ideologists of Gush Emunim, its topographical features were cast as national metaphors. A constructed way of seeing sought to re-establish the relation between terrain and sacred text. Topography turned into scenography and formed an exegetical landscape with a mesh of scriptural signification that must be read, instead of simply viewed. The mountain region of the West Bank therefore became both a physical entity and an imagined, mythical geography. Far from evoking solemn contemplation, the 'biblical' panorama formed the centrepiece of a religious ritual causing a sensation of sheer ecstasy. Menorah Katzover, the wife of a prominent settler leader, said of the view of the West Bank mountains from her living room windows in the settlement of Homesh. 'It causes me such excitement that I cannot even talk about in modesty.'[68]

The settlement of Shiloh[69] advertised itself on its website in the following way: 'Shiloh spreads up the hills overlooking Tel Shiloh [Shiloh archaeological Mound], where over 3,000 years ago the Children of Israel gathered to erect the Tabernacle and to divide by lot the Land of Israel into tribal portions . . . This ancient spiritual centre has retained its power as the focus of modern day Shiloh.'[70] The landscape, imbued with religious signification, establishes the link that helps people relive and re-enact religious-national myths in a way that juxtaposes, on the very same land, ancient with modern time. In 1981, its spiritual leader, Rabbi

Marine Hougnier, film still from 'Territories II', 2005.

Yoel Bin-Nun, one of the founder members of Gush Emunim whose chosen surname (referring to that of Yehoshua Bin-Nun who occupied the same area for the Israelites) reflects a similar relation between the biblical period and the present project, announced with great fanfare the discovery of the precise location of the Tabernacle. With donations gathered from Jewish communities and Christian evangelists in the United States he initiated the construction of the 'Synagogue of the Dome of the Divine Presence', whose architecture was based on construction guidelines he found in the Bible. From afar, the building bears some approximate resemblance to contemporary reconstructions of what the Second Temple of Jerusalem might have looked like. Today, the synagogue and the archaeological site have become comical objects of nationalist-religious pedagogy where settlers dressed in biblical period costume organize guided tours for schoolchildren from neighbouring settlements.

A cyclical process of landscape interpretation is thus set in motion: the sites defined by the military as a threat are understood as components of a biblical panorama. The stone houses of Palestinian villages, the olive terraces and the dust roads are read as cultural-historical signifiers. A gap opens between what the military and the government want settlers to see (sites of national strategic importance and human objects of state control); what the settlers think they see (a pastoral biblical landscape and its figures); and what settlers really do see – the daily life of Palestinians and their poverty under occupation. Within this panorama lies a cruel paradox: the very thing that renders the landscape 'biblical' or 'pastoral' – its traditional habitation and cultivation in terraces, olive orchards, stone buildings and the presence of livestock – is produced by the Palestinians, the very people whom the settlers would like to displace. Like a theatrical set, the panorama is seen as an edited landscape put together by invisible stagehands who must step off the set as the lights come on. On different occasions, Palestinians could exist between the visual resisters of danger, biblical authenticity, native pastorality and political invisibility. This lacuna of the latter register has been best demonstrated by Sa'adia Mandel, the head of the architecture department in Ariel College in the West Bank, who claimed that his architecture students watching out of their classroom windows 'see the Arab villages, but don't notice them. They look and they don't see. And I say this positively.'[71]

Palestinian border control at the Allenby Bridge terminal. Miki Kratsman, 1999. Kratsman says of this photograph: 'When I positioned myself over the shoulder of the Palestinian border policeman to take this photograph, I suddenly heard voices calling behind me: "Zooz! Zooz!" ("Move, Move" in Hebrew). Only then did I realize that behind the mirror were the Israelis. When I tried to take a photograph of the mirror, I was removed from the terminal by the angry Palestinian policeman.'

5.

Checkpoints: The Split Sovereign and the One-Way Mirror

Without drawing a single line, the Israeli and Palestinian peace bureaucrats meeting in Oslo in the summer of 1993 conceived one of the most complex architectural products of the occupation. Article X of the first Annex to the Gaza-Jericho Agreement (also known as Oslo I) is called 'Passages'; it is concerned with the interfaces between a variety of differently defined territories, in particular the border connections between the 'outside' world and the areas handed over to limited Palestinian control.[1] The architecture of the terminals connecting these territories sought to resolve the structural paradox that resulted from the seemingly contradictory desire to enable the functioning of Palestinian autonomy while enabling Israel to maintain overall control of security. For the Palestinian negotiators, the border terminals and the process of passing through them were important symbols of an emergent, autonomous national self-government. For the Israeli military officers leading the negotiations, the terminals were to articulate a new security concept that delegated direct, on-the-ground control of West Bank and Gaza Palestinians to the nascent Palestinian Authority under Israel's overall 'invisible' control. Israeli security personnel and Palestinian politicians considered various options; the architecture finally agreed upon reflected a last-minute compromise achieved shortly before the planned signing ceremony at the White House on September 1993. This architecture allowed Israel to control on a case-by-case basis who would be allowed to pass through the terminal (described in Article X as a large military base), and to keep 'the responsibility for security throughout the passage', but for Palestinians to run the terminal building, and for Palestinian national emblems to be the only ones visible on the ground.[2]

Article X describes in exhaustive detail a flowchart which separates the Palestinian crossings through the border terminals into different colour-coded lanes and sub-lanes. Together, these make up a complex choreography of pathways and security checkpoints that divide passengers according to destinations defined by the geography of the Oslo Accords: by the end of the Oslo process, the several hundred separate enclaves, about 40 per cent of the territory of the West Bank, under autonomous Palestinian self-rule (areas A and B); the rest of the West Bank under Israeli control (area C); Gaza; and East Jerusalem. Incoming Palestinians would not see the Israeli security personnel who exercise overall control: Article X stipulated that the Israeli security agents, although present throughout the terminal building, would be separated from travellers by one-way mirrors.[3] The travel documents of Palestinians were to be 'checked by an Israeli officer who [would] also check their identity indirectly in an invisible manner'.[4] Within the terminal, Palestinian police officers would conduct some security checks, but provision was made for Israeli security personnel to emerge into the main hall from behind the mirror in the event of what they perceive to be an emergency situation. As a 'last resort', they were permitted to use their firearms.[5]

The unassuming Allenby Bridge, which spans the Jordan River on the historical Amman–Jerusalem–Jaffa road, is the main connection between the West Bank and Jordan. At the western end of the bridge, on the Israeli-controlled bank of the Jordan River, the existing old terminal was expanded and remodelled, according to Article X in the following manner: several interconnected rooms, partly glazed with one-way mirrors, were positioned at different intersections within the terminal's various pathways. Access to the rooms concealed by the mirrors was provided by a back door. In accordance with Article X, incoming Palestinians would see only 'a Palestinian policeman and a raised Palestinian flag'. They would also see a Palestinian police counter in front of one of several large mirrors facing the 'incoming passengers' hall. The mirrors were positioned so that Israeli security behind them could observe, unseen, not only the Palestinian passengers but also the Palestinian police personnel themselves.

The waiting room itself is a large open hall with rows of plastic benches fixed to the tiled floor. In 1996, at the height of the Oslo process, the Palestinian poet and PLO activist Mourid Barghouti described the scene when he crossed the bridge back to Palestine for the first time after thirty years of exile: 'I entered a large hall, like the arrival hall in an airport . . . a row of windows to deal with people going to the West Bank and those going to Gaza . . . Thousands of Palestinians like me passing with their bags for a summer visit or leaving for Amman to get on with their lives.' Barghouti goes on to describe a hall crowded with large families and many children. There was a very long wait to be checked. On the benches, on their mothers' laps, or on the floor, children were sleeping.

– '"Where do I go now?"
– '"To the Palestinian officer, of course."'[6]

The Palestinian border policeman, standing behind a large counter, receives the passport of an incoming passenger, examines it, and then slips it into a drawer hidden behind the counter, which is then opened on the other side by the Israeli security staff. There, the information of the passport is processed, a decision regarding entry is made, and the passport is pushed back with one of two coloured paper slips denoting whether or not an entry permission could be given. The Palestinian police officer subsequently welcomes the passenger or denies him or her entry, and stamps the passport accordingly.[7] On the other side of the terminal is the usual commotion of emotional meetings, vendors, kiosks, buses and taxis.

More than a mere solution to a specific security/political problem, the architecture of the terminal is a diagram of the new power relations articulated throughout the Oslo process (1993–2000).[8] Embodied in the architecture of the terminals was the very military, political and economical logic of the Oslo process, one that sought to replace direct occupation and management of the occupied Palestinians, and thus direct responsibility for them, with the creation of a Palestinian Authority – a prosthetic political system propped up by the international community – and the delegation of local functions to it. According to this logic of governance, Israel remained in control of the Palestinians by regulating their movement through space, without resorting to managing their lives within the separate enclaves it sealed around their towns and villages. In assuming the duties of day-to-day governance within the enclaves under its control, the Palestinian Authority has freed Israel of its obligations as an occupying power by international law.[9]

The architecture of the Allenby Bridge terminal incorporated within the scale of a building the principle of surveillance that dictated the distribution of settlements and military bases across the Occupied Territories. However, unlike these mechanisms of surveillance and discipline, which, following principles set up in the nineteenth century, called for power to be 'visible but unverifiable,'[10] the architecture of the terminal is designed to hide from the passengers the mechanism of power and control altogether. Here, power should be neither visible nor verifiable. The aim of the terminal's architecture is not to discipline the Palestinian passengers but rather to mislead them as to the effective source of power, to make them believe that they are under the control of one authority, whereas they are in fact under the control of another. Significantly, it was not the Palestinian passenger, but the agent of the Palestinian Authority, who had to internalize the disciplinary power of surveillance and be under the gaze of the Israeli security personnel. This hierarchy of surveillance could be understood in relation to the almost maternal rhetoric with which Israel argued the Oslo agreement as an attempt to inaugurate the Palestinian Authority into a differentiated world, where, after taking its first steps in supervised self-government, it would, in due time, function separately from Israeli power.[11]

Modulating flows

Israel's conception of security has always included a complex territorial, institutional and architectural apparatus, conceived in order to manage the circulation of Palestinians through 'Israeli' space. The Israeli writer-activist Tal Arbel has called this 'Israel's mobility regimes'.[12] Until 1966, Israeli military administration was imposed on Palestinian citizens of Israel, with checkpoints located in and around their towns and villages, denying them the possibility of travelling without special permits. After 1967, Minister of Defence Moshe Dayan's 'open bridges policy' extended the 1966 easing of travel restrictions on Palestinian citizens of Israel going to the Occupied Territories by allowing West Bank and Gaza Palestinians to travel to Jordan and to enter Israel. It was part of a general policy he called 'the invisible occupation', the goal of which was that 'a local Arab can live his life . . . without needing to see or speak to an Israeli representative'. Dayan wanted to allow for a situation whereby Palestinians would run their own lives and societies under imperceptible but overall Israeli control. In the context of this policy the Israeli military was to avoid patrolling Palestinian cities, keep Israeli flags to a minimum, and avoid interfering in Palestinian daily life.[13] The policy also sought to incorporate Palestinian laborers into the Israeli workforce. Dayan's initiative was argued as 'humanitarian' but the ability to open and close the Allenby Bridge was also, according to Dayan's coordinator of government activity in the occupied territories Shlomo Gazit, part of a behaviouristic 'carrot and stick' policy, which allowed the 'denial of privileges' when the security or political situation demanded.[14] In reality, more often than intended, the bridges between the West Bank and Jordan were closed, or open in one direction only – allowing only the departure of Palestinians. Throughout the years of occupation, restrictions on Palestinian movement gradually increased. Travel permits were first introduced with the creation in 1981 of the Civil Administration – a subsidiary of the IDF tasked with governing the Palestinians in the West Bank and Gaza. Their use accelerated during the first Intifada (1987–91), when villages, towns and cities were placed under curfew for extended periods.[15] In 1991, for the duration of the first Gulf War, Israeli Prime Minister Yitzhak Shamir ordered the closure of the entire Occupied Territories for the first time from Israel and the rest of the world.

During the Oslo years, the politics of closure was further extended, perfected and normalized. During 1994, Israeli security control retreated into the roadways that connected centres of Palestinian population. Between 1994 and 1999, Israel installed 230 checkpoints and imposed 499 days of closures.[16] Israeli sovereignty was exercised in its ability to block, filter and regulate movement in the entire Occupied Territories, and between it and the 'outside'. The occupation effectively shifted to the road network, working as a system of on/off valves of checkpoints and roadblocks. The Israeli occupying forces further ruled by modulating flows of other kinds: labor, goods, energy and waste. Even the level of flow in the water pipes connecting the separate Palestinian enclaves throughout the territories was controlled by the Civil Administration.[17]

The Allenby Bridge terminal was merely one node in the complex legal-spatial-ideological apparatus of Oslo. The governing system not only comprised a network of civilian structures (although, as we have seen, the number of buildings in the settlements doubled during the Oslo years[18]) and new roads reserved for the exclusive use of settlers, other Israelis and the military. Significantly, it was also composed of an array of 'legal' and bureaucratic procedures that attempted to manage the Israeli settlers and the Palestinian inhabitants of the Occupied Territories as two territorially overlapping but increasingly insular, autarkic networks.

Indeed, the bureaucratic infrastructure of the Oslo process sought to replace an 'occupation' with 'management'. The Israeli sociologist Yehouda Shanhav recounted how during the Oslo years, the Israeli military launched an experimental project: the implementation of Total Quality Management (TQM) for the administration of all relations between Israeli security and Palestinians in Gaza. TQM is a client-oriented 'management approach . . . based on participation, aiming at long-term success through customer satisfaction, and benefits to all members of the organization . . .'[19] The system is internationally used in manufacturing, education and the service industries. It was first introduced to the IDF in 1991 by Ehud Barak, then Chief of Staff, in order to manage military staffing and supplies. In 1995, a young officer and recent graduate of an MBA programme managed to convince the IDF command in Gaza to apply this management approach to its relations with the Palestinians. Following this system the military occupation was reinterpreted as the provider of services and security, and the Palestinians and settlers as its customers. In this way, Israeli–Palestinian interactions, which by the standards of international law were still performed within the framework of belligerent occupation, were depoliticized into a smilingly neo-liberal 'service economy', a mere business transaction.[20] The aim of TQM and the Oslo process in general was to reduce 'friction' between the various groups that inhabited the Occupied Territories (Palestinian residents, Palestinian police, Israeli soldiers, settlers, even tourists) and avoid, as much as possible, the application of Israeli military force.

Within this larger system of control the architecture of the border terminals operated as valves regulating the flow of Palestinian passengers under Israel's volatile regime of security; simultaneously, and to those who passed through them, the terminals became an ideological apparatus that aimed to naturalize and normalize the powers of the Palestinian Authority.

Transparent border

Unlike the one-way mirrors we become accustomed to seeing in almost every police station, detention facility and control room worldwide, the one-way mirror system of the terminal/camp of Allenby Bridge was more than the mere apparatus of control – it functioned also as an international border of sorts. In fact, not only did the mirror demarcate a border, but in its positioning and function it created a new conceptual border to the concept of sovereignty. It is in this context that one-way mirrors have become important components in the redesigning of sovereignty across the frontiers of the 'war on terror', enabling, for example, the United States' 'politics of deniability' (almost Clintonian in style) that allows US agents to engage in torture without resorting to physical contact. The process which the Bush administration calls 'extraordinary rendition' was conceived in order to bypass the outlawing of 'cruel, inhuman and degrading treatment of prisoners in US custody' by turning terrorist suspects over to foreign governments that do engage in torture.[21] The one-way mirror behind which US agents and behavioural science consultants observe and perhaps even guide the process of torture in Saudi Arabian, Moroccan or Syrian prisons has effectively become an extension of US borders, acting as the physical and optical medium across which a previously unified sovereignty has now been split.[22]

A similar, if more complex, prosthetic power relation was established through the one-way mirror of the Allenby Bridge terminal. Although Article X renders the Palestinian Authority's border procedures mere performance, the nature of this performance is nevertheless significant. The Oslo process was designed in such a manner that Palestinians would no longer identify themselves merely as the individual *objects* exposed to military power but also as political *subjects* of another. If Israeli security control was always directed at the occupied Palestinians, the same was not true of the Israeli ideological project. The attempt to 'produce' and discipline a political subject remained distinct from the security control that dominates the individual via threats and violence.[23] Under the Oslo Accords, Palestinians were still, as before, subjugated to Israeli security domination in that they were exposed to the threats of its military actions, but encouraged to believe themselves the subjects of their own political authority. (This had the effect of directing Palestinians' anger and frustration for the deterioration of their freedoms and economy at their own Palestinian Authority rather than

Checkpoint. Pavel Wolberg, 2002.

at Israel.) This separation between the functions of direct discipline and indirect control no longer fits the theoretical narrative that presupposes an evolution from 'disciplinary societies' to 'control societies',[24] and makes these two systems of domination coexistent as two components of a vertically layered sovereignty, which is here horizontally separated across the sides of the one-way mirror.

Throughout the second Intifada, the 'exception' clause in Article X, which allowed Israelis to break temporarily into the terminal in order to enforce 'security', was permanently in effect. On the rare occasions that the terminal was open to traffic, Palestinians needed to appeal directly to Israeli border police without the mediation of Palestinian border policemen. Palestinians became exposed to the naked, overt military power. If they cooperated, acquiescently complied with military orders or lowered their eyes in front of the architectural machine, they did so out of fear of violence rather than by internalizing a citizen-like relation of subjugation.

The architecture of checkpoints

The discontinuous lines of fences, ditches, concrete walls and high-tech sensors – referred to by the Israeli government as the 'seam-line obstacle', by the general Israeli public as the 'separation fence', and by those Israelis and Palestinians opposing it as the Wall or sometimes as the 'Apartheid Wall' – are only the most visible and mediatized barriers built in a frenzy of fortification construction that has pockmarked the entire West Bank since the beginning of the Oslo Process in 1993, with the aim of separating Palestinians from Israelis at every opportunity.

Since the beginning of the second Intifada in September 2000, Israeli attempts to isolate and fragment Palestinian resistance and limit the possibility of suicide bombers arriving in Israeli cities have further split the fragile internal matrix of Palestinian society and the geography of the Oslo Accords. Using a complex, ever-present system of closures and traffic restrictions, the Israelis brought the Palestinian economy to a virtual standstill. This system relied upon an extensive network of barriers that included permanent and partially manned checkpoints, roadblocks, metal gates, earth dykes, trenches, 'flying' or mobile checkpoints, all of which were operated according to a frequently changing assortment of bans and limitations. According to a report prepared by OCHA – the UN Office for the Coordination of Humanitarian Affairs, which has been monitoring this policy of traffic restrictions – by September 2006 the number of these restrictions comprised a system of 528 physical obstacles. During one week in December 2006, OCHA researchers registered 160 new 'flying checkpoints' and an extra 38 kilometres of roadways that were fenced off to prevent use by Palestinians.[25] These barriers sustained the creation of a new geographic, social and economic reality.[26] Although the checkpoint system gradually emerged as a series of local responses to what military officers saw as a series of tactical necessities, it has gradually assumed an overall strategic layout, constituting a complete territorial system whose main aim is to dominate and manage the lives of the Palestinians, without having to encroach on their cities, towns and villages, and (mostly) without need for overt violent force. The various barriers splintered the West Bank into a series of approximately 200 separate, sealed-off 'territorial cells' around Palestinian 'population centres' (roughly corresponding to the boundaries of the Oslo era, areas A and B) with traffic between these cells channelled through military-controlled bottlenecks. Palestinians have to apply for more than a dozen different travel permits, each allowing different categories of persons to travel to different categories of space through different categories of checkpoints. Palestinians are, furthermore, barred from the Jordan Valley, Jerusalem and the enclaves trapped between the Wall and the Green Line unless they have still further kinds of almost-impossible-to-get permits.[27] The checkpoint system is also designed to impose and maintain a policy of total closure – complete prohibition on movement from the Occupied Territories to Israel. This is put into effect whenever there is an alert or suspicion of a terror attack, but also as a matter of routine on Jewish festivals and holidays, often on Muslim festivals and holidays, on special occasions (such as the death of Yassir Arafat), or when there are large, international sports events in Israel, such as a European basketball championship match. (This alone should be a good enough reason for international sports bodies to rethink agreeing to stage events in Israel.) According to the Union of Palestinian Medical Relief Committees, 85 per cent of people in the West Bank did not leave their villages during the Intifada's first three years due to the curfews and closures.[28]

The security rationale for the checkpoint system is further founded on the belief that the less Palestinians are permitted to circulate through space, the more secure this space will be.[29] As director of the GSS (General Security Service, or Shabak), Avi Dichter was one of the strongest advocates of the checkpoint system to the degree of accusing those military officers who removed some checkpoints, when they felt they were unnecessarily punishing entire cities, of murder.[30]

Machsom (checkpoint) *Watch* – an organization of women dedicated to monitoring human rights abuse at military checkpoints – has painstakingly recorded and reported the violence and humiliation caused by the checkpoint system; the delaying of the sick, the elderly, and infants needing medical care, the births and deaths occurring on the hard shoulder; the manner in which the circulation regime penetrated and violated every aspect of Palestinian daily lives, delaying, humiliating and exhausting people in a daily struggle to survive, attempting, as they claimed, to make Palestinian political resistance beyond their capacity to undertake.[31] At Huwwara checkpoint south of Nablus, *Machsom Watch* activists reported the arbitrary and random nature of Israeli orders designed to make travelling by Palestinians an uncertain experience, and often discourage it altogether. For example, on 6 September 2004 Israeli soldiers decided to detain every ninth adult male wishing to cross the checkpoint, on the 19th of the same month, every man whose name was Mohammad was detained, which accounted for very large numbers. Sometimes, again at random, some passengers were asked to wait four hours; at others, without warning or announcement, the checkpoint would be closed. While the queues of Palestinian passengers stretch on both sides of the checkpoints, Jewish settlers cruise unhindered through separate gates and down protected corridors that lead to segregated Jewish-only roads.

The checkpoint system has become so omnipresent and intrusive that it has grown to govern the entire spectrum of Palestinian life under occupation. In *Checkpoints*, the recent book by the Palestinian-Israeli member of parliament, writer and political activist Azmi Bishara, Israel is no longer called by its name but termed 'the state of the checkpoints', the Occupied Territories are the 'land of checkpoints', the Israelis 'owners of checkpoints' and the Palestinians 'the people of the land of checkpoints'. 'The checkpoint takes all that man has, all his efforts, all his time, all his nerves . . . the checkpoint is the chaos and the

Erez terminal, Gaza. Nir Kafri, 2004.

order, it is within the law and outside of it, operating by rationality and idio-syncrasy through both order and disorder.'[32] The long wait to pass through check-points has given rise to a secondary economy, which feeds off the arbitrariness of the first – an improvised food and goods market that Palestinian passengers sardonically call 'the duty-free'. Because of the deep depression of the Pales-tinian economy, these markets have gradually expanded to become almost the only functioning Palestinian public space. The neighbourhoods, cities or villages that the checkpoint cut apart have become its suburbs.

> In the beginning the checkpoint was made up of large tin barrels filled with stones
> . . . the barrels were later filled with concrete. They were soon replaced by red and
> white plastic road barriers, which were later themselves replaced with concrete road
> barriers, to which large concrete cubes were added, to which fencings of barbed
> wire were added and then rocks of many sizes . . . In the beginning soldiers stood
> under the open skies; later on, a steel tower was erected next to them with a plastic
> water container on its top. The field-tent was replaced by a pre-fabricated struc-
> ture . . . From time to time the soldiers used rocks or dust bins as a creative touch
> to their art work.[33]

The checkpoints not only carve up space, but divide up time as well. Israel changes to daylight-saving time a month after the rest of the world because of coalition

HOLLOW LAND

agreements with ultra-Orthodox parties whose constituency's hours of prayer are governed by celestial composition and level of daylight. The Palestinian Authority shifts its clocks to daylight-saving time in tune with the rest of the northern hemisphere. In spring, a one-hour time difference opens up across the two sides of the checkpoints, creating two time zones.[34] 'The working day ends at 6pm local time but 7pm checkpoint time. The checkpoint shuts at 7pm its time. Until everybody got used to move the clock backwards and finish work an hour earlier, the checkpoint was blocked with hundreds of winter time people begging the summer-time soldiers to allow them back home.'[35]

Humanitarian design

In the middle of 2003 the IDF inaugurated the programme 'Another Life' whose aim was to 'minimize the damage to the Palestinian life fabric in order to avoid the humanitarian crisis that will necessitate the IDF to completely take over the provision of food and services to the Palestinian population'.[36] This programme has turned 'humanitarianism' into a strategic category in Israeli military operations, and influenced the design of its various instruments of control. In January 2004 Ariel Sharon appointed Baruch Spiegel, a recently retired IDF officer working at the Ministry of Defence, as 'IDF director of civilian and humanitarian issues'. One of Spiegel's tasks was to overhaul the inefficiencies and humanitarian problems caused by the checkpoint system. Upon assuming his post, Spiegel sent Israeli representatives all over the world to examine technologies of control along the borders between Finland and Russia, on the borders of China, between Malaysia and Singapore, the United States and Mexico; even the French-German border arrangements after World War II were studied.[37] Two months later, in March 2004, Spiegel published the first part of a plan devised ostensibly to 'ease the lives of Palestinians in the West Bank and Gaza'. Spiegel's plan, written in English to placate foreign governments, severely criticized the harshness and inefficiencies of IDF soldiers at checkpoints, and proposed some significant changes.

Spiegel's plan followed military terminology in referring to checkpoints according to two general categories: the 'envelope checkpoint' (Machsom Keter), a checkpoint that regulates movement between different Palestinian 'territorial cells', whose total number Spiegel wanted to reduce; and the 'closure checkpoint' (Machsom Seger) that regulates movement between the Palestinian areas and the western side of the Wall, usually called the 'Israeli' side – even though it is sometimes located within the occupied areas. According to the Spiegel plan, twelve permanent 'closure checkpoints' were to be built along the length of the Wall, to be operated by the Israeli Airport Authority as if they were international borders.[38] Their construction was to be partially funded by the '2005 US Emergency Aid to the Palestinians' which was intended, according to President Bush, 'to support Palestinian political, economic, and security reforms'. However, the 'pro-Israeli' US Congress made it difficult for the White House to hand out any of this aid directly to the Palestinian Authority. Out of $200 million allocated for the use of Palestinians in 2005, Israel received $50 million to help fund the construction of the terminals.[39] American money meant to help Palestinians was therefore used to fund one of the most blatant apparatuses of the occupation, demonstrating how distorted American perception could be when they believe, contrary to all evidence gathered during four decades of occupation, that Israel knows best how to spend Palestine's money on its behalf, and that oiling the cogs of the occupation is somehow in Palestinian interest.

An 'artist's impression' of one of the terminals, Sha'ar Ephraim, near the Israeli-Palestinian town of Taibeh, in the northwest part of the West Bank, designed for the Airport Authority by the Haifa-based architectural firm Loyton-Shumni, gives the impression of a respectable international border crossing. It appears to be clad in tiles and glass like a giant suburban shopping mall. It has a parking lot with disabled parking spaces, gardens, and a series of spacious halls that can accommodate hundreds of passengers. The architectural impression of the Sha'ar Ephraim terminal appears under the heading 'humanitarian concerns' on the Ministry's of Defence website, which also promises that the terminals 'will employ advanced technological systems that will minimize human friction'.[40] The Ministry of Defence further announced on 15 January 2006 that, in order 'to lessen the existing friction in the security checks, humanize the process and improve standards of service', security will be privatized and civilians rather than soldiers will conduct all security checks.[41] Spiegel called this privatization 'taking the army out of the checkpoints'.[42]

It would later become clear that this and other plans of a 'humanitarian' nature that were aimed at reducing the extent of closures sustained by the checkpoint system, or making it more efficient, would either not be implemented by the military officers in command, or would make the treatment of Palestinians harsher. In fact, according to OCHA, the number of physical barriers throughout the West Bank has steadily increased since the Spiegel report was released.[43]

Towards the middle of 2004, the improvised checkpoint system began to be regularized. Whereas previously there was chaos now things appeared to operate according to strict procedures. At this time revolving gates or turnstiles started to be installed in many of the permanent checkpoints throughout the West Bank, ostensibly to make more ordered, efficient, secure and 'human' the process of passage. The turnstiles became the centrepieces of a new 'design' for the checkpoint system that attempted to slow, regulate and organize the crowded mass of Palestinians seeking to cross the checkpoints into sequenced and ordered lines in which one Palestinian at a time would face the soldier checking his permits and baggage. In most cases, the checkpoint had two sets of turnstiles with space between them. The first set was placed several tens of metres away from Israeli military positions so as to keep the congestion away from them. Soldiers regulate the pace of passage by using an electrical device that controls the turning of the gates. One person at a time passes through at a push of a button. Every few seconds soldiers stop the rotation of the turnstiles, so that several people remain caged between the gates. Sometimes they trap people within the arms of the turnstiles. Tal Arbel discovered that the manufacturer of these turnstiles had been asked by Ministry of Defence contractors to change their production specifications and reduce the length of their metal arms from the Israeli standard of 75–90cm (used at universities, swimming pools, railway stations, etc.) to a mere 55cm in the West Bank and Gaza,[44] so that the turnstiles physically press against the passengers' bodies, ensuring there is nothing under their clothes. According to testimony from *Machsom Watch*, the tight turnstiles ended up causing more harm and chaos. 'People got stuck, parcels got crushed, dragged along and burst open on the ground'. Heavier people got trapped in the narrow space, as were older women and mothers with small children.'[45] It is hard to imagine the cruelty imposed by a minor transformation of a banal, and otherwise invisible architectural detail, ostensibly employed to regulate and make easier the process of passage.

The upgrade of the Qalandia terminal crossing, which connects (or rather disconnects) Jerusalem from Ramallah, was completed, according to the principles of the Spiegel plan, at the end of 2005. The new system includes a labyrinth of iron fences that channels passengers en route to Jerusalem via a series of turnstiles. All commuters must go through five stages: the first set of turnstiles, the X-ray gates, the second set of turnstiles, the inspection booth and an X-ray machine for the bags. This entire process is captured by a dense network of cameras, and the passenger is given instructions via loudspeakers. From their protected booths, Israeli security personnel operate the revolving gates remotely, regulating the rate of passenger flow. The inspection booths are encased in bulletproof glass. The glass is so thick that it tends to reflect the outside light rather than letting it through, thereby obscuring the security personnel inside, and effectively functioning as a one-way mirror. Palestinians must insert their identity cards and travel permits into a small slot under the windows. Communication takes place through push-button speakers. Still in the process of installation, new detectors operated by biometric cards will eventually make even this minimal interaction redundant. After crossing this checkpoint, the passenger is allowed through another turnstile and then through the Wall. Near the exit of the terminal a large sign mockingly greets in Hebrew, Arabic and English: 'The Hope of Us All'. Some Israeli anti-occupation activists have sprayed on it the words 'Arbeit Macht Frei'.

Each of the large terminals also includes what the military calls 'humanitarian gates'. These gates have a small waiting area with a bathroom and a water cooler, designed for the passage of those in wheelchairs, parents with baby strollers and people over the age of 60.[46] Indeed, 'humanitarian' has become the most common adjective in matters of occupation-design: 'humanitarian gates', 'humanitarian terminals', 'humanitarian technology' and 'humanitarian awareness', as well as – according to a procedure already in effect since the beginning of the Intifada – a 'humanitarian officer' (usually a middle-aged reserve soldier) employed at checkpoints to smooth the process of passage and mediate between the needs of Palestinians and the orders of soldiers. The 'humanitarian' rhetoric of the current phase of the occupation is part of a general attempt to normalize it. The urgent and important criticism that peace organizations often level at the IDF – that it is dehumanizing its enemies – masks another more dangerous process by which the military incorporates into its operations the logic of, and even seeks to cooperate directly with, the very humanitarian and human rights organizations that oppose it. In March 2006, Chief of Staff Halutz received some members of *Machsom Watch* at a mediatized meeting where he claimed he was ready to hear their suggestions with a view to improving IDF conduct at its checkpoints and to addressing the problems of the Palestinians under occupation in general. Cases of colonial powers seeking to justify themselves with the rhetoric of improvement, civility and reform are almost the constant of colonial history. Currently, moreover, the massive presence of humanitarians in the field of military operations means that the military no longer considers them as bystanders in military operations, but factors them into the militarized environment, just like the occupied population, the houses, the streets and the infrastructure. Beyond that, as we have already seen, the new terminals built according to Spiegel's plan are the physical infrastructure that sustains a political illusion: two states politely separated by a border and connected by a terminal.

The most extreme act of architectural-political camouflage, however, must surely be the new terminal in Rafah, between Gaza and Egypt. In November 2005, following the Israeli withdrawal, 'The Agreed Principles for the Rafah Crossing' were reached after another last-minute compromise was brokered by US Secretary of State Condoleezza Rice. The logic of the Agreed Principles recreated, this time electronically, the spatial logic of the one-way mirror terminals of the Oslo era terminal.[47] The document specified that the Rafah terminal 'will be operated by the Palestinian Authority on its side and Egypt on its side

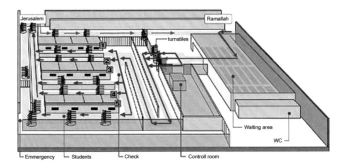

Flow Diagram of Qalandia Crossing. IDF, 2005.

according to international standards' but that the entire process of passage will be overseen by Israeli security. 'A liaison office, led by the 3rd party [i.e not Israelis or Palestinians] would, according to the agreement, receive real-time video and data feed of the activities at Rafah . . . [and] resolve any disputes arising from this agreement.'[48] A Joint Control Room was thus constructed off-site within Israel and was staffed by European observers and Israeli security officers. The control room receives constant live video streams from a network of CCTV cameras operating at the terminal. The face of each passenger standing in front of the Palestinian border police is thus transmitted to the control room as well as the real-time video feed from the machines X-raying luggage. From the control room the Israeli and European observers can communicate with the on-site Palestinian security, demand a rescan or a search in this or that bag, or halt the transit of suspected passengers altogether.[49] When Israel wants the terminal closed it simply denies the European observers access to the control room. According to the agreement, Egyptian border police must then close the passage on their side. In this way, Israel has kept the Rafah crossing, the only gateway Gaza has to the outside world, closed for 86 per cent of the time since June 2006 when an Israeli soldier was kidnapped and taken into Gaza.

But neither the architecture of the Oslo-era Allenby Bridge terminal, nor Israel's pseudo-'border terminals', and not even the new Rafah crossing should be mistaken for metaphors for new forms of domination exercised by Israel; rather they should be seen as components in its ubiquitous and fractalized logic. The logic of the late occupation is not represented by but embedded and saturated within these structures. The Wall itself reiterates some of these built physiognomies. It is not only an instrument of partition but also an apparatus of observation and control, a sensitive linear sensor directed at Palestinian towns and cities. The biometric passes that will soon be used to permit Palestinians to

The Israeli/Palestinian village of Jisr al Zarka and the landscape feature separating it from the town of Caesarea. Eyal Weizman, 2004.

travel through the Wall will make Israel's demographic data on Palestine more complete than the data Palestinians themselves could ever hope to compile.[50]

Enclaves exclaves

The open frontier of conflict has spread this politics of separation throughout the entire Israeli political territory. In Israeli cities, manned checkpoints and guarded entrances have been erected to protect bus stations, shopping malls and inner-city residential neighbourhoods from suicide attacks. Even entry into shops and coffee houses generally requires an identity check. Physical and manned fortification systems (electronic surveillance alone is no longer seen as adequate in face of the intensity and immediacy of threats) are available to the public on the open market, and to the global security market as Israeli 'innovations'. Exported globally, these Israeli practices and technologies have connected the uniqueness of the conflict with worldwide predilections to address security anxieties through 'circulation management', applied now, to state but two examples, along the shifting external borders of the EU as well as along the United States–Mexico and United States–Canada borders.

Within Israel, the barriers between Jews and Palestinian citizens of Israel have had, for legal reasons, to camouflage their real motivations. The high earth rampart, which was raised in 2003 between the poor Palestinian coastal village of Jisr al-Zarqa and the very wealthy town of Caesarea, half an hour's

HOLLOW LAND

drive north of Tel Aviv, was planted with trees and flowers and presented as a supposedly innocent landscape feature in order to disguise its real function of national-economic separation. Following this example, the affluent, previously agricultural and presently suburban Moshav Nir Ziv, quarter of an hour's drive east of Tel Aviv, demanded that the government construct a 1.5-kilometre long and 4-metre high 'acoustic wall', which would in effect separate it from the inhabitants of the predominantly Palestinian-Israeli, government-neglected and drug-plagued neighbourhoods of the city of Lod. Residents of Moshav claim that Lod's inhabitants bother them, steal from them and generally disturb their quality of life. The territorialization of Israel's demographic phobia has generated increasing numbers of barriers between Jewish and Arab communities in neighbouring villages or shared cities, and has led to the further fractalization and fragmentation of the terrain into an archipelago of enmity and alienation.

The physical exclusion of Palestinian citizens of Israel from Israeli space obviously mirrors their increased political exclusion. That the inner borders of the conflict are constantly multiplying is not surprising given the fact that Israel's own Palestinian minority, comprising more than 20 per cent of its population, have been cast as second-class citizens. They are included within the Israeli economy (mainly, but not only, to provide cheap labor and services), but are increasingly excluded from other spheres of life – and are often even described as a 'demographic problem' that upsets rather than forms part of an Israeli public.[51] New legislation forbidding Palestinian married couples (even if one of them is an Israeli citizen) to reside in Israel and subsequently become naturalized citizens is part of this cognitive and practical system that sees the physical separation of Jews and Arabs, and the total control of Palestinian movement, as an important component of Jewish collective security.[52]

Prosthetic sovereignty

Although the terror of the second Intifada heralded a security response of 'permanent emergency', and led to the total breakdown of political negotiations and to the current Israeli policy of unilateral action, the most important aspect of the Oslo Accords' articulation of sovereignty remained in place: a Palestinian government is still apparently in charge of all civil matters under Israel's overarching security control. Whether the Palestinian Authority under Hamas recognizes Israel, or whether Israel is at all willing to negotiate with it, are secondary questions to the facts created and daily confirmed by the very existence of such a Palestinian Authority. The victory of Hamas in the January 2006 Palestinian legislative elections demonstrates not the collapse of the system of prosthetic sovereignty but, paradoxically, its culmination. The Hamas government's ideology and practice of resistance confirm more than anything else an independent agency, external to Israeli sovereignty.

Why should Israel's security control seek to appear invisible? The Fourth Geneva Convention of 1949, which defines the international laws of belligerent occupation, demands that an occupying power assume responsibility over the management of the institutions – welfare, healthcare, judiciary and education, among others – that govern the life of the occupied Palestinians. Of special relevance is Article 55 of the Fourth Geneva Convention: 'To the fullest extent of the means available to it, the Occupying Power has the duty of ensuring the food and medical supplies of the population . . .'[53] Inscribing Palestinian lives under Israel's military regime made them objects of state responsibility. This responsibility operated as a mechanism of restraint in moderating military violence, as it was Israel itself that had to face the consequences of any destruction it inflicted.[54] However, considering the costs of day-to-day government of 3.5 million Palestinians, and of the violent resistance during the two Intifadas (1987–93 and 2000 to the present), Israel has wanted to absolve itself of the responsibilities it had assumed as the occupying power, without losing overall 'security control'. If Israel's excessive security actions had previously been moderated, however lightly, by considerations of an economic and functional nature, since the Oslo Accords, increasingly since the start of the Intifada and increasingly still, in Gaza, since the evacuation of August 2005, Israel's security control could be assumed without the duties of governance, and could freely penetrate every aspect of Palestinian life, consequently aggravating the desperate Palestinian economic situation without having to pay the price in an adverse impact on its own economy. That this logic was guiding the politics of Israeli retreats from Palestinian-populated areas during the Intifada became apparent in Sharon's speech of May 2003, delivered to Likud Party members ahead of his decision to evacuate Gaza. Surprisingly echoing the rhetoric of the Israeli centre-left, Sharon stated that 'the occupation cannot go on indefinitely', and further asked his colleagues to make their choice: 'Today there are 1.8 million Palestinians fed by international organizations. Would you like to take this upon yourselves? Where will we get the money?'[55]

By assuming a degree of political autonomy, the Palestinian economy and the mobility of its labor force have become completely dominated by Israeli security considerations.[56] The temporary/permanent policy of road and checkpoint closure and traffic restrictions effectively disconnected the Occupied Territories from the labor market in Israel and brought the Palestinian economy to a virtual standstill. By imposing itself from above and diffusing throughout the territories from within, Israel's security devastated the Palestinian economy and any

Huwwara checkpoint. Nir Kafri, 2005.

possibility of effective local government. Indeed, since the Oslo Accords, the Israeli economy, benefiting from wider access to the global markets, has been rapidly expanding while the Palestinian economy, with restricted access to the Israeli and global economy, was actually shrinking.[57] According to the UN Office for the Coordination of Humanitarian Affairs, the closure system is presently the primary cause of poverty and humanitarian crisis in the West Bank and the Gaza Strip.[58]

The costs of managing this crisis were (conveniently for Israel) subcontracted to the international community. Increasingly since 2000, international aid to the West Bank and Gaza has been cast as crisis management, with much of the funding allocated for emergency aid, and directed to essential provisions, hospitals and infrastructure, which would otherwise have collapsed. The ensuing crisis has been regarded (in both Israel and the international community) as 'humanitarian', as if it had an unforeseen natural cause, although its reasons are in fact clearly embedded in the political-security situation described above. Recasting the crisis in terms of 'humanitarian politics' was itself a political decision by the European and American donor countries; in doing so, they effectively released Israel from its responsibilities according to international law and undermined their own potential political influence in bringing the occupation to an end. Between 1994 and 2000 the donor community disbursed $3.2 billion – the equivalent of 20 per cent of the GDP of the West Bank and Gaza Strip; between 2000 and 2006, the level of aid averaged about $800 million per year.

An existing Palestinian Authority with an elected 'government' and 'parliament' disguises a reality of social and political fragmentation and total chaos within Palestinian society. Government control was lost to armed organizations (and the conflicts between them) and local gangs on the one hand and to international and humanitarian organizations on the other, with the effective services and provisions bypassing the mechanisms and bureaucracy of the Palestinian Authority altogether.[59] Most of the $800 million annually donated to the Palestinian Authority since the start of the Intifada by the international community has been spent on crisis management, some of it – amazingly enough – earmarked to repair the damage caused by periodic and ongoing Israeli military incursions. Israel could therefore indiscriminately bomb indispensable Palestinian infrastructure safe in the knowledge that its excessive violence would be mitigated, and the damage caused repaired by other states. Another way of manipulating the involvement of international organizations and independent NGOs engaged in humanitarian relief efforts in the occupied areas was through the checkpoint system. 'Internationals' must obtain 'security clearance' from Israel in order to enter the Occupied Territories and move through Israeli-controlled checkpoints. Israel can simply suspend or withhold these permits from organizations and individuals it doesn't like.[60] Certain international aid organizations, in particular the International Committee of the Red Cross (ICRC), questioned whether their mandates included performing actions that international law defined as the responsibility of Israel as the occupying power; they even engaged in several one-day strikes to protest over the conditions of their work.[61]

Ariella Azoulay has claimed that although the Israeli government has brought the Occupied Territories to the verge of hunger, it tries to control the flow of traffic, money and aid in such a way as to prevent the situation reaching a point of total collapse, because of the international intervention, possibly under a UN mandate, that might follow.[62] The 'occupation' of Gaza has been thus reconceptualized as 'crisis management' modulated by Israel through the opening and closing of checkpoints and terminals. It is through this regulation of international aid, under the guise of security, that Israel still controls the Palestinian economy – and, in effect, life – in Gaza and the West Bank.

The illusion that the policies of Israel after Oslo were instrumental in the 'production' of the Palestinians as sovereign *subjects* – proto-citizens of their own political representation – has paradoxically led to them becoming the *objects* of humanitarian assistance. From the perspective of these subjects/objects, it is precisely when, starting in the Oslo years, they perceived themselves to be almost liberated from repressive occupation that they have become most exposed to its unrestrained powers.

Given these conditions, Palestinians are right to question whether it would not be better if the Palestinian Authority dismantled itself completely until conditions for full sovereignty are met. Dismantling the Authority would place responsibility for government of the territories squarely in Israeli hands. Israel would have a choice of either recognizing its obligations as the occupying power under international law, thus using its own budget to cater for the occupied people, or desisting immediately from its policy of intentional economic strangulation and ending the occupation, in all its various dimensions. From the Palestinian perspective, accepting a walled off, aerially policed, infrastructurally dependent and security-controlled territory as a 'state' is bound to perpetuate the logic of the one-way mirror rather than mark an effective stage to full sovereignty. A call to reconnect the concepts of security control and government, and amend the split described within the function of sovereignty, is not a call for a return to nineteenth-century type imperialism, with its technologies of government and production of colonial subjects. It is rather a call for power either to assume the expensive full responsibility for the people under its security control or to avoid 'security' action when it cannot, is unable or unwilling to do so.

The Palestinian sociologist Elia Zureik has noted that the Palestinian passengers crossing the Allenby Bridge terminal in the late 1990s were in fact fully aware of its architecture.[63] The final perspective of this chapter will therefore be theirs. Late in the afternoons, when sunlight falls through the outside window of the Israeli control room facing west, the balance of light between the control room and the now-darkened hall is rendered almost equal by the setting sun. This makes the one-way mirror transparent enough to expose the silhouette of the Israeli security agents behind it, and with it the designed charade of prosthetic sovereignty. On his return to Palestine, Mourid Barghouti was similarly not fooled by the architectural manipulation of the terminal. 'I did not concern myself for long with the odd situation of the [Palestinian police]man. It was clear that the Agreements had placed him in a position in which he could make no decision.'[64]

The Wall, Jerusalem region, graphic illustration on newsprint.

6.

The Wall: Barrier Archipelagos and the Impossible Politics of Separation

At the 2004 annual convention of Israel's Architects Association, the architect Gideon Harlap, campaigning unsuccessfully for the chairmanship of the association, delivered a speech highlighting the fact that 'no architect [had] been employed on the project of the Wall'.[1] Harlap had previously been associated with plans, thought by some to be quite crazy, for the construction of a synagogue on the Haram Al Sharif/Temple Mount on behalf of an organization of Temple-Faithfuls.[2] As a result of the Israeli government's reluctance to incorporate architects into the design process, he claimed, the Wall 'looked clumsy and ugly', whereas it could have been an attractive structure, 'potentially as beautiful as the Great Wall of China'. According to Harlap, the fact that the Wall had become an aesthetic eyesore was the main reason for the fierce international opposition to the project. Furthermore, the government's exclusion of architects from the process denied them 'much work and significant potential revenue from the most expensive project in the history of the state' – $3 billion and counting as these lines are written – at a time when the building industry was in deep recession.

That the Wall, a barrier constructed through the entire West Bank to separate Jewish settlements and Israeli cities from Palestinian towns and villages, was not designed by any pedigreed architect does not mean, however, that it has no architecture. The components that alternately or simultaneously comprise the Wall – 8-metre-high concrete slabs, electronic fences, barbed wire, radar, cameras, deep trenches, observation posts and patrol roads – have been devised and sequenced by the Department of Regional and Strategic Planning of the IDF's Central Command.[3] Since 1994, this department, staffed by civil engineers specializing in 'security design', has been under the direction of Danny Tirza, an expert map-maker, reserve officer and national-religious West Bank settler, who was involved in outlining the changing borders of Palestinian enclaves (Areas A and

B) during the Oslo era. Tirza liked to think that he was a personal friend of Sharon, styling himself the 'Defence Ministry's Chief Architect for the West Bank Security Fence'. The role of the Department of Regional and Strategic Planning was to adapt the general political outline of the Wall's path, authorized by the government, to the precise topographical conditions of its various sites. However, by being in charge of detailed design Tirza managed to influence the path and nature of the entire project.

The project was announced in April 2002 and was put under the charge of the Ministry of Defence, which acted, together with the Department of Regional and Strategic Planning, as its general contractor. In the early stages of planning, the projected route was divided into subsections, each a few dozen kilometres long, which were separately tendered out to one of twenty-two private contractors on the Ministry of Defence's lists. The contractors competed among themselves on quality, price and speed. The construction of the Wall began in June 2002 and was undertaken incrementally: while some segments were built, others were still, or even not yet, planned. The government's initial authorization of the project as a concept rather than as a precise, complete route allowed different interested parties to interfere with and influence the route of the as yet unbuilt sections. Although the very essence and presence of the Wall is the obvious solid, material embodiment of state ideology and its conception of national security, the route should not be understood as the direct product of top-down government planning at all. Rather, the ongoing fluctuations of the Wall's route, as this chapter will demonstrate, registers a multiplicity of technical, legal and political conflicts over issues of territory, demography, water, archaeology and real estate, as well as over political concepts such as sovereignty, security and identity. They reflect as well the effect of a multiplicity of organizations and agents – Palestinian 'popular farmers' committees', Israeli real estate developers, settler associations and their political lobbies, environmental activists, Jewish religious organizations, political and human rights groups, armed paramilitaries, local and international courts, and international diplomacy. Throughout the process of its construction, the Wall was continuously deflected and reoriented, repeatedly changing its route along its length, and could thus be seen, as Tirza himself noted, as 'a political seismograph gone mad'. Not merely a reflection of the government's political vision, the folds, deformations, stretches, wrinkles and bends in the route of the Wall plotted the influences of these different political interests and the actions they could have brought to bear.

Israeli public opinion overwhelmingly supports the politics of separation embodied in the Wall.[4] However, each different strand within the Israeli political spectrum promotes its 'own route', which runs somewhere between the Green Line (the closer to the Green Line the more left-leaning the proposal) and a fragmented patchwork of territory around Palestinian 'demographic centres'. Most opposition to the Wall does not address the fundamental idea and politics of separation, but rather focuses on which route it should take to cut through Palestinian lands. Although the settler organizations initially rejected the idea of the Wall, understanding that it would eventually put a limit on their territorial ambitions and ultimately concede parts of the West Bank to the Palestinians, the majority has since grown to accept it and learned to manipulate its route according to their interests. Mostly, they have managed to radicalize the project, making it more invasive, encapsulating more settlements and even areas meant for the potential expansion of already existing settlements. Palestinian inhabitants of the 'seam-line' – the area around the route of the Wall – and political activists have brought the anguish of Palestinians to international attention. The American administration limited Israeli territorial appetite and demanded modifications to its path and rerouting in several places. The Israeli High Court of Justice called for 'proportionality' between the state 'security' needs and Palestinian human rights, and allowed no other consideration to be taken into account, ordering, in cases where other considerations were blatantly present, the dismantling of sections of the Wall and the rerouting of its path. Changing governments and coalitions have caused yet more transformations. It sometimes seems as if the Israeli state was acting out its social and political conflicts in a tug-of-war over the Wall's route.

The diffused 'authorship' of the project was made possible by its 'elasticity' – a category that does not imply the built Wall's physical softness or pliability, but rather that the outline of the project has continuously accommodated political pressures of various kinds into its changing path. Complex political processes do not of course fully articulate themselves in formal and material organization, but the Wall's changing layouts can potentially reveal the micro-structure of the conflicts that saturate its environments, and thus add a significant layer to our understanding of the nature of the political force-field of the late occupation. In this chapter, the changing contours of the Wall's path will be read as the design of its many and various 'architects'.

Political shaping forces

In April 2002, while military bulldozers were carving new roadways through the refugee camp of Jenin, and with all other major Palestinian cities under military control, Sharon 'surrendered' to public pressure and to the demands of the Labor ministers in his unity government, and announced his decision to construct what he called 'the seam-line obstacle'. His initial intention was a 'security area' – a deep fortified zone rather than a fortified line. The decision was approved by the government – although the exact nature of the project was clear neither to them nor to the general public. Two months later, in June 2002, Defence Minister Binyamin Ben-Eliezer cut the ribbon on the first phase of the Wall's construction – a 4-kilometre long and 100-metre wide sequence of various fortifications and sensors – in the north of the West Bank along the east-facing slopes of an olive orchard, between the Palestinian-Israeli village of Salem and the Jenin region. At the centre of the fortification system stood a 3-metre-high touch-sensitive 'smart fence', immediately west of it ran a trace road where foot-prints of intruders could be imprinted, while along patrol roads, trenches and pyramid-sectioned barbed-wire fences stretched on both sides.

The idea of a separation barrier between Israel and the West Bank had first been proposed some years earlier, in 1999, by Prime Minister Ehud Barak and Minister of Internal Affairs Haim Ramon, via Barak's Oslo era 'Peace Bureau'. The idea was founded on the following assumption: if a final status agreement could be reached with the Palestinians along Israel's proposed territorial outlines, all well and good – the barrier would stand on undisputed state land. If, however, an agreement could not be reached, Israel would be ready for unilateral separation. Immediately after the collapse of the Camp David talks in July 2000, Barak, pursuing unilateral separation, proposed two barriers, one along the international Green Line and the other deep within the West Bank, meandering around settlement blocks and separating them from the Palestinian towns and villages next to them.

Although in the spring of 2002 it might have appeared that Sharon was bowing to military contingencies and political pressures by transforming his politics of territorial expansion, and adopting the proposals of his political rivals, his initial route for the Wall suggested otherwise. He did not at first like the idea of parti-tion, but he believed that if somebody had to do it there was no better man for the job than he. When the project was under construction, Sharon fell in love with the very act of its creation, becoming again 'Sharon the Bulldozer', spending hours studying maps and plans, cruising the terrain from the air and on the ground, trekking from hill to hill with the large entourage of security personnel and reporters who hung on his every word, theatrically drawing rough outlines on nylon-covered maps ('I want everybody to pay attention to what I do here') or tracing imaginary paths against the horizon with his finger. The first path drawn by Sharon incorporated roughly half of the West Bank.[5] In these plans, the Wall was routed not only to the west of the Palestinian-populated mountain region, but also behind, east of it, through the western slopes of the Jordan Valley. The plan Sharon presented to the public showed a redrawing of the contours of the settlement plan he had prepared with architect Avraham Wachman back in 1977 as the 'Double Column' or the 'H' Plan.[6] According to the contem-

The Wall, Jerusalem region. Nir Kafri, 2005.

porary variation of this scheme – different segments of the Wall would enclose several discrete enclaves of Palestinian territory around each of the major West Bank cities. Moreover, the plan ensured that the Palestinians would not only be surrounded on the terrain's surface, but would also be enveloped vertically, both above and below. Israel would keep effective control over the mountain aquifer beneath the Palestinian areas, and of the airspace above them. Gradually – as and when political and security circumstances 'allow' – this archipelago of sealed enclaves would become what the George Bush-sponsored 'roadmap' called the 'Palestinian state within temporary borders' – a 'soft' Palestinian sovereignty within temporary borders which the Palestinians, if they so desired, would be free to call a state.[7] However, as Sharon and the government soon came to realize, different political pressures impacted on the planned route. As the following months began to reveal the horrific impact of the Wall on the daily lives of Palestinians, a diffused global campaign waged via the UN, the Israeli High Court of Justice, local and international NGOs, the International Court of Justice, the media, and scores of foreign governments acting along visible or backstairs diplomatic channels managed to deflect the sweep of the lines drawn on Sharon's original plan. European leaders demanded the cancellation of the project and American officials proposed significant reroutings. The American administration was particularly 'worried' by the loop designed to encapsulate the rapidly expanding

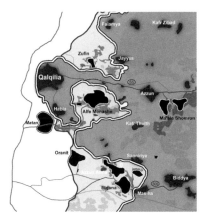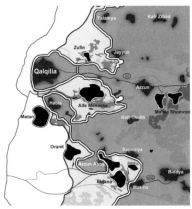

The path of the Wall in Qalqilya region. Left: Government-approved path, August 2002. Right: Approved path March 2003, completed July 2003 (Israeli settlements outlined in white).

settler towns of Ariel and Karnei Shomron in the centre of the West Bank, east of the Tel Aviv metropolitan region, and even threatened to reduce loan guarantees as a penalty if construction went ahead.[8]

In response to political criticism, Tirza claimed that the detailed path of the Wall he had drawn up using Sharon's outlines was not designed in accordance with political considerations – such as the desire to set a unilateral borderline – but was 'generated' as a mathematical (perhaps algorithmic) response to a variety of 'security' issues and geographical conditions. His detailed design of the Wall's path sought, he insisted, to optimize security considerations in terms of local geographical singularities and generate a path of maximum efficiency, allowing for what the military calls a line of 'topographic command and control' – a situation in which armed patrols could visually dominate the Palestinian towns and villages located on the other side of the barrier. As Tirza summed up: 'From a security perspective, mountains dominate valleys. To provide security, [the Wall] must control the high ground in order to dominate the area and not have others dominate us.'[9] Latitude is indeed an important tactical consideration in the positioning of fortification lines. According to the IDF's practice of border fortification and fencing, however, a defensible line should not run on top of a mountain ridge but at about three-quarters of its height, on the slope facing the threat. The reason for this is to prevent the silhouettes of military patrols driving along the ridge from appearing against the background sky (driving slightly lower would make them disappear against the dark background of the ridge). It would also deny the enemy the possibility of accessing the summit and looking over the hill into Israeli territory. The military naturally prefers fencing systems to concrete walling as fences allow soldiers to see and shoot through them. Concrete walling is, however, the default option when the Wall is routed through urban environments without 'tactical depth', and when Palestinian areas have a direct line of sight (and fire) to Israeli settlements or roads. Because patrol roads run along the Wall's length, its path must also conform to the limitations of vehicular movements, one of which is a maximum gradient no steeper than nine degrees. According to Tirza, the detailed design for the route of the Wall was generated by a calculation that took into account these factors in relation to the topography of the western slopes of the West Bank, the density and distribution of settlements, their infrastructure and the location of Palestinian villages. The claim that the Wall followed the 'ideal' path from a purely security perspective formed the Israeli state's most prominent argument when the Israeli High Court of Justice was asked to rule on various segments of the Wall. Both Israeli and international law tend to tolerate acts defined according to the logic of security.

Notwithstanding Tirza's explanations, the Wall's route was influenced by other considerations. In fact, at the beginning of 2006, Tirza was severely reprimanded by the High Court of Justice (and suspended from his job) for misleading it during a case brought before it by a Palestinian whose land was requisitioned. Tirza had 'forgotten' to mention that the section of the Wall in question was routed to incorporate an area designed for the planned expansion of several settlements and where several real estate investors had a vested interest.

The first attempts to influence the route of the Wall came from a variety of settlement lobby groups. As the Wall drew closer to their region, settlement councils started to apply political pressure for the route to loop around their communities and absorb them into the safer, 'Israeli' side of the Wall. However, settlers also created pressure in ways other than lobbying. The logic behind the recent frenzy of outpost construction in the West Bank lies in the settlers' desire to influence the Wall's path by seeding the terrain with 'anchor points' around which it might loop. The settling of outposts east of the settlement-town of Ariel was an attempt to create settlement continuity that would force the Wall even deeper into the West Bank.[10] A particularly strong outcry came from the settlement of Alfei-Menashe, a relatively wealthy suburban community of 5,000 residents, a quarter of an hour's drive east of Tel Aviv metropolitan region. It was the first settlement to lobby the government and has since encouraged a number of other settlement councils to do the same. Plans authorized in June 2002 for the northern path of the Wall left Alfei-Menashe 'outside' it, on the eastern, Palestinian side. Local panic about being 'abandoned' was mediated through political pressure and ultimata from right-wing ministers in the government. The head of the settlement council, Eliezer Hisdai, opposed the Wall on ideological grounds, as he believed its presence would curtail the Zionist project of expansion, but he also knew his settlers wanted protection. He tagged along with one of Sharon's mediatized West Bank tours and pleaded with him, in front of running TV cameras, to run the Wall around his settlement. On the spot, aware of the cameras, but unaware of the complicated implications, and that such a move ran contrary to military opinion, Sharon announced that Alfei-Menashe would be incorporated into the 'Israeli' side of the Wall, a decision that forced Tirza's office to revise the path and to extend a loop to envelop and incorporate the settlement. This loop meant, however, that the road connecting Alfei-Menashe with Israeli territory also had to be rerouted to pass through the suburban community of Matan hugging the Green Line within Israeli territory.[11] The infuriated residents of Matan in turn decided to engage in a legal battle to protect their private community from becoming a thoroughfare for the residents of Alfei- Menashe. They assembled a powerful legal team that successfully petitioned against the routing of the road, resulting in yet another rerouting of both the path of the Wall and the road. As a result, the neighbouring Palestinian towns of Qalqilya and Habla, which were not engaged in lobbying and complicated legal battles, a few hundred metres apart as the crow flies, were cut apart and walled off in two sealed dead-end enclaves. Families were separated, children were cut off from their schools, residents from services and shops – all in order to allow the settlers' road to pass safely between the two towns, and for the residents of Matan to complete their *schlafstunde* undisturbed a few hundred metres away.

A report jointly published at the end of 2005 by the human rights organization B'Tselem, and an Israeli planning rights group, Binkom, demonstrated that one of the primary reasons for the Wall's routing in the area of Alfei-Menashe was not only to surround and grab the settlements themselves, but also to grab hilltops intended for their expansion, and that this route was dictated at the expense of the very security principles, defined by the military, that formed the whole basis for the Wall's conception.[12] In some cases, the report claimed, reasons for routing reflected the interests of real estate companies with existing construction contracts on the land on which they had already made a large investment. The annexation of colonized lands had the potential to yield enormous profits. That there was much money to be made – or lost – by the routing of the Wall intensified the conflict over its path.[13] Indeed, following the principles of Israel's capitalist colonization, prices of properties left to the east of the Wall immediately lost 10–15 per cent of their value – in addition to a considerable drop in their prices following the outbreak of the second Intifada in September 2000.[14] In settlements left to the west of the Wall, as the Israeli historian and activist Gadi Algazi noted, 'real-estate developers could promise middle class Israelis the luxury and security of gated communities, with the local Palestinian inhabitants barricaded out of sight'.[15]

There were further influences on the route of the Wall. In 2003 religious parties succeeded in pressuring the government to alter its path south of Jerusalem. A small concrete loop, a few hundred metres in length, was formed which cut through the built fabric of Bethlehem in order to snatch and grab an archaeological site believed to be the biblical-era tomb of Rachel. On one occasion, when pressed by the High Court of Justice, Tirza was himself forced to admit that 'archeological factors generated changes in the route of the barrier'.[16] Indeed, ten archaeological sites, including one complete ancient Egyptian city, were unearthed when the Wall's foundations were dug, and in some cases the route was changed to incorporate these sites on the 'Israeli' side.[17]

In one particularly strange case, some of the residents of the settlement of Sal'it near the Green Line protested, without success, that the Wall's path separated them from the nearby village of Ar-Ras, where their Palestinian housemaids lived. Elsewhere, the desire to link the Wall with subsurface resources resulted in the incorporation of the water extraction points of the mountain aquifer 'inside' the Wall, while the desire to look after Israel's aerial interests led the Ministry of Defence to attempt to force a rerouting that would include those areas located within shoulder-missile range of the paths of international flights into Ben-Gurion airport.[18]

Along a ridge on the northern edge of the West Bank, one rerouting responded to pressure from Israeli environmentalists, who believed that the protection of a nature reserve of rare irises could only be guaranteed if it were to remain under Israeli control; they also argued that the Wall should not cut through the ancient forest of Abu Sudah, near Bethlehem, but run around it. In fact (and contrary to Gideon Harlap's assertions), some landscape considerations were taken into account, and architects were indeed involved in the project, mainly as landscape designers and advisers to the Department of Regional and Strategic Planning. The association of Israeli landscape designers published an article by one such architect, who claimed that 'although human security is the main consideration in the routing of the barrier, other considerations take into account the values of landscape and nature and their relation to topography . . . in many places the route has been changed to preserve special and sensitive areas like cliffs and springs or eagle nests . . . my hope is that the route of the separation barrier will become a landscape route in the state of Israel, a touristic route, crossing various kinds of landscapes'.[19] On the Israeli team responsible to the liberal, but unofficial, 'Geneva Initiative' – a blueprint for peace negotiated by teams of Israelis and Palestinians led by former ministers Yossi Beilin and Yasser Abed Rabbo – which proposed the path of separation to run through the centre of Jerusalem between Jewish and Palestinian neighbourhoods, was an architect named Ayala Ronel, who, besides being in charge of drawing the maps, proposed

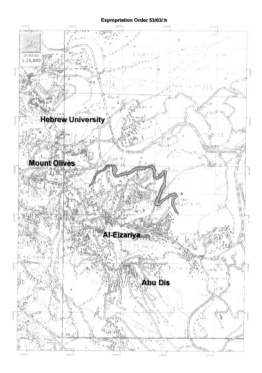

IDF expropriation order for land for the construction of the Wall in the area of Jerusalem.

'original' ideas for wall-like devices. These included camouflaging the partition as landscape elements or as thick vegetation. At some places, where Israel was to be bordered out of very striking landscapes, she envisaged transparent plastic partitions, while at others she suggested marking the border by terracing, generating height differences between one side and another, a kind of present day ha-ha, as conceived by England's romantic landscape designers to blend landscape and properties.

Al-Quds University President Sari Nusseibah, who still maintained good relations with Israeli politicians, managed to convince the government to order another rerouting of the planned path of the Wall in the eastern outskirts of Jerusalem, to avoid splitting the university in two and separating it from the rest of the city, although the revised path did separate the campus from the homes of many of the students on the other side of the Wall. However, few other Palestinians managed to force such reroutings when the Wall cut whole communities off from their schools and clinics. Along the built and proposed paths of the Wall, the fabric of Palestinian life has been completely deracinated, while the economy of the zone around the Wall has already ground to a stand-still. People have been separated from their farmland and water sources, from their families, friends and places of work, from recreation areas and universities. The visibly devastating effect of the Wall helped mobilize Palestinian, Israeli and international groups. The Popular Committee against the Wall was an organization of Palestinian farmers from the villages of Jayyous, Biddu, Dir Ballut and Budrus, who had lost their fields, orchards and vineyards to the wild meanderings of the Wall in the Modi'in area northwest of Jerusalem, near the northern Tel Aviv–Jerusalem road. Its members gathered every Friday, together with Israeli peace activists, in non-violent demonstrations in front of the developers' bull-dozers and the accompanying soldiers. At the beginning of 2006 they even set up an 'outpost', mimicking those of the settlers; but unlike settlers' outposts, they were immediately dispersed by the military.[20] The physical appearance of the Wall helped the opposition to the project gain further support from international organizations and private volunteers. Whereas the images of mundane, almost benign, red-roofed suburban settlements might not have been menacing enough to mobilize a global campaign, images of barbed-wire fencing and high concrete walls cutting through pastoral olive orchards, wheatfields and vineyards, or through the fabric of towns and cities, brought home the plight of Palestinians to an international audience. Beyond its impact on the ground, the Wall functioned very effectively as a powerful image within a media-economy of the conflict, one resonating within a Western historical imagination still engaged with unresolved memories of its colonial and Cold War legacies. The different semantics of the names given to the project – whether a 'fence', a 'wall', a 'Wall' or a 'barrier' – also played a major role.[21] It has also become particularly associated with the word 'apartheid', although even at the height of its barbarity, the South African regime never erected such a barrier.[22]

Constructing volatility

Throughout the process of the Wall's construction, the High Court of Justice has been an arena for these conflicts over its route. Responding to petitions submitted by Palestinians and Israeli civil rights groups against land requisition orders for the building of the Wall, the HCJ has so far ruled four times that the state must reroute several sections in order to take into account the negative impact it would have on the lives of Palestinians in the surrounding area. The legal principle followed by HCJ rulings on this matter was that of 'proportionality'. According to this principle, the state must find a route that balances security needs (which, controversially, also includes the security of the West Bank settlers) against the livelihood of the Palestinian inhabitants, and that no other consideration could be taken into account. The first petition ruled on June 2004 was the *Beit Sourik Village Council vs. The Government of Israel and the Commander of the IDF Forces in the West Bank*.[23] The HCJ ruled that some 30 kilometres of the Wall northwest of Jerusalem, between the settlements of Maccabim-Giveat Ze'ev and the Jerusalem–Modi'in–Tel Aviv road (Road 443), constructed on lands belonging to farmers from Beit Sourik, should be rerouted and the segments already built dismantled. Tirza, who was called upon to testify to the court, responded to a reporter's question by saying it was 'a dark day for the State of Israel'. He redrafted the entire route of the yet-to-be constructed sections of the Wall, ordering the rerouting of some sections that had already been built but were considered vulnerable to further petitions. However, other fortifications had to be built east of the Wall. The Israeli-only Road 443, now running on the eastern side of the Wall, itself became a massive barrier with high concrete elements running along both sides, and with all Palestinian entrances to it blocked by earth mounds. Although it later became clear that these were only Pyrrhic victories, the concentrated action of Palestinian activists and international diplomacy had for almost the first time been visibly effective in transforming the 'elastic' geography of Israeli domination.[24] To give a general idea, the 2002 route of the wall would de facto annex 900 square kilometres to Israel, about 16 per cent of the West Bank. (This figure includes only the western part of the Wall, not the one planned at the same time along the Jordan Valley – with the latter the figure would be closer to 50 per cent.) Estimates made at the end of 2006 put the figure at 360 square kilometres, about 6 per cent of the West Bank.[25]

In order to requisition land for the Wall's route, the government had to argue that the barrier was a 'temporary security measure' – a similar argument to that used by Israeli governments in the late 1970s to requisition land for settlement. On the Israeli Ministry of Defence website there is still an announcement stating that 'the anti-terrorist fence [the Wall] is a passive, *temporary* . . . measure, not a permanent border' (my emphasis) and that decisions regarding its nature and path are designed to address 'urgent security needs'.[26] This claim attempts to portray the Wall as an instrument of contingency in a temporary state of emergency. Barriers are indeed different to borders: they do not separate the 'inside' of a sovereign, political or legal system from a foreign 'outside', but act as contingent structures to prevent movement across territory. Such measures are legally tolerated precisely because they are temporary. However, the very logic of military rule in the West Bank and Gaza has always perpetuated itself through ever-new, seemingly 'temporary' facts.[27] It is the very definition of the occupation as 'temporary', and the definition of every violation of rights as merely 'temporary' evils, that has allowed Israeli society and its courts to ignore these ongoing acts.[28] When the government was challenged in court as to how such a massive construction could be considered 'temporary', it cited its various reroutings as proof that the Wall could be further rerouted and even removed altogether – when the 'security situation permits'. It was thus the 'elastic' property of the Wall that affirms its 'temporariness'. What the temporary 'state of emergency' is to time, this elasticity became to space. According to this principle the Israeli planning system has learned to use ever-developing and fast-transforming security threats to erect temporary security measures that can be explained at every stage as an ad hoc reaction, but which finally add up to comprise and embody a coherent strategic reality.

This use of 'temporariness' as a legal measure exposes the underlying paradox behind Israel's system of domination and control: in order to pacify the territories, 'temporary' security measures must be employed, but since the Palestinians rebel against the very security measures (the settlements) that were originally put in place to pacify them, further 'temporary' security measures (the Wall) are erected to manage the radicalizing resistance and violence, and so forth. The definition of all Israeli military activities as responses to security threats therefore perpetuates the condition that justifies their further deployment.[29] Violence becomes a necessary condition for the constant application of seemingly ad hoc but actually strategic security measures, and is the very justification for the suspension of state budgetary constraints and the allocation of massive funds for the purpose of security. The combination of security emergencies and economic recession during the early years of the second Intifada prepared the ground for the radical budget restructuring and the deep cuts in government spending (on all public projects but security) that typified the neo-liberal reforms promoted in 2002 by Minister of Finance Benjamin Netanyahu. Revealingly, Netanyahu called the first such plan 'Economic Defensive Shield', insinuating that neo-liberal restructuring must be seen as an emergency measure comparable to the military operation 'Defensive Shield' of April 2002, which led to the destruction of the institutions of the Palestinian Authority and of many Palestinian urban areas, and which was extremely popular in Israel.[30]

The changes to the Wall's route imposed by the HCJ managed to alleviate slightly the harsh living conditions of Palestinian communities along its path. In relieving pain and suffering any action is commendable and must be supported; however, as the legal scholar Aeyal Gross has pointed out, the regime behind the Wall has gained judicial and moral legitimacy as a result of the HCJ rulings.[31] The Israeli HCJ's imposed 'improvements' in the path made the entire regime imposed by the Wall seemingly 'tolerable', or at least aimed to make it tolerable to the Palestinians. The moderating influence of the HCJ also helped the government withstand international

Left: Palestinian areas surrounded by the path of the Wall as planned in 2003. Right: projected path with 'depth barriers' and settlement fences.

media criticism, and in particular political demands that it abide by the Advisory Opinion of the International Court of Justice (ICJ) in The Hague. Handed out in July 2004, less than a month after the first rerouting case was ruled upon in Israel's HCJ, the ICJ statement declared the entire project, constructed on occupied lands, and the Wall's associated regime, to be in contravention of international law.[32] Because of the fierce international criticism, it was always in the interest of the Israeli government to resolve the humanitarian problems arising from the Wall's construction, thereby deflecting attention from the fundamental political and legal illegitimacy of the entire project. Although it often seemed as if the Israeli HCJ adopted a profoundly adversarial position towards the government, by amending segments of the route and 'balancing' human rights against security, the HCJ has effectively taken part in its design. Furthermore, when, in the aftermath of the rulings, the military itself began using the vocabulary of international law, principles such as 'proportionality' started to become compatible with military goals such as 'efficiency' and 'necessity', generating a more sustainable route for the Wall, helping make military action more economical.[33] Indeed, the frequent reroutings cost the government an extra $200 million, and Tirza was put under pressure to create a route that would be 'immune' to petitions.[34]

Danny Tirza himself paraded the 'humanitarian' approach he adopted at a late stage in the Wall's design:

> Israel's High Court of Justice said we had to give greater weight to the daily life of the Palestinians, so we changed the route in some places . . . We also understand that we have to take the needs of people into consideration, and we sometimes have to build new roads for the villagers. We have also replanted more than 90,000 trees in the area to try to minimize the damage to local farmers . . . [and] provided services for people living east of the fence. In one place we gave land for a school so pupils won't have to cross a checkpoint every day. In other places we have to build clinics so the population won't have to cross into Jerusalem. We deal with these questions every day, everywhere along the fence . . .[35]

These statements, in which Tirza seems to have completely adopted the language and operational aims of humanitarianism, do not of course reflect a sense of altruism or care for the Palestinians; rather, they form part of a legal-moral rhetoric that attempts to pre-empt possible restrictions on or delays to the project. The 'lesser evil' approach towards the villagers thus allowed a 'greater evil' to be imposed on the Palestinian people as a whole.

From the perspective of those opposing it, the 'elastic' nature of the Wall is thus simultaneously empowering and frustrating. It is empowering because bringing pressure to bear on the route, in protests and court petitions, has been demonstrated to alleviate conditions on the ground, and further pressure may be effective in pushing the Wall further westwards, closer to the international border of the Green Line and making marginally more tolerable the lives of Palestinians who are suffocating under the weight of its regime. However, the principle of 'elasticity' is also frustrating because it demonstrates that any action directed against the Wall's route, rather than against its very concept, presence and essence (the approach the ICJ has taken), not only legitimizes it and confirms it as a fact, but effectively takes part in its making – the frontier continually remoulds itself to absorb and accommodate opposition, which gradually becomes part of its discourse and contributes to its efficiency. Oppositional action has therefore played a part in the collective, albeit diffused, authorship of the architecture of the Wall.

Extraterritorial islands

As international pressure against the Wall mounted, so did the pressure of the settlers' lobbies for more intrusive routing for the incorporation of their settlements 'inside' the Wall. In a curious role reversal, after several High Court of Justice cases were won and the route of the Wall altered to a less injurious path, the settlers themselves started appealing against route changes. Using language similar to that which won the Palestinian cases, they started claiming that the new path would now leave them – the settlers – landlocked within isolated enclaves, 'separated from their land, work and services'.[36] At one small section along Road 443, northwest of Jerusalem, where the Wall was adjusted to a route less injurious to Palestinians, it was later rerouted again due to the counter-petitions of Jewish settlers.

The political forces around the Wall started echoing each other in a loop of ever-radicalizing feedback. But pressure from settlers' groups to incorporate many settlements within loops in the Wall, together with the military intention to route the Wall through strategically important territory, were not compatible with the diplomatic and legal pressures to place it as close as possible to the internationally recognized Green Line. No longer able to translate the intensely contradictory force-field into a complex, albeit linear, geometry, the Wall also ceased being a singular, contiguous object, and broke into separate shards, fragments and discontinuous vectors. Like a worm sliced into segments each assuming a renewed life, the fragments of the Wall started to curl around isolated settlement blocks and along the roads connecting them. Each of these separate segments, dubbed 'depth barriers' by the Ministry of Defence, comprised a sequence of fortifications and sensors similar to that of the main section of the Wall, and were designed to provide specific material responses to the 'local security problems' that could not be addressed by the main, linear section. In September 2004, the fragmentation of the Wall's route prompted the Israeli government to release an apparently contradictory statement, in which four major settlements, Ariel, Emanuel, Qedumim and Karnei Shomron, housing about 50,000 settlers on the western slopes of the West Bank, 'would be on the Israeli side of the barrier [the Wall] . . . but the barrier would not be connected to the main section'.[37] These, as well as other large settlement blocks, would become Israeli 'extraterritorial islands' within Palestinian space. With public attention, demonstrators and clashes directed exclusively on the visible, linear part of the Wall, its offspring 'depth barriers' remained largely invisible to international criticism. In fact, the further west the opposition succeeded in moving the Wall's path, the more 'depth barriers' were constructed to resolve security problems left within the depth of the territory, the more fragmented the West Bank terrain effectively became, and the more disrupted life has become for Palestinians. A pact of convenience has seemingly been established between Israel and international opposition to the Wall: Israel will move the main section of the Wall closer to the Green Line,

Left: Underpass connecting the two parts of Palestinian Beit-Tzafafa, under the road connecting Jerusalem city centre with the neighbourhood of Gilo. Eyal Weizman, 2001. Right: Underpass connecting Habla to Qalqilya under the settler-only road to Alfei Menashe. OCHA, 2005.

following HCJ guidelines, but will not be censured over the series of politically invisible barriers it places in depth.

Although none of the maps released by the media or independent right organization actually shows it, and all photographs of it depict a linear object resembling a border (and which all foreigners from territorially defined nation states will immediately understand as such), the Wall has in fact become a discontinuous and fragmented series of self-enclosed barriers that can be better understood as a prevalent 'condition' of segregation – a shifting frontier – rather than one continuous line neatly cutting the territory in two. With the rapid multiplication of 'depth barriers' the face of the territory has grown to resemble maps more redolent of Scandinavian coastlines, where fjords, islands and lakes make an inconclusive separation between water and land.

Current projections of the Wall's route leave fifty-five settlements, twelve of them Jewish neighbourhoods in East Jerusalem, contiguous with Israeli territory on the inside of the Wall.[38] In Jerusalem the Wall did not separate Israelis from Palestinians but Palestinians from Palestinians. Sharon, fearing accusations about 'partitioning the city' included within the Wall around Jerusalem most of the Palestinian neighbourhoods that belong to the municipal area.

More than a hundred settlements, however, are left east of the main section of the Wall; since the start of the second Intifada, about 700 kilometres of fencing have been built around these settlements – totalling about the same projected length as the main section of the Wall. The settlement islands encircled by 'depth barriers' were declared by the IDF to be 'special security zones' and the area extending 400 metres around them to be 'sterile'. Beyond the hygiene neurosis suggested by the term, its definition means that the military and the settlements' civil militias may, without warning, shoot-to-kill any Palestinian who happens to stray into these zones.[39]

Several dozen Palestinian villages with a total population of around 60,000 inhabitants were trapped in enclaves west of the Wall, between it and the Green Line. In October 2003, the IDF declared these Palestinian enclaves 'closed military zones', enforcing this arbitrary new status with extra barriers between the enclaves and the Green Line. Simultaneously, IDF orders have forced on their residents the new legal status of 'temporary residents', which prevents them from entering either Israel in the west or the rest of the West Bank to the east without special permits. Together with those Palestinians left on the 'Israeli' side of the Wall in Jerusalem, altogether about 250,000 Palestinians will be trapped in this inter-border zone.

The result of the Wall's fragmented route is a mutual extraterritoriality, a condition of double enclosure. Settlements in the 'special security zones', like the Palestinian communities in the 'closed military zones', are territorial 'islands' physically and legally estranged from their immediate surroundings. Under this arrangement, the traditional perception of political space as a contiguous territorial surface, delimited by continuous borderlines, is no longer relevant.

The function of the respective barriers that enclose these islands must not be confused, however. The walls around 'Israeli islands', where Israeli law applies, are meant to protect the lives of settlers and exclude a threatening exterior. Gates within the fences open onto protected fast and wide traffic corridors, effectively integrating the settlers economically and politically with Israel. The fences, walls, ditches, dykes and all sorts of other territorial apparatuses and inventions placed around Palestinian territorial islands, on the other hand, are conceived to prohibit 'security threats' from leaking out.[40] By designating and constraining habitats, by physically marking out the limit of different legal jurisdictions, these barriers function mainly as administrative apparatuses of population control. More than merely a fortification system, they became bureaucratic-logistical devices for the creation and maintenance of a demographic separation.

The Israeli fantasy of separation seeks to create a defensible and homogeneous Israeli political space that will guarantee, if not protection from Palestinian attacks, a space of Jewish demographic majority and control. Why is this fantasy? Because although unilateral evacuation of more settlements was discussed until very recently, mainly in the context of Prime Minister Ehud Olmert's now discarded unilateral 'realignment plan' (the name of which inadvertently confirmed the elasticity of the Wall), no Israeli government has ever displayed the desire or the political resolve to dismantle the large blocks of settlement-islands within the West Bank or the Jewish neighbourhoods in the annexed part of Jerusalem.[41]

Their future incorporation into Israeli territory was furthermore implicit in a letter sent by President Bush to Ariel Sharon in April 2004.[42] Without these evacuations the terrain would remain fragmented and non-contiguous. Although, and perhaps because, the Wall is unable to create a contiguous political border, it attempts to display the reassuring iconography of one. Notwithstanding the constant shifting of its route, in its massive physical presence that has made it the largest and most expensive project in the history of the state, the Wall seeks to appear as a heavily fortified border. The illusion that with a set of unilaterally fortified lines reinforced with concrete, barbed wire and surveillance technology, Israel and Palestine could both become ordinary, territorially defined nation states, disguises the violent reality of a shifting colonial frontier.[43]

Hollowed land

After the Wall has coalesced around a permanently temporary Palestinian state, scattered in an archipelago of landlocked 'sovereign zones', and itself further perforated with islands of state-claimed Israeli territory, yet another paradox will have to be resolved. The fragmentation of Palestinian jurisdiction is apparently incompatible with Sharon's public pledge of 2003, and his assurances to President Bush in 2004, that with the implementation of the Bush-sponsored 'roadmap', he will carve out a 'contiguous area of territory in the West Bank that would allow the Palestinians to travel from Jenin [the northernmost city in the West Bank] to Hebron [the southernmost] without passing any Israeli roadblocks'. When bewildered reporters asked how the two apparently contradictory terms of continuity and fragmentation could be accommodated within a single territorial reality, Sharon responded (probably with one of his notorious winks) that this would be accomplished with a 'combination of tunnels and bridges'.[44]

If this type of continuity – first given substance by Sharon in 1996 when, as Minister of National Infrastructure under Benjamin Netanyahu, he inaugurated the 'Tunnel Road' – cannot be achieved on the surface of the terrain alone, it must be accomplished in three dimensions. The 'Tunnel Road' connects Jewish Jerusalem with the West Bank settlement of Gush Etzion and, further south, with the Jewish settlements of Hebron. As it leaves Jerusalem it cuts a straight line through mountains and valleys much like the nineteenth-century colonial routes designed by the engineers of France's School of Highways and Bridges (to tame an arbitrary nature and express the 'Cartesian logic' of the empire and the goals of Reason). To accomplish this feat in Palestine, the 'Tunnel Road' performs a double contortion: it spans as a bridge over Palestinian-cultivated valleys, and dives into a tunnel under the Palestinian town of Beit Jalla. Meron

A reconstruction of the path of the Wall around the Tunnel Road. Daniel Bauer, 2003 (illustration by Eyal Weizman, 2004).

Benvenisti, who first wrote about this 'engineering wonder', described its territorial effects as the 'crashing of three dimensions into six: three Israeli and three Palestinian'.[45] Although the road is under Israeli control, both the valley it spans and the city it runs beneath are areas under Palestinian control. As the road threads itself through this folded, topographical arrangement of different jurisdictions, Israeli territory finds itself alternately above and below the Palestinian. This physical separation of transport infrastructure also cuts through the territorial labyrinth created by the Oslo Accords. The tunnel and bridge are under full Israeli control (Area C), the valley below the bridge is under Palestinian civilian control (Area B), while the city above the tunnel is under Palestinian civilian and military control (Area A). When the bridge's columns rest on Palestinian ground, the 'border' runs, presumably, through the thermodynamic joint between the column and the beams.[46]

Following this principle of partition in three dimensions, the Department of Regional and Strategic Planning conceived of a mesh of two parallel road networks throughout the West Bank, separated along national lines, to be inaugurated with 'a pilot' of thirty-five roads. At places where two road networks cross, a vertical interchange of bridges and tunnels will separate the traffic systems, and Palestinians from Israelis. Twenty-six such interchanges of vertical separation have already been constructed; the other nineteen are currently being planned or are under construction.[47] The neighbouring West

Bank towns of Habla and Qalqilya, cut apart by the Wall into two separate enclaves in 2003, were reconnected the following year according to this principle by a subterranean tunnel constructed by Ministry of Defence contractors, running under the Wall and the Israeli road.

Danny Tirza explained this logic of separation by saying that 'the dangerous friction' between the settlers and the Palestinians 'could be reduced if certain interchanges enabled Palestinians to enter the area from one side [and settlers from another]. We would drive above and they would drive below, and vice versa.'[48] This separation of the road system is a complementary project to that of the Wall. It facilitates the possibility of contiguous walled-out Palestinian territories without the need to evacuate the Israeli settlements. Although the traffic networks pass by each other, the physical arrangements deny even the possibility of a cognitive encounter. According to Tirza, Israelis should be able to travel through the upper highways 'without even noticing the Palestinian traffic underneath'.[49]

Indeed, Israelis driving along Road 443 from Tel Aviv via Modi'in to Jerusalem pass through a section of the road surrounded by high concrete walls on both sides. In 2004, the road became a border itself, and the concrete walls lining its sides, while painted with idealized images of the surrounding landscape, were raised to protect the passengers from the perils of the real landscape. These walls also conceal from Israeli commuters the fact that this part of the road is a bridge that spans an entire Palestinian village – Al-Muwahil (or the Mud Neighbourhood).[50]

Another of the most ambitious instruments of vertical separation is the new Jerusalem eastern ring road, currently under construction. The road is a bottleneck in the system, serving both settlers and Palestinians (the latter would have to use it when travelling from Bethlehem to Ramallah, because they are not allowed into walled-off Jerusalem). The road is split down its centre by a high concrete wall, dividing it into separate Israeli and Palestinian lanes. It extends across three bridges and three tunnels before ending in a complex volumetric knot that untangles in mid-air, channelling Israelis and Palestinians separately along different spiralling flyovers that ultimately land them on their respective sides of the Wall.[51]

A new way of imagining space has emerged.[52] After fragmenting the surface of the West Bank by walls and other barriers, Israeli planners started attempting to weave it together as two separate but overlapping national geographies – two territorial networks overlapping across the same area in three dimensions, without having to cross or come together. One is an upper-land – the land of the settlements – a scattering of well-tended hilltop neighbourhoods woven together by modern highways for the exclusive use of its inhabitants; the other, Palestine – crowded cities, towns, and villages that inhabit the valleys between and underneath the hills, maintaining fragile connections on improvised underpasses.[53] Within this new political space, separate security corridors, infrastructure, bridges and underground tunnels have been woven into a bewildering and impossible Escher-like territorial arrangement that struggles to multiply a single territorial reality. However, in the over-complexity it requires, the system of tunnels and bridges clearly demonstrates the very limitation of the politics of separation. Out of the endless search for the forms and mechanisms of 'perfect' separation emerges the realization that a viable solution may not necessarily lie within the realm of territorial design.

IDF engineers in the refugee camp of Tulkarm. Nir Kafri, 2003.

7.

Urban Warfare: Walking Through Walls

I have long, indeed for years, played with the idea of setting out the sphere of life
– bios – graphically on a map. First I envisaged an ordinary map, but now I would
incline to a general staff's map of a city centre, if such a thing existed. Doubtless
it does not, because of the ignorance of the theatre of future wars.

Walter Benjamin[1]

I no longer know what there is behind the wall, I no longer know there is a wall,
I no longer know this wall is a wall, I no longer know what a wall is. I no longer
know that in my apartment there are walls, and that if there weren't any walls,
there would be no apartment.

Georges Perec[2]

Go inside, he ordered in hysterical broken English. Inside! – I am already inside!
It took me a few seconds to understand that this young soldier was redefining
inside to mean anything that is not visible, to him at least. My being 'outside' within
the 'inside' was bothering him.

Nuha Khoury[3]

The manoeuvre conducted by Israeli military units in April 2002 during the attack
on the West Bank city of Nablus, was described by its commander, Brigadier
General Aviv Kochavi, as 'inverse geometry', which he defined as the reorganization of the urban syntax by means of a series of micro-tactical actions. Soldiers
avoided using the streets, roads, alleys and courtyards that define the logic of
movement through the city, as well as the external doors, internal stairwells and
windows that constitute the order of buildings; rather, they were punching holes
through party walls, ceilings and floors, and moving across them through 100-
metre-long pathways of domestic interior hollowed out of the dense and
contiguous city fabric. Although several thousand Israeli soldiers and hundreds

Balata refugee camp. Nir Kafri, 2002.

of Palestinian guerrilla fighters were manoeuvring simultaneously in the town, they were saturated within its fabric to a degree that they would have been largely invisible from an aerial perspective at any given moment. This form of movement is part of a tactic that the military refers to, in metaphors it borrows from the world of aggregate animal formation, as 'swarming' and 'infestation'. Moving through domestic interiors, this manoeuvre turned inside to outside and private domains to thoroughfares. Fighting took place within half-demolished living rooms, bedrooms and corridors. It was not the given order of space that governed patterns of movement, but movement itself that produced space around it. This three-dimensional movement through walls, ceilings and floors through the bulk of the city reinterpreted, short-circuited and recomposed both architectural and urban syntax. The tactics of 'walking through walls' involved a conception of the city as not just the site, but as the very *medium* of warfare – a flexible, almost liquid matter that is forever contingent and in flux.

According to British geographer Stephen Graham, since the end of the Cold War a vast international 'intellectual field' that he calls a 'shadow world of military urban research institutes and training centres' has been established in order to rethink military operations in urban terrain.[4] The expanding network of these 'shadow worlds' includes military schools, as well as mechanisms for the exchange of knowledge between different militaries such as conferences, workshops and joint training exercises. In their attempt to comprehend urban life, soldiers take crash courses in order to master topics such as urban infrastructure, complex systems analysis, structural stability and building techniques, and study a variety of theories and methodologies developed within contemporary civilian academia. There is therefore a new relationship emerging within a triangle of interrelated components that this chapter seeks to examine: armed conflicts, the built environment and the theoretical language conceived to conceptualize them. The reading lists of some contemporary military institutions include works dating from around 1968 (in particular, the writings of those theorists who have expanded the notion of space, such as Gilles Deleuze, Félix Guattari and Guy Debord), as well as more contemporary avant-garde writings on urbanism and architecture that proliferated widely throughout the 1990s, and relied on postcolonial and post-structuralist theory. According to urban theorist Simon Marvin, the military-architectural 'shadow world' is currently generating more intense and better funded urban research programmes than all university programmes put together.[5] If some writers are right in claiming that the space for criticality has to some extent withered away in late twentieth-century capitalist culture, it surely seems to have found a place to flourish in the military.

Seeking out the destiny of the discipline of architecture in another – the military – this chapter will examine Israel's urban warfare strategies throughout the second Intifada, and the emergent relationship between post-modern critical theory, military practice and institutional conflicts within the IDF that it brought about; in analysing these developments it will also offer a reflection on the ethical and political repercussions of these practices.

Following global trends, in recent years the IDF has established several institutes and think-tanks at different levels of its command and has asked them to reconceptualize strategic, tactical and organizational responses to the brutal policing work in the Occupied Territories known as 'dirty' or 'low intensity' wars. Notable amongst these institutes is the Operational Theory Research Institute (OTRI), which operated throughout the decade extending from the beginning of 1996 to May 2006, under the co-directorship of Shimon Naveh and Dov Tamari, both retired brigadier generals. OTRI employed several other retired officers, all at the rank of brigadier general, from the different corps of the IDF. Besides ex-soldiers, it employed several young researchers, usually doctoral candidates in philosophy or political science from Tel Aviv University. Until 2003, its core course, 'Advanced Operational Approach', was obligatory for all high-ranking Israeli officers. In an interview I conducted with him, Naveh summed up the mission of OTRI: 'We are like the Jesuit order. We attempt to teach and train soldiers to think . . . We have established a school and developed a curriculum that trains "operational architects".'[6] Former Chief of Staff Moshe Ya'alon, who promoted the activities of OTRI, described the significance of the institute after its closure in May 2006: 'The method of operational assessment that is used today in the Regional Commands and in the General Staff was developed in collaboration with OTRI . . . OTRI also worked with the Americans and taught them the methods we had developed.' The collaboration between OTRI and the US armed forces was confirmed by Lt. Col. David Pere of the US Marine Corps, who is now writing the corps' 'operational doctrine manual': 'Naveh and OTRI's influence on the intellectual discourse and understanding of the operational level of war in the US has been immense. The US Marine Corps has commissioned a study . . . that is largely based on Shimon [Naveh]'s [work]. One can hardly attend a military conference in the US without a discussion of Shimon's [work] . . .' According to Pere, the British and Australian militaries are also integrating the concepts developed at OTRI into their formal doctrines.[7]

One of the main reasons why Israeli military doctrine on urban operations became so influential among other militaries is that Israel's conflict with the Palestinians since the Intifada has had a distinct urban dimension. The targets of both Palestinian and Israeli attacks were primarily the cities of the other. Israel's new methods of ground and aerial raids were honed during the second (Al-Aqsa) Intifada and especially in 'Operation Defensive Shield', the series of military raids on Palestinian cities launched on 29 March 2002, following a spate of Palestinian suicide attacks in Israeli cities. The attacks targeted different kinds of Palestinian urban environments: a modern city in Ramallah; a dense historic city centre in the Kasbah of Nablus; an international holy city in Bethlehem; and the refugee camps of Jenin, Balata and Tulkarm. The urban setting of these attacks was the reason they were keenly observed by foreign militaries, in particular those of the USA and UK, as they geared up to invade and occupy Iraq.[8] Indeed, during 'Operation Defensive Shield' the West Bank has become a giant laboratory of urban warfare at the expense of hundreds of civilian lives, property, and infrastructure.

In my interview with Naveh, he explained the conditions that led the Israeli military to change its methods during the early years of the second Intifada: 'Although so much is invested in intelligence, fighting in the city is still incalculable and messy. Violence makes events unpredictable and prone to chance. Battles cannot be scripted. Command cannot have an overview. Decisions to act must be based on chance, probability, contingency and opportunity, and these must be taken only on the ground and in real time.'[9] Indeed, as far as the military is concerned, urban warfare is the ultimate post-modern form of warfare. Belief in a logically structured and single-track battle plan is lost in the face of the

Path of IDF attack on Nablus, April 2002. Diagram: OTRI, 2004.

complexity and ambiguity of the urban mayhem. Those in command find it difficult to draw up battle scenarios or single-track plans; civilians become combatants, and combatants become civilians again; identity can be changed as quickly as gender can be feigned: the transformation of a civilian woman into a militant can occur at the speed that it takes an undercover 'Arabized' Israeli soldier or a camouflaged Palestinian fighter to pull a machine gun out from under a dress.

Indeed, military attempts to adapt their practices and forms of organization has been inspired by the guerrilla forms of violence that confront it. Because they adapt, mimic and learn from each other, the military and the guerrillas enter a cycle of 'co-evolution'. Military capabilities evolve in relation to the resistance, which itself evolves in relation to transformations in military practice. Although the mimicry and reappropriation of military techniques represent the discourse of a common experience, the Israeli and Palestinian methods of fighting are fundamentally different. The fractured Palestinian resistance is composed of a multiplicity of organizations, each having a more or less independent armed wing

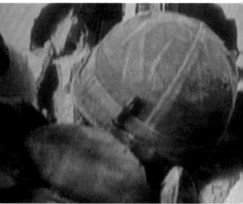

– *Iz Adin al-Qassam* for Hamas, *Saraya al-Quds* (the Jerusalem Brigades) for Islamic Jihad, *Al-Aqsa Martyrs Brigade, Force-17* and *Tanzim al-Fatah* for Fatah. These are supplemented by the independent *PRC* (Popular Resistance Committees) and imagined or real members of *Hizbollah* and/or *Al-Qaeda*. The fact that these organizations shift between cooperation, competition and violent conflict increases the general complexity of their interactions and with it their collective capacity, efficiency and resilience. The diffused nature of Palestinian resistance, and the fact that knowledge, skills and munitions are transferred within and between these organizations – and that they sometimes stage joint attacks and at others compete to outdo each other – substantially reduces the effect that the Israeli occupation forces seek to achieve by attacking them.

According to Naveh, a central category in the IDF conception of the new urban operations is 'swarming' – a term that has, in fact, been part of US military theory for several decades. It was developed in the context of the Revolution in Military Affairs (RMA) after the end of the Cold War and in particular in the doctrine of Network Centric Warfare which conceptualized the field of military operations as distributed network-systems, woven together by information technology.[10] Swarming seeks to describe military operations as a network of diffused multiplicity of small, semi-independent but coordinated units operating in general synergy with all others.

According to the RAND Corporation theorists David Ronfeldt and John Arquilla, who are credited with much of the development of this military concept, the main assumption of low-intensity conflict, particularly in cities, is that 'it takes a network to combat a network'.[11] The term is in fact derived from the Artificial Intelligence principle of 'swarm intelligence'. This principle assumes

Breaking through walls. Film Stills, IDF, 2002.

that problem-solving capacities are found in the interaction and communication of relatively unsophisticated agents (ants, birds, bees, soldiers) without (or with minimal) centralized control. 'Swarm intelligence' thus refers to the overall, combined intelligence of a system, rather than to the intelligence of its constituent parts. A swarm 'learns' through the interaction of its constitutive elements, through their adaptation to emergent situations, and in reaction to changing environments.[12]

Instead of linear, hierarchical chains of command and communications, swarms are polycentric networks, in which each 'autarkic unit' (Naveh's term) can communicate with the others without necessarily going through central command. The swarm manoeuvre is perceived by the military as non-linear in *temporal* terms as well. Traditional military operations are chrono-linear in the sense that they seek to follow a determined sequence of events embodied in the idea of 'the plan' which implies that actions are preconditioned to some degree on the successful implementation of previous actions. The activity of a swarm, by contrast, is based upon simultaneous actions which are dependent but not preconditioned on each other. The narrative of the battle plan is thus replaced by what Naveh calls 'the toolbox' approach, according to which units receive the tools they need to deal with emergent situations and scenarios, but cannot predict the order by which these events would actually occur. By lowering the thresholds of decision-making to the immediate tactical level, and by the encouragement of local initiative, different parts of the swarm are supposed to provide answers to the forms of uncertainty, chance and uncontrolled eventualities that the nineteenth-century military philosopher Carl von Clausewitz called *friction*.[13]

The concept of the swarm is a central component of the Israeli military's

Left: Balata refugee camp, IDF image, 2002. Right: Nablus, Miki Kratsman, 2002.

concerted attempt to adopt the language of 'de-territorialization' and transform what they perceived as their organizational and tactical 'linearity' into 'non-linearity'. In this regard, a major historical reference for the teaching of OTRI was the military career of Ariel Sharon. Not only was Sharon the prime minister, and thus visible as the 'commander in chief' throughout most of the Intifada, but his military career[14] has been characterized by attempts to break away from traditional military organization and discipline. The tactics for punitive raids on Palestinian villages and refugee camps that he developed and exercised in 1953 as commander of Unit 101, and later those that enabled his brutal counter-insurgency campaign in the Gaza refugee camps in 1971–72, in many ways prefigured Israeli tactics in dealing with the present Intifada. An indication of the historical interest that OTRI had in Sharon's military career was the last work-shop organized at OTRI in May 2006, 'The Generalship of Ariel Sharon', which was a form of homage to the dying Sharon, and his influence on the IDF.[15]

The attack on Balata

The Israeli security establishment has always tended to see the refugee camps as both the locus of and the urban condition for the 'breeding' of resistance. The camps have thus been projected in Israel's simplified geographic imaginary as evil and dangerous places, 'black holes' that the IDF dare not enter.[16] The IDF's avoidance of the Jenin and Balata refugee camps throughout the first (1987–91) and second intifadas allowed them to evolve into extraterritorial enclaves surrounded by Israeli military power; indeed, the military codename for the Jenin camp, in which resistance groups were most strongly entrenched, was 'Germania'. Whether in reference to Tacitus' ambivalent description of the barbarians,[17] or in reference to the Nazi regime, this term encapsulates Israeli fear of the 'evil' it believes is bred. After becoming prime minister in March 2001, Ariel Sharon persistently mocked the military for not daring to enter the refugee camps: 'What is happening in the Jenin and Balata camps? Why don't you go in?' Sharon never tired of telling military officers how, in the 1970s, he 'made order' in the refugee camps of Gaza with a combination of commando raids, assassinations and bulldozers.[18]

The method of 'walking through walls' employed by the IDF in the attacks of 'Operation Defensive Shield' had already been part of its tactical manual in matters of small-scale operations and arrests where the doorway of a home was suspected of being booby-trapped. However, as the defining mode of military manoeuvre in large-scale operations, it was first tested out in early March 2002 in a raid commanded by Aviv Kochavi of the paratroop brigade on the refugee camp of Balata at the eastern entrance of Nablus, just a few weeks before Operation Defensive Shield commenced. It was employed in response to tactical necessity. In anticipation of an impending Israeli attack, militants from different Palestinian armed organizations had blocked all entries to the refugee camp, filling oil barrels with cement, digging trenches and piling up barricades of rubble. Streets were mined with improvised explosives and tanks of gasoline, and entrances to buildings on these routes were booby-trapped, as were the interior stairwells, doorways and corridors of some prominent structures. Several lightly armed independent guerrilla groups were positioned within the camp in houses facing major routes or at major intersections.

In a briefing called by Kochavi prior to the attack, he explained to his subordinate officers the problems they would encounter in the impending operation. Kochavi apparently told his officers (as paraphrased by Naveh): 'The Palestinians have set the stage for a fighting spectacle in which they expect us, when attacking the enclave, to obey the logic that they have determined . . . to come in old-style mechanized formations, in cohesive lines and massed columns conforming to the geometrical order of the street network.' After analysing and discussing this situation with his officers, Kochavi included the following instruction in his battle command: 'We completely isolate the camp in daylight, creating the impression of a forthcoming systematic siege operation . . . [and then] apply a fractal manoeuvre swarming simultaneously from every direction and through various dimensions of the enclave . . . Each unit reflects in its mode of action both the logic and form of the general manoeuvre . . . Our movement through the buildings pushes [the insurgents] into the streets and alleys, where we hunt them down.'[19] Israeli troops then cut off electrical, telephone and water connections to the camp, positioned snipers and look-outs on the mountains and the high buildings surrounding the area, and cordoned off a large perimeter around the battle arena.[20] Soldiers departing from their assembly zones in the settlements of Har Bracha and Elon Moreh overlooking Nablus were greeted and hugged by the settlers. Divided into small units the soldiers then entered the refugee camp from all directions simultaneously, punching holes through walls and moving through the homes of civilians rather than along the routes where they were expected. They thus managed to take hold of the camp, but allowed the guerrillas to retreat.

For anyone who might imagine that moving through walls constitutes a relatively 'gentle' form of manoeuvre, it is worth describing the IDF's tactical procedures: soldiers assemble behind a wall. Using explosives or a large hammer, they break a hole large enough to pass through. Their charge through the wall is sometimes preceded by stun grenades or a few random shots into what is usually a private living room occupied by its unsuspecting inhabitants. When the soldiers have passed through the party wall, the occupants are assembled and, after they are searched for 'suspects', locked inside one of the rooms, where they are made to remain – sometimes for several days – until the military operation is concluded, often without water, sanitation, food or medicine. According to Human Rights Watch and the Israeli human rights organization B'Tselem, dozens of civilian Palestinians have died during the attacks.[21]

The Palestinian writer Adania Shibli described her visit to the Balata refugee camp and her meeting with Salma, an older lady, in the aftermath of the raid:

> She took us around to see the holes that the soldiers had left behind as the house was set suddenly on fire when the main electric cable was hit by shrapnel from a hand grenade that they threw into the house, and they ran away, leaving behind them a fire that burnt up the half-finished wreckage. Along with her children and grandchildren, she had been forced to evacuate the house when the army stormed in, but her husband remained nearby watching the house, and when he saw it burning he rushed over and tried in vain to put out the flames. He was asphyxiated and lost consciousness but did not die; just something happened to his brain because it didn't get enough oxygen for a long while, and he lost his mind.[22]

The unexpected penetration of war into the private domain of the home has been experienced by civilians in Palestine, just like in Iraq, as the most profound form of trauma and humiliation. Aisha, a Palestinian woman interviewed in the *Palestine Monitor* in the aftermath of the attack in November 2002, described the experience:

Imagine it – you're sitting in your living room, which you know so well; this is the room where the family watches television together after the evening meal . . . And, suddenly, that wall disappears with a deafening roar, the room fills with dust and debris, and through the wall pours one soldier after the other, screaming orders. You have no idea if they're after you, if they've come to take over your home, or if your house just lies on their route to somewhere else. The children are screaming, panicking . . . Is it possible to even begin to imagine the horror experienced by a five-year-old child as four, six, eight, twelve soldiers, their faces painted black, submachine guns pointed everywhere, antennas protruding from their backpacks, making them look like giant alien bugs, blast their way through that wall?'

Pointing to another wall now covered by a bookcase, she added: 'And this is where they left. They blew up the wall and continued to our neighbour's house.'[23]

The ability of Israeli soldiers to 'occupy' the Balata refugee camp led IDF Central Command (in charge of the West Bank) to adopt this form of manoeuvre as the mode of attack on Nablus old city centre (the Kasbah) and the Jenin refugee camp, which commenced on 3 April 2002.

An Israeli soldier described to me the beginning of the battle of Jenin: 'We never left the buildings and progressed entirely between homes . . . we carved out several dozen routes from outside the camp into its centre . . . we were all – the entire brigade – inside the homes of the Palestinians, no one was in the streets . . . we hardly ventured out . . . We had our headquarters and sleeping encampments in these buildings . . . even vehicles where placed in carved out areas within homes.'[24] Another soldier, who later wrote a book about his experiences during this attack, described in detail the movement through walls: 'We studied an aerial photograph to find a wall connecting the house we were in with the house to its south. Peter took the hammer and started working, but the wall wouldn't break – for the first time we faced a wall that was built of concrete rather than of cinder blocks . . . using demolition explosive was the most sensible way. We detonated at least four demolition blocks [of explosive] until the hole became big enough to go through.'[25] Since Palestinian guerrilla fighters were themselves manoeuvring through walls and pre-planned openings, most fighting took place in private homes. Some buildings became like layer-cakes, with Israeli soldiers both above and below a floor where Palestinians were trapped. For a Palestinian fighter caught in the crossfire of the Israeli attack on Nablus in April 2002, Israelis seemed 'to be everywhere: behind, on the sides, on the right, and on the left . . . How can you fight that way?'[26]

The IDF has recently completed the production of 3-D computer models of the entire West Bank and Gaza, which provide intricate detail of individual houses, including the location of internal doors and windows. In 2002, however, soldiers were still using aerial photographs on which each house was given a four-digit designation number to facilitate the communication of positions. Orientation was aided by global positioning systems (GPS) and centrally coordinated by commanders using images from unmanned drones. When soldiers blasted a hole through a wall, they crudely sprayed 'entrance', 'exit', 'do not enter', 'way to . . .' or 'way from . . .' on the wall in order to regulate the traffic of soldiers and to find their way back through the labyrinth they carved out through the bulk of the city.

A survey conducted by the Palestinian architect Nurhan Abujidi, after the Nablus and Balata attacks, showed that more than half of the buildings in the Nablus Kasbah had routes forced through them, resulting in anything from one to eight openings in their walls, floors or ceilings, creating several haphazard cross-routes. Abujidi saw that the routes could not be understood as describing simple linear progression; they indicated for her a very chaotic manoeuvre without clear direction.[27] Not all movement was undertaken through walls and between homes, many buildings were bombed from the air and completely destroyed, including historic buildings in the old city centre, amongst which were the eighteenth-century Ottoman Caravanserai of al-Wakalh al-Farroukkyyeh, and both the Nablusi and the Cana'an soap factories. The Abdelhade Palace, the Orthodox Church and the al-Naser Mosque were also badly damaged.[28]

The Kasbah of Nablus was the site of a radical experiment that took military activity beyond that of a mere manoeuvre. IDF officers had expressed their frustration over the fact that the quick invasion and occupation of Palestinian urban areas, such as Balata, had led to guerrillas disappearing and emerging again after the IDF's eventual withdrawal. In a war council at IDF Central Command headquarters in preparation for 'Defensive Shield' at the end of March 2002, Kochavi insisted on the need to redirect the operation and make its aim the killing of members of Palestinian armed organizations, rather than allowing them to disappear or even to surrender. Kochavi's intentions were no longer to capture and hold the Kasbah, but to enter, kill as many members of the Palestinian resistance as possible and then withdraw.[29] Military operations with the sole aim of killing were in accordance with clear guidelines laid down at the political level. In May 2001, only two months after he assumed office, Sharon summoned Chief of Staff Shaul Mofaz, Avi Dichter and their deputies for an urgent meeting at his private ranch. Sharon was explicit: 'The Palestinians . . . need to pay the price . . . They should wake up every morning and discover that they have ten or twelve people killed, without knowing what has taken place . . . You must be creative, effective, sophisticated.'[30]

The following day Mofaz spoke to a gathering of field commanders at a 1967 war memorial in Jerusalem ('Ammunition Hill'). After ensuring that his words were not being recorded, Mofaz stated that he wanted 'ten dead Palestinians every day, in each of the regional commands'. In an exceptional bypassing of military hierarchy he later called lower-ranking field commanders individually on their mobile phones, saying that he wanted 'to wake up every morning to hear that you went on operations and killed . . .'[31] An atmosphere of indiscriminate revenge killing was in the air. On Mofaz's direct orders, 'unnecessary killing' and the killing of civilians was rarely investigated and soldiers who killed civilians were hardly ever punished.[32] The horrific frankness of these objectives was confirmed to me in an interview with Shimon Naveh. Naveh described how in this period 'the military started thinking like criminals . . . like serial killers . . . they got allocated an area and researched it . . . they study the persons within the enemy organization they are asked to kill, their appearance, their voice [as heard in telephone tapping], their habits . . . like professional killers. When they enter the area they know where to look for these people, and they start killing them.'

During the attack on Nablus, Kochavi ignored Palestinian requests to surrender and continued fighting, trying to kill more people, until Mofaz ordered the attack over. It was the political and international pressure brought to bear in the aftermath of the destruction of Jenin that brought the entire campaign to a quick halt. Gal Hirsh, another graduate of OTRI and Chief of Operations in Central Command during the battle, later boasted that 'in 24 hours [the Palestinians] lost more than 80 of their gunmen and they could never identify where we were.'[33] After the attack, Defence Minister Ben Eliezer called Kochavi on his mobile phone to congratulate him; another 'well done' was passed on from Sharon.[34] Kochavi later claimed that if the political establishment had allowed him to continue fighting, his troops would have killed hundreds. The attack on Nablus was considered a success, both in terms of the number of Palestinians killed and in demonstrating both to the Israeli military and to the Palestinians that the IDF could now enter Palestinian camps and city centres at will. Kochavi's forces went on demonstrating this and entered Nablus and the Balata camp eight more times in the same way. It is mainly, but not exclusively, his enthusiastic laying out and enacting of Israeli security objectives that explain international calls for Kochavi to face a war-crimes tribunal.[35]

Inverse urban geometry

Like many other career officers, Kochavi had taken time off from active service to earn a university degree. Originally intending to study architecture, he ultimately pursued philosophy at the Hebrew University, and claimed that his mili-

The labels in the image read:
- Main "Bridge Houses" controlling the traffic arteries in the western part of the Kasbah
- Hadera Mosque
- Church
- Girls' Elementary School
- Girls' Middle School

The attack on Nablus, April 2002; the stars signify Palestinians killed. Diagram: OTRI, 2004.

tary practice had been considerably influenced by both disciplines; as a military officer, he also attended OTRI courses.[36] Kochavi's description of the attacks, delivered in the context of an interview I conducted with him, is a rare and astonishing manifestation of the relation between military theory and practice.

This space that you look at, this room that you look at [he refers to the room where the interview took place, at a military base near Tel Aviv], is nothing but your interpretation of it. Now, you can stretch the boundaries of your interpretation, but not in an unlimited fashion – after all, it must be bound by physics, as it contains buildings and alleys. The question is, how do you interpret the alley? Do you interpret it as a place, like every architect and every town planner does, to walk through, or do you interpret it as a place forbidden to walk through? This depends only on interpretation. We interpreted the alley as a place forbidden to walk through, and the door as a place forbidden to pass through, and the window as a place forbidden to look through, because a weapon awaits us in the alley, and a booby trap awaits us behind the doors. This is because the enemy interprets space in a traditional, classical manner, and I do not want to obey this interpretation and fall into his traps. Not only do I not want to fall into his traps, I want to surprise him. This is the essence of war. I need to win. I need to emerge from an unexpected

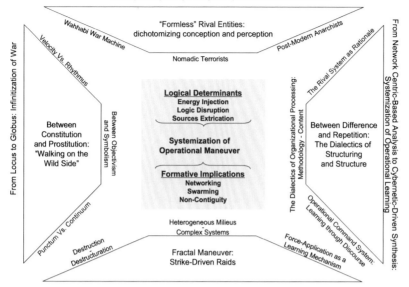

Presentation slide, OTRI, 2004.

place. And this is what we tried to do.

This is why we opted for the method of walking through walls . . . Like a worm that eats its way forward, emerging at points and then disappearing. We were thus moving from the interior of [Palestinian] homes to their exterior in unexpected ways and in places we were not anticipated, arriving from behind and hitting the enemy that awaited us behind a corner . . . Because it was the first time that this method was tested [on such a scale], during the operation itself we were learning how to adjust ourselves to the relevant urban space, and similarly how to adjust the relevant urban space to our needs . . . We took this micro-tactical practice [of moving through walls] and turned it into a method, and thanks to this method, we were able to interpret the whole space differently . . . I said to my troops, 'Friends! This is not a matter of your choice! There is no other way of moving! If until now you were used to move along roads and sidewalks, forget it! From now on we all walk through walls!'[37]

Beyond the description of the action, the interview is interesting for the language Kochavi chose to articulate it with. The reference to the need to interpret space, and even to re-interpret it, as the condition of success in urban war, makes apparent the influence of post-modern, post-structuralist theoretical language. War, according to the sophisticated, sanitizing language of Kochavi is a matter of reading, and (conceptually) deconstructing the existing urban environment, even before the operation begins.

Referring to the context of Kochavi's 'success', Naveh explained that: 'In Nablus, the IDF started understanding urban fighting as a spatial problem.' With regard to OTRI's influence on these tactics he said that 'by training several high-ranking officers, we filled the system with subversive agents who ask questions . . . Some of the top brass are not embarrassed to talk about Deleuze or [the deconstructive architect Bernard] Tschumi.' When I asked him, 'Why Tschumi?!' (in the annals of architectural history a special place of honour is reserved to Tschumi as a 'radical' architect of the left) he replied: 'The idea of disjunction embodied in Tschumi's book *Architecture and Disjunction*[38] became relevant for us . . . Tschumi had another approach to epistemology; he wanted to break with single-perspective knowledge and centralized thinking. He saw the world through a variety of different social practices, from a constantly shifting point of view . . .' I then asked him, if so, why does he not read Derrida and deconstruction instead? He answered, 'Derrida may be a little too opaque for our crowd. We share more with architects; we combine theory and practice. We can read, but we know as well how to build and destroy, and sometimes kill.'

In a lecture in 2004, Naveh presented a diagram resembling a 'square of oppo-sition' that plotted a set of logical relationships against certain propositions relating to military and guerrilla operations. Headings such as *Difference and Repetition – The Dialectics of Structuring and Structure; 'Formless' Rival Entities; Fractal Manoeuvre; Velocity vs. Rhythms; Wahhabi War Machine; Post-Modern Anarchists; Nomadic Terror-ists,* and so on, employed the language of French philosophers Gilles Deleuze and Félix Guattari.[39] Reference to Deleuze and Guattari is indicative of recent transformations within the IDF, because although they were influenced by the study of war, they were concerned with non-statist forms of violence and resist-ance, in which the state and its military are the arch-enemy. In their book, *A Thousand Plateaus,* Deleuze and Guattari draw a distinction between two kinds of territoriality: a hierarchical, Cartesian, geometrical, solid, hegemonic and spatially rigid state system; and the other, flexible, shifting, smooth, matrix-like 'nomadic' spaces.[40] Within these nomadic spaces they foresaw social organizations in a variety of polymorphous and diffuse operational networks. Of these networks, *rhizomes* and *war machines* are organizations composed of a multiplicity of small groups that can split up or merge with one another depending on contingency and circumstances and are characterized by their capacity for adaptation and metamorphosis. These organizational forms resonated in themselves with mili-tary ideals such as those described above.

Naveh observed that 'Several of the concepts in *A Thousand Plateaus* became instrumental for us [in the IDF] . . . allowing us to explain contemporary situations in a way that we could not have otherwise explained. It problematized our own paradigm . . . Most important was the distinction [Deleuze and Guattari] have pointed out between the concepts of "smooth" and "striated" space . . . [which accordingly reflected] the organizational concepts of the "war machine" and the "state apparatus". In the IDF we now often use the term "to smooth out space" when we want to refer to operation in a space in such a manner that borders do not affect us. Palestinian areas could indeed be thought of as "striated", in the sense that they are enclosed by fences, walls, ditches, roads blocks and so on . . . We want to confront the "striated" space of traditional, old-fashioned military practice [the way most military units presently operate] with smoothness that allows for movement through space that crosses any borders and barriers. Rather than contain and organize our forces according to existing borders, we want to move through them.' When I asked him if moving through walls was part of it, he answered that 'travelling through walls is a simple mechanical solution that connects theory and practice. Transgressing boundaries is the definition of the condition of "smoothness".'

Design by destruction

The professed effortless 'smoothness' of the raids on Balata and Nablus must be compared with the difficulties, 'striation' and physical destruction that the IDF attack brought on Jenin. The refugee camp of Jenin is located on the hill-slopes west of the city of Jenin, in the north of the West Bank close to the Green Line. Its proximity to Israeli cities and villages was the reason many attacks on Israeli civilians and the military originated from it, and the military was under much government and popular pressure to attack the Jenin camp. In preparation for an impending IDF attack, the commander of the camp's defences, Hazam Kubha 'Abu-Jandel', a former police officer, divided the camp into 15 zones, and assigned each to several dozen defenders, including Palestinian police officers, who prepared hundreds of improvised explosives from fertilizers.[41] The attack began concurrently with that on Nablus, on 3 April, and started with Israeli soldiers employing rather similar methods. Military bulldozers drove into the edges of the camp, piercing holes within the external walls of inhabited peripheral buildings. Armoured vehicles then reversed into these homes, offloading soldiers through these openings directly into Palestinian homes, thereby protecting them from snipers. From there, soldiers tried to progress from house to house through party walls. As long as the fighting took place within and between homes, the Palestinian fighters, moving through tunnels and secret connections in the lower

New routes carved through the Jenin refugee camp, stills from Palestinian 'home' video April 2002.

storeys where Israeli helicopter fire could not reach them, managed to hold back an entire IDF division trying to break in through the edges. The Israeli soldiers who formed the vanguard of this attack were mostly a collection of random units of reserve troops, with less military experience than the force that attacked Balata and Nablus. Within the chaos of battle, civilians and fighters were intermingled, and fighting occurred in and among the ruins of daily life.[42] Much of the fighting consisted not of major assaults but of relentless, lethal small-scale conflicts, of ambushes among buildings and ruins. Palestinian snipers learnt to shoot from deep within the buildings, locating themselves a few metres away from walls and shooting through openings they had cut through them – sometimes shooting through holes cut through several layers of walls.

The massive destruction of Jenin's centre started after IDF attacks failed to bring about the rapid collapse of the camp's defence. On 9 April, about a week after the beginning of the attack and with the IDF making little progress, Palestinian militants had their biggest success, blowing up and collapsing a row of buildings on an IDF patrol, in the Hawashin district at the heart of the camp, killing thirteen soldiers. Unwilling to risk further losses and unable to subdue the resistance in any other way, IDF officers ordered giant armoured D9 Caterpillar bulldozers to start destroying the camp, burying its defenders and remaining civilians in the rubble. One of the bulldozer operators, Moshe Nissim, described his experiences: 'For three days, I just destroyed and destroyed. The whole area. Any house that they fired from came down. And to knock it down, I tore down some more . . . By the end, I cleared an area as big as [the Jerusalem football stadium of] "Teddy" [named after Jerusalem mayor Teddy Kollek].'[43] At times, bulldozers

Construction in Jenin. Construction works in the Jenin refugee camp (left): UNRWA engineer Ahmad A'bizari (right).

piled earth and rubble onto buildings or between them, sealing areas off and changing the topography of the battle space. As the centre of the camp succumbed, a thick cloud of dust started to fill the streets and alleys, and lingered there throughout the remaining days of the battle. Only when the dust finally dispersed could international organizations and the media fully comprehend the scale of destruction caused by the IDF. Fifty-two Palestinians were killed, more then half of them civilians. Some, including those who were elderly or disabled, couldn't escape in time and were buried alive under the rubble of their homes.

Inspection of the aerial photographs taken after the battle revealed that the destruction of more than 400 buildings, in an area of 40,000 square metres, was informed by the logic of military planning.[44] This must be understood not only as the response to the contingencies of battle but also as the creation of a radically new layout for the camp. During the battle, the IDF widened the existing narrow alleyways and cut new ones through existing buildings in order to allow tanks and armoured bulldozers to penetrate the camp's interior. An open space was cleared out at the camp's core, where the new routes came together. This was also the area, the Hawashin district, where the resistance made its last stand, and which Palestinians later called 'ground zero'. Along these new and widened roads the Israeli military could easily re-enter the camp, a fact that undid its status as an impenetrable enclave and 'a haven for the resistance'.

UN-sponsored reconstruction efforts started almost immediately. The plans for reconstruction, however, sparked off a series of arguments between Palestinian representatives of the refugee camp and UN engineers concerning the direct

All video stills, Nadav Harel, Anselm Franke, Eyal Weizman, 2004.

relationship between design, military logic and destruction.[45]

The United Arab Emirates' Red Crescent had donated $29 million which was allocated to allow the UN Relief and Works Agency (UNRWA) to implement a new masterplan for the camp's layout, and replace most of the destroyed homes with new ones. The project was dedicated to Sheikh Zayed Bin Sultan al-Nahyan, the late President of the United Arab Emirates. Upon the release of the reconstruction plans, a controversial issue concerning the road layout immediately became apparent. The UNRWA engineer in charge of the project's streets and infrastructure, Ahmad A'bizari, wanted to 'take advantage of the destruction and widen the roads to 4–6 metres across . . .'[46] This new width of the roads would better serve the camp, he thought, but would also obviously provide enough space for Israeli tanks, if they returned, to move through without smashing into house walls, and getting stuck between the buildings. However, this widening of the roads meant that between 10 and 15 per cent of the original ground area of private properties along the roads would be re-registered as public land. In some cases the UNRWA plan sought to achieve road widening by pushing back the front walls of buildings at street level a metre or so into the boundary line of their respective lots, so that some of the upper floors would overhang parts of the street. The loss of private space at the camp's ground level was to be compensated for by the addition of more floors and by expanding the camp's overall size into surrounding agricultural land purchased by UNRWA.

Although UNRWA's proposal was argued as a simple improvement to the camp's traffic management, the camp's popular committee,[47] in which the armed organizations have crucial influence, protested that the widening of the roads would allow Israeli tanks to penetrate the camp easily whenever they wanted. One of the committee members insisted that 'it should be made more, not less difficult for Israeli tanks to enter the camp'.[48] The debate ended with UNRWA exercising its sovereignty over the camp's affairs and pushing on with construction of the wider roads regardless of the residents' protests. In an apologetic afterthought, Berthold Willenbacher, UNRWA's second project director, observed that 'We designed a way for Israelis to get through with tanks and we shouldn't have done that because the armed guys have less chance of getting away than if it's narrow alleys. We didn't take their views into consideration.'[49]

A tragic demonstration of the dangers of facilitating tank access to the camp took place six months later in November 2002, when Israeli tanks re-entered the camp. One of their gunners shot and killed the first UNRWA project director, Briton Iain John Hook, claiming to have mistaken him for a Palestinian and his mobile phone for a grenade.

By taking responsibility for the well-being and maintenance of architecture in a situation of ongoing conflict, UNRWA's planning programme was exposed to one of the more obvious cases of the 'humanitarian paradox' – namely, that humanitarian help may end up serving the oppressing power. Moreover, the new homes were built to a standard not previously seen at the camp, and for the first time UNRWA had an opportunity to replace the inadequate water and sewage arrangements destroyed by the IDF.[50] It is in this context that we can understand a statement made by one of the members of Jenin camp's popular committee who, after seeing the UN's newly built cream-coloured permanent-looking homes, that seemed to him to undo the camp's very status of temporariness, declared: 'we have lost the right of return'.[51]

'Smart destruction'

Given the international outcry that followed the rampant destruction of the Jenin refugee camp, the Israeli military realized that its engineering corps had to improve its 'art of destruction' which had seemingly spun out of control. This led to further investment in alternative 'smarter' ways of urban warfare, such as, but not exclusively, those methods employed at the beginning of the battle of Jenin, and successfully in Balata and Nablus and in the work of OTRI.

As part of this new approach, two months after 'Operation Defensive Shield', in June 2002, the military started to upgrade a small mock-up town located at the IDF's base of Tze'elim in the Negev desert, named Chicago (invoking the bullet-ridden myth of the American city), turning it into what was then the world's largest mocked-up oriental city used for practising military assaults. Chicago

HOLLOW LAND

Urban warfare training site Chicago (Tze'elim base), in the Negev desert. The interior view shows pre-cast holes in walls (Adam Broomberg and Oliver Chanarin, 2005). The history of Chicago has shadowed much of the military history in the Middle East since the 1980s, reflecting changes in the IDF's conception of security and its relation to cities. Chicago's history can be understood in the gradual alteration of its signified environment. The core of Chicago was built in the mid-1980s as a small training site simulating a Lebanese village during the Israeli occupation of a Lebanon. It was later extended into a larger urban environment to provide a setting for the training of Israeli special forces before their aborted operation (abandoned after several Israeli soldiers were killed in an accident) to assassinate Saddam Hussein in the Iraqi town of Tikrit in 1992. In 2002, it was further expanded to simulate all different types of Palestinian urban environment, and now includes an area called the Kasbah, a dense market area with narrow alleys, a section simulating a refugee camp, a downtown area with broader streets and a neighbourhood resembling a rural village. In the summer of 2005 it was used to simulate the Jewish settlements of Gaza in training sessions for their evacuation.

includes an area called the Kasbah: a dense market area with narrow alleys, a section simulating a refugee camp, a downtown area with broader streets and tanks, and a neighbourhood resembling a rural village. Holes have been cut through the walls of homes to allow soldiers to practise moving through them. In certain training sessions the military enlisted the stage-set designer of a well-known Tel Aviv theatre to provide the relevant props and organize the special effects.

During this period other transformations were manifest in the realm of military engineering. At a military conference held in March 2004 in Tel Aviv, an Israeli engineering officer explained to his international audience that, thanks to the study of architecture and building technologies, 'the military can remove one floor in a building without destroying it completely [sic], or remove a building that stands in a row of buildings without damaging the others'.[52] However exaggerated, this statement testifies to the new emphasis placed by the military on what it perceives as the 'surgical' ability to remove elements of buildings supposedly without destroying the whole – essentially the military engineer's adaptation of the logic of 'smart weapons'.

Un-walling the Wall

In historical siege warfare, the breaching of the outer city wall signalled the destruction of the sovereignty of the city-state. Accordingly, the 'art' of siege warfare engaged with the geometries of city walls and with the development of equally complex technologies for approaching and breaching them. Contemporary urban combat, on the other hand, is increasingly focused on methods of transgressing the limitations embodied by the domestic wall. Complementing military tactics that involve physically breaking and 'walking' through walls, new methods have been devised to allow soldiers not only to see, but also to shoot and kill through solid walls. The Israeli R&D company Camero developed a hand-held imaging device that combines thermal images with ultra-wideband radar that, much like a contemporary maternity-ward ultrasound system, has the ability to produce three-dimensional renderings of biological life concealed behind barriers.[53] Human bodies appear as fuzzy 'heat marks' floating (like foetuses) within an abstract blurred medium wherein everything solid – walls, furniture, objects – has melted into the digital screen. Weapons using standard NATO 5.56mm rounds are complemented by use of 7.62mm rounds, which are capable of penetrating brick, wood and sun-dried brick (adobe) without much deflection of the bullet's trajectory. These practices and technologies will have a radical effect on the relation of military practices to architecture and the built environment at large. Instruments of 'literal transparency' are the main components in the search to produce a military fantasy world of boundless fluidity, in which the city's space becomes as navigable as an ocean (or as in a computer game). By striving to see what is hidden behind walls, and to fire ammunition through them, the military seems to have sought to elevate contemporary technologies to the level of metaphysics, seeking to move beyond the here and now of physical reality, collapsing time and space.

This desire to unveil and 'go beyond' the wall could itself explain military interest in transgressive theories and art from the 1960s and the 1970s. Most literally, the techniques of walking through walls bring to mind what the American artist Gordon Matta-Clark called the 'un-walling of the wall'.[54] From 1971 until his death in 1978, Matta-Clark was involved in the transformation and virtual dismantling of abandoned buildings. In this body of work known as 'building cuts', and his approach of *anarchitecture* (anarchic architecture) using hammers, chisels and bow saws, he sliced buildings and opened holes through domestic and industrial interiors.[55] This could be understood as his attempt to subvert the repressive order of domestic space and the power and hierarchy it embodies. The 'building cuts' of Matta-Clark were featured in OTRI's presentation material – juxtaposed with IDF holes cut through Palestinian walls.

Other canonical references of urban theory, touched on by OTRI, are the Situationist practices of *dérive* (a method of drifting through the different ambiances of the city that the Situationists referred to as psychogeography) and *détournement* (the adaptation of buildings to new sets of uses or purposes, other than those they were designed to perform). These ideas were conceived by Guy Debord and other members of the *Situationist International* as part of a general approach that was intended to challenge the built hierarchy of the capitalist city. They aimed to break down distinctions between private and public, inside and outside, use and function, to replace private space with a fluid, volatile and 'borderless' public surface, through which movement would be unexpected. References were also made to the work of Georges Bataille, who spoke of a desire to attack architecture: his own call to arms was meant to dismantle the rigid rationalism of a postwar order, to escape 'the architectural straitjacket', and liberate repressed human desires. These tactics were conceived to transgress the established 'bourgeois order' of the city as planned and delivered, in which the architectural element of the wall – domestic, urban or geopolitical (like the Iron Curtain that descended upon Europe) – projected as solid and fixed, was an embodiment of social and political order and repression. Because walls functioned not only as physical barriers but also as devices to exclude both the visual and the aural, they have, since the eighteenth century, provided the physical infrastructure for the construction of privacy and bourgeois subjectivity.[56] Indeed, architectural discourse tends to see walls as architecture's irreducible givens. If the walls attempt to harness the natural entropy of the urban, breaking it would liberate new social and political forms.

Although representing a spectrum of different positions, methods and periods, for Matta-Clark, Bataille, the Situationists and Tschumi it was the repressive power of the capitalist city that should have been subverted. In the hands of the Israeli military, however, tactics inspired by these thinkers were projected as the basis for an attack on the little protected habitat of poor Palestinian refugees under siege.

In this context the transgression of domestic boundaries must be understood as the very manifestation of state repression. Hannah Arendt's understanding of the political domain of the classic city would agree with the equating of walls with law and order. According to Arendt, the political realm is guaranteed by two kinds of walls (or wall-like laws): the wall surrounding the city, which defined the zone of the political; and the walls separating private space from the public domain, ensuring the autonomy of the domestic realm.[57] The almost palindromic linguistic structure of law/wall helps to further bind these two structures in an interdependency that equates built and legal fabric. The un-walling of the wall invariably becomes the undoing of the law. The military practice of 'walking through walls' – on the scale of the house or the city – links the physical properties of construction with this syntax of architectural, social and political orders. New technologies developed to allow soldiers to see living organisms through walls, and to facilitate their ability to walk and fire weapons through them, thus address not only the materiality of the wall, but also its very concept. With the wall no longer physically or conceptually solid or legally impenetrable, the functional spatial syntax that it created collapses. In 'the camp', Agamben's well-known observation follows the trace left by Arendt, 'city and house became indistinguishable'.[58] The breaching of the physical, visual and conceptual border/wall exposes new domains to political power, and thus draws the clearest physical diagram to the concept of the 'state of exception'.

Lethal theory

Military use of contemporary theory is of course nothing new. From Marcus Aurelius to Robert McNamara,[59] power has always found ways to utilize theories and methodologies conceived in other fields. The 'soldier-poet-philosopher' is also a central figure of Zionist mythologies. In the 1960s, when an academic education became the standard component of a career in the Israeli military, high-ranking officers returning from studies in the United States invoked philosophy to describe the battlefield, sometimes literally the Spinozan concept of 'extension' with respect to the 1967 battles of occupation.

Military use of theory for ends other than those it was meant to fulfil is not dissimilar to the way in which progressive and transgressive theoretical ideas were applied in organizing post-modern management systems in business and as efficiency indicators in technological culture. Education in the humanities, often believed to be the most powerful weapon against capitalist imperialism, could equally be appropriated as a tool of colonial power itself. This is a particularly chilling demonstration of what Herbert Marcuse warned of as early as 1964: that, with the growing integration between the various aspects of society, 'contradiction and criticism' could be equally subsumed and made operative as an instrumental tool by the hegemony of power – in this case, the absorption and transformation of post-structuralist and even post-colonial theory by the colonial state.[60]

This is not to place blame for Israeli's recent aggression in the hands of radical theorists and artists, or to question the purity of their intentions. It is also not my aim here to try to correct imprecisions and exaggerations in the military 'reading', use and interpretation of specific theories. I am concerned primarily with understanding the various ways by which theory, taken out of its ethical/political context, may perform within the military domain.

The practical or tactical function of theory, the extent to which it influences military tactics and manoeuvres, is related to more general questions about the relation between theory and practice. However, if the new tactics of the IDF are the result of a direct translation of post-modern theory to practice, we should expect to see these tactics amounting to a radical break with traditional ones. However, they rather constitute a continuation of many of the procedures and processes that have historically been part of urban military operations. Describing acts of war as new, unprecedented, or claiming that military strategy is deeply rooted in contemporary or ancient philosophy illustrates how the language of theory itself could become a weapon in the contemporary conflict, and the institutional ecologies that sustain them. Although the concept of 'walking through walls', 'swarming' and other terms referring to military non-linearity may indeed imply some structural changes in military organization, claims that these developments constitute radical transformations are largely overstated. This, in itself, should bring into question the real place of theory as a generative source for the actual transformations of military practice.

The defenders of the Paris Commune, much like those of the Kasbah of Algiers, Hue, Beirut, Jenin and Nablus, navigated the city in small, loosely coordinated groups, moving through openings and connections between homes, basements and courtyards, using alternative routes, secret passageways and trapdoors. Gillo Pontecorvo's 1966 film *The Battle of Algiers*, and Alistair Horne's book on Algeria, *A Savage War of Peace*,[61] both describe such manoeuvres and are both now part of US military and IDF curricula.

The technique of moving through walls was first recorded in writing by Marshal Thomas Bugeaud's 1849 military manual, *La Guerre des Rues et des Maisons*, in the context of anti-insurgency tactics used in the class-based urban battles of nineteenth-century Paris. 'Are the barricades too strong to be broken down by the *tirailleurs* [light infantry manned usually by soldiers drawn from France's colonies]? Then one enters into the first houses that line either side of the street, and it is here that the detonator is a great advantage because he quickly achieves the goal. One climbs up to the top floor and systematically blasts through all the walls, finally managing to pass the barricade.'[62] On the other side of the barricades and a decade later, Louis-Auguste Blanqui wrote this micro-tactical manoeuvre into his *Instructions pour une prise d'armes*.[63] For Blanqui, the barricade and the mouse-hole were complementary elements employed for the protection of self-governing urban enclaves. This was achieved by a complete inversion of the urban syntax. Elements of circulation – paving stones and carriages – became elements of blockage (barricades), while the existing elements of blockage – walls – became routes. The fight in the city, and for the city, was thus equated with the ability to interpret and re-interpret it. No longer merely the locus of war, the city became its medium and finally its apparatus. Similarly, the idea of walking through walls, as Israeli architect Sharon Rotbard insisted, has been invented anew in almost every urban battle in history, and in response to local necessities and battle conditions.[64] In Palestine it may first have been used during the April 1948 battle for the occupation of Jaffa by the Zionist *Irgun* or 'Begin Gang', as the British called it. Its sappers cleared 'overground tunnels' between house walls through the city's contiguous built fabric, planted explosives along its path and blew it up to make a wide swathe of rubble all the way to the sea, cutting off Jaffa's northern neighbourhood, Manshiya, from the rest of the city.[65]

Claims for the 'non-linearity' and the 'breakdown of vertical hierarchies' in contemporary warfare are also largely exaggerated. Beyond the rhetoric of 'self-organization' and the 'flattening of hierarchy', military networks are still largely nested within traditional institutional hierarchies, units are still given orders, and follow plans and timelines. Non-linear swarming is performed at the very tactical end of an inherently hierarchical system.[66] In the case of the West Bank, some non-linear manoeuvres could be undertaken because the Israeli military still controls all linear supply lines – the roads within the West Bank and those that connect it to its large bases within Israel proper, as well as the ever-increasing multiplicity of linear barriers that it has constructed throughout the terrain. In fact, what the military refers to as 'networks' (implying non-hierarchical cooper-

HOLLOW LAND

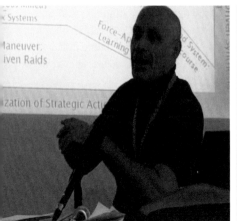

Left: Shimon Naveh. Right: Aviv Kochavi. Video stills, Nadav Harel and Eyal Weizman, 2004.

ation of dispersed parts) should technically be referred to as 'systems', which are distributed structures with centralized command.

Furthermore, 'swarming' and 'walking through walls' may be successful primarily when the enemy is relatively weak and disorganized, and especially when the balance of technology, training and force is clearly on the side of the military. During the years of Intifada, the occupation forces went on imagining the attack of poorly armed Palestinian guerrillas and attacks on frightened civilians in their ramshackle homes, as 'battles', boasting of their achievements as significant military accomplishments. The hubris of those crowned as the heroes of these operations can only temporarily conceal the very impasse and long-term futility of this strategizing, the political stupidity, the military crudeness and the waste of life and dignity.

The years spent attacking the weak Palestinian organizations, a sort of 'Great Game' for the IDF, was no doubt one of the reasons for the incompetence demonstrated by the same Israeli soldiers and officers when they faced the stronger, better armed and well-trained Hizbollah fighters in Lebanon in summer 2006. Indeed, the two officers most implicated in these failures in both Gaza and Lebanon are none other than the two Israel military 'whizz kid' graduates of OTRI and veterans of the 2002 Balata and Nablus attacks, Aviv Kochavi (in summer 2006 commander of the Gaza Division) and Gal Hirsh (in summer 2006 commander of the Northern Galilee Division 91). The abduction in June 2006 of an Israeli soldier by Palestinian guerrillas who were tunnelling under IDF fortifications was undertaken when Kochavi was in command, and Hizbollah's kidnapping of two Israeli soldiers the following month was undertaken in Hirsh's area of command. Kochavi, who directed the punitive attacks on Gaza that followed, insisted on sticking to his obfuscating language: 'we intend to create a chaos in the Palestinian side, to jump from one place to the other, to leave the area and then return to it . . . we will use all the advantages of "raid" rather than "occupation." '[67] Although he succeeded in inflicting hundreds of civilian casualties, and destroying essential infrastructure, the attack failed to bring back the soldier or put an end to Palestinian rocket fire. In a remarkable echo of the Lebanon front, Hirsh too called for 'raids instead of occupation', ordering the battalions newly attached to his command (and unused to the language he acquired at OTRI) to 'swarm' and 'infest' urban areas in south Lebanon. In one of his later widely mocked operational commands for the attempted takeover of the southern Lebanese town of Bint Jbeil, Hirsh wrote the following complex set of instructions: 'Forces must conduct wide-scale infiltration in low-signature raid; quickly establish themselves on the controlling areas, then create lethal contact with the built-up areas (by "swarming"), then create a shock-and-awe effect that would freeze the entire space of action, then shift mode to domination, all while engaging in systemic-spatial deconstruction of the enemy infrastructure ("occupation").'[68] However, his subordinate officers did not understand what these terms meant, and were left clueless as to what they were expected to do. After the 2006 Lebanon war, Hirsh was criticized for arrogance, 'intellectualism' and being out of touch, and was forced to resign from military service.

Pondering the results, Naveh himself publicly admitted that 'the war in Lebanon was a failure and I had a great part in it. What I have brought to the IDF has failed.'[69] The Israeli campaign in Lebanon was indeed in chaos. Continuous and intensive bombardment by the increasingly frustrated Israeli military gradually transformed Lebanese villages and border towns into a jagged topography of broken concrete, glass and twisted metal. Within this alien landscape, the hills of rubble were honeycombed with cavities of buried rooms, which offered more cover to the defenders. Hizbollah fighters, themselves effectively swarming through the rubble and detritus, through underground basements and the tunnels they had prepared, studied the movements of Israeli soldiers, and attacked them with anti-tank weapons at precisely the moment when they entered the interior of homes and tried to walk through walls in the manner they were used to in the cities and refugee camps of the West Bank.

Institutional conflicts

Although, as I showed before, the Israeli military hardly needed Deleuze to attack Nablus, and in the reality of military operations, as Paul Hirst once sarcastically remarked, 'war machines run on petrol and coal'[70] and 'bodies without organs' denote casualties, theory, in the case of its contemporary transformation in the

IDF, did provide the military with a new language with which to speak to itself and others. It has helped articulate new ideas and sensibilities, but it was primarily used to help explain, justify and communicate ideas that emerged independently within disparate fields of military experience and practical knowledge. If we leave aside for the time being the operative aspect of practice-based theory, we can perhaps understand the way in which the military's use of theoretical language reflects upon the military itself as an institution.

In this respect, one of Naveh's answers to my question in the interview was revealing. When I asked Naveh about the incompatibility of the ideological and political foundations of the theories he employs, he answered: 'We must differentiate between the charm, and even some values within Marxist ideology and what can be taken from it for military use. Theories do not only strive for a utopian socio-political ideal with which we may or may not agree, but are also based on methodological principles that seek to disrupt and subvert the existing political, social, cultural, or military order. The disruptive capacity in theory [elsewhere Naveh talked of the "nihilist capacity of theory"] is the aspect of theory that we like and use . . . This theory is not married to its socialist ideals.'

When Naveh invokes the terms *disruptive* and *nihilist* to explain his use of theory, something other than an attack on the Palestinians is at stake. Theory functions here not only as an instrument in the conflict with the Palestinians, but primarily as an instrument in the power struggles within the military itself. Critical theory provides the military (as it has at times in academia) with a new language with which it can challenge existing military doctrines, break apart ossified *doxas* and invert institutional hierarchies, with their 'monopoly' on knowledge.

Throughout the 1990s when Western militaries were undergoing restructuring and specialization through the use of high technology and computerized management, such as the transformation promoted by neo-conservatives such as Donald Rumsfeld, they faced strong opposition from within their respective institutions. Since the early 1990s the IDF has similarly undergone institutional conflicts in the context of its development and transformations. In the context of these institutional conflicts, the language of post-structuralist theory was used to articulate the critique of the existing system, to argue for transformations and to call for further reorganizations.[71] Naveh admitted this when he claimed that OTRI 'employed critical theory primarily in order to critique the military institution itself – its fixed and heavy conceptual foundations . . .'

Something of these internal conflicts within the IDF was exposed publicly in the context of the mediatized controversy that surrounded the closing down of OTRI in May 2006, and the suspension of Naveh and his co-director Dov Tamari weeks before the war in Lebanon broke out and culminated with Hirsh's resignation a few months after it. These debates brought to light existing fault lines within the IDF, between officers associated with OTRI, for whom Naveh functioned as a kind of guru, and officers who resisted him, his methods and language.

Officially, Naveh's suspension came as the response by Chief of Staff Dan Halutz to an early draft of the report of State Comptroller Michael Lindenstrauss on the state of IDF officer training. The report accused OTRI staff of delivering their teaching orally, in lectures and seminars, without publishing a book or a lexicon of terms that would facilitate the comprehension of their complicated and ambiguous terminology, and that therefore their concepts remained vague and faced the 'danger of different interpretations and confusions . . .' (this in itself could be read as an implied compliment to post-modern scholars). Other sections in the report accused Naveh and Tamari of some management irregularities of which they were later cleared.[72] The closing of the institute had much to do with the fact that OTRI was associated with former Chief of Staff (and Halutz's rival) Moshe Ya'alon, who had placed the institute at the centre of the IDF's process of transformation. Halutz did not directly confront the theoretical concepts produced by OTRI, but the critique was articulated by the former commander of the National Defence Colleges, Ya'akov Amidror. Amidror, now a security analyst in civilian life, was one of the first IDF generals affiliated to the National-Religious movement and the right-wing settler movement. Amidror's position on territorial control is diametrically opposed to that of OTRI: he repeatedly claimed that 'there is no way to fight terror without physical presence and control of the territory',[73] and was therefore consistently opposed to territorial withdrawals in the Occupied Territories. Concerning OTRI, he believed that 'theoretical complexity' stands in absolute contradiction to the operational logic of power: 'It is good that the institute [OTRI] closed down, because its effects on the military were catastrophic . . . it talked "mumbo-jumbo" instead of clear language . . . it was unwilling to differentiate true from false according to the best of the post-modern tradition that it introduced into the IDF . . . I really envy anyone that does manage to understand [what they teach], as this is far beyond my capacity.'[74] In Naveh's view, Amidror conversely epitomizes IDF 'idealization of military empiricism, rejection of the value of theoretical study and critical inquiry . . . impatience for conceptual discourse, disregard for literary theory and intolerance for philosophical discourse'. Regardless of other reasons that may have been at play, Naveh presented his dismissal as 'a coup against OTRI and theory'.[75]

This military debate was thus tied in with current political differences within Israeli society at large. Naveh, together with most of his former colleagues at OTRI, are aligned with what is referred to in Israel as the 'Zionist left', which supports territorial withdrawals. Kochavi, who enthusiastically accepted the command of the military operation to evacuate and destroy the Gaza settlements, is similarly understood as a 'leftist' officer regardless of the atrocities of which he was accused in Gaza the following year. Some of the conflict about theory within the IDF resonated thus with political ones within the military.

But readers should not mistake the 'leftist' Israeli officers for a hopeful alternative to the brutality of the IDF at large; in fact, the contrary may be true. A comparison between the two attacks in 2002, on Jenin and on Nablus, could reveal the paradox that may render the overall effect of the 'de-territorial', 'smart' officers more destructive: a hole in the wall may indeed not be as devastating as the complete destruction of the home, but if the occupation forces are not able to enter refugee camps without having to destroy them as they have done in Jenin, and considering local and international opposition, they will most likely avoid attacking refugee camps, or will at least not attack them as frequently as they do now that they had found the tool to do so 'on the cheap' – which is presently almost daily. In this way, the militaristic logic of the Israeli left has presented the government with a tactical solution to a political problem.

One of the primary aims of the new tactics developed by OTRI is to release Israel from the necessity of being physically present within Palestinian areas, but still able to maintain control of security. According to Naveh, the IDF's operational paradigm should seek to replace presence in occupied areas with a capacity to move through them, and produce in them what he called 'effects', which are 'military operations such as aerial attacks or commando raids . . . that affect the enemy psychologically and organizationally'. The tactics developed at OTRI and other institutes with IDF command, thus have the aim of providing tools for replacing the older mode of territorial domination with a newer 'de-territorial' one, which OTRI called 'occupation through disappearance'.

Israel's preconditions for any territorial compromise – partial withdrawal and the drawing of temporary borderlines – as the recent invasion of Gaza after its evacuation has demonstrated, are based on being able to annul it and enter the territories in the event of a situation it considers to be an emergency. Under the terms of the Oslo Accords, Israeli withdrawal from Palestinian cities and villages was accompanied by a clause of exception that guaranteed its right, under certain circumstances which it could itself declare, for 'hot pursuit', that is, to break into Palestinian-controlled areas, enter neighbourhoods and homes in search of suspects, and take these suspects into custody for purposes of interrogation and detention in Israel.[76]

On the Wall that may grow to mark out the border of a fragmented, temporary Palestinian state, Naveh claimed that 'Whatever path they [the politicians] can agree to build the fence [Wall] along is okay with me – as long as I can cross this fence. What we need is not to be there, but . . . to [be able to] act there . . . Withdrawal is not the end of the story.'

The IDF precondition for withdrawal – articulated by Naveh's comment '. . . as long as I can cross this fence' – implies a conditional withdrawal that could be annulled as immediately as it is undertaken. This undoubtedly undoes much of the perceived symmetrical nature of borders, embodied by the iconography of the West Bank Wall, and in all the recent diplomatic rhetoric that would like to regard whatever polity remains (fragmented and perforated as it may be) on the other side of this Wall as a Palestinian state. As long as the Wall is seen as constantly permeable and transparent from one side only, Israel should still be considered sovereign in Palestinian territories, if only because it is Israel itself that can declare the exception that would allow it to annul the legal status of this 'border'. In this respect, the large 'state wall' has been conceptualized in similar terms to the walls of houses within the territories: a transparent and permeable medium that allows the Israeli military to move 'smoothly' through and across it. When Kochavi claims that 'space is only an interpretation', and that his movement through and across urban fabrics reinterprets architectural elements (walls, windows and doors) and when Naveh claims that he would accept any border as long as he could walk through it, they are both using a transgressive theoretical approach to suggest that war fighting is no longer about the destruction of space, but rather is about its 'reorganization'. The 'inverse geometry' that was conceived to turn the city 'inside out', shuffling its private and public spaces, would now similarly fold the 'Palestinian state' within Israeli security conceptions and subject it to constant transgressions seeking to un-wall its Wall.

A parade in Gaza; the model is about to be burned. Reinhard Krauss, 2001.

8.

Evacuations:
De-Colonizing Architecture

On the morning of 12 September 2005, Israeli forces completed their withdrawal from the Gaza Strip. The gate through which Brigadier General Aviv Kochavi, commander of the Gaza Division, the last to have left the strip, was promptly buried in deep sand by military bulldozers. Kochavi, who would order his forces to re-enter Gaza nine months later, convened a small press conference at which he prematurely announced: 'Our mission has been completed . . . Israel's 38-year presence [in Gaza] has come to an end.'

Behind it, the military left the bulldozed rubble of more than 3,000 buildings – mainly single-family homes, but also public buildings, schools, military installations, and industrial and agricultural facilities built for the benefit of the twenty-one settlements and the scores of military bases that protected them – incidentally, around the same number as the Palestinian homes destroyed by the Israeli military in Gaza since the start of the second Intifada in 2000.[1] An Israeli journalist who visited the Gaza settlements a few days before the evacuation was completed described seeing 'mounds of building rubble piled at the centre of what used to be private gardens . . . the disturbing stench of food remains . . . pools of water and sewage . . . endless swarms of flies . . . and miles upon miles of nylon packing rolls'.[2] Hundreds of disoriented stray cats were left wandering the apocalyptic landscape to die of hunger and thirst. The only structures remaining afloat on the swamp of debris and liquid waste were the nineteen synagogues of Gaza, whose destruction was halted by an Israeli High Court of Justice ruling and a last-minute government vote. One of the synagogues – designed as a three-dimensional extrusion of a Star of David and built of reinforced concrete (in order that, as its architect Gershon Shevah stated, 'Jews [can] rid themselves of their diasporic complex') – best embodied the aesthetic immediacy and inevitable fate of the art of Israeli occupation.[3] A day after the withdrawal, Palestinian youths completed what the High Court of Justice had left undone, and torched the synagogue buildings. Thousands of Palestinian flags of

all organizations, and banners displaying images of many Palestinian leaders and 'martyrs' were raised over the settlement rubble. The Palestinian Authority organized guided tours and renamed some of the ruined settlements after dead militants and leaders. The ruins of Neve-Dekalim became Yasser Arafat City, and those of Kfar Darom, Sheikh Ahmed Yassin City. After the celebrations were over and everything that could be reused had been taken, most of the destroyed settlements were occupied by militant organizations; those close to the border were used as launching sites for home-made Qassam rockets against Israeli towns and villages adjacent to Gaza. Bombing by the Israeli Air Force and the constant pounding from Israeli artillery routinely shuffled the remaining mounds of rubble, reinforcing what the Israeli military called, in leaflets dropped from its fighter jets, an 'aerially enforced closure' meant to put the evacuated areas 'off limits' to all Palestinians.

Prior to the withdrawal, and ignorant of the impending destruction of the settlements, a number of local and international interested parties speculated upon several alternative scenarios for the possible reuse of buildings in the settlements. The impending evacuation opened up a unique arena of speculation, in which, between April 2004 when the plans for evacuation were firmed up and August 2005 when they were carried out, some of the world's most powerful international players grappled with questions that normally belong to the domain of architecture and planning. Although the evacuation was conceived and undertaken as a unilateral Israeli operation, the fate of the settlement buildings was debated by the United States, the EU, the UN, the World Bank, the International Monetary Fund (IMF), some of the wealthiest Arab property developers, a variety of NGOs and some security and policy think-tanks. In addition, the various political parties within Pales-

Gaza Evacuation. Miki Kratsman, August 2005.

tine and Israel also had differing opinions, ideas and proposals. In the political rhetoric that surrounded the period immediately prior to evacuation, homes have alternately been referred to as physical entities embodying power relations, as symbols of a set of ideologies, as sentient (even haunted) active agents, as military weapons or ammunitions, as bargaining chips, as economic resources, accumulations of toxic waste or as the instruments of a crime.

Although all aspirations to reuse the settlement architecture were later flattened into the debris of their destruction, these visions are nevertheless valuable in contemplating the potential reuse of Israel's architecture of occupation, if and when the rest of the Occupied Territories are reclaimed (militarily or peacefully) by Palestinians. Furthermore, these plans present us with a rare opportunity to examine more general problems associated with the reuse of the architecture of exclusion, violence and control, at the moment when such architecture is unplugged from the socio-political-military power that created and sustained it. The ritual destruction, reuse, 'redivivus' or 'détournement' of the single-family house may even suggest a possible repertoire of actions for its possible transformations at large.

State of architectural emergency

The economy of the Gaza settlements had been based mainly on agriculture, in particular hot-house crops for European export, sustained by low-paid workers from China and Thailand who gradually replaced Palestinian workers following the commencement of the Oslo process. Seventeen of the settlements were

Evacuated settlements, Nir Kafri, September 2005.

concentrated within the large enclave of Gush Katif on the southwestern beach-front of Gaza, the rest were strategically positioned as isolated strongholds near Palestinian cities and refugee camps, or as traffic valves on the main routes connecting them. The more 'isolated' settlements also acted as bridgeheads for military operations in Palestinian urban areas. After the start of the second Intifada in September 2000, some of the settlements were surrounded by 8–12-metre-high concrete walls constructed of the same modular components used to build the Wall in the West Bank. Hundreds of Palestinian homes and hundreds of acres of Palestinian orchards surrounding the settlement walls were destroyed in what the IDF called 'landscape exposure operations', aiming to remove cover for putative Palestinian attacks. Seen from the air, the settlements appeared as pleasant, green islands, resting in the middle of a series of concrete cylinders (the surrounding walls) and woven together by a thick web of infrastructure (roads for the exclusive use of settlers).

In the weeks leading up to the August 2005 evacuation, the architects and planners of the Palestinian Ministry of Planning operated under 'state of emergency' regulations: all holidays and weekend vacations were postponed, and routine work suspended. The fact that architecture and planning was seen as a service essential enough to be included in a 'state of emergency' – a measure usually reserved for security forces and valuable industries – demonstrates the prominent status of the built environment and its transformations in this context. The ministry became the centre of intense meetings between Palestinians and a variety of NGOs, different UN agencies, the World Bank, foreign governments and international investors, who outlined their proposed use for the evacuated settlements. The building itself appeared like a fortified beehive too small to contain all of these delegations, especially since the number of people making up each delegation doubled when foreigners were obliged by insurance companies to maintain personal bodyguards.

Israeli discussions about the fate of the settlement buildings focused on the potential symbolic effect of Israeli architecture under Palestinian control. Representing the attitudes of the right-wing faction of the Likud Party, Benjamin Netanyahu – who later resigned his office as Finance Minister in protest at the evacuation – demanded that all settlement homes be destroyed. This was purportedly in order to avoid the broadcast of what he felt were ideologically destructive images: Arabs living in the homes of Jews and synagogues tuning into mosques. The Palestinians 'will dance on our rooftops', Netanyahu warned, referring to broadcasts aired on Israeli TV during the 1991 Gulf War, which showed Palestinians standing on rooftops in Ramallah cheering Iraqi Scud missiles aimed at Israeli cities – overlooking the fact that the roofs of most settlement homes are in fact pitched and tiled. His rhetoric conjured up images of a murderous Palestinian mob storming the gates of settlements, looting and reoccupying the homes of 'decent' settlers. This 'apocalyptic scenario', he feared, would become the image for a reversal – and thus imply the reversibility – of a Zionist project previously characterized by the seizure, destruction and, in some cases, reoccupation of Palestinian dwellings that became highly prized real estate among an 'orientalized' Israeli bourgeoisie. Images, broadcast internationally, of the evacuated settlements taken over by Palestinians may also have triggered barely repressed middle-class anxieties at the root of the suburban project itself: the internally ordered, well-serviced outposts of a 'first world' collapsing in the face of a 'barbaric' surge of the 'third world' irrupting on it from the outside. Together with a vision of technological superiority, it may have been this fear that prompted a high-ranking Israeli military officer, inspired by newly developed techniques for physically relocating buildings, to propose rolling settlement homes across the border on steel tracks. In an equally bizarre scenario, when a rabbi from one of the settlements petitioned the High Court of Justice to oppose the destruction of his Gaza synagogue, the government proposed to examine an option for the relocation of the nineteen synagogues of the Gaza Strip which would involve airlifting parts of them out by helicopter.

The US administration was firmly opposed to the destruction of the settlements. Handing over homes, public buildings, agricultural and industrial assets was seen by President Bush and Condoleezza Rice as more than a mere economic stimulus.[4] What could better fit the American agenda of civilizing the Middle East into a liberal society with broad middle-class values than having Palestinians live in American-style single-family homes? In response to US demands, the Israeli government announced that it would reconsider its decision to demolish settlement homes. Deputy Prime Minister Shimon Peres sought to sell them to the Palestinians or to give them 'on account' of any claims Palestinians might make for the homes they were forced to leave behind in 1948 in areas now under Israeli control.[5] Mohamed Alabbar, the flamboyant Arab businessman (who is slated to be the equivalent of Donald Trump in the pan-Arab TV show version of *The Apprentice*), arrived in Israel six months prior to the evacuation, met with Shimon Peres and briefly with Sharon, and offered to buy all the homes and other real estate assets in the settlements of Gush Katif for $56 million. Alabbar is the chairman of Emaar Properties, a gigantic real estate company registered in the United Arab Emirates which has been a central player in the frantic development of Dubai, specializing in rapid construction of themed onshore tourist and residential projects. He imagined Katif as the site for a possible tourist enclave.[6] This resulted in bizarre and grotesque plans for Dubai-style, large high-rise hotel complexes, and settler homes becoming part of a set of tourist villages, on what was now dubbed 'the best beach resort of the Mediterranean'; had they come to fruition, such complexes would no doubt have become extraterritorial enclaves set against the deep poverty that surrounded them. These fantasies never got very far. But, together with other proposals for wholesale privatization, they would have robbed Palestinians of the evacuated public land to which they were entitled, and desperately needed.

It was therefore no wonder that, when Palestinians were asked to pay for the structures by which the occupation of their lands was perpetuated – or, considering Israel's price offer, to over-pay for them – or even to allow the allocation of money that could have otherwise been earmarked for their use, they responded angrily. Palestinian Minister Saeb Erekat stated that the Palestinians were not interested in purchasing the infrastructure and told Israel simply to 'dismantle the houses and take them away'.[7] Jihad Alwazir, permanent secretary at the Palestinian Ministry of Planning, claimed that 'the settlements are an alien body that was forced on the Palestinians', and that if it were up to him, he would 'have a big bonfire [of the settlements] . . . where every Palestinian should come with a hammer and bang on a building'.[8] In Israel, these and other similar

Palestinian pronouncements were interpreted – as are many Palestinian state-ments – as a double bluff in the context of haggling over the price of the homes, rather than as sincere rejection; accordingly, Israel continued to 'play poker' over the price of the settlements right up to the final weeks before the evacuation.

In November 2004, I attended a discussion regarding the fate of the Gaza settlements in Sham'l, the Palestinian Diaspora and Refugee Centre in Ramallah. There, proposals that Palestinians should reside in evacuated settlement homes were met with objection, even aversion: 'How could anyone expect us to reside in the same homes, look out of the same windows, use the same rooms, that our oppressors have used?' Architecture was commonly understood to be one of the direct instruments of occupation. For one of the speakers the settlements even seemed to be haunted – a settlement site in the West Bank was referred to as Tel A Jnein, 'hill of the demons'. In Palestine/Israel – where almost every act of settlement is an act of erasure and re-inhabitation – each side considers different locations to be haunted. Here, no one is ever the 'first' or 'original' occupier; but being a subsequent occupier – either to one's present-day enemies or to an imagined or real ancient civilization – is a condition that turns the inhabitation of old cities, archaeological sites, battlegrounds and destroyed villages into culturally complex acts of co- or trans-habitation.[9] Buildings have them-selves acquired an active role in the unfolding political drama. Not only were the settlement houses seen as haunted sites containing 'ghosts', but they also seemed to have acquired a kind of subjectivity in which architectural elements – roofs, windows, doors and walls – were seen as living organs. To be exorcized, archi-tecture must burn; in Alwazir's view, this would produce a 'cathartic release'.[10]

Other grounds for objection to the re-inhabitation of settlement homes were articulated in the typical language of planning. While settlement homes might suit families of three to six, an extended family in Gaza is typically more than double this size. Furthermore, the 1,500 homes that were to be evacuated were seen as almost irrelevant in the face of the urgent housing needs of more than half a million Palestinians.

Plans drawn up by the Palestinian Ministry of Planning anticipated the destruc-tion of most settlements and the re-ruralization of the evacuated areas. I was shown the masterplans for the area of the coastal Katif settlement block by Khalil Nijem, Director-General of the Ministry of Planning in Ramallah; they were coloured with different shades of solid and hatched green, delineating the nature reserves, recreational areas and beaches that would replace the evacuated settlements. This *tabula rasa* scenario resonated well with an awakened nostalgia for the period before the occupation, when Gazans had access to such sites located among the white sand dunes on the shores of the Mediterranean.[11]

Several months before the evacuation was scheduled to begin, the appointment of James Wolfensohn, formerly president of the World Bank, to the newly created office of Special Envoy for Gaza Disengagement on behalf of the 'Quartet' of the US, UN, EU and the Russian Federation testified to the broad international commitment to and engagement with the project. However, it also highlighted the kind of economic approach the Quartet wanted to adopt. Although Wolfensohn initially attempted to broker a 'peaceful handover of all structures', and even gave half a million dollars of his own money to help buy back Israeli greenhouses for the use of Gazan farmers, other economic prospects caused him to change his mind. Working in cooperation with the World Bank under the presidency of the arch-neo-conservative Paul Wolfowitz, and in line with its reflex response of privatization, Wolfensohn assembled a coalition of wealthy property developers, including Mohamed Alabbar, who were prepared to invest large sums of money in exchange for long leases on the evacuated and vacant land for various schemes of private development.[12]

De-camping refugees

Seeing other prospects for development, the EU's foreign policy coordinator, Javier Solana, wanted the 'settlement villas' destroyed and removed in order 'to make way for high-rise construction'[13] for the housing of refugees. The Palestinian Ministry of Planning itself examined proposals submitted to it by the Foundation for Middle East Peace, a think-tank based in Washington DC, which proposed, in the context of similar evacuations in the West Bank, that refugees should be resettled in settlements close to Palestinian cities.[14]

Those who proposed housing Palestinian refugees in the abandoned settlement homes, or in European-style housing blocks built in their place, were treading on a political minefield. Attempts to implement permanent housing for refugees would be perceived by many Palestinians as the undoing of the temporary nature of the refugee camps and with it the physical proof of the urgency of the Palestinian claim for a return to the places from whence they were deported in 1948. For many refugees, having an address in the camp maintains the address in the lost city or village. Building a new house in the camp is sometimes seen as a betrayal of the national cause, and it is primarily the younger generation that rejects plans for reconstruction.[15] A sense of temporariness is often maintained by Palestinian political organizations, in their insistence on keeping infrastructure in camps to a bare minimum. Sewage often runs overground, trees are not planted, and other signs of permanence are avoided.[16] The refugee camp is thus kept in an Orwellian 'endless present' without past and with no future. This policy became apparent in the 1970s, when, under the influence of Marxist ideology, then prevalent within the PLO, domestication was seen as anathema to the Palestinian revolution. The 'permanent revolution' relied on the negation of the home as a sign of bourgeois culture. Maintaining the temporary, harsh conditions in the camps also formed part of revolutionary guerrilla warfare which is termed in French 'la politique du pire' – the politics of making conditions worse: the worse things get, the deeper the crisis, the faster political change will arise.[17]

It is thus not surprising that counter-revolutionary approaches often tried to induce domestication. From the British-built 'New Villages' in Malaysia through to the Portuguese 'Aldeamentos' in Angola, and the French 'Douars' in Algeria to the US-built 'Strategic Hamlets' in Vietnam, resettlement projects have been carried out as central components of strategies of 'counter-insurgency' and pacification, demonstrating that the default response to the violence of the colonized has always been increased spatial discipline. These housing projects were seen as part of a general colonial policy variously referred to as 'modernization', 'urbanization', 'civilization', 'hygienization', 'de-peasantization' or, as in our context, the 'de-camping' of refugees.

In the eyes of the IDF, refugee camps were seen not only as the place in which the resistance is located and organized, but as the socio-physical environment that creates it. Throughout the occupation, periodic attempts by the IDF to upgrade infrastructure and living standards in the very places it believed its enemies were located sought to eradicate what were believed to be the breeding grounds of discontent, but also to bring about a process of forced *embourgeoisement* which was meant to create the very vulnerabilities that may reduce the motivation of the urban population to support active resistance.

According to a comprehensive study conducted by Palestinian sociologist Norma Masriyeh Hazboun, it is for this very reason that the rehousing of refugees has been a central part of Israeli strategic thinking since the end of the 1967 war, when Israel gained control over Gaza and the West Bank where many refugee camps were located.[18] For Israeli politicians and military officers, turning refugees into city- or village-dwellers was thought to be a solution to 'the refugee problem', itself seen as the main precondition of the conflict, and reflected their belief that political problems can be reduced to social-economic or even urban ones. Indeed, the first proposals for construction in the occupied territories, debated by the Israeli government immediately after the 1967 war, were not only for the building of Israeli settlements, but for the provision of new homes for Palestinian refugees from Gaza.[19] A central component of the Allon plan[20] sought to 'liquidate the refugee problem' by the gradual evacuation of the camps into new, specially conceived towns and villages to be built by Israel with the help of international funding in some particularly arid parts of the West Bank and in northern Sinai. The plan included outlines for the construction of three pilot settlement-towns on the eastern slopes of the Hebron Desert where the authorities would monitor whether or not Palestinian refugee families could adapt to the area's harsh climate.[21] In 1968, Prime Minister Levy Eshkol was hesitant and ambiguous about these resettlement projects but reminisced how, when he was in Africa, he 'saw how to settle primitive nations' and supported 'the building of some kind or another of prefabricated houses [in the Occupied Territories] . . .'.[22] These early plans all came to nothing because the government believed that it was the international community that should fund these schemes; however, with objections from the Arab states, little international help was forthcoming.

Attempts to rehouse the refugee have thus taken a coercive, violent turn. The destruction in Shati, Jebalia and Rafah refugee camps in 1971–72 by military forces under Ariel Sharon, then Chief of Southern Command, was undertaken with the intention not of widening the internal roadways and creating a controllable urban plan[23] but of making the refugees homeless and in need of new homes – and thereby forcing the government to implement a refugee resettlement programme. In his autobiography Sharon later explained that the camps 'bred the most serious problems . . . It would be to our great advantage to eliminate them once and for all . . . [and] we should take pains to provide decent housing . . .'.[24] The destruction of 6,000 homes in the refugee camps of Gaza was intended, in the words of Shlomo Gazit, 'to evacuate one-third of the Strip's refugee population, about 60,0000–70,000 people, to new places . . .'.[25] Out of the 160,000 refugees in Gaza in 1971, Sharon suggested that the government should resettle 70,000 within new neighbourhoods to be built within the towns of Gaza; another 70,000 should be settled in the cities and towns of the West Bank, and 20–30,000 more, controversially, within Palestinian towns in Israel.[26] The idea was not accepted by the government, but other attempts to house refugees were nevertheless implemented with the support of Minister of Defence Moshe Dayan. Between 1972 and 1979 four new neighbourhoods for refugees were constructed adjacent to the large camps of the Gaza Strip. They included Israeli-style dense housing schemes, simply replicating existing plans provided by the Israeli Ministry of Housing, constructed by Palestinian developers. The Israeli government took foreign visitors on tours to show off the new housing schemes, claiming they demonstrated their enlightened rule and attempts solve the 'refugee problem' by providing decent housing. But Dayan also explained the behaviouristic logic of this policy when he claimed that 'as long as the refugees remain in their camps . . . their children will say they come from Jaffa or Haifa; if they move out of the camps, the hope is that they will feel an attachment to their new land'.[27] In 1974 another approach

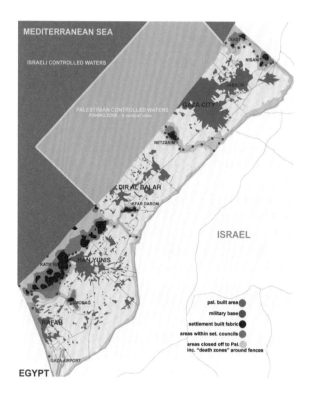

Israeli settlements in Gaza, Eyal Weizman 2005.

for the resettlement of refugees was implemented with a program in which refugees were provided with plots of 250 square metres and given the means to build their own homes. Financial assistance was handed out on condition that refugees physically demolished their older homes in the camps.[28] Methods used by Israeli occupation authorities to convince reluctant refugees included threats and random demolitions within the camps as well as visits by Palestinian collaborators to refugee households. The PLO forbade refugees to accept these Israeli offers and killed some of those who did, as well as many of the Palestinian collaborators.[29] The programme received its final impetus in 1981–2 when Ariel Sharon served as Minister of Defence, and died out after he was fired from government at the beginning of 1983 for his role in the Christian Falangist Massacre in the Palestinian refugee camps of Sabra and Shatila in Lebanon. According to UNRWA records, throughout the entire duration of the programme, a total of some 10,000 homes for refugees were provided by Israel, but barely keeping up with the natural annual demographic growth in the existing camps.[30] Although, some neighbourhoods for refugees – such as

EVACUATIONS   231

the Sheikh Radwan resettlement scheme north of Gaza City – were success-fully constructed and inhabited and even named by the occupation authorities Kfar Shalom (the Village of Peace, but referred to mockingly by Palestinians as Sharon's Neighbourhood) – the programme failed to subdue Palestinian resistance, and some of the new populated housing areas themselves became centres of resistance.[31]

Re-inhabiting de-colonized architecture

The Palestinian rejection of proposals to re-inhabit the evacuated Gaza settle-ments in 2005 was to resist as well a strong temptation present throughout the history of decolonization. Colonial buildings and infrastructure left behind when imperialist regimes were dismantled were usually appropriated by newly formed postcolonial administrations. Such repossession tended to reproduce some of the colonial power relations in space: colonial villas were inhabited by new finan-cial elites and palaces by political ones, while the evacuated military installations of colonial armies were often used to prop up new national regimes. Frantz Fanon, pondering the possible corruption of national, postcolonial governments, warned during the Algerian liberation struggle that, if not destroyed, the phys-ical and territorial reorganization of the colonial world may once again 'mark out the lines on which a colonized society will be organized'.[32]

In the British Mandate of Palestine, during the Arab Revolt of 1936–9, British forces erected a string of military installations near or within Palestinian cities. Most of the British military infrastructure that remained in Israeli terri-tory after the 1948 war later served as police stations and military bases. Some of these bases, built within Palestinian areas, were perfectly placed to continue the tactical task of population control for which they were originally built.[33]

Some participants at the round-table discussions in Sham'l in Ramallah warned that following these patterns of colonial reuse, the postcolonial adaptation of the evacuated Israeli settlements in Gaza might reproduce something of the alienation, hostility and violence of the occupation by turning them into 'luxury' Palestinian suburbs. They feared that the system of walls, fences, and surveil-lance technologies around them would hasten their seamless transformation into gated communities for the Palestinian returnee elites.

But evacuated colonial architecture does not necessarily reproduce its previous power structures. Some evacuated British military infrastructure in the West Bank and Gaza became the nuclei for refugee camps. The Balata refugee camp, at the eastern entrance to the city of Nablus, and the Rafah refugee camp, at the southern edge of the Gaza Strip, were both established within evacuated

British military bases. Laid out according to a gridded, military geometry, these bases-turned-refugee camps have surrendered to the formless topologies of everyday human activity. Unable to expand, they have overgrown their original layout, forming dense maze-like environments.

The subversion of the original use of evacuated colonial settlements was apparent in the fate of the first Israeli settlements to be evacuated. The town of Yamit and the agrarian settlements surrounding it on the Rafah Salient on Sinai's northern Mediterranean coast were razed to the ground after an evacuation conducted by Minister of Defence Ariel Sharon, in 1982 following the 1978 peace accord with Egypt. Sharon's rationale was his wish to avoid an 'Egyptian town of a hundred thousand on Israel's border'.[34] However, the Israeli settlements of Sinai's Red Sea coast – Neviot (Nuweba), Di Zahav (Dahab) and Ophira (Sharm el-Sheik) – were left intact and met different fates. Around the military and civilian infrastructural nucleus of the former Israeli town of Ophira, Sharm el-Sheikh has grown into an international tourist town, hosting more than a million tourists annually. The airport of Sharm el-Sheikh, busy with charter flights bringing European package holidaymakers, is an ex-Israeli military airport, strangely still carrying the name Ophira. Neviot, a small cooperative agricultural settlement of the Moshav type, has become home to Egyptian police personnel and their families. The evacuated Moshav settlement and desert retreat of Di Zahav provided the infrastructure for the expansion of the tourist Bedouin village of Dahab.

In the spring and summer of 2005 I took part, together with Palestinian and Norwegian planners (the latter have been employed as advisers in the ministry since the Oslo Accord) from the Palestinian Ministry of Planning, in the architectural formulation of another approach to the reuse of the Gaza settlements. In this scheme, the settlement buildings would be reused but for a function other than housing: they would be transformed into public institutions – hospitals, clinics, schools, academies, training centres, educational centres and cultural centres. If the geography of occupation was to be liberated, we thought, its potential should be turned against itself.

Four months before the evacuation was scheduled to take place, in May 2005, the Ministry of Planning succeeded in convincing the rest of the Palestinian government – each of its ministries themselves having claims on and plans for the settlements – to allocate the building of three of the settlements, Morag, Netzarim and Kfar Darom, to public institutions. From the Israeli perspective, these three smaller colonies, strategically built like frontier outposts outside the main settlement-blocks, were considered 'isolated'; however, in relation to the Palestinian towns they were built to confront, they were very close, almost contiguous and potentially an extension of their fabric. The architectural challenge was to rationalize a set of public institutions within the repetitive domestic shells of evacuated settlement homes. To this end, the settlement of Morag was designated an agricultural education centre, an extension of the University of Gaza. Its single-family homes were to be adapted as classrooms, libraries and storage facilities. Some of the small private gardens, surrounding fields and greenhouses were to be devoted to horticultural education. The built infrastructure of Kfar Darom, meanwhile, was to be assigned to the International Committee of the Red Cross for use as a hospital and medical campus. The large agricultural storage facilities of Netzarim settlement, the closest to Gaza City, were designated to provide facilities for the port of Gaza that was to be built on a nearby stretch of coast. The domestic part of the Netzarim, comprising about fifty small, single-family homes, was to be converted into an education centre. Here, we allocated space for a growing archive of documents, testimonies, films and photographs that had been widely collected by local and international organizations and NGOs throughout the occupation.

Public institutions occupying the mundane fabric of suburban structures could spawn a new type of institution. It was possible to imagine the subversion of the entire geography of occupation in the West Bank, with each of the evacuated residential settlements used to a different end from that it had been designed and built for.

In the end, however, there was nothing to reuse. Responding to its inner destructive impulses and fearing attempts by settlers to return to their homes, the Israeli government ordered the military to demolish the settlements in their entirety. The World Bank estimated the total amount of rubble generated from this destruction to be about 1.5 million tons, between 60,000 and 80,000 truckloads. The demolition and the removal of the rubble posed a complex logistical problem as some of the older structures contained large quantities of asbestos. At the end of 2005, Israel and the UN Development Program (UNDP) signed an agreement in which Israel would pay the UNDP $25 million, which, in turn, would pay Palestinian contractors to sort, clear, compact and store the rubble from the destroyed settlement buildings. With no international investment, with no possibility of working in Israel, and with no opportunity to export goods on account of an endless Israeli siege, this financing of the clearing up of the mess it had left behind was presented by Israel in a mockingly philanthropic tone as a project 'aimed at boosting the economy of the Gaza Strip'.[35]

This rubble – composed of the crushed mixture of the homes, public buildings, synagogues, fortifications and military bases that until recently made up Israel's colonial project in Gaza – is now being gradually wheeled into the Mediterranean and deposited there in the form of a large arch, as a wave-breaker around

the site where the planned deep-sea port of Gaza is to be built. Standing idle –
as the port construction will forever await Israeli security clearance – this giant
earthwork-jetty may after all demonstrate the best use of the architecture of
Israeli occupation.

The remnants of a car after an Israeli targeted assassination, Khan Yunis, Gaza. Miki Kratsman, 2005.

9.

Targeted Assassinations:
The Airborne Occupation

The fighter plane is the quintessence of modern civilization . . . It soars above good and evil, a celestial goddess with an insatiable thirst for sacrificial tribute.

Azmi Bishara

On 13 September 2005 – the 'day after the day after' – when the Israeli evacuation of the Gaza Strip was complete, the ground bases of the occupying forces were translocated to the airspace over the Strip, to the territorial waters off its coastline and to the border terminals along the fences that cut it off from the rest of the world. The geography of occupation thus completed a ninety-degree turn: the imaginary 'orient' – the exotic object of colonization – was no longer beyond the horizon, but now under the vertical tyranny of a western airborne civilization that remotely managed its most sophisticated and advanced technological platforms, sensors and munitions in the spaces above.

Since the beginning of the second Intifada, limitations on its ability to maintain a permanent ground presence throughout the Palestinian territories had reinforced Israel's reliance on a tactical logic that sought to disrupt Palestinian armed and political resistance through targeted assassination – namely, extra-juridical state executions, undertaken most frequently from the air.[1] In fact, the tactical precondition for Israel's policy of territorial withdrawal was that its security services be able to maintain domination of the evacuated areas by means other than territorial control. An IDF think-tank called the 'Alternative Team' (as if it were a group of comic-book heroes) was involved in rethinking Israeli security after the evacuation of Gaza. They admitted: 'whether or not we are physically present in the territories, we should still be able to demonstrate our ability to control and affect them . . .'[2] They, and other military planners, referred to the occupation that will follow the Occupation – i.e. the domination of Palestinians after the evacuation of the ground space of the Gaza Strip and parts of the West

Bank is completed – as the 'invisible occupation', the 'airborne occupation' and/or 'occupation in disappearance'.[3]

The ability of the Israeli Air Force to maintain a constant 'surveillance and strike' capability over Palestinian areas was one of the main reasons for the Sharon government's confidence, and popular support, in pursuing unilateral ground withdrawals and accordingly transforming the logic of occupation. Sharon's sacking of Chief of Staff Moshe Ya'alon and his replacement with the pilot and former Air Force Commander Dan Halutz, several months before the ground evacuation of Gaza, testified to the perceived shift of military emphasis from the ground to the air, and of the Israeli government's acceptance of Halutz's mantra: 'technology instead of occupation'.[4] Until the result of the 2006 war in Lebanon made him realize otherwise, Halutz was known to be the strongest proponent of the belief that air-power could gradually replace many of the traditional functions of ground forces. In a lecture he delivered at the military National Security College in 2001 he explained that 'the capability of the Air Force today renders some traditional assumptions – that victory equals territory – anachronistic'.[5]

Indeed, throughout the years of the second Intifada, major efforts were directed at the development and 'perfection' of the tactics of airborne targeted assassinations. From a 'rare and exceptional emergency method' it has become the Air Force's most common form of attack. According to Ephraim Segoli, a helicopter pilot and former commander of the Air Force base at Palmahim, located halfway between Tel Aviv and Gaza, from which most helicopter assassination raids have been launched and currently the location of the largest fleets of remote-controlled killer drones, airborne 'liquidations are the central component of IDF operations and the very essence of the "war" it is waging'. Segoli, speaking in May 2006, claimed, furthermore, that 'the intention to "perfect" these operations meant that Israel's security industries have . . . started concentrating [much of their effort] on the development of systems that primarily serve this operational logic'.[6]

Most states at one time or another have engaged in assassinations of their enemies' military and political leadership. Israel is no exception and has used assassinations in its conflict with Palestinian and Lebanese resistance for many years.[7] However, since the beginning of the Al-Aqsa Intifada in September 2000 and increasingly since the evacuation of Gaza, targeted assassinations have become the most significant and frequent form of Israeli military attack. From the beginning of the Intifada to the end of 2006, 339 Palestinians were killed in targeted assassinations. Only 210 of those were the intended targets, the rest were Palestinians whose daily lives brought them to the wrong place at the wrong time; 45 of them were children.[8] The assassinated also included most of the political leaders of Hamas.

The policy of targeted assassinations, as this chapter seeks to show, cannot be understood according to the logic of terrorist prevention alone; rather, it has become a political tool in Israel's attempt to maintain control in the Palestinian areas from which it has territorially withdrawn, and so has a territorial dimension.

'Technology instead of Occupation'

Perennial over-optimism regarding air power has led successive generations of airmen – from the early theorist of aerial bombing, Italian Giulio Douhet, at the beginning of the twentieth century, through to the present – to believe that unprecedented technological developments would allow wars to be won from the air, bombing to intimidate politicians into submission, and native populations to be managed by air power. The fantasy of a cheap aerial occupation, or 'aerially enforced colonization', is thus as old as air forces themselves. In the 1920s, Winston Churchill, as Minister of War and Air, was fascinated with what he perceived to be the economically efficient, quick, clean, mechanical and impersonal alternatives that air power could provide to the otherwise onerous and expensive tasks of colonial control. Emboldened by a murderous aerial attack on a tribal leader in Somaliland in 1920 that had put down a rebellion, he suggested that aircraft be further adapted to the tasks of policing the Empire. In 1922 Churchill persuaded the British government to invest in the Air Force and offered the Royal Air Force £6 million to take over control of the Mesopotamia (Iraq) operation from the army, which had cost £18 million thus far.[9] The policy, called 'control without occupation', saw the Royal Air Force successfully replacing large and expensive army contingents. Sir Percy Cox, the high commissioner in Baghdad, reported that by the end of 1922 'on [at least] three occasions, demonstrations by aircraft [have been sufficient to bring] tribal feuds to an end. On another occasion, planes . . . dropped bombs on a sheik and his followers who refused to pay taxes, held up travellers and attacked a police station.'[10] Arthur 'Bomber' Harris (so-called for his infamous bombing campaigns on German working-class districts when commander of the RAF's bomber wing during World War II) reported after a mission in Iraq in 1924: 'The Arab and Kurd now know what real bombing means, in casualties and damage. They know that within 45 minutes a full-sized village can be practically wiped out and a third of its inhabitants killed or injured.'[11] The methods pioneered in Somaliland were also applied by the RAF against revolutionaries in Egypt, Darfur, India, Palestine (mainly during the 1936–9 Arab Revolt)[12] and in Afghanistan in Jalalabad and Kabul. Anticipating the logic of targeted assassinations, Harris later boasted that the latter war was won by a single strike on the king's palace.[13]

Similar belief in 'aerially enforced occupation' allowed the Israeli Air Force to believe it could replace the network of lookout posts woven through the topography by translating categories of 'depth', 'stronghold', 'highpoint', 'closure' and 'panoramas' into 'air-defence in depth', 'clear skies', 'aerial reconnaissance', 'aerially enforced closure' and 'panoramic radar'. With a 'vacuum cleaner' approach to intelligence gathering, sensors aboard unmanned drones, aerial reconnaissance jets, attack helicopters, unmanned balloons, early warning Hawkeye planes and military satellites capture most signals emanating from Palestinian airspace. Since the beginning of the second Intifada, the Air Force has put in hundreds of thousands of flight hours, harvesting streams of information through its network of airborne reconnaissance platforms, which were later placed at the disposal of different intelligence agencies and command-and-control rooms.

Where previously the IDF had cordoned off an area with fences and earth works, and placed checkpoints on the approach roads, today the airborne occupation of Gaza enforces its closures by leafleting villages and refugee camps around the area to be shut off, declaring it to be off limits – and then targeting whoever tries to enter. In this very manner the evacuated settlements of the northern part of Gaza have remained 'off limits' ever since the 2005 evacuation. Following the evacuation, another procedure (code-named 'a knock on the door') replaced military bulldozers with bomber jets for the purpose of house demolition. This new method involves an Air Force operator telephoning the occupants of the house to be demolished – as happened on 24 August 2006 at the A-Rahman family home in Jebalia refugee camp:

> On Thursday 24 August 2006, at 23:30, someone telephoned the house of Abed A-Rahman in Jebalia claiming to be from the IDF. The phone had been disconnected because the bill had not been paid to the Palestinian phone company, but was activated for the sake of this conversation. The wife of Abed A-Rahman, Um-Salem, answered the phone . . . [on the other side of the line a voice] said 'evacuate the house immediately and notify the neighbours'. She asked 'Who is talking?' and was answered: 'The IDF'. She asked again but her interlocutor had hung up. Um- Salem tried to use the phone but it was disconnected again . . . the entire family left the house without having the possibility to take anything with them. At 24:00 the house was bombed by military helicopters and was completely destroyed.[14]

Operational planning

The operational aspects of airborne targeted assassinations rely on military developments that originated in Israel's war in Lebanon during the 1980s and 1990s. In February 1992 Hizbollah Secretary-General Sheikh Abbas Mussawi was the first to be killed in an airborne assassination when a group of Israeli helicopters flying inland from the Mediterranean Sea, attacked his convoy, killing him and his family. The first airborne targeted assassination in Palestinian areas took place on 9 November 2000 when an Israeli Apache helicopter pilot launched a US-made 'Hellfire' anti-tank missile at the car of a senior member of the Tanzim al-Fatah organization, Hussein Muhammad Abayit, in Beit-Sahur near Bethlehem, killing him and two women, Rahmeh Shahin and 'Aziza Muhammed Danun, who happened to be walking by the car when it exploded in the middle of their street. The IDF's spokesperson announced that the killing was part of 'a new state policy'.[15] In recent years it is Gaza, however, that has become the world's largest laboratory for airborne assassinations. The US administration made feeble protestations about the Israeli assassinations, diplomatically demanding that Israel merely 'considers the results of its actions', and suggesting that different branches of the US security forces, themselves engaged in unacknowledged assassinations using unmanned drones in the Middle East, 'examine Israeli Air Force performances and results in order to draw lessons for its own wars'.[16]

Ephraim Segoli explained that targeted assassinations were 'a success story based upon a high degree of cooperation between the General Security Service (GSS or Shin Bet) and the Air Force'.[17] Above all, the mechanistic operation of targeted assassinations was fed by the information and organizational powers that the GSS developed under Avi Dichter, who gained considerable public popularity and earned the respect of Sharon as a result of their 'success'. The efficiency of the operations relied on close networking between the intelligence provided by the GSS, fast-tracked political decisions and the strike capacity of the Air Force. The GSS drafts the death-lists and prioritizes targets (once included, rarely has a named target been removed from the list), provides files on each person to be liquidated (including details of their involvement in resistance and their preceived danger to Israel); a special ministerial committee gives its approval (the typical length of deliberation is fifteen minutes, and there are generally no objections); and the Air Force does the killing.

Each targeted assassination is a large-scale operation that integrates hundreds of specialists from different military branches and security apparatuses. Beyond its reliance on background intelligence, targeted assassination depends on sharing real-time information between various agents, commanders, operators and different military planes, and their ability to act upon it. After a Palestinian is put on the death list he is followed, sometimes for weeks, by a 'swarm' of various unmanned aircraft. Often, different swarms would follow different people simultaneously in different areas of the Gaza Strip. In this way, the security services establish the targeted person's daily routines and habits, and maintain continuous visual contact with him until his killing.[18] As well as being cheaper to operate, unmanned drones have the advantage over manned planes or helicopters in that they can remain in the air around the clock, some for as long as thirty hours, and because their formations circulate in relatively small areas while providing a multiplicity of angles of vision. Moreover, drones are quiet and barely visible to the human eye. This is the reason why, from 2004, the Air Force started to shoot its missiles from drones rather than from its more visible attack helicopters or jets. A swarm of various types of drones, each circulating at a different altitude, up to 30,000 feet, is navigated by a GPS system and woven by radio communication into a single synergetic reconnaissance and killing instrument that conducts the entire assassination operation. Some drones are designed to view the terrain vertically downwards in order to establish the digital coordinates of a targeted person, while others look diagonally, in order to distinguish facial features or identify a vehicle's licence plates. Some drones are designed to intercept radio signals and mobile phones, others can carry and shoot missiles. With the development and proliferation of drone technology, there remains, as Shimon Naveh put it, 'very few Israeli soldiers in the airspace over Gaza . . . the air is mainly filled with Golems . . . an army without soldiers'. Although until 2004, military jets and helicopters carried out the assassinations, they are now largely used to divert attention from the real area of operations by flying over other parts of the Gaza Strip when the assassinations take place.[19] During the second Intifada, Israel's Armament Development Authority – Rafael – developed the 'Spike' missile to replace the US-made 'Hellfire' laser-guided, anti-tank missile for the purpose of targeted assassinations. The Spike is itself a small joystick-navigated 'kamikaze' drone with an 'optical eye'.[20]

Targeted assassinations often rely on cooperation from the ground. The clandestine Unit 504, jointly operated by military intelligence and the GSS, is responsible for the recruitment and direction of foreign agents, and for forcing Palestinians to collaborate. From one of its bases south of Haifa – where it also maintains Facility 1391, a Guantanamo Bay-style secret prison for 'administrative detainees' – Unit 504 trains groups of Palestinian commandos to mark targets, plant and detonate bombs, or 'shake the tree for the Air Force'.[21] In previous years, members of this Palestinian military unit of the IDF would splash ultraviolet paint on the roof of a car to identify the target for a pilot to destroy.

The planning of a targeted assassination follows the traditional principles of Air Force operational planning. The unit of 'operational analysis', part of the Israeli Air Force's 'operational group', is responsible for optimizing bombing missions. At the simplest level, this involves matching munitions with targets, and calculating what size and type of bomb is needed to destroy a particular target. In this role it has twice been criticized for incompetence: first for an operation on 23 July 2002 when it proposed a one-ton bomb to destroy a residential building in Gaza where the leader of Hamas' military wing Salah Shehadeh was spending the night, causing the building to collapse, killing Shehadeh and an additional fourteen Palestinian civilians, more than half of them children.[22] The second, two years later, was for allocating a quarter-ton bomb for the attack on a meeting of Hamas leaders. The bomb failed to collapse the building, allowing the leaders to escape unharmed from the ground floor.

The unit's function extends beyond physical destruction. It attempts to predict and map out the effect that destruction of a particular target might have on the enemy's overall system of operation. Following the principles of 'system analysis',[23] the enemy is understood as an operational network of interacting elements. Unlike state militaries, much of whose power is based on physical infrastructure and equipment, the effectiveness of the Palestinian resistance is grounded in its people: political and spiritual leaders, spokespersons, financiers, commanders, experienced fighters, bomb-makers, suicide volunteers and recruiters. The killing of a key individual, much like the destruction of a command-and-control centre or a strategic bridge in 'conventional wars' is intended to trigger a sequence of 'failures' that will disrupt the enemy's system, making it more vulnerable to further Israeli military action.[24] 'Killing', according to Shimon Naveh, 'injects energy into the enemy system, disrupting its institutional hierarchies . . . "operational shock" is best achieved when the rhythm of these operations is rapid and the enemy system is not given time to recover between attacks'. Although 'there can be no precise prediction of the outcome of these killings', the effect, according to Naveh, is a degree of institutional and political chaos that allows Israeli security forces to sit back and see 'how the cards fall'.[25]

When the opportunity for an assassination arises, or when an emergency situation develops, information about the targeted person's location, direction and speed is transferred as radio and image data between the drones and the control room where members of the GSS, the General Staff and Air Force oversee the operation on multiple screens. After the GSS identifies the target, and the chief of the Air Force authorizes the operation, two missiles are simultaneously fired from two different drones. The missiles aim most often at a vehicle, but increasingly, and since Palestinians now often take the precaution to walk, at pedestrians. Each assassination thus juxtaposes different spaces and domains: a control room in central Tel Aviv in which young soldiers pilot drones and missiles remotely, as in a live computer game, into the narrow dusty alleys of Gaza's refugee camps where young Palestinians end their lives. The code for 'hit' is Alfa and for 'kill' is 'Champagne'. Cheap Israeli versions of the latter are traditionally served by the GSS after a successful operation.

One of hundreds of counter-points to these digitized visions of 'precision' killing was provided by 'Aref Daraghmeh, a witness to an August 2002 targeted assassination in the village of Tubas in the West Bank:

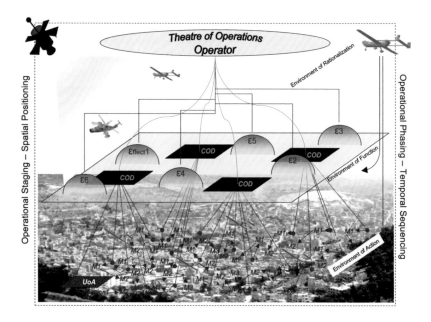

Presentation slide, OTRI, 2004.

The helicopter . . . fired a third missile towards a silver Mitsubishi, which had four people in it. The missile hit the trunk and the car spun around its axis. I saw a man escaping the car and running away. He ran about 25 meters and then fell on the ground and died. The three other passengers remained inside. I saw an arm and an upper part of a skull flying out of the car. The car went up in flames and I could see three bodies burning inside it. Three minutes later, after the Israeli helicopters left, I went out to the street and began to shout. I saw people lying on the ground. Among them was six-year-old Bahira . . . She was dead . . . I also saw Bahira's cousin, Osama . . . I saw Osama's mother running towards Bahira, picking her up and heading towards the a-Shifa clinic, which is about 500 meters away. I went to the clinic and saw her screaming after seeing the body of her son, Osama.[26]

Legalizing killing

The IDF employs the sanitizing term 'focused obstruction' or 'focused pre-emption' to describe these assassinations. Such rhetoric is repeated by most of the popular Israeli media, which conceals as far as possible the real impact of the killings, mostly avoiding to mention the names of Palestinian civilians killed in Israeli attacks and the display of the corpses, blood and body parts – the very images on which it lingers when covering the aftermath of a Palestinian terror attack. Indeed, the Israeli media's use of selective imagery allows it to project assassination not only as necessary, but also as ethical, rhetorically legalizing it by what Neve Gordon called 'the discursive production of a pseudo-judicial process'.[27] Clips from the 'kamikaze' camera on 'smart missiles' and from other airborne sensors are later broadcast in the popular media to support IDF refutations of Palestinian accusations about indiscriminate killing, and to focus political and public resolve for the further application of this tactic. The images and videos from these munitions are as much a media product as they are 'operation footage'. It would be unsurprising if their ability to produce 'broadcast-able' images were not actually specified in the briefs of their technological development.[28]

Another factor helping maintain a high level of popular support was the daily terror alerts which Dichter's GSS routinely released. Their average during the height of the Intifada, from 2001 to 2003, was between forty and fifty a day, and Israeli public support for targeted assassination stood at about 80 per cent.[29]

Targeted assassinations were presented to the public by the GSS according to a *vindictive* logic that insisted that the victims had 'blood on their hands'. However, press releases describing a victim as the 'most wanted' or the most senior individual in a particular Palestinian organization were issued so frequently that even the bellicose Israeli public started to question their accuracy.

Revenge is clearly not a legitimate argument for state killing. When challenged in the Israeli High Court of Justice over the killings, government representatives justified assassination with a preventive logic that described the targeted individual as an imminent danger, a 'ticking bomb' about to explode in an impending terror attack, often even in a 'mega terrorist attack'.[30] The legal framework for targeted assassinations has developed in response to the pace of events. Immediately after the start of the second Intifada, the head of the IDF's legal branch, Colonel Daniel Reisner, stated that due to the heightened level and frequency of Palestinian violence, Israel could start defining its military operations in the Occupied Territories as an 'armed conflict short of war', which placed the Intifada in the context of international law rather than criminal law.[31] Such a definition implied that, for the purpose of their killing (but not their internment), members of militant Palestinian organizations could be seen as combatants and thus attacked at will, not just when in the process of a hostile action or while resisting arrest.[32] Given that distinctions in international law between 'inside' and 'outside' regulate the logic of security operations ('internal' operations are perceived as policing or security work; external ones as military) and that the definition of 'inside' depends upon whether a state has 'effective control' over the territory in question,[33] the unilateral evacuation of the Gaza Strip strengthened Israel's conviction that targeted assassinations were legal and has therefore made their use more frequent. Politically, Israel expected that once it had evacuated settlements and retreated to the international border around Gaza, the international community would be more tolerant of these forms of military action.[34]

The politics of killings

Many of the people involved in the development and promotion of assassination methods, and in the extension of this tactic from an exceptional emergency measure into state policy, were former members of *Sayert Matkal*, a military elite commando and assassination unit whose ex-members form Israel's military and political 'elite'. They include former Prime Minister Ehud Barak and former Prime Minister Benjamin Netanyahu, former Defence Minister and current Deputy Prime Minister Shaul Mofaz, former Chief of Staff Moshe Ya'alon and GSS chief Avi Dichter, now Minster of Internal Security. As prime minister, Ehud Barak renewed orders for targeted assassination of Palestinian activists a month after the outbreak of the second Intifada. However, the policy was to gain greater momentum during the premiership of Barak's successor, Ariel Sharon, himself former commander of *Sayert Matkal*'s precursor, Unit 101.[35] After he assumed office, Sharon allowed this tactical operation to become the centre of Israel's security services response to Palestinian terror, but found ways to let it be used also as an alternative to negotiations with the Palestinians, and even as a method of derailing diplomatic initiatives. For targeted assassinations to assume this pre-eminence, they had to rely not only on the maturing of operational and technological developments, but also on legal and popular support. When all these components were put in place, less than a year after the beginning of the Intifada, targeted assassinations assumed an appetite and a life of their own, spinning beyond the ability of the military, the government, parliament, media or judiciary to restrain them.

Given the high level of Israeli public support for this tactic, no government minister could afford to let slip any opposition to the policy or the timing of a particular assassination, as recommended by the GSS, lest it be leaked by the media. The obsession with assassination gripped the entire Israeli security system and political leadership, so much so that in a 2002 meeting called to discuss the assassination of several Palestinian leaders, a military officer suggested conducting one killing every day as a matter of policy. The Minister of Defence thought it was 'indeed an idea' and Sharon seemed excited, but the GSS recommended the idea be dropped on the grounds that it was the GSS, not the military, who should decide where and when Palestinians were to be killed (at that point, in any case, killings were already being carried out at an average rate of one every five days).[36] The Israeli government, confident of its ability to hit anybody anywhere at any time, started publishing in advance the names of those to be killed.[37]

Israel's operational planning always saw the potential of targeted assassinations as more than a tactical response to imminent dangers, and rather as a component of a larger political project.[38] Military operational planning has continuously tried (and always in vain) to model the possible impact that assassinations may have on political developments.[39] From the very start of the Intifada, Palestinian political leaders were themselves assassination targets. At the end of August 2003, government authorization was given to kill the entire political leadership of Hamas in Gaza without further notice. The method was referred to as the 'hunting season' – the first leader to reveal himself would be the first to be killed. The first one to be killed was Ismail Abu Shanab, a relatively moderate political leader of Hamas, who was targeted on 21 August 2003. On 22 March 2004, Israel assassinated the spiritual leader of Hamas, Sheikh Yassin. A month later, on 17 April 2004, Yassin's successor, Abd al-Aziz Rantissi, was killed. Dichter and the Israeli government explained that the reason for these assassinations was to strengthen the position of Abbas and the moderates in the 'Palestinian street'. At the beginning of 2006, when the 'moderates' were ousted by the newly elected Hamas government, Defence Minister Shaul Mofaz repeated the warning, promising that 'no one will be immune', including the Palestinian Prime Minister Ismail Haniyeh.[40]

The government still believed that targeted assassinations provided it with 'military solutions to situations that were thought of as militarily unsolvable'.[41] It was, however, security operatives who filled the political vacuum of the Intifada, dictating political developments. The way these operatives sought to generate a political effect was in fact no different to the way Palestinian militant groups timed their terror attacks to maximize political impact. Every time a political initiative, local or international, seemed to be emerging, threatening to return the parties to the negotiation table, an assassination followed and derailed it. The list demonstrating this is long, so only a few examples are given here: on 31 July 2001, the Israeli Air Force bombed an apartment building in Nablus, in which a Hamas office was located, killing two Hamas leaders, Jamal Mansour and Jamal Salim, and two boys, bringing an end to the nearly two-month-long Hamas cease-fire. The January 2002 killing of Ra'ad Karmi, a leader in Fatah's own militant group – *Tanzim* – in preparation for which the GSS had already invested millions, could not have been stopped or postponed by anyone within the political system, although the killing was certain to bring about the collapse of a cease-fire that started in December 2001and would certainly bury an American diplomatic initiative. The assassination achieved this aim, leading to the spate of Palestinian suicide attacks of February and March 2002. On 23 July 2002, the day before the *Tanzim* was to announce a unilateral cease-fire, Salah Shehadeh was assassinated, foreclosing this development. A year later, at the beginning of the summer of 2003, another type of cease-fire, the *Hudna*, was declared and another American diplomatic initiative was launched. On 10 June 2003, while this initiative was in the process of being formulated, the military attempted to assassinate Rantissi with missile fire. A few weeks later, Israeli security forces targeted *Tanzim* militant Mahmoud Shawer in Qalqilya, derailing the initiative completely. On 1 December 2003, the same day that the Geneva Initiative was launched, the IDF conducted a massive operation attempting to kill Sheikh Ibrahim Hamed, head of Hamas in Ramallah. In June 2006, just as Mahmoud Abbas was about to declare a referendum vote on a progressive political initiative of the 'prisoners' document', Israel targeted Jamal Abu Samhadana, the commander of the Popular Resistance Committees in Gaza and the idea for the referendum was shelved.

'Radical' Palestinian leaders could thus be assassinated to open the way for a more 'pragmatic' form of politics. 'Pragmatic' leaders could be assassinated to open the way for direct confrontation or to stave off a diplomatic initiative. Other assassinations could be undertaken in order to 'restore order', others still to 'create chaos'; some assassinations would be undertaken simply because they could be undertaken, because too much money was already invested in the manhunt, because security forces enjoyed the thrill, wanted to impress foreign observers, test new technological developments or keep themselves in practice. It is the same people, members of the same organizations, who train for these operations, the same agents and officers who need 'successful' kills in their resumé to gain promotions, who are also those in charge of assessing their effects, and, based on their own assessments, continue demanding that the government authorize more attacks. In fact, the assassinations have been supervised by no one but the executioners.

A considerable part of Israel's security logic of assassinations is grounded in the bias of Israel's intelligence agencies towards personality analysis. The Israeli sociologist Gil Eyal demonstrated that, following a long orientalist tradition, the Israeli intelligence services have tended to seek motives for political developments, as well as for terror attacks, not in response to a history of repression or in pursuit of rational political goals, but in the personal irrationalities, idiosyncrasies and inconsistencies of Arab leaders.[42] When undertaken, political and economical analysis generally only provided the background context for the work of psychological profiling.[43] The natural consequence of this logic was the belief that in killing, Israel's security services remove not only a leader but also the cause of a political or security problem.

Although so much effort has been put into modelling enemy behaviour, and the security services remain confident of their methods, years of targeted assassinations have not managed to limit violence, nor have they reduced Palestinian motivation for resistance, or strengthened the hand of President Mahmoud Abbas or 'reinforced the moderates in the Palestinian street'. Indeed, these killings have never managed to 'sear the Palestinian consciousness' regarding the futility of resistance. On the contrary, assassinations have fed the conflict by creating further motivation for violent retaliations, and dramatically increased Palestinian popular support for acts of terror.[44]

The power of targeted assassination to affect politics has been most strongly felt, however, within the Israeli political system itself. In the half year from the beginning of 2004, when the political debates regarding the evacuation of Gaza settlements began, to 6 June 2004, when the 'disengagement plan' came to a vote and was authorized by the Israeli government, targeted assassinations were accelerated, leading to the death of 33 Palestinians.[45] In anticipation of the evacuation operation itself, scheduled for August 2005, the level of assassinations increased again, with July 2005 being the bloodiest month of the year.[46] This bloodshed helped Sharon present himself as 'tough on terror' while pursuing a policy that was understood in Israel as 'left leaning'. In this manner, targeted assassination paradoxically increased the support for 'territorial compromise'.

The 'humanitarian war'

In the months following the evacuation (and before the abduction of the Israeli soldier), targeted assassinations remained almost the sole form of attack that the Israeli military, now deployed around Gaza's fences and in the airspace over it, could undertake. Palestinian home-made Qassam rockets were fired into Israeli development towns. The rate of assassinations further increased, with 52 Palestinians killed during such attacks in the period to April 2006.[47]

In March 2006, the Israeli Air Force was criticized for a particularly horrific attack in which unmanned drones fired missiles at an ice-cream van in order to kill two Islamic Jihad militants who had taken refuge in it. In the event, a man and two children – brothers Ra'ad and Mahmoud Al-Batash – were killed along with the militants. In response to widespread condemnation of the attack, the chief of Israel's Air Force, Eliezer Shakedy, called a press conference in which he claimed that the Air Force makes 'super-human efforts in order to reduce the number of innocent civilian casualties in aerial strikes'.[48] To prove his claims he projected charts that numerically 'demonstrated' how the Air Force had reduced the ratio between the victims of aerial raids it defined as 'combatants', and those victims it was willing to concede were 'non-combatants' or 'uninvolved civilians'.

Data collected by the Israeli human rights organization B'Tselem shows that the military figures were skewed – largely because the military included within the definition of 'combatants' all men of combat age who happened to be in the vicinity of the assassination.[49]

Since the end of 2003, in response to ongoing international and local protests over the killing of many bystanders in targeted assassinations, and significantly since the refusal of several Israeli Air Force pilots to fly on these missions,[50] the military has begun to employ operatives whose task is to minimize 'collateral deaths'. Using cameras on auxiliary drones, they observe the surrounding context of an impending attack in order to judge the 'safest' moment to launch missiles. These specialists have effectively become the 'trigger' of the operation, deciding the level of danger to which Palestinian bystanders can be acceptably subjected. As one of these operators explained to me, they see their work not as facilitating assassinations but as saving lives; minimizing the slaughter that would undoubtedly occur were they not there to maintain vigilance.[51] Following this trend, in the summer of 2006, a new type of explosive began to be used in missiles deployed in targeted assassinations. That new munitions were being used became apparent when doctors in Gaza hospitals started receiving Palestinian victims with horrifying burn wounds, loss of limbs and internal burns never seen before. A former Israeli Air Force officer and head of the IDF's weapons-development programme Yitzhak Ben-Israel, explained that these are new munitions – referred to as 'focused lethality munitions' or 'munitions of low collateral damage' – which are designed to produce a blast more lethal, but also of smaller radius than traditional explosives. 'This technology allows [the military] to strike very small targets . . . without causing damage to bystanders or other persons . . .'[52]

At the end of November 2006, again in response to local and international protests regarding the killing of civilians, the government wanted to demonstrate it was acting to further regulate targeted assassinations. It established a 'legal committee' to rule on the assassination of individuals, with the assassination of senior political leaders subjected to the opinion of the Attorney General. A few weeks later, on 14 December 2006, in response to petitions by the Public Committee Against Torture in Israel, and the Palestinian Society for the Protection of Human Rights and the Environment (known by its Arabic acronym, LAW), the Israeli High Court of Justice issued a ruling in which other regulatory directives were outlined: assassinations could take place only if there is 'well-founded, strong and persuasive information as to the identity [of the person to be assassinated] and his activity'; if they could help curtail terror attacks; if other more moderate use of force, such as an arrest, cannot take place without gravely endangering the lives of soldiers; and if it will not lead to a 'disproportionate harm to innocent civilians'.[53]

Whether or not these measures will reduce the deaths of bystanders in targeted assassinations, a critical perspective must contend with the *claims* that these, and military developments in the technology, techniques and proficiency of targeted assassination will eventually bring about fewer unintended deaths, without having this possible outcome exonerate the act. Lacking another mode of critique to justify or oppose military actions, one would have to accept the Israeli terms of a *necro*-economy in which a 'lesser evil' or 'lesser evils', represented in a lower body count, should be measured against an imaginary or real 'greater evil', represented by more suffering and death on both sides.[54]

The theoretical terms of this argument were articulated by the human rights scholar and now a leader of the Liberal Party of Canada, Michael Ignatieff. Ignatieff claimed that in a 'war on terror', democratic societies may need to breach some basic human rights and allow their security services to engage in other covert and unsavoury state actions – in his eyes, a 'lesser evil' – in order to fend off or minimize potential 'greater evils', such as terror attacks.[55] Ignatieff is even willing to consider Israeli targeted assassinations under conditions similar to those articulated by the Israeli HCJ as 'qualifying within the effective moral-political framework of the lesser evil'.[56]

In the terms of this *necro*-economy, targeted assassinations are to be understood as the 'lesser evil' alternatives to possible greater evils that could occur to both Israelis and Palestinians. Israel, which undertakes these operations, would like Palestinians to understand that because it uses targeted assassinations it restrains its more brutal measures that would affect the entire population, killing only, or mostly, those who are 'guilty'. According to former Chief of Staff Ya'alon, 'focused obstructions are important because they [communicated to the Palestinians that we] make a distinction between the general public and the instigator of terror'.[57] From the perspective of Israelis, by allowing their state to undertake extra-juridical executions, they are simply acting to save their lives.

However, as Israeli philosopher Adi Ophir suggested, this concept of the 'lesser evil' raises a problem of a different nature: a less brutal measure is a measure that may easily be naturalized, accepted and tolerated. When normalized, this measure could be more frequently applied. Because it helps normalize the low-intensity conflicts, the overall duration of this conflict could be extended and, finally, more 'lesser evils' could be committed.[58]

The quest to make war more 'humane' – which has been written into different conventions and laws of war since the nineteenth century – may under certain conditions similarly result in making it more imaginable, more frequent. By regulating violence, the laws of war and the other moral rules that societies voluntarily impose upon themselves, society may end up legitimizing war, and even prolonging it. An example of this paradox can be found in the IDF's use of rubber-coated steel munitions. Soldiers believe that 'rubber bullets' are non-lethal munitions and that their use demonstrates restraint in non-life-threatening situations. But this perception leads to their more frequent and indiscriminate use, causing the death and permanent injury of many Palestinian demonstrators, mainly children.[59]

The military belief that it can perform 'controlled', 'elegant', 'pinhead accurate', 'discriminate' killing may thus bring about more destruction and death than 'traditional' strategies because these methods, combined with the manipulative and euphoric rhetoric used to promulgate them, induce decision-makers to authorize their frequent and extended use. The illusion of precision, here part of a rhetoric of restraint, gives the military-political apparatus the necessary justification to use explosives in civilian environments where they could not be used without injuring or killing civilians. The lower the threshold of violence a certain means is believed to possess, the more frequent its application might become.

The promoters of the instruments, techniques and rhetoric supporting such 'lesser evils' believe that by developing and perfecting them they actually exercise a restraining impact on the government and on the rest of the security forces, which would otherwise succeed in pushing for the further radicalization of violence. They believe that targeted assassinations are the more moderate alternative to the devastating capacity for destruction that the military actually possesses and which it would unleash in the form of a full-scale invasion or the renewal of territorial occupation, should the enemy exceed an 'acceptable' level of violence or breach some unspoken agreement in the violent discourse of attacks and retaliations. Confirming this logic, Air Force chief Shakedy, when arguing for targeted assassinations, explained, only a few weeks before the June 2006 invasion of Gaza, that 'the only alternative to aerial attacks is a ground operation and the reoccupation of Gaza . . . [targeted assassinations] is the most precise tool we have'.[60]

The reoccupation of Gaza starting in June 2006 and the Lebanon war of July–August 2006 both demonstrated that more destructive alternatives are always possible, especially when the 'unwritten rules' of the low-intensity conflict are perceived to have been broken. Since the kidnapping of an Israeli soldier in Gaza on 25 June 2006, over 500 Palestinians have been killed, including 88 minors, and more than 2,700 injured;[61] furthermore, infrastructure valued at $46 million, including a power plant, 270 private houses and residences, was destroyed. The killing of civilians, the displacement of communities, the intentional destruction of property and infrastructure – including airports, power stations and bridges – in both Gaza and Lebanon should be understood as eruptions of violence that sustain the threat of even greater force.

Military threats function only if gaps are maintained between the *possible* destruction an army can inflict in the application of its full destructive capacity, and the *actual* destruction it does inflict.[62] Restraint is what allows for the possibility of further escalation. A degree of restraint is thus part of the logic of almost every conventional military operation: however bad a military attack appears to be, they can always get worse.

Naturally, I am not suggesting that 'greater evils' should be preferred to lesser ones, or that war should be more brutal, rather that we should question the very terms of the economy of evils. These terms are not only part of the nature of military planning, but are integral to political 'militarism' – a culture which sees violence as permanent as a rule of history and thus military contingencies as the principal alternative available to politicians. Israeli militarism has accordingly always sought military solutions to political problems.[63] Locked within the limits defined by the degrees of violence, it continuously forecloses the exploration of other avenues for negotiations and participation in a genuine political process. At the beginning of 2006, Chief of Staff Dan Halutz expressed this world view when he stated that 'the Intifada is part of an un-resolvable . . . permanent conflict between Jews and Palestinians that started in 1929'. The military, according to Halutz, must therefore gear itself to operate within an environment saturated with conflict and a future of permanent violence. With this he echoed an often-recurring claim within the Israeli security discourse: in June 1977 Moshe Dayan, then foreign minister, declared that the presumption that Israel's conflict with the Palestinians could be 'solved' was fundamentally flawed. 'The question was not, "What is the solution?" but "How do we live without a solution?"' In the absence of both options – a political solution or the possibility of a decisive military outcome – the Israeli military would merely be 'managing the conflict'. At the beginning of 2006, Halutz still thought that the precision method of the Israeli Air Force would help keep the conflict 'on a flame low enough for Israeli society to be able to live and to prosper within it'.[64] This prediction of an ongoing conflict will, in all likelihood, go on fulfiling itself.

Hollow land

The territorial logic of Israel's occupation of Palestine is increasingly manifested by a creeping progression along a vertical axis, in opposing directions. The more efficient the destructive capacity of the Israeli Air Force has become, the deeper the resistance has had to retreat below ground. This reality sustains the last symmetry of the asymmetrical conflict: absolute control of air space and outer space (as the US military has already painfully learned in Vietnam, and the Soviets in Afghanistan) is mirrored by the enemy's mastering of subterranean warfare.[65]

Although political sovereignty is traditionally expressed in the state's control of ground territory, at present the most effective and contested political sphere is the airspace over Palestinian territories. In the context of all political negotiations to date, Israel insisted that any territorial concessions it undertakes on the ground would be on the condition that it maintains control of the airspace above it.[66] Thus, in both the Oslo process and the Camp David negotiations, Israel demanded the right to the 'use of the airspace [over Palestine] and [its] electromagnetic spectrum and their supervision'.[67] Although Avraham Shay, former director of the Israel Aviation Administration and adviser on the July 2000 Camp David negotiations, would have liked Israel's 'occupation of Palestinian airspace' defined as a matter of security, practicality and flight safety, the demand for 'overriding control' amounted in fact to a vertical limitation on the sovereignty of a future Palestinian state.[68] Even the liberal Geneva Initiative reserved the right of Israel's Air Force to conduct 'high-altitude military exercises' in the airspace over Palestine. Because it would be practically impossible to monitor what the activities are in which the Israeli Air Force might be engaged under the guise of training, Israel could locate airborne sensors and air power over Palestinian ground with impunity.[69]

President Arafat's dependency on airspace in travelling among the fragmented patchwork of Palestinian territories was the prime motivation behind Prime Minister Ehud Barak's decision to close off Gaza international airport at Dahania, at the start of the second Intifada in 2000, thereby preventing flights from the West Bank to Gaza. In December 2001 Sharon went further down this route, completely shutting off Palestinian airspace by bombing the Palestinian runways, and destroying the entire Palestinian air fleet – Arafat's presidential aircraft and his two helicopters.[70]

In its last military action before it withdrew completely from the Egyptian Sinai Peninsula in 1982, the IDF carved out a wide security corridor, codenamed Philadelphi, 10 kilometres long and several tens of metres wide, through the built fabric of the border city of Rafah, separating the town into two parts: Palestinian and Egyptian. Since the creation of this barrier, the subsurface of the border zones has been hollowed out by hundreds of tunnels that bypass the Israeli fortifications and connect the two estranged parts of what was once a single town. Tunnels that were initially dug by families who had members on both sides of the border have come to be used for a variety of purposes: as smuggling routes for cheap Egyptian cigarettes, household goods and even prostitutes; and as the main supply lines for weapons, explosives and armed recruits for the Palestinian resistance. The use of tunnels accelerated after the start of the second Intifada, when Israel completely sealed off the Gaza Strip from the

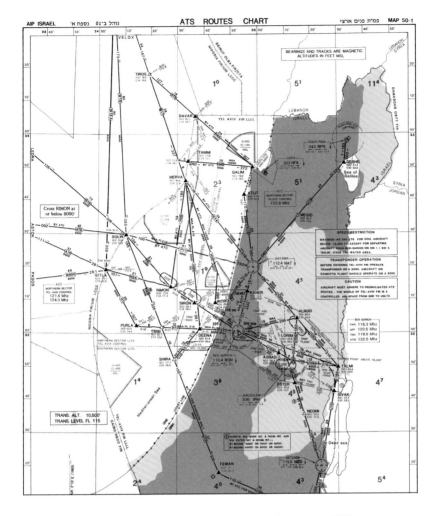

Aerial routes over Israel and the West Bank, Israel Aviation Administration, 2002.

outside world, and the demand for weapons rose. To avoid being spotted, the tunnel entrances and exits are generally located inside buildings on both sides of the border. Indeed, most tunnels have several access points and routes, starting in several homes or in chicken coops, joining together into a main route, and then branching off again into several separate passages leading to buildings on the other side. In this way, if one entrance is spotted and shut down, or a tunnel collapses through poor construction or by Israeli earth-penetrating bombs, others can still be used, and new access tunnels can be dug and connected with the main route.

Most tunnels are constructed and operated by private contractors who employ their own diggers and engineers; the contractor rents out the completed tunnels for private or military use, or sells the smuggled goods to military organizations and small businesses. Given the almost complete collapse of Gaza's economy, tunnelling has become extremely lucrative and is the main source of income in this border area for those involved.[71] The process of tunnel construction is complex and risky. Typically, a contractor rents the use of several rooms in the homes of private families, whose inhabitants must live in the house throughout the tunnel's construction so as not to arouse suspicion. Excess landfill is stored within rooms or packed into sacks and transported to remote locations. It is through the trail of excess sand that the IDF, using overhead drones to keep the area under constant surveillance, and through its collaborators on the ground, generally identifies houses that conceal tunnel entrances. However, paradoxically, the massive destruction inflicted upon the area and the huge quantities of rubble still lying around makes it easier to hide the excavated earth.

Because GPS systems do not work underground, navigation is undertaken with compasses and tape measures, aided by hand-drawn maps or markings on downloaded satellite imagery. But since tunnels are not centrally regulated, collisions between tunnels often inadvertently occur, leading to conflicts that are resolved above ground. The pace of tunnelling – between 6 and 12 metres a day, which is relatively fast for a single hand-digger – is enhanced by the fact that Gaza's soil is primarily sandy earth. But the softness of the ground can be dangerous and the tunnels need to be reinforced and shored up.

Air is pumped into the tunnel using vacuum cleaners and through ventilation shafts. The ventilation shafts, often constructed from flexible plastic hosing bored up from the tunnel and through the ploughed-up no-man's-land of the Philadelphi strip, are the most vulnerable part of a tunnel. When Israeli soldiers used to spot these shafts they threw in smoke grenades and liquid explosives. The route and depth of the tunnel must itself be carefully calculated to avoid the underground water table, Israeli touch-sensitive deep foundations of walls, and Israel's earth-penetrating radar (which requires tunnels to be at a depth of at least 15 metres).

Developments in Palestinian tunnelling techniques have also been deployed for other purposes. Israeli Air Force bombing of Gaza's cities forced weapon laboratories and ammunition depots into underground bunkers hollowed out beneath the cities and refugee camps. Tunnels have also been used to carry out subterranean attacks. In the first of these, on 26 September 2001, Palestinians detonated a 200-kilogram bomb inside a tunnel underneath the IDF border outpost of Termit on the Philadelphi corridor; it was almost completely destroyed. On at least three other separate occasions during the second Intifada Palestinians managed to burrow under military installations and blow them up with substantial quantities of explosive.[72] In another attack near Rafah on 12 May 2004, an armoured vehicle disappeared into a crater when a charge was blown underneath it.

The IDF has gradually grown to realize that its most vulnerable and porous borders are not those that it has tirelessly erected across the terrain, but rather the surface of the earth that separates it from the uncontrollable and wild subterranean spaces below it. The IDF has therefore geared itself up to fight this war in the depths of the ground. According to B'Tselem, in the context of its fight against tunnelling, the IDF has demolished about 1,800 homes since the beginning of the Al-Aqsa Intifada, in the Rafah area alone,[73] mainly on the pretext that they might conceal underground tunnels. (It is in the context of this type of destruction in Rafah that International Solidarity Movement [ISM] activist Rachel Corrie was run over by an Israeli bulldozer on 16 March 2003, when attempting to protect a house from demolition.) In 2004, the IDF claimed to have uncovered more than a hundred tunnels in Rafah since the outbreak of the Intifada.[74]

When uncovering a tunnel mouth, IDF engineering units or a contractor hired by the Egyptians on their side sometimes pour raw sewage down the tunnel, so that it continues to emit poisonous fumes for months afterward.[75] Often concrete is used to seal the tunnel, poured through long hoses along its length. Because of the seemingly endless proliferation of the tunnel networks, such casting work can never be complete. If ever uncovered, years from now, and craned out, the frozen network of concreted tunnels, a solidification of complex subterranean movement, would appear like bouquets of giant corals.

An Israeli Air Force officer, writing in the IDF journal *Ma'arachot*, suggested that the military establish a specialist subterranean unit. Presumably influenced by Palestinian tactics, he proposed that the unit should use tunnels to access buildings from underground to kidnap wanted persons or release hostages, and to place explosives or listening devices under enemy positions.[76] This unit has not yet been formed, but the events of the summer of 2006 may yet influence the IDF top brass into giving it the go-ahead.

The frontier wars of summer 2006 demonstrated how effective subterranean warfare could be. On 25 June, a 650-metre-long tunnel that had been dug under the fences surrounding Gaza, and which passed beneath the bombed Palestinian 'International Airport' of Dahania (remarkably demonstrating how tunneling has replaced flying), allowed Palestinian guerrillas to emerge close to IDF positions and return to Gaza with a kidnapped Israeli soldier. With a few spades, buckets and some hundreds of working hours, Palestinian militants thus made the $3 billion dollar phantasm of 'hermetic enclosure' seem remarkably pervious.

On the other battlefront of summer 2006, Hizbollah's resilience in the face of Israeli air raids was similarly enhanced by its control of the subsurface. Since the Israeli military withdrawal from Lebanon in 2000, a dispersed network of 'underground villages' had been constructed with the help of Iranian advisers of the 'Al-Quds Force' of the Revolutionary Guard. These comprise hundreds of bunkers, some of which are 40 metres deep, and include living quarters, command centres, storage facilities and camouflaged rocket-launching positions. The Lebanon war, was waged between the two spheres of extraterritorial sovereignty: an 'upper Lebanon' of Israeli-controlled airspace, and 'lower Lebanon', dug beneath villages, civilian neighbourhoods and open land. When Israeli jets finished raining down their bombs from near stratospheric altitudes, Hizbollah guerrillas climbed out of their bunkers to launch more rockets against Israeli cities and villages.

In military terms, the subterranean diggers of Gaza and Lebanon may have indeed defeated the builders of walls and the masters of airspace, but the border separating the parties and the elements, the thin crust of the earth where civilians struggle to live, seems now more vulnerable than ever.

HOLLOW LAND

Postscript

From the 'primitive' habitats in the exhibition 'Architecture without Architects'[1] to the glitzy casinos and social phenomenon of mass culture in *Learning from Las Vegas*,[2] architectural research from the mid-1960s onwards was devoted to breaking the bonds of modernist traditions, and reinvigorating architectural design with symbolic, communicative and semiotic contents. These exhibitions inaugurated a lineage of architectural research that can still be seen in contemporary avant-garde practices. In an increasingly sophisticated manner, contemporary architectural research tends to look for inspiration in the phenomena of global urbanization and the 'vernaculars of capitalism'. These practices involve turning observations into concepts, concepts into tools and tools into design methodologies applied in the construction of buildings. The 'learning' in *Learning from Las Vegas*, as much as in the learning from all other contemporary cities, phenomena and places, implies that the prime motivation for architectural research is still in its application in a design scheme, that architectural research is at its core projective applied research.

The aims of this book are very different. Committed architectural research in zones of conflict make the premise of applied research methods cynical at best. What should creative architectural research 'learn from the domination of Gaza' and apply in London? However, forms of research and practice in conflict zones imply other problems. In Palestine, architects and planners, mostly affiliated to independent organizations such as the Applied Research Institute of Jerusalem[3] (ARIJ) and Bimkom (Planners for Planning Rights),[4] document and appeal against the violation of Palestinian rights through the transformation of the built environment. Other architects, operating especially through humanitarian organizations and different UN agencies, help in the designing and improvement of Palestinian refugee camps, in the reconstruction of destroyed homes and public institutions, and with the relocation of clinics and schools cut apart from their communities by the West Bank Wall. The former are acts of advocacy aiming to put pressure on the Israeli government to end the occupation; the latter are direct interventions that aim to make somewhat more bearable the lives of Palestinians under Israel's regime of occupation. But as this book has sought to demonstrate,[5] clearing and amending the disastrous mess created by the occupying forces raises problems of a different kind. Poorly considered direct intervention, however well intentioned, may become complicit with the very aims of power itself. Interventions of this kind often undertake tasks that are the legal – though neglected – responsibility of the military in control, thus relieving it of its responsibilities, and allowing it to divert resources elsewhere. Furthermore, by moderating the actions of the IDF they may make the occupation appear more tolerable and efficient, and thus may even help, by some accounts, to extend it. This problem is at the heart of what came to be known as the 'humanitarian paradox'.[6]

The 'humanitarian paradox' impacts upon all practitioners of the humanitarian, usually international non-governmental, community – a sphere that has expanded in recent years into a multi-billion dollar 'aid industry'. One of the most important innovations in this field has been conceived by members of Médecins sans Frontières (MSF) and was best articulated by one of its founder members, Rony Brauman. MSF's code of practice insists that humanitarian organizations, which sometimes gain access to environments and information to which others, including journalists, have no access, must be prepared not only to perform their professional tasks but also 'to bear witness to the truth of injustice, and to insist on political responsibility'. According to Brauman, medical experts 'go into the field with a medical kit and return in order to bear witness'.[7] In drawing up its code, MSF politicized a medical profession that had previously been committed to Hippocratic neutrality. Acts of witnessing can be undertaken as unmediated visual testimony – registering what members see as taking place – or as medical testimony from the specialized perspective of professional expertise and medical knowledge.[8] MSF's method is simple but innovative: in doubling up the role of the medical expert with that of the witness, their members can work with the paradoxes present in conflict zones rather than surrender to them.

Architectural practice in conflict zones could similarly incorporate the ethical motivations, and the methodological capacities, for bearing professional witness to those crimes conducted through the transformation of the built environment. The conflation of the roles of a specialized expert and that of witness should be undertaken in a way that does not leave the two aspects distinct from each other, but that rather allows them to work together in a mutually supporting way. The work of the Israel Committee Against House Demolition[9] (ICAHD) provides an example of this mode of action. ICAHD is a direct action group founded to help protest against the destruction of Palestinian homes by Israel, and to rebuild them. These are mainly homes built 'illegally' as a result of the refusal by Jerusalem municipality to grant anything like sufficient numbers of building permits in the city's Palestinian neighbourhoods. ICAHD increasingly works also as an information centre in order to expose the bureaucratic, deliberately obfuscating planning processes that sustain these practices of occupation. ICAHD's intervention, in the form of applying for planning permissions and 'illegally' reconstructing homes destroyed by the municipality of Jerusalem, might simultaneously qualify as humanitarian aid and investigative research. The former is obviously essential, providing shelter and assistance to those who need it. The latter is manifest in the effect their work has had in inducing Jerusalem's planning system to reveal its inherently colonial nature.[10] This form of provocative intervention places these activists simultaneously inside and outside: as players within the conflict, but are also in a position to analyse and critique it. As a model for a different type of research, ICAHD's practices turn the traditional notion that research leads to construction (or theory to practice) on its head. ICAHD not only conducts research in order to build, but builds in order to tease out the very information it is seeking on planning practices and legislation. This form of architectural research thus carves out possible spaces of agency within a paralysing and powerful system of apparent impossibilities, in the process becoming a form of radical critical practice. Its methods shows that research, produced from within architecture, can itself become architecture – moreover, architectural practice that turns against architecture. Although most ICAHD members are not qualified architects, their work may help define a fresh embodiment of the activist-architect, a role that should be accommodated in the very education of architects if the profession is to maintain its cultural-political relevance.[11]

During my involvement in this conflict, a particular set of projects opened up different points of view and provided most of the human connections and source material for this book. These included work I carried out with the human rights organization B'Tselem, a period of involvement with the Palestinian Ministry of Planning in Ramallah, a series of publications and exhibitions I co-curated with Anselm Franke and Rafi Segal, and extensive filmed and recorded interviews undertaken with the military theorists of the IDF. I mention these in order to acknowledge the diverse means through which the perspectives and analysis within this book have been put together.

In 2001 Yehezkel Lein, a researcher from B'Tselem, invited me to collaborate on the production of a comprehensive report, *Land Grab*, which aimed to demonstrate violations of Palestinian human rights through the built environment, especially in the planning of Israeli settlements. Analysing series of drawings, regulations, policies and plans, undertaking a number of on-site measurements and oversite flights, we identified human rights violations and breaches of international law in the most mundane expressions of architecture and planning. Besides the fact that Israel has undertaken construction in the Occupied Territories in breach of international conventions and law, it was the architectural and planning methods by which this construction was implemented that directly and negatively impacted on the lives and livelihood of Palestinians. The crime was undertaken by architects and planners in the way they drafted their lines in development plans. The proof was in the drawings. Collecting evidence for this claim against the complicity of architecture in the occupation, we synthesized all drawings and collated all the masterplans onto a single map.[12] We found recurring patterns that embodied an aggressive intent. Both in their form and their location, settlements were designed to bisect a Palestinian traffic artery, at others to surround a village; to overlook a major city or a strategic crossroad. Formal manipulation and spatial organization are the very 'stuff' of architecture and planning. In its overall logic and in the repetition of its micro conditions, the role of architects and planners in the 'civilian occupation' was critically exposed.[13]

When the map was published in May 2002, at one of the peaks in the violence of the second Intifada, it became one of the geographical tools for advocacy actions against the Israeli government.[14] However, at that time, the geography of occupation was in constant flux, with the reality described on that map, much like any subsequent maps based upon it,[15] becoming a mere snapshot in a process of continuous transformation. The physical organization of the terrain proved to be both rigid and elastic. Rigid in its immediate material effect on every aspect of daily life in Palestine, elastic in its ability to incorporate further political changes into its organization and form.

Establishing its perspective with the triangulations of high points of the terrain, later with aerial photography and satellite imagery, mapping has until recently been almost exclusively associated with the mechanisms of colonial power. However, since the start of the Intifada, it has increasingly become more commonly associated with attempts to oppose and disrupt it. Although at the beginning of the second Intifada Edward Said was correct to suggest that the organization of the Occupied Territories was largely hidden from the Palestinians and their supporters, which gave the occupation forces a clear advantage,[16] in recent years a 'spatial turn' in the discourse surrounding the occupation has helped extend our political understanding of the conflict to a physical, geographical reality, and led to the production of a wide range of maps, drawn and distributed by a multiplicity of political and human rights groups.

We posted the map on the internet in a format that could easily be converted into a graphic file. This, and similar postings by other activists and organizations, helped the diffused project of 'mapping the occupation' acquire something of the nature of a dynamic 'open source' process. Each organization, dealing with an aspect of the spatial regime of occupation – roadblocks, settlements, outposts, military raids, the Wall – used, updated and posted its data in such a way that its graphic content could be shared. The combined research project led to the near-instantaneous transparency of the physical facts of the territory, and its transformation by the occupying forces. Thanks to these studies, we believe that the geographical realities of the occupation are relatively well mapped and, considering the effort invested in further mapping and constant updating, we can assume that we will continue to be informed about future transformations of the terrain. The task with which we are still largely left to deal is that of interpreting these territorial facts, understanding the logic by which the occupation works.

Based on the collaboration with B'Tselem, in 2002 my office partner Rafi Segal and I curated a small exhibition and edited its accompanying catalogue, entitled *A Civilian Occupation*. The project included work by Israeli architects, historians, photographers and journalists, and analyzed several key episodes in the planning history of Zionism. As is now well known, the Israeli Association of Architects, who commissioned the project, prevented it from being shown at the 2002 UIA Berlin Architectural Congress and destroyed the 5,000 copies of the catalogue.[17] The banning of the original show led to a series of other commissions worldwide. The first showing of the exhibition, co-curated with Sarah Herda, opened in February 2003 at the Storefront Gallery for Art and Architecture in New York City. Further work on this topic was later included in a larger exhibition – *Territories* – three months later, which was co-curated with Anselm Franke at the KW Institute for Contemporary Arts in Berlin. Although Rafi Segal and I initially saw the invitations for these exhibitions as opportunities to extend our research, we quickly realized the unique critical involvement and the insightful and specialized perspective of our art-world partners. Working with Anselm Franke taught us how the practice of curating could become a method of producing and assembling visual and other forms of knowledge, allowing us access to different understandings of political issues. Updated versions of *Territories* opened at the Witte de With Centre for Contemporary Art in Rotterdam (November 2003), at Berkeley University Gallery in San Francisco (March 2004), at the Konsthall in Malmö (May 2004), at the B'tzalel gallery in Tel Aviv and the Sham'l Centre in Ramallah (November 2004). The project also led to several conferences, the most significant of which, 'The Archipelago of Exception', dealing with the proliferating phenomena of extraterritorial zones, was organized with Thomas Keenan and Judit Carrera at the Centre for Contemporary Culture, Barcelona in 2005.[18]

Parts of this research were first published in March 2002 as 'The Politics of Verticality' on OpenDemocracy.net.[19] A year after it was banned by the AIUA in June 2002, *A Civilian Occupation* was published by Verso Books and Babel Publishers. In this collection, the chapter 'Mountain Settlements: Principles of Building in Height', co-authored by Rafi Segal and me, was largely based on the chapter 'Optical Urbanism' that was previously published in 'The Politics of Verticality'. This chapter was extended, updated and appears in this book as Chapter 4. The three volumes of the catalogue *Territories*, co-edited with Anselm Franke (and published by Walther Koening Press in Cologne), also contained material that is updated and expanded in this book.

Among the people who helped publish other parts of this research in their respective edited books, journals and magazines, I would like to thank: Shumon Basar, Ole Bouman, Denise Bratton, Sarah Breitberg-Semel, Haim Bresheeth, Eduardo Cadava, David Cunningham, Cynthia Davidson, Daniela Fabricius, Stephen Graham, Haifa Hammami, Brian Holmes, Branden W. Joseph, Christian Höller, Bechir Kenzari, Walther Koening, Rem Koolhaas, Aaron Levi, Markus Miessen, Philip Misselwitz, Sina Najafi, Adi Ophir, Andreas Ruby, Sharon Rotbard, Meike Schalk, Felicity Scott, Michael Sorkin and Sven-Olov Wallenstein.

I would like to thank Michael Sorkin again for giving me, in the summer of 1999, my first opportunity to speak publicly on the topic of architecture and the Israel–Palestine conflict and for greatly supporting this research as it progressed. Of the other people who invited me to give lectures related to this research I would especially like to thank Lindsay Bremner and the Faculty of Architecture at Witwatersrand University in Johannesburg, South Africa, for the invitation to deliver the Rusty Bernstein Memorial Lecture in 2004; Annabel Wharton and the Faculty of Art, Art History and Visual Studies at Duke University for the invitation to deliver, together with Rafi Segal, the three Benenson Lectures of 2005; the Faculty of the School of Architecture at the University of Michigan for its invitation to deliver the Raul Wallenberg Studio Lecture in 2005; and the Canadian Centre for Architecture and the London School of Economics for hosting the James Stirling Memorial Lectures in 2006 and 2007. I would also like to thank Andrew Benjamin, Stefano Boeri, David Campbell, Lieven De Cauter, Patricia Clough, Teddy Cruz, Catherine David, Zvi Efrat, Steve Fagin, Jeff Halper, Shirine Hamadeh, Abe Hayeem, Thomas Keenan, Declan McGonagle, Dan Monk, Roger Owen, Nezar Al-Sayyad, Hans Ulrich Obrist, Walid Ra'ad, John H. Smith, Neil Smiths, Anthony Vidler, Mark Wigley and Alejandro Zaero-Poro for inviting me to give lectures at their respective institutions and for stimulating discussions.

I would like to thank Nadav Harel with whom I made several incomplete documentary films, parts of which were shown in the context of the *Territories* exhibition, and produced material that informed this book. I would like to thank the photographers: Adam Broomberg, Oliver Chararin, Marine Hougonier, Nir Kafri, Miki Kratsman, Bas Princen, Daniel Bauer and Zohar Kaniel for showing me, through their images, things I was unable to see with my own eyes. I would like to thank Zvi Efrat and Zvi Elhyani for allowing me to use the archives of Israeli architecture they have put together, namely the archive of the 'Israeli Project' and the 'Elhyani Archive of Israeli Architecture'.

I would like to thank the academic members of the London Consortium,[20] and especially Paul Hirst, for providing me with an academic home and the scholarship to complete my PhD dissertation. This book is not the PhD, but the dissertation formed the basis of several of the chapters in this book. Paul Hirst, Mark Cousins and Steven Connor helped frame a productive interaction between public action (exhibitions, mapping, publications, human rights work) and academic research. I would have very much liked Paul to see this book and hope it would have made him pleased with the result of our long conversations. Jacqueline Rose and Robert Jan van Pelt examined the thesis rigorously and lovingly, and provided generous and valuable insights.

Much of this research is based on interviews with Palestinian and Israeli architects, planners, academics, government officials, soldiers and activists that I met in Palestinian Israeli or European cities. Amongst these people I would to thank Khalil Nijem, Director General of the Palestinian Planning Ministry; Knut Felberg, a Norwegian planner working at the same ministry; Sari Hanafi from the American University of Beirut; Akram Ijla from the Ministry of Antiquity in Gaza; Adania Shibli, a Palestinian writer based in London; and Omar Yussuf, an architect from Jerusalem. I would like them and everyone who helped me by telling me what they know, to understand how grateful I am for their generosity and help. Interviews were conducted as well with several serving or retired Israeli military personnel. When reading the book, non-Israeli and non-Palestinian readers may wonder about access to military personnel and first-hand military information. Anyone living in, visiting Israel or living under its regime is well aware of the diffusion of the military in all spheres of life. Many officers and soldiers were willing to talk, mostly anonymously, about military operations, tactics and procedures. Amongst the most fertile sources for this work were interviews with Shimon Naveh, a retired officer and former director of the military Operational Theory Research Institute (OTRI). I thank him for being forthcoming even though (and perhaps because) he understood the position from which this book is written. Shlomo Gazit and Arie Shalev, of the first military governors of the Occupied Territories, were interviewed at the Jaffee Centre for Strategic Studies at Tel Aviv University.

I would like to thank two of my friends and mentors in Israel – Zvi Efrat[21] and Sharon Rotbard,[22] each of whom transformed, in his own particular way, the discourse of Israeli architecture by infusing it with cultural, critical and post-colonial studies. A great debt of gratitude must go as well to Meron Benvenisti, Adi Ophir and Ariella Azoulay for pointing out, whether directly or through their inspiring work, unexpected directions and insights.

Eitan Diamond, Anselm Franke, Manuel Herz, Sharon Rotbard and Alberto Toscano read drafts of this book and commented on it. Their ideas and insights are in the text. I enjoyed the critical enthusiasm of the fabulous Tom Penn at Verso who, under the guise of a commissioning editor, became a real partner in the making of this book.

My sister Elian Weizman undertook research in the last months of the book's making. Although we share the same gene-pool, her competence, intelligence and meticulous eye were what I lacked at these crucial moments. Ines, my wife, read so many drafts, heard so many lectures, critiqued, commented and suggested improvements so often that I can no longer be sure where her ideas stop and mine begin.

Those acknowledged here have been generous and genuine collaborators; they have influenced, personally or institutionally, the development of this project, and to a large degree made it possible. They have each in their own way taught me that in generous professional collaboration there is always also a degree of friendship.

Notes

Preface

1 Lahav Harkov, 'Retired General Calling Israel "World Champion of Occupation" sparks outrage', Jerusalem Post, 1 September 2016. Gadi Shamni led the IDF's Central Command from 2007 to 2009 and left the army in 2012.

2 Peace Now, Settlement Watch Program, peacenow.org.il/en/settlements-watch/settlements-data/population, accessed 3 March 2017.

3 There are approximately 20 Israeli-administered industrial zones in the West Bank. Human Rights Watch, 'Occupation, Inc.: How Settlement Businesses Contribute to Israel's Violations of Palestinian Rights', 19 January 2016.

4 Naomi Klein, 'Laboratory for a Fortress World', Nation, 14 June 2007.

5 Britain, the United States, France, and Germany acted in different ways against the boycott of Israel. Oliver Wright, 'Israel Boycott Ban: Shunning Israeli Goods to Become Criminal Offence for Public Bodies and Student Unions', Independent, 14 February 2016; Michael Wilner, 'US Congress Passes Rare Law Targeting Boycotts of Israel', Jerusalem Post, 24 June 2015; Benjamin Dodman, 'France's Criminalisation of Israel Boycotts Sparks Free-Speech Debate', France 24, 21 January 2016.

6 Information about settlements and settler numbers is usually disaggregated according to the different administrative areas into which the occupation is divided, and differs slightly between different estimates. According to B'tselem, there are currently between 300,000 and 350,000 settlers in the occupied areas of East Jerusalem (up from 189,708 in 2007) and 406,302 in the rest of the West Bank (up from 276,500 in 2007). According to the state's population registry, in 2005 the number of settlers in the West Bank (not including Jerusalem) was 254,000. During the last decade this number has grown by 167,000 or 66 per cent. As of 2016 there were 422,000 Jewish settlers in the West Bank. In 2016 the Jewish population in the West Bank grew by 15,675 people or 3.9 per cent, double the national population increase. The number 750,000 is the sum of the average in B'tselem's estimate for the occupied parts of Jerusalem and the state's population registry numbers for the West Bank. The state's population registry does not provide separate statistics for occupied Jerusalem because the area has been officially annexed to Israel and its numbers refer to Jerusalem as a whole. In Gaza, since the evacuation of 2005, there were no (and still aren't any) settlers. In 1993, when the Oslo Accords were signed, there were approximately 110,000 Israeli settlers living in the West Bank and 146,000 living in East Jerusalem. See: B'tselem, Statistics on Settlements and Settler Population, btselem.org/settlements/statistics, updated 11 May 2015. The settlement numbers quoted above are from the Settlement Watch Program of Peace Now, available at peacenow.org.il/en/category/settlement-watch.

7 Yael Berda, The Bureaucracy of the Occupation in the West Bank: The Permit Regime 2000–2006, Jerusalem: Van Leer Institute, 2012 (in Hebrew). Human Rights Watch, 'Israel/West Bank: Separate and Unequal: Under Discriminatory Policies, Settlers Flourish, Palestinians Suffer', 19 December 2010; B'tselem, 'A Palestinian Charged in a Military Court is as Good as Convicted', 21 June 2015; Noam Sheizaf, 'Conviction Rate for Palestinians in Israel's Mili-

tary Courts: 99.74%', +972 magazine, 29 November 2011; B'tselem, 'The Occupation's Fig Leaf: Israel's Military Law Enforcement System as a Whitewash Mechanism', 25 May 2016; Gili Cohen, 'Citing IDF Failure to Bring Soldiers to Justice, B'Tselem Stops Filing Complaints on Abuse of Palestinians', Ha'aretz, 25 May 2016.

[8] Eyal Weizman and Fazal Sheikh, The Conflict Shoreline: Colonization as Climate Change in the Negev Desert, Göttingen: Steidle and Cabinet, 2015. Forensic Architecture's investigation of a police killing in the illegalized Bedouin village of umm al-Hiran is here: forensic-architecture.org/case/umm-al-hiran.

[9] Uri Blaue and Yotam Feldman, 'Consent and Advice', Ha'aretz, 1 January 2009.

[10] United Nations, 'Gaza in 2020: A Liveable Place?', August 2012; UN figures can also be found here: unrwa.org/gaza-emergency.

[11] Shaul Arieli, 'The Two-state Solution to the Israeli-Palestinian Conflict Remains Viable', Ha'aretz, 31 December 2016.

[12] Eyal Weizman, 'Introduction to The Politics of Verticality', Open Democracy, 23 April 2002.

[13] B'tselem, 'The Water Crisis', 28 September 2016; United Nations, 'Occupied Palestinian Territory Slides into Recession, Gaza Becoming Uninhabitable', 1 September 2015.

[14] Nir Hasson, 'In a Tunnel Beneath Jerusalem, Israeli Culture Minister Gives Obama a Lesson in History', Ha'aretz, 31 December 2016.

[15] Susan Schuppli, 'Uneasy Listening', in Forensic Architecture (ed.), FORENSIS: The Architecture of Public Truth, Berlin: Sternberg Press, 2014.

[16] Tamar Pileggi and Raphael Ahren, 'Rivlin Proposes Israeli-Palestinian "Confederation"', Times of Israel, 3 December 2015.

[17] See: bdsmovement.net; Benjamin Winthal, 'Ban of Ireland Shuts Down Anti-Israel BDS Accounts', Jerusalem Post, 3 October 2016.

[18] Alessando Petti, Sandi Hilal and Eyal Weizman, Architecture After Revolution, Berlin: Sternberg Press, 2014. See also: Alessandro Petti and Sandi Hilal's initiative, Campus in Camps (campusin-camps.ps).

[19] Eyal Weizman, Forensic Architecture: Violence at the Threshold of Detectability, New York: Zone, 2017. See also: forensic-architecture.org.

Introduction: Frontier Architecture

[1] Patrick Kieller, London (film), 1994.

[2] Mourid Barghouti, I Saw Ramallah, Ahdaf Soueif (trans.), London: Bloomsbury, 2005, p. 31.

[3] The full sentence, captured and immortalized in sound recordings of Chief of Southern Command in 1967, Yeshayahu Gavish, was 'Sadin adom nu'a nu'a sof'. The code for the beginning of the Israeli attack on 5 June 1967 was 'sadin adom' (red bedsheet). 'Nu'a nu'a sof' (move move out) implied the transfer of most command authority from staff officers to field officers operating on the ground.

[4] The Ministry of Construction and Housing paid as well for a paved access road. The streetlights and a double fence with dogs chained at 20-metre intervals were paid for by the military. Dror Etkes, 'Construction in unauthorized outposts: April–August 2006'. Peace Now, http://www.peacenow.org.il/site/en/peace.asp?pi=61&docid=1936.

[5] Talya Sasson, 'A interim legal opinion submitted to Prime Minister Ariel Sharon on the subject of illegal outposts in the West Bank'. In Hebrew: http://www.pmo.gov.il/NR/rdonlyres/0A0FBE3C-C741–46A6–8CB5–F6CDC042465D/0/sason2.pdf. In English: http://www.peacenow.org/hot.asp?cid=390.

[6] Agence France Presse, 15 November 1998.

[7] BBC: 'Activists demolish West Bank outpost', 8 September 2004. The operation was undertaken by Dror Etkes of Peace Now. The aim was to demonstrate that the reluctant ministry could enforce the law and government promises and remove outposts if it really wanted.

[8] On 26 September 2006, human rights lawyer Michael Sfard sent a letter to Minister of Defence Amir Peretz and Central Command Head Major General Yair Naveh on behalf of the Palestinian landowners of Migron, demanding the immediate evacuation of the illegal outpost and the return of the land to its legal owners.

[9] Despite a common perception, the frontier did not originate with the expansion of Europe into

America, Australia or Africa. It was part of the territoriality of pre-modern empires. The margins of the ancient Roman and Chinese Empires, as well as those of the Aztecs and the Incas, were deep, shifting and scantily defined domains of cultural exchange and warfare, where battles took place with people defined since Ancient Greece as 'barbarians'. These empires were based upon a flexible relationship between centre and periphery, defined by power, commerce and affiliation rather than by territorial proximity. See Paul Hirst, *Space and Power, Politics, War and Architecture*, London: Polity, 2005, pp. 63–4.

[10] Sharon Rotbard, 'Preface', in *A Civilian Occupation, The Politics of Israeli Architecture*, London and Tel Aviv: Verso and Babel, 2002, pp. 15–16.

[11] Conflict can be seen as a force field. For Nietzsche, territory, like a cosmic sphere composed of fields of invisible energies, is '*a substratum of force*'. See: Friedrich Nietzsche, *The Will to Power*, fragment 545, Walter Kaufmann (ed. and trans.), New York: Random House, 1967, p. 293. According to Gilles Deleuze's reading of Michel Foucault's work: '*Power . . . is not an attribute but a relation: the power-relation is the set of possible relations between forces, which passes through the dominated forces no less than through the dominating*.' See Gilles Deleuze, *Foucault*, Minneapolis and London: University of Minnesota Press, 1988, p. 27. See as well p. 36 where Deleuze uses the term 'map of relations between forces'. Following Deleuze, the architect and theorist Greg Lynn describes flexibility as the continuous development and transformation of form: 'Pliancy allows architecture to become involved in complexity through flexibility . . .' And elsewhere: 'curvilinear sensibilities are capable of complex deformations in response to programmatic, structural, economic, aesthetic, political and contextual influences'. See Greg Lynn, *Folds, Bodies & Blobs, Collected Essays*, Brussels: La Lettre Volée, 1998, pp. 110, 115. Lynn's process-driven approach was modelled as well on D'Arcy Thompson's dictum that 'form is a diagram of forces'. Since 'shaping forces' – the political rationalities, practices of space formations and range of expertise – are embedded in space, spatial analysis could to be employed to extract and reveal them. The latter statement must be qualified when applying this approach outside the virtual world of the computer and into the world of politics and action. Political forces do not obviously manifest themselves *fully* in material organization. The complexity of politics, its responsiveness to specificities, idiosyncrasies, singularities and chance, leaves spatial transformations indeterminable and thus unmappable. Because frontiers are everywhere in contact with friction and chance, their analysis could never fit the framework of geographical determinism or 'the rule of forms'.

[12] The term 'archival probe' has been used in Sanford Kwinter and Daniela Fabricius, 'Urbanism: An Archivist's Art?' in Rem Koolhaas, Stefano Boeri, Sanford Kwinter, Nadia Tazi and Hans Ulrich Obrist, *Mutations*, Barcelona: Actar, 2001, pp. 495–503.

[13] Two of the most prominent Israeli 'celebrity activists' operating in the context of the conflict within the West Bank – Dror Etkes of Peace Now and Jeff Halper of the Israel Committee against House Demolition (ICAHD) – have often been able to deal significant blows to Israeli government policy in the West Bank and transform some realities on the ground. In 2005 the US administration, usually relying upon its network of satellites for every task, decided not to photograph the expansion of Israeli settlements, stating 'we do not use our satellites against our allies'. The main source of information for the US Administration are the internet sites of Peace Now, B'Tselem, and to a lesser degree, ICAHD. In 2006 Jeff Halper was nominated for the Nobel Peace Prize.

[14] The legal formal ambiguity is exemplified by the difference between the different versions of UN Resolution 242 calling Israel to retreat from 'areas occupied' (as in the English version) or from 'the areas occupied' (as in the French version). Within the frontier of the West Bank, various rules and military regulations apply differently to the separate categories of individual who inhabit the West Bank – 'Israeli Jew', 'Israeli non-Jew' (there are Palestinian citizens in Israel of course), 'settler' (uber-citizen, enjoying greater benefits and rights), 'soldier', 'security personnel' (private mercenaries), 'Arabs' (subjects), 'uninvolved civilian' (Palestinians killed during military operations, whose innocence must be proven), 'temporary resident' (Palestinians living on the western side of the Wall), 'foreign' (automatically suspected as European Palestinian sympathizers), 'guest worker' (many of the workers in the agrarian settlements are from China and Thailand), 'leftists' (yes – there are areas in the West Bank, mainly near the hard-core settlements of Hebron, that are closed by the military to Israelis with a liberal-secular 'look'), 'terrorist' (any member of a Palestinian organization that has a military wing) and so on. In some of the strange paradoxes of the conflict, a Palestinian can be an IDF soldier while a soldier on weekend leave can be a political activist.

[15] According to an Israeli law enacted in 1992, the Minister of Interior is not permitted to

award the status of a local council to communities with a population of fewer than 3,000 residents, or to award the status of a municipality to communities with a population of fewer than 20,000. However, the law grants the minister discretion to act otherwise 'if special conditions and circumstances exist'. As of the end of 2001, four of the fourteen local councils in the West Bank had a population of fewer than 3,000 residents, and two of the three municipalities had a population of fewer than 20,000. See Lein and Weizman, *Land Grab*, Jerusalem: B'Tselem, 2002.

[16] In his review of *A Civilian Occupation*, the political theorist David Campbell highlighted the difference between settlement typologies (relying on information he gathered in the human rights report *Land Grab*, which I prepared with Yehezkel Lein) and pointed out some distinctions between their etymological roots, but generally failed to grasp the political agenda that benefited from, further manipulated and accentuated this 'complexity' in order to blur the borders between Israel and the territories it occupies. Campbell thus fell into the same linguistic trap set up for the Israeli public. David Campbell, 'Construction Site: Architecture and Politics in Israel/Palestine', *Theory and Event* 7:4, 2004.

[17] Ilan Pappe, 'Occupation Hazard', *Bookforum*, 13 February 2006.

[18] Derek Gregory, *The Colonial Present*, Oxford: Blackwell, 2004.

[19] Makram Khoury-Machool, 'Losing the battle for Arab hearts and minds', www.opendemocracy.net, 10 May 2003.

[20] See figures given by B'Tselem: 683 people killed in the conflict in 2006, http://www.btselem.org /english/Press_Releases/20061228.asp, 28 December 2006.

[21] IDF generals, serving or retired, in fact governed the entire peace process with the Palestinians in Oslo and in Camp David. Another example of the way in which 'peace' and 'security' are intrinsically related in Israeli perception occurred during the 1996 and 1999 elections, when the alternatives with which the voters were presented were 'Peace with Security' and 'A Secure Peace'. See Baruch Kimmerling, *The Invention and Decline of Israeliness: Society, Culture and the Military*, Berkeley, CA: University of California Press, 2001, pp. 227, 209.

[22] Ron Pundak in interview, Peres Institute for Peace, Tel Aviv, 12 February 2002.

[23] Nadav Shragai, 'Dividing Jerusalem', *Ha'aretz*, 28 May 2002. The Geneva initiative was based almost entirely on the Clinton Guidelines for Jerusalem. A team of Israeli and Palestinian traffic engineers and planners, including the Israeli architect Ayala Ronel, set out to resolve the details of the Clinton Guidelines in Jerusalem. In many places they found that it could only be resolved if 'national traffic' was rerouted over or under the other's territory and homes. The examples they outlined included the main road leading from the city centre to the Jewish neighbourhood of French Hill, Pisgat Ze'ev and Ramot, the road between Mount Scopus and Ma'ale Adumim, and to connect the Palestinian neighbourhoods of Beit Hannina, Shuafat and Beit Tzafafa. They have also explored the possibility of constructing a bridge between the road running along the southeastern edge of the Old City walls to the Mount of Olives and the ancient Jewish cemetery there. See Menachem Klein, *The Geneva Initiative – an Insider View*, Jerusalem: Carmel, 2006, pp. 160–5 (in Hebrew).

[24] Gilead Sher in interview at the British Library, London, 23 February 2002.

[25] Annex I of the 'Interim Agreement' signed in 1995 stipulates: 'In order to maintain the territorial integrity of the West Bank and the Gaza Strip as a single territorial unit, and to promote their economic growth and the demographic and geographical links between them, both sides shall implement the provisions of this Annex, while respecting and preserving without obstacles, normal and smooth movement of people, vehicles, and goods . . . between the West Bank and the Gaza Strip.' See http://www.mideastweb.org/meosint.htm.

[26] Quoted in Eli Kamir, 'Safe passage', *Ma'ariv*, 8 April 1998.

[27] Ministry of Regional Cooperation, 'The Safe Passage', internal publication, 1999. Cost estimates for the project prepared by Yoram Shimon, an Israeli bridge-engineer, projected a bridge, resting on columns spaced 50–60 metres apart costing about US$1 billion dollars. Calculations were based on a similar bridge built over water leading to New Orleans which is also about 50 kilometres long. See Shai Elias, 'An expensive solution, but still possible', *Ma'ariv*, 8 April 1998.

[28] Doug Suisman, *The Arc: A Formal Structure for a Palestinian State*, Santa Monica, CA.: Rand Corporation, p. 33.

[29] Recognizing the inevitable economic disruption that would be caused by the partitioning of such a small area, the UNSCOP report recommended an economic union between the states of Israel and Palestine. Currency and customs would be administered in common. The communication

network – railway systems, highways, postal, telephone and telegraphic services, seaports and airports – would be bi-national. See Avi Shlaim, *The Politics of Partition: King Abdullah, the Zionists and Palestine 1921–51*, Oxford: Oxford University Press, p. 166. The complex path of the partition plan of 1947 was based on the UN's belief that complex borders would create interdependency and thus foster peace and economic cooperation between the two states. This arrangement is rather similar to that of European states within the EU. See Gideon Biger, *Land of Many Borders*, Beer Sheva: Ben-Gurion University Press, 2001, p. 220 (in Hebrew).

[30] Meron Benvenisti, 'An Engineering Wonder', *Ha'aretz*, 5 June 1996. This editorial later appeared in French in *Pre/occupations d'espace/ Jérusalem au Pluriel*, Marseille: Image En Manoeuvres Editions, 2001, pp. 171–3.

[31] Jules Verne, *Journey to the Centre of the Earth*, London: Griffith and Farran, 2000 [1864] Edgar Allan Poe, *The Narrative of Arthur Gordon Pym of Nantucket*, London: Penguin, 2000 [1850].

Interlude – 1967

[1] Yigal Allon, *Curtain of Sand*, Tel Aviv: Hakibbutz Hameuchad, 1988 (1959). [Hebrew] pp. 52, 61–82, 366–7. Allon distinguishes between three types of counter attacks: a 'responsive counter-attack', a 'parallel counter-attack', and a 'preemptive counter-attack'. He favoured the latter which he defines as 'the taking of initiative against enemy concentrations, the capture of strategic areas on enemy territory at the time the enemy is organizing for attack' (p. 62). Allon distinguishes this strategy from 'preemptive war' which takes place between nations in peace, and while acknowledging the paradox in conflating the terms 'preemptive' and 'counter-attack' attributes it to the fact there is a state of 'war' between Arab states and Israel. It is interesting to note the similarity between Israel's defence doctrine and those of Germany between the end of the nineteenth century and the middle of the twentieth. Germany's strategic location at the centre of Europe made it vulnerable to invasions or blockades and led to the fear of an *Einkreisung* (encirclement). Before World War I, Admiral Alfred Tirpitz viewed Germany's strategic situation as that of a 'mollusc without a shell'. The famous plan prepared by Count Alfred Schlieffen before World War I, aimed to keep the surrounding armies from meeting on German soil. In 1894 the Count reckoned that Germany could survive only after a speedy and decisive victory, which he planned to achieve by launching a holding action against Russia in the east while defeating France in a lightning attack in the west. See Stephen Kern, *The Culture of Time and Space, 1880–1918,* Cambridge, MA: Harvard University Press 2003, pp. 249–51.

[2] Israel 'cleansed' two areas in the West Bank of their Palestinian inhabitants, the Jordan Valley (excluding Jericho) and the Latrun enclave on the road to Jerusalem, ostensibly to secure this road. Out of an estimated 300,000 Palestinians who were made to leave to Jordan only about 17,000 were ultimately allowed to return.

[3] In 1967, 385,000 Palestinians lived in the Gaza Strip, more than half of them refugees. Before the 1967 war the West Bank had about a million inhabitants, of whom almost 300,000 fled east of the Jordan during and after the conflict. Of the present population of the West Bank, 2.5 million, about a third, are refugees; of Gaza's population of about 1.5 million, about half are refugees.

[4] Accordingly, a complex legal system composed of Ottoman, British Mandatory (particularly the emergency regulations of 1945), Jordanian and Egyptian law (depending on the region), Israeli and military rules was put in place and applied together or separately, to regulate the lives of Palestinians and promote the settlement of Israelis there. The commanders were vested with powers not only to enact laws, but to cancel and suspend them, which enabled them continuously to reshape the legal system in accordance with Israel's political objectives. During the occupation, the military commanders issued at least 2,500 such orders regulating every aspect of the occupied population's life. See Neve Gordon, *Israel's Occupation: Sovereignty, Discipline and Control*, Berkeley, CA: California University Press, forthcoming (Introduction).

[5] More than sixty springs and wells have been left west of the Wall. See Jane Hilal and Sandra Ashhab, 'The H2O Factor', in Philipp Misselwitz and Tim Rieniets (eds), *City of Collision*, Basel and London: Birkhauser, 2006, pp. 184–92.

[6] Yoav Peled, 'Zionist Realities: Debating Israel–Palestine', *New Left Review* 38, March–April 2006.

[7] The Oslo Accords, still in effect regarding water issues, transferred responsibility for the Palestinian water sector to the Palestinian Authority. But a Joint Water Committee (JWC), comprising an equal number of representatives of Israel and the Palestinian Authority, was set up to oversee and approve every new water and sewage project in Palestinian areas. What otherwise seemed a

sensible compromise meant in effect that through the Committee, Israel could veto any Palestinian request to drill a new well or to obtain the additional waters stipulated in the water section of the Oslo Accords. Jewish settlements on the other hand have access to pumping wells, which do not require JWC permission, and thus cannot be scrutinized by Palestinians. Consequently, Israeli settlers utilize on average six times more water as the West Bank Palestinians. See Yehezkel Lein, *Thirsty for a Solution, The Water Crisis in the Occupied Territories and its Resolution in the Final-Status Agreement*, Jerusalem: B'Tselem, July 2000, www.btselem.org.

[8] Shlomo Swirski, *The Price of Occupation*, Tel Aviv: Mapa Publishers, 2005 [Hebrew], p. 28.

[9] As a consequence of this policy, as well as the poor condition of the infrastructure that Israel handed over to the Palestinian Authority in 1995, 40 per cent of the water carried through the pipes is lost by leakages. As of June 2006, some 215,000 Palestinians in 220 villages lived in communities without a running-water network. See B'Tselem, 'The water crisis', http://www. btselem.org/English/Water/Index.asp.

[10] Amiram Cohen, 'Eitam prohibits Palestinians from drilling for water in West Bank', *Ha'aretz*, 10 February 2005.

[11] Since the beginning of the Oslo Process the international community has committed over $230 million for wastewater infrastructure in the West Bank. IDF military operations led to the destruction of much of this infrastructure. Israeli bombing of Palestinian electricity supplies in June 2006 led to the deactivation of electric pumps and to an overspill in the three sewage treatment facilities in Gaza. Since the Intifada, and increasingly since Hamas came to power in 2005, many other internationally sponsored projects have been delayed or obstructed. Darryl Li and Yehezkel Lein, *Act of Vengeance: Israel's Bombing of the Gaza Power Plant and its Effects*, Jerusalem: B'tselem, 2006. Sometimes, Israeli approval of internationally funded water and sewage projects was made conditional on extending their service to the settlers. These requests were consistently rejected both by the donor community and the Palestinians and led to further delays and cancellation of projects. Zecharya Tagar and Violet Qumsieh, *A Seeping Time Bomb: Pollution of the Mountain Aquifer by Solid Waste*, Amman, Bethlehem and Tel Aviv: EcoPeace and Friends of the Earth Middle East, January 2006.

[12] Tzafrir Rinat, 'Contamination doesn't stop at the green line', *Ha'aretz*, 14 August 2003.

[13] David Ratner, 'Israel plans to dump tons of garbage in the W. Bank', *Ha'aretz*, 4 April 2005.

[14] Most of the sewage created by the large settlement-town of Ariel has been redirected to flow through the Palestinian town of Salfit. It passes a few metres from a pumping station supplying most of the water used for domestic consumption by the residents of the town. According to the town council's water engineer, Salah Afani, this sewage channel pollutes the waters of the well, and he must occasionally order the municipality to stop pumping when his inspections reveal high levels of pollution. Information based on a conversation with Salah Afani on 30 December 2001 in the context of a tour I conducted with Yehezkel Lein at the West Bank city of Salfit. The sewage of Qalqilya on the western slopes of the West Bank flows under the Wall into Israel proper. The sewage of Tul Qarem and Nablus mixes with the waters of the Alexander River, which meanders downstream through the Israeli coastal plains. Mixing domestic with industrial outflows, sewage flows out of Hebron to the outskirts of Be'er Sheva, passing through a number of Bedouin villages. According to Friends of the Earth Middle East, the complete non-cooperation approach by Israel and the international community, adopted after Hamas came to power, has seriously aggravated the condition of Palestinian sewage works and has led to further spills into Israel. See Tagar and Qumsieh, *A Seeping Time Bomb*.

[15] Mary Douglas, *Purity and Danger: An Analysis of the Concepts of Pollution and Taboo*, London: Routledge and Kegan Paul, 1966.

[16] The members of the evacuated Jahalin tribe were only allowed to settle close to a pirate dump site, set beside the Palestinian village of Azaria. Gideon Levy, 'The sewage of Ma'ale Edummim', *Ha'aretz*, 22 February 1998.

[17] Dominique Laporte, *History of Shit*, Cambridge, MA: MIT Press, 1993, p. 56.

[18] Amos Harel, 'A cummunition of careful fraternity', *Ha'aretz*, 11 February 2005.

[19] Quoted in Eitan Felner, *A Policy of Discrimination: Land Expropriation, Planning and Building in East Jerusalem*, Jerusalem: B'Tselem, 1995.

[20] Quoted in Elli Wohlgelnerter, 'Follow the Cobblestone Road', *Jerusalem Post*, 10 June 1998.

Chapter 1 Jerusalem: Petrifying the Holy City

[1] The Palestinian inhabitants of the area annexed were given the option of becoming Israeli citizens, but in order to do so they had to relinquish their Jordanian citizenship. Only a small number complied. Nonetheless, all of the inhabitants were made permanent Jerusalem residents and could vote for municipal elections. Eitan Felner, *A Policy of Discrimination, Land Expropriation, Planning and Building in East Jerusalem*, Jerusalem: B'Tselem, 1995.

[2] The borders were determined by a military committee headed by General Rehavam Ze'evi, at the time an assistant to the head of the Operations Branch of the General Staff. The guiding consideration was that they would ultimately become the state's borders. Everything beyond them, so it was thought at this time, would be returned to Jordan after a peace agreement. See Felner, *A Policy of Discrimination: Land Expropriation, Planning and Building in East Jerusalem*, p. 10.

[3] Quoted in Shlomo Gazit, *The Carrot and the Stick: Israel's Policy in Judea and Samaria, 1967–68*, New York: B'nai B'rith Book Service, 1995, p. 226.

[4] Avia Hashimshoni, Yoseph Schweid and Zion Hashimshoni Municipality of Jerusalem, *Masterplan for the City of Jerusalem*, 1968 (1972).

[5] Jeff Halper, 'The Key To Peace: Dismantling The Matrix Of Control' at http://icahd.org/eng/articles.asp? menu=6&submenu=3.

[6] Hashimshoni et al., *Masterplan 1968*.

[7] Geologically, the stone referred to as 'Jerusalem Stone' comes from indigenous Cretaceous and Tertiary rocks belonging to the Turonian period and consisting mainly of limestone, dolomite and sometimes chalk. The texture on the stone's surface and the one giving it its particular character is caused by the abundance of marine carbonate sediments.

[8] Hashimshoni et al., *Masterplan 1968*, p. 13.

[9] Upon entering Jerusalem Allenby declared: 'today the wars of the Crusaders are completed', and The *Times* celebrated his victory with a cartoon of Richard the Lionheart looking down at Jerusalem above the caption: 'At last my dream come true.' www.keepmedia.com.

[10] Ronald Storrs, *Orientations*, London: I. Nicholson & Watson, 1939, p. 405.

[11] Charles Robert Ashbee (ed.), *Jerusalem 1918–1920 Being the Records of the Pro-Jerusalem Council during the First Two Years of the Civil Administration*, London: John Murray, 1924, pp. 33–9.

[12] William H. McLean, *City of Jerusalem – Town Planning Scheme, Explanatory Note*, 1918. See also the discussion of the McLean plan in Henry Kendall, *Jerusalem: the City Plan. Preservation and Development During the British Mandate 1918–1948*, London: HMSO, 1948.

[13] McLean, *Town planning Scheme*, p. 20.

[14] Storrs, *Orientations*, p. 44.

[15] Jerusalem District Building and Town Planning Commission, Town Planning Ordinance, 1936. By the time of the British Mandate, the contradictions between the traditionalist and modernist traditions were already embodied by an architectural style that crossed modernism and orientalism, one exemplified at its best by the work of Erich Mendelsohn in Palestine. For Mendelsohn, 'Palestine . . . forms part of the Arabian world. The problem that confronts the Jew in Palestine is how to reach equal rank among his neighbors; how to become a cell of the future Semitic commonwealth, to which they in fact belong by their race, tongue and character.' Quoted in Heinze-Greenberg, *Architecture in Palestine*, New York: Monacelli Press, 1999, pp. 206–7. See also, Alona Nitzan-Shiftan, 'Contested Zionism – Alternative Modernism: Erich Mendelsohn and the Tel-Aviv Chug in Mandate Palestine', *Architectural History* 39; 1996, pp. 154–8.

[16] Jerusalem Town Planning Ordinance, 1936; and Jerusalem outline town planning scheme [modification], 1944. See also the discussion in Arthur Kutcher, *The New Jerusalem, Planning and Politics*, London: Thames and Hudson, 1973, pp. 51–4.

[17] Plan No. 64 of the 1955 Israeli-devised Jerusalem masterplan.

[18] Kutcher, *The New Jerusalem*, p. 91.

[19] Elli Wohlgelnerter, 'Follow the cobblestone road', *Jerusalem Post*, 10 June 1998.

[20] Although he incorporated into his buildings a variety of oriental motifs, including domes, Mendelsohn's Hadassah-Hebrew University medical complex in Jerusalem, constructed between 1934 and 1939, applied its stone cladding in a challenging gesture. Polished limestone tiles, visually different from the kind of stone used in traditional construction, were laid in vertical rather than horizontal stripes, making sure the cladding was not mistaken for solid stone construction.

The building ushered in an architectural fashion for the 'creative subversion' of the stone bylaw. The best example of its influence can be found in the Hebrew Union College Building designed by Hainz Rau and inaugurated in 1963. Its stone cladding is made of modular sawn stone in vertical strips.

[21] Hashimshoni et al., *Masterplan 1968*.

[22] Yosef Sharon, *The Supreme Court Building*, Jerusalem: Yad Hanadiv, Rothschild Foundation, 1993, p. 94.

[23] Meron Benvenisti, *City of Stone, The Hidden History of Jerusalem*, Berkeley and Los Angeles: University of California Press, 1996, p. 147.

[24] Ibid., p. 147.

[25] Azmi Bishara, *Checkpoints, Fragments of a Story*, Michael Goggenheimer (trans.), Tel Aviv: Babel, 2006, p. 14. City planners and scores of architectural critics, acknowledging some of the idiosyncrasies represented in the bylaw, usually conceded its effectiveness in moderating the ugliness of architectural monstrosities. In this context, most recently, the stone bylaw was enthusiastically embraced in Frank Gehry's design for the 'Museum of Tolerance' – a hallucinatory initiative of the Simon Wiesenthal Center (for a city in which tolerance could indeed be only placed in a museum). The building, located – of all places – on the site of a Muslim graveyard, combines Gehry's signature titanium cladding with a massive wall clad in stone.

[26] Zvi Efrat, *The Israeli Project, Israeli Planning and Construction 1948–1973*, Tel Aviv: Tel Aviv Museum of Art, 2000 (as exhibition) and 2005 (as catalogue).

[27] Alona Nitzan-Shiftan, 'Seizing Locality in Jerusalem', in Nezar AlSayyad (ed.), *The End of Tradition?*, London and New York: Routledge, 2004, pp. 231–55.

[28] The main theoretical reference for this transformation was paradoxically the writing of Martin Heidegger. The most relevant text was 'Building Dwelling Thinking' in *Poetry, Language, Thought*, Albert Hofstadter (trans.), New York: Harper Colophon Books, 1971. See treatment of this issue in Nitzan-Shiftan, 'Seizing Locality', p. 238.

[29] Wohlgelnerter, 'Follow the cobblestone road'.

[30] Simone Ricca, *Inventing the Jewish City: The Reconstruction of Jerusalem's Jewish Quarter After 1967*, London: IB Tauris, 2007, p. 150.

[31] Kutcher, *The New Jerusalem*, pp. 54, 87–9.

[32] Quoted in Gazit, *The Carrot*, p. 53.

[33] Tom Segev, *Israel in 1967*, Jerusalem: Keter Books, 2005, p. 511.

[34] Peter Bogud, 'The Cardo – the Jewish Street and Habad Road', in Amiram Harlap (ed.), *Israel Builds*, Jerusalem: Ministry for Construction and Housing, 1977, p. 173.

[35] Nitzan-Shiftan, 'Seizing Locality', p. 241–2.

[36] David Ben-Gurion, *Recollections*, New York: Macdonald & Co., 1970, p. 70.

[37] Immediately upon the establishment of the state, David Ben-Gurion appointed the Governmental Names Committee to 'Judaize' the country through the use of Hebrew names. See Meron Benvenisti, *Sacred Landscape: The Buried History of the Holy Land Since 1948*, Berkeley and Los Angeles: University of California Press, 2000, pp. 11–54. After the 1967 war, one of the first such settlements was developed in the West Bank city of Hebron close to an ancient mosque believed to be the 'Tomb of the Patriarchs'. A more recent Jewish settlement within Hebron is Tel Rumeida, built in 1999 over an excavated Bronze Age site believed to be the 'City of David'. Tel Rumeida is the most literal embodiment of the relationship of Israeli settlements to archaeology. As the contested subterrain erupted onto the surface of a densely populated Palestinian neighbourhood, the area was declared an archaeological site and was immediately requisitioned by the military for the purpose of urgent and temporary 'rescue excavation'. Columns were placed beside the dig to support a large cement roof. Coming to power just as this construction was completed in March 2001, Ariel Sharon's unity government immediately allowed a group of settlers to build a small outpost composed of seven mobile homes – six new apartments and a Torah study hall – on top of the roof, which itself was perched over the small archaeological site. Shimon Riklin, *Israeli History in Palestinian Hands*, Makor Rishon, 11 September 1998; Gideon Samet, 'The hidden threat of the outposts', *Ha'aretz* 23 October 2002; Akiva Eldar, 'Unnatural growth', *Ha'aretz*, 1 May 2001; Nadav Shragai, 'Tel Rumeida getting permanent housing', *Ha'aretz*, 3 September 2002; Nadav Shragai, 'Sharon orders new Hebron Jewish housing', *Ha'aretz*, 19 November 2002.

[38] In the practice of Israeli biblical archaeology the chronological classification has acquired national significance. The Bronze Age was designated as the 'Canaanite period' while the Iron Age has become the 'Israelite period'. See Colin Renfrew and Paul Bahn, *Archaeology, Theories, Methods and Practice*, London: Thames and Hudson, 2000, pp. 20–5.

[39] Neil Asher Silberman, *Between Past and Present: Archaeology, Ideology, and Nationalism in the Modern Middle East*, New York: H. Holt, 1989; Shulamit Geva, 'Biblical Archaeology at its Infancy', *Zmanim* issue 42, 1992; Nadia Abu El-Haj, *Facts on the Ground: Archaeological Practice and Territorial Self-Fashioning in Israeli Society*, Chicago: University of Chicago Press, 2001.

[40] Along the arc that stretches from Egypt, through Palestine, Lebanon, Syria, Turkey, Greece, the Balkans and Italy, the formation and consolidation of national identities, as well as a series of irredentist claims and conflicts, were often argued on overlapping historical narratives and myths that archaeology was called upon to resolve, substantiate and propagate. Lynn Meskell (ed.), *Archaeology Under Fire*, London and New York: Routledge, 1998, pp. 3–9.

[41] The British Palestine Exploration Fund, founded in May 1865 for 'investigating the archaeology, geography, geology, and natural history of Palestine', also furnished the cartography which facilitated the British conquest of Palestine. Some of the surveys and maps that enabled the defeat of the Ottoman armies had been prepared between 1913 and 1914 by two officers who had been seconded to the Palestine Exploration Fund by the War Office – Herbert Horatio Kitchener and T.E. Lawrence (of Arabia). These 'legendary' soldier-archaeologists surveyed and mapped the area under the guise of a religiously inspired archaeological investigation of the Holy Land. In the theological context of the nineteenth century, archaeology was seen as a sub-discipline of biblical research, combining excavation with textual study in attempts to match Bronze Age material ruins with biblical narratives. In the early 1920s, William Foxwell Albright's excavation work in Palestine turned biblical archaeology into a rigorous scientific discipline. But the archaeological excavations he led – such as the pompous 1924 expedition to the Dead Sea in search of Sodom and Gomorrah, accompanied by ceremonially dressed representatives of each of the ethnic communities in Jerusalem – still possessed some of the showmanship of earlier religious pilgrimages.

[42] Anita Shapira, 'Ben-Gurion and the Bible: the Forging of an Historical Narrative?', *Journal of Middle Eastern Studies*, 33 (4), 1997, pp. 645–74. Early Israeli biblical archaeologists saw the Bible through a fundamental paradox: it was both a historical document that was called upon to reconstruct a national past and direct them to ancient sites, and was also the source in need of verification by such discoveries. By contrast, ultra-Orthodox Jewish communities – their faith in the Bible never in need of physical proof – routinely objected to digs, and even petitioned in court against them, for fear that they might desecrate ancient Jewish graves. Shlomo Bunimovitz, 'Cultural Interpretation and the Bible: Biblical Archaeology in the Postmodern Era', *Cathedra*, August 2001, p. 33.

[43] Israeli biblical archaeology emerged in the 1950s, under the figurehead of Yigal Yadin, the Israeli Defence Force's second Chief of Staff. Seeking to supply nascent Israeli society with historical parallels to the 1948 War of Independence, Yadin focused his digging on the biblical period of 'Occupation and Settlement' of the Israelites in Canaan, on wars and monumental fortification works carried out by the kings of the First and Second Temple periods and on the Bar Kokhba revolt in places that were, or thereafter became, sites of epic national mythology – Hazor, Megiddo and Massada. Three years after the 1967 war, Yadin became Director of the Institute of Archaeology at Jerusalem's Hebrew University, in which capacity he led several digs across recently occupied territories. Another prominent soldier-archaeologist during these years was Moshe Dayan. Throughout his career in the military and as Defense Minister, he pursued archaeology as his private hobby. After 1967 his activities expanded to the Occupied Territories, which until 1974 were under his direct command as Defense Minister. Dayan pillaged more than thirty-five sites across the West Bank, Gaza and the Sinai, using military personnel, helicopters and trucks to transfer artefacts to his home in a Tel Aviv suburb. Neil Asher Silberman, *A Prophet from Amongst You: The Life of Yigal Yadin: Soldier, Scholar, and Mythmaker of Modern Israel*, Boston, MA: Addison Wesley Publishing, 1993; Raz Kletter, 'A Very General Archaeologist': Moshe Dayan and Israeli Archaeology', *The Journal of Hebrew Scriptures*, 4, 2003; Shabtai Teveth, *Moshe Dayan*, New York: Quartet Books, 1972, p. 202.

[44] Neve Gordon, *Israel's Occupation: Sovereignty, Discipline and Control*, Berkeley, CA: California University Press, forthcoming (chapter five). Although international law prohibits archaeological digs in occupied territories (other than rescue digs) and forbids the findings to be removed from those territories, since 1967, about 5,000 archaeological sites in the West Bank have been surveyed. After the first Intifada, Israeli academics began to abstain from carrying out digs in the West Bank, and most excavations were undertaken under the military's own 'staff officer for archaeology', a position held for the past twenty-five years by Yitzhak Magen. See Meron Rapoport, 'Buried Treasure that's kept in the Dark', *Ha'aretz*, 17 December 2006.

45 Shulamit Geva, *Biblical Archaeology*, p. 93.

46 Quoted in Nadia Abu El-Haj, *Facts on the Ground, Archeological Practice and Territorial Self Fashioning in Israeli Society*, Chicago: University of Chicago Press, 2001, p. 182.

47 'The Restoration of the Hurva: a Symposium' in David Casuto (ed.), *The Hurva Reconstructed: Comments and Criticisms on the Restoration of the Synagogue of 'Hurvat Rabi Yeduda Hahasid'*, Jerusalem: Ministry of Education and Culture, 1970.

48 Shimon Gardi, 'Rehabilitation of the Jewish Quarter,' in Harlap, *Israel Builds*, p. 161; Peter Bogud, 'The Cardo – the Jewish Street and Habad Road,' in Harlap, *Israel Builds*, p. 173.

49 Efrat, *Israeli Project*, p. 935.

50 Ram Karmi, 'Human Value in Urban Architecture,' in Harlap, *Israel Builds*, p. 31. A recent book by Karmi repeats some of these concepts: Ram Karmi, *Lyric Architecture*, Tel Aviv: Ministry of Defense Press, 2001 [Hebrew].

51 Karmi, *Human Value*, p. 31.

52 Ibid. p. 35.

53 Nitzan-Shiftan, 'Seizing Locality', p. 242.

54 Abu El-Haj, *Facts on the Ground*, p. 153. See also Gil Eyal, 'Between East and West: The Discourse on the "Arab Village" in Israel', in Yehuda Shenhav (ed.), *Coloniality and the Postcolonial Condition: Implications for Israeli Society*, Jerusalem: Van Leer Institute and Hakibbutz Hameuchad Publishing House, 2004, pp. 208, 217, 39–55 (in Hebrew).

55 Ella Shohat, *Forbidden Reminiscences, A Collection of Essays*, Tel Aviv: Kedem Publishing, 2001, p. 321. Moshe Dayan similarly described how, as a young man, the Palestinian farmers, working their lands with a pair of oxen, near Moshav Nahalal where he was raised, appeared to him like biblical figures displaced by time and made him think of his ancient 'forefathers and the heroes of our nation'. Moshe Dayan, *Living with the Bible*, New York: W. Morrow, 1978.

56 Bernard Rudofsky, *Architecture without Architects: A Short Introduction to Non-Pedigreed Architecture*, Albuquerque, New Mexico: University of New Mexico Press, 1987 [1964]. For excellent analysis of this work see Felicity Scott, 'Bernard Rudofsky: Allegories of Nomadism and Dwelling', in Sarah Goldhagen and Réjean Legault, *Anxious Modernisms: Experimentation in Postwar Architectural Culture*, Cambridge MA: MIT Press and Montreal: Canadian Center for Architecture, 2000, pp. 215–37; Felicity Scott, 'Underneath Aesthetics and Utility: The Untransposable Fetish of Bernard Rudofsky', *Assemblage* 38, April 1999 pp. 58–89; Felicity Scott, 'Revisiting Architecture without Architects', *Harvard Design Magazine*, Fall 1998, pp. 69–72.

57 Eran Tamir-Tawil, 'To Start A City From Scratch: An Interview with Architect Thomas M. Leitersdorf', in Rafi Segal and Eyal Weizman (eds), *A Civilian Occupation, The Politics of Israeli Architecture*, Tel Aviv and London: Verso Press and Babel Press, 2003, p. 160.

58 Gil Eyal, 'Arab Village', p. 208.

59 Esther Zandberg, 'Stepping down off the fence', *Ha'aretz*, 18 April 2006.

60 HCJ 5601/94, '*Odeh A'ida Abu Tier et al. v. The Prime Minister et al.* In 1994 the Israeli High Court of Justice was called upon to address the discriminatory expropriation policy in East Jerusalem, in the form of a petition filed by attorney Daniel Seidemann on behalf of residents of two Arab neighbourhoods, Umm Tuba and Bet Sahur. The petition concerned the land expropriated in April 1991 to build a new Jewish neighbourhood, to be known as 'Har Homah'. See Lein and Weizman, *Land Grab*.

61 Lein and Weizman, *Land Grab*.

62 Yaski and Co., Architects, 'Gilo, Housing Cluster 7, *in Harlap*,' *Israel Builds*, pp. 206–7.

63 Efrat, *Israeli Project*, p. 935. Demonstrating this tendency, the neighbourhood 'David's Village' outside the city walls was designed by the architect Moshe Safdie in neo-oriental style as a biblical village for wealthy foreign residents. It includes terraced buildings of two or three storeys with a variety of domes, arches and the streets named 'Sweet Singer' or 'Shepherd of Flocks'.

64 Minutes of meeting of the Local Planning and Building Committee, quoted in Eitan Felner, *A Policy of Discrimination: Land Expropriation, Planning and Building in East Jerusalem*, Jerusalem: B'tselem, 1995.

65 For most recent references to this policy, see Jerusalem Institute for Israel Studies, *The Jerusalem Metropolis – A Master Plan and Development Plan*, Jerusalem, 1994, and The Municipality of Jerusalem, *Jerusalem City Plan 2000*.

66 The Rome Statute of the International Criminal Court. (See the complete statute at: http://www.un.org/law/icc/statute/romefra.htm.) Article 8.3.b.viii forbids 'The transfer, directly or indirectly, by the Occupying Power of parts of its own civilian population into the territory it

occupies, or the deportation or transfer of all or parts of the population of the occupied territory within or outside this territory'.

[67] Crimes relating to the organization of the built environment, originating on computer screens and drafting tables, may call for architect/planners, for the first time, to be placed on the accused stand at an international tribunal. It is revealing that the Israeli Attorney-General Elyakim Rubinstein urged the Israeli Knesset to retreat from ratifying the ICC lest 'every building (in the Occupied Territories) start to be considered a war crime,' and Israeli planners, architects, constructors, suppliers, or residents in the settlement be indicted. Allen Baker, then the legal adviser to the Foreign Office, put it in bolder terms: 'Every person who is involved in decision making regarding the setting of citizens on occupied area may be arrested, from the prime minister down to the last citizen.'

[68] Nathan Marom, *The Planning Deadlock: Planning Policies, Land Regularization, Building Permits and House Demolition in East Jerusalem*, Jerusalem: Bimkom–Planners for Planning Rights and Ir Shalem, 2004 (in Hebrew). A summary of the report was published in English, see Nathan Marom, 'The Planning Deadlock: House Demolition in the Palestinian Neighborhoods of East Jerusalem', in Philipp Misselwitz and Tim Rieniets (eds), *City of Collision*, Basel and London: Birkhauser, 2006, pp. 347–52.

[69] According to a study undertaken by the architect Nathan Marom, more than 18,000 buildings – half of all Palestinian housing units in East Jerusalem – are 'illegally' built. Between 1987 and 2004 about 500 of these homes were demolished. Since the beginning of the second Intifada the rate of destruction has increased: in 2004 alone, 120 homes were pulled down. See Nathan Marom, *The Planning Deadlock*. Also see Rassem Khamaisi, 'Villages under Siege,' in Misselwitz and Rieniets (eds), *City of Collision*, esp. p. 123. For a constant update of these data and more, see the website of the Israel Committee against House Demolition on http://icahd.org/eng.

[70] Rassem Khamaisi and Rami Nasrallah, *The Jerusalem Urban Fabric: Demography, Infrastructure and Institutions*, Jerusalem: International Peace and Cooperation Center, 2003, p. 126. See also the summary of this work in Rassem Khamaisi, 'Villages under Siege', and Rassem Khamaisi and Rami Nasrallah, 'Jerusalem: From Siege to a City's Collapse?', in Misselwitz and Rieniets (eds), *City of Collision*, pp. 120–9 and pp. 163–9.

[71] Sarah Kaminker, *Planning and Housing Issues in East Jerusalem*, Jerusalem: Report Prepared for the Society of St. Yves, in Response to High Court Petition 1091/94, 1994, p. 15. Quoted in Felner, *A Policy of Discrimination*.

[72] Nathan Marom, *The Planning Deadlock*.

Chapter 2 Fortifications: The Architecture of Ariel Sharon

[1] Israeli politicians touching upon populist sentiments routinely described the cease-fire lines of 1949 as an existential danger to the state. Even the dovish Foreign Minister Abba Eban (although later retreating from the statement) referred to Israel's international borders as nothing less than 'Auschwitz lines'. Benny Morris, *Righteous Victims*, London: John Murray, 2000, p. 308. For more on the fear of a Second Holocaust prior to the 1967 war, see Idith Zertal, *Death and the Nation: History Memory Politics*, Or Yehuda: Dvir Publishing House, 2002. The perception of 'indefensible lines' did not truly reflect the military realities at the time. Moshe Dayan made this point: 'The road leading from Damascus to Tel Aviv is not shorter then the road between Tel Aviv and Damascus.' Quoted in Martin van Creveld, *Defending Israel*, New York: St. Martin's Press, 2004, p. 9.

[2] Although the cease-fire lines included many of the Jewish holy sites, they did not coincide with any of the several biblical definitions of the Holy Land. In their maximal form, these were often perceived as extending from the Euphrates River in the north to Sinai in the south, from the Jordanian desert in the east to the Mediterranean in the west.

[3] From the West Bank, the political outlines of the Allon plan sought the annexation by Israel of a strip about twenty kilometres in width along the Jordan Valley, with a further transport corridor passing through Jerusalem connecting it with the Israeli coastal plain. These two parts, according to the plan, would eventually become a self-governed Palestinian area confederated with the Kingdom of Jordan. The Allon plan sought to further annex two other areas of the West Bank – the Etzion Settlement Block southwest of Jerusalem, where Zionist settlements fell in the 1948 war, and Arab East Jerusalem. Between 1967 and 1977, fifteen settlements were established along

the Jordan River, twenty in the Golan Heights and five in the Sinai Desert according to Allon's plan.

4 NAHAL is the Hebrew acronym for 'Noar Halutzi Lohem' – Fighting Pioneer Youth. It is a military corps which combines military service in a combat unit with civilian service in a new outpost. NAHAL soldiers spend about eight hours a day farming with a few extra hours training.

5 The increased utilization of aquifers water affected Palestinian villages on the mountain range. The water consumption of 6,200 settlers in the Jordan Valley was equivalent to 75 per cent of the water consumption for domestic and urban uses of the entire Palestinian population of the West Bank. See B'Tselem, *Not Even a Drop, The Water Crisis in Palestinian Villages Without a Water Network*, July 2001. www.btselem.org.

6 Avraham Adan, *On Both Sides of the Suez*, Jerusalem: Idanim, and Yediot Aharonot editions, 1979, p. 47 [Hebrew].

7 Lt. General Sa'ad El Shazly, *The Crossing of the Canal*, San Francisco: American Mideast Research, 2003, p. 329. In 1983 Shazly was sentenced in absentia to three years of hard labor in an Egyptian military prison for allegedly divulging military secrets in this book but in effect for his implicit criticism of Sadat and of the peace process with Israel. In 1992 Shazly returned to Egypt after fourteen years in exile in Algeria, and was arrested.

8 'The fourth barrier was a secret one. Deep inside the sand rampart the enemy had embedded reservoirs filled with inflammable liquid, their outlets controlled from the nearest forts. In minutes, the liquid could gush into the Canal, turning its surface into an inferno.' In effect that secret weapon never worked. Egyptian divers may have blocked it, as Shazly claimed, or it may have failed due to a technical problem in its mechanisms, as some Israeli generals claimed. Shazly, *Crossing*, pp. 7–8.

9 A similar debate took place in the spring of 1944 between Erwin Rommel and General von Rundstedt's over the *Wehrmacht* defences along the Atlantic coast. Rommel believed that the only chance of beating back an Allied invasion was to confront them on the water's edge: 'the main battle line will be the beach!' Rundstedt advised for defence in depth. See Friedrich Ruge, *Rommel in Normandy*, San Rafael, CA: Presidio Press, 1979, p. 4.

10 Adriana Kemp, 'Border Space and National Identity in Israel', *Theory and Criticism, Space, Land, Home, On the Normalization of a 'New Discourse'*, issue no. 16, Spring 2000, p. 282 [in Hebrew].

11 Ibid., p. 19.

12 Ibid., p. 23.

13 According to Benny Morris, this was a continuation of previous tendencies of Israeli command during the 1948 war. Wary of the rule of law or that of history, it only took David Ben-Gurion to wish for the expulsion of the Palestinians known to IDF top brass in 1947–8 for them to launch into action. See Benny Morris, *The Birth of the Palestinian Refugee Problem, 1947–1949*, Cambridge: Cambridge University Press, 1987.

14 Gorenberg, *The Accidental Empire*, New York: Times, 2006 p. 227.

15 Uzi Benziman, *Sharon, an Israeli Caesar*, London: Robson Books, 1985, pp. 115–16.

16 Ariel Sharon with David Chanoff, *Warrior, the Autobiography of Ariel Sharon*, New York: Simon & Schuster, 2001, p. 219.

17 Zeev Schiff and Eitan Haber, *Israel, Army and Defence, A Dictionary*, Jerusalem: Zmora, Bitan, Modan–Publishers, 1976, p. 542 [in Hebrew].

18 Sharon, *Warrior*, p. 208.

19 Martin van Creveld, *Command in War*, Cambridge MA: Harvard University Press, 1985, p. 204.

20 In fact what the military calls 'networks' (implying a non-hierarchical structure) should technically be referred to as 'systems' (distributed structures with centralized command). Military 'networks' are thus most often 'systems' in disguise.

21 Shimon Naveh, *In Pursuit of Military Excellence, The Evolution of Operational Theory*, London and New York: Frank Cass, 2004 [1997], pp. 269–71.

22 Adan, *Both Sides of the Suez*, p. 47; Uzi Benziman, *Sharon*, p. 110.

23 Sharon, *Warrior*, p. 219.

24 Benziman, *Sharon*, p. 111.

25 Baruch Kimmerling, *Politicide: Ariel Sharon's War Against the Palestinians*, London: Verso, 2003, p. 65.

26 Stephen Graham, 'Constructing Urbicide by Bulldozer in the Occupied Territories', in Stephen Graham, *Cities, War and Terrorism*, Oxford: Blackwell, 2004, p. 333.

27 'The Generalship of Ariel Sharon', a round table discussion at the Operational Theory Research

Institute (OTRI) of the IDF's Academy of Staff and Command, 24–25 May 2006.

28 Norma Masriyeh Hazboun, *Israeli Resettlement Schemes for Palestinian Refugees in the West Bank and Gaza Strip since 1967*, Shaml: Palestinian Diaspora & Refugee Centre, http://www.shaml.org/publications/monos/mono4.htm, Richard Locke and Anthony Stewart, *Bantustan Gaza*; London: Zed Books, 1985.

29 Galal Nassar, *Dam-busters on the Bar Lev Line*, an interview with Maj. Gen. (retired) Gamal Mohamed Ali, commander of the military engineers corps before and during the October War, *Al-Ahram Weekly* On-line, http://weekly.ahram.org.eg.

30 Shazly, *The Crossing*, p. 222.

31 Ibid., pp. 55–6, 226.

32 Ibid., p. 55.

33 According to Shazly, 1,020 tanks, and 13,500 vehicles were ferried across the canal in the first day of operations. See ibid., p. 234.

34 The breaking of the Bar Lev Line was a further affirmation, if one was needed, of Carl von Clausewitz's warning against linear defence. In order to defend the entire length of a line, he claimed: 'positions became more and more extended, and their front became proportionately weaker . . . the attacker . . . no longer tried to outflank the enemy by outextending him, but massed his strength against a single point and pierced the line.' Carl Von Clausewitz, *On War* (edited and translated by Michael Howard and Peter Paret), London: Everyman's Library, 1993, pp. 503–4.

35 Benziman, *Sharon*, p. 163.

36 Quoted in Ronen Bergman and Gil Meltzer, *The Yom Kippur War – Moment of Truth*, Tel Aviv: Miskal–Yedioth Ahronoth Books and Chemed Books, 2002, pp. 152, 199 [Hebrew].

37 Ronen Bergman and Gil Metzer, 'Bulldozer: A New Research Opens up the War over History', *Yediot Aharonot* weekend supplement, 13 January 2006 [Hebrew].

38 Benny Morris, *Righteous Victims*, London: John Murray, 2000, p. 421.

39 Abraham Rabinovich, *Yom Kippur War: The Epic Encounter That Transformed the Middle East*, Westminster, MD: Knopf Publishing Group, 2004, pp. 416–33.

40 Basil Liddell Hart, *Strategy*, London: Plume, 1991. 'In strategy the longest way round is often the shortest way there; a direct approach to the object exhausts the attacker and hardens the resistance by compression, whereas an indirect approach loosens the defender's hold by upsetting his balance.'

41 Rabinovich, *Yom Kippur War*, p. 505.

42 Naveh, *Military Excellence*, pp. 252–3.

43 'The Generalship of Ariel Sharon'.

44 The debate around the manual marked, according to Shimon Naveh, 'the prelude to the longest, most intoxicating and creative professional debate which ever occurred in the history of American military thought'. See Naveh, *Military Excellence*, pp. 258, 263–4.

45 John. L. Romjue, 'The Evolution of the Airland Battle Concept', *Airpower*, June 2006: http://www.airpower.maxwell.af.mil/airchronicles/aureview/1984/may-jun/romjue.html.

46 The result of these developments was captured in a new economic model developed recently by the political economists Jonathan Nitzan and Shimshon Bichler and titled 'accumulation through-crisis'. According to Nitzan and Bichler, the sectors to have financially benefited most from the 1973 war were the OPEC states, large oil companies, military contractors, infrastructure companies and key financial institutions. Over the 1974–84 period, the annual arms trade rose 136 per cent, with roughly 53 per cent of the total going to the Middle East and Africa, taking over as the world's leading market for imported weaponry representing over one-third of the global trade. Jonathan Nitzan and Shimshon Bichler, *The Global Political Economy of Israel*, London and Sterling, VA: Pluto, 2002, pp. 25, 217–46.

47 About 30 per cent of the Israeli security budget was dedicated to military research and development in information-based weapons manufacturing, around which emerged a network of business services which later gave birth to Israel's robust high-tech industry. See Shlomo Swirski, *The Price of Occupation*: Tel Aviv: Mapa, 2005, p. 67 [Hebrew].

48 Antonio Gramsci, *Selections from the Prison Notebooks* (edited and translated by Quintin Hoare and Geoffrey Nowell Smith), London: Lawrence and Wishart, 1998 [1971], pp. 229–39.

49 Ibid., p. 238.

50 Tamar Herman, 'Social Protest in State and Security', in Anat Kurz (ed.), *Thirty Years Later: Challenges to Israel since the Yom Kippur War*, Tel Aviv: Jaffee Centre for Strategic Studies, 2004, p. 47 [Hebrew].

[51] The Israeli Black Panthers (HaPanterim HaShkhorim) was a protest movement of second-generation Jewish immigrants from Muslim countries (Mizrahi Jews), set up in 1971 in Jerusalem to work against state discrimination. They received the name Black Panthers as a nickname based on the African-American Black Panthers and then eventually adopted it as their official name.

[52] If before the turnabout, the state was characterized by the cultural and social proximity between the elite groups and a symbiosis between so-called 'free' intellectuals and state politicians, after it the Likud government distanced itself from 'high' culture but this distance unintentionally brought about a more liberal cultural approach, where some in the media and academia joined in critical debate on security matters. The stand-off contributed to their autonomy and gave rise to a critical culture that accentuated differences and ethnicities, shook the foundational myths of Zionist 'national unity' and formed movements or schools of thought that, decades later, were labelled post- and anti-Zionist. Shlomo Sand, *Intellectuals, Truth and Power From the Dreyfus Affair to the Gulf War*, Tel Aviv: Am Oved, 2000, pp. 162–73 [Hebrew].

[53] Mark Heller, 'The PLO and the Israeli Question', in Kurz, *Thirty Years Later*, p. 28.

[54] James Rosenau, *Turbulence in World Politics*, New York: Harvester Wheatsheaf, 1990.

[55] Jacqueline Rose, *The Question of Zion*, Princeton, NJ: Princeton Press, 2005.

[56] Under the spiritual leadership of Rabbi Zvi Yehuda Kook, Gush Emunim followers were taught that they lived in the beginning of messianic times, in which the redemption of the entire Land of Israel is essential for the redemption of the world. Each person, friend or foe, is divinely ordained to help bring about the world's redemption. See Baruch Kimmerling, *Invention and Decline of Israeliness: Society, Culture and the Military*, Berkeley and Los Angeles: University of California Press, 2001, p. 124.

[57] Compare the classic and much contested representation of the American frontier in Frederick J. Turner, 'The Significance of the Frontier in American History', originally read at the meeting of the American Historical Association in Chicago, 12 July 1893. It was first published in the *Proceedings of the State Historical Society of Wisconsin*, 14 December 1893. It is accessible on the web at www.fordham.edu/halsall/mod/1893turner.html.

[58] Yehezkel Lein and Eyal Weizman, *Land Grab: Israel's Settlement Policy in the West Bank*, Jerusalem: B'Tselem, May 2002. Published online on www.btselem.org.

[59] Sharon, *Warrior*, p. 358.

[60] It is rather incredible that in the context of critiquing my work in 2002, Wachman was quoted as saying that those who see too close a link between architecture and politics are misguided: 'Whether Israeli architects and planners design sprawl or architectural gems, it is irrelevant to the bitter geopolitical dispute.' See Simona Fuma Shapiro, 'Debate Builds Over the Politics of Israeli Architecture', *Forward*, 25 October 2002, www.forward.com.

[61] The Wachman plan was actually first submitted to Prime Minister Rabin in 1976 at the time Sharon was his Special Advisor on Security under the title: 'Headlines for a territorial solution and a long term physical plan'. The plan, which he later called the 'Double Column Plan', sought to spread Jewish population along two longitudinal columns: an 'eastern column' which, similar to the Allon plan was to be stretched along the Jordan River, and the 'western column' along the western edge of the West Bank. Several latitudinal connections would connect the two columns. With various generations these plans would come to be known throughout the late 1970s and early 1980s as the 'H-Plans'. Avraham Wachman, *The 'Double Column' Plan*, Haifa: University of Haifa, Horizons in Geography, Vol. 3, 1977 [Hebrew].

[62] Elisha Efrat, *Geography of Occupation, Judea, Samaria and the Gaza Strip*, Jerusalem: Carmel Press, 2002, pp. 65–7 [Hebrew]. This arrangement was based on principles current in Israeli practices of rural planning since the 1950s, originating in the 'Central Place Theory' of the German geographer Walter Christaller. This theory, developed in Christaller's 1939 PhD thesis, formed the basis for the development of Nazi territorial *Raumordnung* ('the spatial order') in occupied Poland. According to these principles, new rural villages and towns were not autarkic entities but part of a distributed synergetic network of cities, towns and villages. Considering the use of this theory, and its applicability to a situation of colonization, it is amazing that Christaller's theories are still being taught in architectural and planning schools worldwide and in particular at the Technion in Haifa, without much critical/historical discussion of its source. See Efrat, *The Israeli Project*, pp. 998–1000 [Hebrew]; Gerhard Fehl, 'The Nazi Garden City', in Stephan Ward (ed.), *The Garden City: Past, Present and Future*, London: Spon, pp. 88–103; Walter Christaller, *Die zentralen Orte in Sueddeutschland*, Jena: Gustav Fischer, 1933. Translated in part by Charlisle W. Baskin, as *Central Places in Southern Germany*, Prentice Hall, 1966.

[63] This may have originated from similar discussions undertaken by Deleuze and Guattari. They illustrated the difference between a network- and a line-based geography by comparing the game of Go with that of chess. If the aim of Go is the 'bordering, encircling, shattering . . .' of the opponent, it implies 'a war without battle lines, with neither confrontation nor retreat, without battle even: pure strategy'. Deleuze and Guattari, *A Thousand Plateaus*, pp. 389–90.

[64] Jeff Halper, *Dismantling the Matrix of Control*, Israel Committee Against House Demolitions, 2004, http://www.icahd.org/eng/articles.asp?menu=6&submenu=3.

[65] Aluf Benn, 'This is how the evacuation plan was born', *Ha'aretz*, 30 December 2006.

[66] Emmanuel Sivan, 'The lights of Netzarim', *Ha'aretz*, 7 November 2003.

[67] Sharon, *Warrior*, p. 366.

[68] Ibid., p. 219.

[69] Ibid., pp. 357–9.

Chapter 3 Settlements: Battle for the Hilltops

[1] Zvi Efrat, 'The Plan', in Rafi Segal and Eyal Weizman (ed.), *A Civilian Occupation*, London and New York: Verso Press, 2003, p. 61.

[2] Interview 15 April 2006, Jaffee Centre for Strategic Studies, Tel Aviv University.

[3] David Newman, *Jewish Settlement in the West Bank: The Role of Gush Emunim*, Durham: Centre for Middle Eastern and Islamic Studies, 1982, pp. 40–3. Daniella Weiss became general-secretary of Gush Emunim in 1985 and is currently the head of Qedumim municipality.

[4] Ari Shavit, 'A leader awaits a signal', *Ha'aretz*, 22 March 2002.

[5] In later years it would become clear that the settlers of Gush Emunim have been the vanguard of the colonization of the mountain district of the West Bank, but never formed the bulk of it. At present, the proportion of Gush Emunim settlers among the total number of settlers in the West Bank is less than 10 per cent. See Shlomo Swirski, *The Price of Occupation*, Tel Aviv: Mapa Publishers, 2005 [Hebrew], p. 51.

[6] Uzi Benziman, *Sharon: an Israeli Caesar*, London: Robson Books, 1985, p. 209.

[7] Ibid., p. 223.

[8] The clashes between Gush Emunim and the government continued during most of the period of the first Likud government headed by Menachem Begin, but ended shortly before the 1981 elections, after the centrist Democratic Movement for Change resigned from the government.

[9] Lein and Weizman, *Land Grab*.

[10] Pierre Bourdieu, *The Logic of Practice*, Stanford, CA: Stanford University Press, 1990, pp. 42–51.

[11] See Chapter 1, 'Petrifying the Holy City', pp. 25–6.

[12] See discussion of the Allon plan in Chapter 2, pp. 58–9.

[13] Martin Van Creveld, *Defending Israel*, New York: St. Martin's Press, 2004, p. 24.

[14] See discussion of the Sharon plan in Chapter 2, pp. 80–5.

[15] Gush Emunim, 'Plan J.S – Masterplan for Major Settlement in Judea and Samaria', 1976.

[16] See Chapter 2, note 13.

[17] Similarly, Noam Chomsky claimed that according to the 'mad man' theory of the CIA, the US Administration must always appear slightly irrational to its enemies. Noam Chomsky, *Rogue States: The Rule of Force in World Affairs*, London: Pluto, 2000, pp. 20–1.

[18] Such a functional approach can be found in the works of German historians Martin Broszat and Hans Mommsen. They have separately claimed that the exterminist dynamic National Socialist was the consequence of the erosion of the formal-legal state. Immediately after the seizure of power, the chaos, fragmentation of government, governmental disorder, duplication and personalization of institutional structures led to a process that Mommsen called 'cumulative radicalization'. Once this 'cumulative radicalization' was unleashed the process became self-generating and ultimately self-destructive. Hans Mommsen, 'Cumulative Radicalization and Progressive Self-Destruction as Structural Determinants of the Nazi dictatorship', in Ian Kershaw and Moshe Lewin (eds), *Stalinism and Nazism, Dictatorships in Comparison*, Cambridge: Cambridge University Press, 1997; Martin Broszat, *The Hitler State: The Foundation and Development of the Internal Structure of the Third Reich*, New York: Longman, 1981; Ian Kershaw, *Hitler* (2 vols), New York: W. W. Norton, 1999; Deborah Dwork and Robert Jan van Pelt, *Holocaust*, New York: W. W. Norton, reprint edition (September 2003), p. 82.

19 The Hague Convention on the Laws and Customs of War on Land, and its attached Hague Regulations of 1907 can be accessed on www.icrc.org/ihl.nsf.

20 International law outlaws *confiscation* of private property by the occupying army, but recognizes the power of the army to temporarily *requisition* land, and that only for the duration of hostilities (Article 46).

21 Under the terms of international humanitarian law, the laws of belligerent occupation come into effect as soon as the government of the occupied territory is no longer capable of exercising its authority and ends when another government is in a position to impose its authority and control over that area. Yoram Dinstein, *Laws of War*, Tel Aviv: Schocken and Tel Aviv University, 1983, pp. 209–20 [Hebrew].

22 Gershom Gorenberg, *The Accidental Empire, Israel and the Birth of the Settlements, 1967–77*, New York: Times, 2005, p. 197.

23 HCJ, 302/72 *Abu Hilo et al. v. Government of Israel et al.* [Rafah Salient]. This section was translated in Gorenberg, *Accidental Empire*, p. 220.

24 Ibid. [HCJ, 302/72].

25 HCJ 258/79 *Abu Hilo et al. v. Government of Israel et al.* [Bet El].

26 Indeed, settlers could never be considered only as passive consumers of IDF security, but as active contributors to it. A decade later, settlers formed armed 'settlement security units'. During the second Intifada the military relocated some of its bases into the settlements, while settlers from the 'security units' were present at military briefings and debriefings.

27 HCJ 390/79, *Dweikat et al. v. Government of Israel et al.* [Elon Moreh].

28 Tower and Stockade settlements were developed by the architect Yochanan Ratner in April 1936, coinciding with the beginning of the Arab Revolt of 1936–9. They combined physical fortifications in the form of a bulletproof stockade with an observation and communication tower. See Sharon Rotbard, 'Wall and Tower', in Rafi Segal and Eyal Weizman, *A Civilian Occupation, The Politics of Israeli Architecture*, London and Tel Aviv: Verso Books and Babel Publishers, 2004, pp. 39–58.

29 Yigal Allon, *Curtain of Sand*, Tel Aviv: Hakibbutz Hameuchad, 1988 [1959], p. 254.

30 Ibid., p. 244.

31 See discussion of Adan's design of the Bar Lev Line in Chapter 2, pp. 60–1.

32 S. Ilan Troen, *Imagining Zion*, New Haven, CT and London: Yale University Press, 2003, p. 65.

33 During the 1948 war, the Moshav gained primacy over the Kibbutz as the main method of absorbing Jewish immigrants from Arab countries without having to resort to long processes of ideological and social preparation which the fully cooperative life of the Kibbutz requires. To this end, Moshavs were primarily established on cleansed Palestinian lands within the areas that came under Israeli control in 1948.

34 Troen, *Imagining*, p. 67.

35 Settlements had no part in the containment of attacks by Arab armies in the 1973 war. In the morning of the concentrated Egyptian Syrian attack on 6 October 1973, the government ordered the civilian population of the Golan Heights – a series of cooperative settlements built along the cease-fire line with Syria according to the northern part of the Allon plan – to be evacuated.

36 HCJ 390/79, *Dweikat et al. v. Government of Israel et al.* [Elon Moreh].

37 Ibid.

38 Lein and Weizman, *Land Grab*.

39 HCJ 258/79 *Abu Hilo et al. v. Government of Israel et al.* [Bet El].

40 Ibid.

41 This was the principle that the High Court of Justice relied upon when it ruled out the appeals of Gaza settlers against their evacuation from their homes in the summer of 2005. HCJ 1661/05 *Hof Azah Regional Council v. The Knesset*.

42 Samera Esmeir, 'Introduction: In the Name of Security', *Adala's Review*, Volume 4, Spring 2004, p. 5.

43 In Hebron, settlers, who pleaded with the military authorities, were given permission to enter the city in April 1968 and stay there for the week of Passover only. Yet they consolidated their presence and have remained there to this very day. When challenged for allowing them to stay, Dayan claimed that it would be a waste of time to fight with settlers regarding issues that will in any case soon be resolved through political decisions and would thus be rendered irrelevant. In the war of 1948, the cleansing of Palestinian communities was similarly argued as a 'temporary' measure under-

taken to secure the traffic arteries for the transportation of military supplies. The expulsion of many other Palestinian villagers was argued as 'temporary' for a variety of other security reasons. Almost sixty years later, those refugees left in Israel are still considered 'present absentees', and those who fled the borders still live in 'temporarily' refugee camps. Mourid Barghouti explained how this 'temporariness' was perceived by Palestinians:

> In the disaster of 1948 the refugees found shelter in neighboring countries as a temporary measure. They left their food cooking on stoves, thinking to return in few hours. They scattered in tents and camps of zinc and tin 'temporarily'. The commandos took arms and fought from Amman 'temporarily', then from Beirut 'temporarily', then they moved to Tunis and Damascus 'temporarily'. We drew up interim programs for liberation 'temporarily' and they told us they had accepted the Oslo Agreements 'temporarily', and so on, and so on. Each one said to himself and to others 'until things become clearer.' Mourid Barghouti, *I Saw Ramallah*, Ahdaf Soueif (trans.), London: Bloomsbury, 2005, p. 26.

44 Adi Ophir, 'A Time of Occupation', in Roane Carey and Jonathan Shainin (eds), *The Other Israel*, New York: The New Press, 2003, p. 60. See also Ariella Azoulay and Adi Ophir, *Bad Days*, Tel Aviv: Resling Press, 2002 [Hebrew].

45 David Kretzmer, *The Occupation of Justice, The Supreme Court of Israel and the Occupied Territories*, New York: State University of New York Press, 2002, p. 120.

46 Leon Shelef, 'The Border of Activism is the Green Line: in the Margin and in the Pathways of High Court of Justice ruling in the occupied territories', *Legal Review*, 17 (2) 1993, pp. 890–757 [Hebrew].

47 HCJ 390/79 [Elon Moreh].

48 Ibid.

49 Ibid.

50 Dror Etkes and Hagit Ofran, *Breaking the Law in the West Bank: The Private Land Report*, Peace Now, November 2006, http://www.peacenow.org.il/site/en/peace.asp?pi=61&fld=191&docid =2024. According to this report, at present nearly 40 per cent of the total land area on which the settlements, outposts and industrial zones in the West Bank are located (a total area of 158 square kilometres) is privately owned by Palestinians. All together, more than 3,400 buildings in settlements are constructed on land that is privately owned by Palestinians.

51 Ronen Shamir, 'Landmark Cases and the Reproduction of Legitimacy: the Case of Israel High Court of Justice', *Law and Society Review*, 24 (3) 1990, p. 788.

Chapter 4 Settlements: Optical Urbanism

1 Mourid Barghouti, *I Saw Ramallah*, Ahdaf Soueif (trans.), London: Bloomsbury Publishing, 2005, p. 29.

2 A Palestinian resident of a village near Ramallah, quoted in Danny Rubinstein, 'Preparing for a civil war', *Ha'aretz*, 18 December 2006.

3 In 1974 the Labor Party wanted to build a settlement in this location. It was part of a general attempt to ring Jerusalem with neighbourhoods within the 1967 extended municipal boundaries and with settlements immediately beyond them.

4 Eran Tamir-Tawil, 'To Start a City from Scratch, An Interview with Architect Thomas M. Leitersdorf', in Rafi Segal and Eyal Weizman, *A Civilian Occupation, The Politics of Israeli Architecture*, London and Tel Aviv: Verso Books and Babel Publishers, 2004, p. 45.

5 Ibid, p. 44.

6 Ibid. The land on which Ma'ale Adumim was constructed belonged to the villagers of Abu Dis, Anata, Azariya, A-Tur and Isawiya. The Bedouin tribe – Jahalleen – that inhabited the hills on which it was built, was forcibly relocated to an adjacent rubbish dump. Ma'ale Adumim is located, as Leitersdorf claimed, 'well within the Israeli political consensus', and is at present home to 32,000 inhabitants – the largest city-settlement in the West Bank with a municipal area larger than Tel Aviv, and with the Wall now routed around it. It has succeeded in its aim: to sever the north of the West Bank from its south, and to isolate Jerusalem from the rest of the West Bank.

7 Ministry of Construction and Housing, *A City in the Desert: Ma'ale Adumim*, 1983 (promotional film).

8 Ebenezer Howard, *Garden Cities of To-Morrow*, London: Faber, 1965 [1902]. The first 'Garden City' was implemented by the architect Raymond Unwin in Letchworth, north of London, and at Hampstead Garden Suburb.

9 Gilbert Werbert and Silvina Sosonovsky, *Bauhaus on the Carmel: The Coming of Modern Architecture to Hadar Hacarmel*, Haifa: The Technion Press, 1985 [Hebrew]; Patrick Geddes, *Cities in Evolution: An Introduction to the Town Planning Movement and to the Study of Civics*, London: Benn, 1968, p. 154.

10 Geddes, *Cities in Evolution*, p. 154.

11 Werbert and Sosonovsky, *Bauhaus on the Carmel*, p. 21.

12 Ibid., pp. 32–3. In 1920 a report entitled 'Haifa Garden Village' was submitted to the World Zionist Organization and the British government, forming the blueprint for the development of Haifa. Later, in 1922, Geddes' guidelines were drawn into a masterplan by the architect Richard Kauffmann, the WZO's leading planner, together with the prominent British planner Abercrombie. Patrick Abercrombie (1880–1957) was later known for the 1943 'London Plan' which recommended the construction of the South Bank Complex – a development which was undertaken together with the Festival of Britain on the site in 1948, and for the 'New Towns' outside London in the post-World War II period.

13 Ministry of Construction and Housing, *Ma'ale Adumim*.

14 Thomas Leitersdorf, 'Development Plan for Neighborhoods A(02), B (04), E (03), Ma'ale Adumim', in Amiram Harlap (ed.), *Israel Builds* Jerusalem: Ministry of Construction and Housing, 1988, p. 164.

15 Tamir-Tawil, 'To Start,' p. 158.

16 See the discussion of this legal arguments in Chapter 3, p. 95–7.

17 Yehezkel Lein and Eyal Weizman, *Land Grab: Israel's Settlement Policy in the West Bank*, Jerusalem: B'Tselem, May 2002. Published online at www.btselem.org.

18 This declaration of uncultivated Palestinian land as land belonging to the state of Israel was based on the 1967 'Order Regarding Government Property', which authorized the Israeli military to take possession of properties belonging to an 'enemy state' and to manage them at its discretion. 'Order Regarding Government Property (Judea and Samaria) (No. 59), 5727–1967', in *Planning, Building and Land Laws*, pp. 520–3.

19 Lein and Weizman, *Land Grab*.

20 On the process of aerial mapping of the West Bank and Israel, see also Moshe Saban, 'Aerial Photography and Photometrics', in Harlap, *Israel Builds*, p. 53.

21 In 1968 alone Israel helped Palestinians in the Gaza Strip plant some 618,000 trees. This should be seen in comparison to over 226,000 trees and more than 10 per cent of Gaza's agricultural land destroyed by Israel during the first three years of the second Intifada. See Neve Gordon, *Israel's Occupation: Sovereignty, Discipline and Control*, Berkeley, CA: California University Press, forthcoming (Introduction). Gordon's own data from *Monthly Statistics of the Administered Territories*, 1, (8) Central Bureau of Statistics, August 1971, pp. xiv–xvi.

22 Quoted in Gorenberg, *Accidental Empire*, p. 174. In 1884, Togo became a German colony. The Germans experimented with scientific cultivation of the country's main export crops (cacao, coffee and cotton) and developed its infrastructure to the highest level in Africa. Dayan also sought to invest Israeli funds in Palestinian hospitals, roads, waterworks and power lines. He believed that the Palestinians would be grateful subjects, and would realize that only under Israeli military rule could Arabs and Jews live together.

23 Gordon, *Israel's Occupation* (Introduction). This went hand in hand with rapid economic growth: between 1968 and 1973 the GNP of the Occupied Palestinian Territories increased by almost 20 per cent.

24 Shlomo Swirski, *The Price of Occupation*, Tel Aviv: Mapa Publishers, 2005, p. 28 [Hebrew]. The result could be summed up by the following statistics: while Israeli farmers managed to water 95 per cent of agriculturally suitable soil within the borders of the state, the Palestinians managed to water only twenty 25 cent of their suitable soil.

25 The reduction was from an estimate of 2,435 km^2 in 1965 to 1,735 km^2 in 1985. Data from Gordon, *Israel's Occupation* (Introduction).

26 Dror Etkes and Hagit Ofran, *Breaking the Law in the West Bank: Israeli Settlement Building on Private Palestinian Property*, Peace Now, November 2006. http://www.peacenow.org.il/site/en/peace.asp? pi=61&fld=191&docid=2024; http://www.peacenow.org.il/data/SIP_STORAGE/files/9/2569.pdf.

27 Saul Ephraim Cohen, *The Politics of Planting*, Chicago: University of Chicago Press, 1993.

28 While the JNF plants new pine trees, under the pretext of security the military uproot olive trees around settlements and bypass roads in operations it has termed 'landscape exposure', purportedly to prevent trees and orchards from being used as cover for Palestinian sniper attacks.

29 The two key military orders granting the Jewish local authorities the status of territorial enclaves of Israeli law were issued in 1979: the Order Regarding the Management of Regional Councils (No. 783), and the Order Regarding the Management of Local Authorities (No. 892). With a few exceptions, these orders replicate Israeli law regarding the local authorities in matters such as elections, composition of the councils, budgets, planning and building, education, and courts for local matters.

30 In fact two types of enclaves of Israeli civil law were created: personal and territorial. While the territorial imbued the thousands of isolated islands of 'state land' on the mountain summits with Israeli law, the personal enclaves effectively meant that any Israeli citizen in the Occupied Territories was subject, wherever they might be, to the authority of Israeli civilian law. This meant that a settler caught in crime within a Palestinian town would be subjected to Israeli law while a Palestinian at the same place would be subjected to military rule. The body of the settler has been legally understood to be an extraterritorial embodiment of the state. Its violation has thus become akin to a territorial violation. See Lein and Weizman, *Land Grab*.

31 Ibid.

32 Ibid. The headquarters of the Civil Administration was located near the settlement of Bet-El, the same settlement that had been legalized as 'strategic' by the HCJ in 1978.

33 Once a plan for a new settlement or for construction in an existing one has gained preliminary approval, notification appears in the local Arabic-language and Hebrew press, and time for objection is set. However, the ability of Palestinian residents to object effectively to the outline plans for a settlement is seriously impaired by their physical difficulty in reaching the planning offices to review the drawings, as they are located within settlements. Another difficulty is in participating in a hearing that takes place in Hebrew. Because of this, many outline plans get approved without any objections whatsoever.

34 The Mandatory outline plans were already a completely unreasonable basis for urban planning at the time of occupation, and they are even more so today. Moreover, British planning for Palestine at the time only recognized four land use categories: agriculture, development, nature reserve and coastal reserve, ignoring all other uses, some of them essential to a modern economy such as industrial zones, tourism areas, etc.. *Jerusalem District Outline Regional Planning Scheme RJ/5*, approved in 1942, and *Samaria Regional Planning Scheme S15*, deposited in 1945 but which never received final approval. For greater detail on this matter, see a planning opinion prepared by Bimkom, 'Villages in Area C Without Outline Plans' [Hebrew], Planning Opinion, June 2001 (unpublished). See Lein and Weizman, *Land Grab*.

35 Gadi Algazi, 'Offshore Zionism', *New Left Review*, 40, July–August 2006.

36 According to the audit, the Ministry of Housing grants about $5,000 to anyone buying a home beyond the Green Line and a loan of up to a further $15,000, half of which is converted into a grant after fifteen years. The Ministry of National Infrastructure grants a 50 per cent reduction in development costs or 69% discount on the leasehold fees. So far the state has spent $2.2 billion on housing, $500 million of which was during 1992, when Ariel Sharon was the Minister of Housing. In addition, the Ministry of Education provides a discount of 90% for tuition fees in nurseries and other benefits. The Ministry of Trade and Industry provides favourable conditions to industry with grants of up to 30 per cent for financing needs, as well as income tax benefits on income from the enterprise. The Ministry of Finance provids a 7% discount on the payment of income tax. In addition, more money is transferred to the local authorities. Despite the fact that the settlements are generally well-off suburban communities, much stronger economically than the average population in Israel, the per capita financial transfers of the government to local authorities in the West Bank is 2.25 times higher than within Israel. Moti Bassouk, 'The price of settlements', *Ha'aretz*, 26 September 2003; Shlomo Swirski, *The Price of Occupation*, Tel Aviv: Mapa, 2005 [Hebrew].

37 According to the plan, twenty-three new communal and rural communities were to be established, as well as twenty NAHAL military settlements. In addition, between 300 and 450 kilometres of new roads were to be constructed in the West Bank, for the exclusive use of its Jewish residents. Ministry of Agriculture and the Settlement Division of the World Zionist Organization, *Master*

Plan for Settlement for Judea and Samaria, Development Plan for the Region for 1983–1986, Jerusalem, 1983. During the period of the plan, the government achieved the objective in terms of the number of new settlements, but failed to meet the population forecast; the actual population by the end of 1986 was just 51,000.

[38] See also Matityahu Drobless, *Masterplan for the Development of Settlement in Judea and Samaria for the Years 1979–1983,* Jerusalem: The Settlement Division of the World Jewish Organization, 1978 [Hebrew].

[39] Matityahu Drobless*, Master Plan for Settlement for Judea and Samaria, Development Plan for the Region for 1983–1986,* Jerusalem: Ministry of Agriculture and the Settlement Division of the World Zionist Organization, 1983 [Hebrew].

[40] Lein and Weizman, *Land Grab.*

[41] Data according to Israel's population management office, January 2007.

[42] The Kibbutz and Moshav vary in terms of the level of equality and extent of cooperation in ownership of property in general, and of means of production in particular. However, these distinctions have become blurred since the 1990s, due to the economic crisis affecting the Kibbutz and Moshav movements and due to changes in the prevailing values of Israeli society. The common feature of this type of settlement, at least during the early phases, is their agricultural character, although since the 1980s many of these settlements have branched out into industry and tourism, while some of their members have begun to work as salaried employees in the adjacent urban centres. See Lein and Weizman, *Land Grab.*

[43] The Israeli Central Bureau of Statistics defines a settlement as 'urban' if its population is 2,000 or more, while rural settlements are those with fewer than 2,000 inhabitants. There are currently twelve settlements defined as rural and thirteen defined as urban.

[44] Oren Yiftachel, *Planning a Mixed Region in Israel: The Political Geography of Arab-Jewish Relations in the Galilee,* Aldershot: Gower Publishing, 1992, p. 376.

[45] The practice originated during the 1948 war, when David Ben-Gurion became concerned about international opinion over the cleansing and annexation of Palestinian land. Having promised that 'there would not be any expropriation of Arab land by the Jewish state' he wanted, through the transfer of lands to the WZO and from it to Jewish Israelis, to bypass his own promise.

[46] Because settlements were against US policy the Jewish Agency was no longer allowed to secure tax exemption for donations raised in the United States. Accordingly, in 1971 the Settlement Division was established within the World Zionist Organization; this body performed the function of the Jewish Agency's Settlement Department in all matters relating to the establishment of settlements in the Occupied Territories. See Lein and Weizman, *Land Grab.*

[47] In 2000 this practice was successfully challenged in the High Court of Justice by a Palestinian-Israeli family – the Ka'adans – who petitioned for their right to live within the 'community settlement' of Katzir, located on the Israeli side of the Green Line. On two separate occasions, the settlement admission committee barred the family of Adel Ka'adan from leasing land in the town because of its national origins. It took the High Court of Justice five years to rule against the settlement and the Jewish Agency and to order the settlement to reconsider the application of Ka'adan. Although they won their case and were awarded the opportunity to purchase land within the settlement (at its 1995 price – when the case was first petitioned) the general practice of exclusion is still largely in place and has not yet been dismantled. In 2003 the Ka'adans were offered a plot in the community, but the construction of the house on this plot is still delayed. See Neta Ziv and Ronen Shamir, 'Politics and Sub-Politics in the Struggle Against Land Discrimination', in Yehuda Shenhav (ed.), *Theory and Criticism, Space, Land, Home,* Tel Aviv: The Van Leer Jerusalem Institute and Hakibbutz Hameuchad, issue no. 16, Spring 2000, p. 281.

[48] The programme was initiated by the first Likud government to enable residents of state housing in development towns to improve their living standards, and was also applied in some settlements. The programme enabled Israeli citizens to lease state land privately, then design and build a private home on a small garden of 250–500 square metres. The project became a popular success. Across Israeli development towns, against the background of the large state-sponsored housing estates, rows of independently designed single-family homes made clear the aesthetic-ideological contrast between the Labor fantasy of collectivity, based on the melting away of previous diasporic identities into the pot of Sabra modernism, and the Likud fantasy of liberalism that often stimulated the 'return' of an ethnic diasporic identity. See description of aims and failure of the project in Dan Raz (Chief Architect, Ministry of Construction and Housing), 'Planning Guidelines for "Build Your Own Home" Neighborhoods', in Harlap, *Israel Builds,* p. 388.

49 Transcription of film research archive of 'The Politics of Verticality', episode 10, *The Panoptic Paradox*, Eyal Weizman and Nadav Harel, 2003.

50 Sylvain Bulle, 'Between War and Peace, Chronicle of a Modern Urban Condition', in Philipp Misselwitz and Tim Rieniets (eds.), *City of Collision*, Basel and London: Birkhauser, 2006, pp. 373–4.

51 Homi Bhabha, 'Of Mimicry and Man: The Ambivalence of Colonial Discourse', *October*, issue 28, spring 1984. See also Yehuda Shenhav, 'Introduction', in *Coloniality and the Postcolnial Condition: Implications for Israeli Society*, Jerusalem: Van Leer Institute and Hakibbutz Hameuchad, 2004, p. 19.

52 Michael Boneh, *Building and Development in the Mountain Regions*, Jerusalem: Ministry of Construction and Housing, 1984. This manuscript was reproduced four years later in Harlap, *Israel Builds*.

53 Small agricultural settlements were recommended for areas with gradients of 15 to 25 per cent, suburban settlements on steeper slopes of between 25 and 50 per cent, while for slopes of 50 per cent or more it recommended only regional towns. Boneh, *Building and Development*, p. 9.

54 Building typologies are divided according to slope gradients: three-storey building: 15–20 per cent: single-family houses: up to 25 per cent; apartment building in terraces: 20–45 per cent; high-rise with two flats per floor: 20–40 per cent; high-rise with four flats per floor: 25–35 per cent. See Boneh, *Building and Development*, p. 10.

55 Ibid., p. 14.

56 Compare with ideas of Jane Jacobs in Jane Jacobs, *The Death and Life of Great American Cities*, New York: Vintage Books, 1992 [1961], pp. 35–6.

57 Louis Althusser, 'Ideology and Ideological State Apparatuses', in Slavoj Zizek (ed.), *Mapping Ideology*, London and New York: Verso, 2000, pp. 105–37 and Louis Althusser, *For Marx*, London: Verso, 2006.

58 See the full quote in the Chapter 3, pp. 99–100.

59 HCJ 258/79, *Abu Hilo et al. v. Government of Israel et al.* [Bet-El].

60 The ability of settlements to generate surveillance is only one element in a more subtle and diffuse system that operates through a series of electronic techniques of demarcation, population control, identity cards, inspections, currency control and so on. See Elia Zureik, 'Constructing Palestine through Surveillance Practices', *British Journal of Middle Eastern Studies*, 2001, pp. 205–7.

61 Avi Mograbi, *How I Learned to Overcome My Fear and Love Arik Sharon*, a documentary film, 1997.

62 Both quotes are from Shlomi Hazoni, the security officer of QAdumim, in an interview with Mira Asseo on 21 November 2002. Mira Asseo has been employed as a research assistant by the author.

63 Amos Harel, 'Soldiers can shoot Gazans spying on Netzarim', *Ha'aretz*, 5 November 2003. An Israeli soldier, Shahar Ginossar, describes such a procedure: 'The open-fire regulations were clear enough: every Palestinian on a roof is supposedly a "lookout," and the snipers shoot him right away . . . At one point we saw somebody standing on a roof. Just standing, without binoculars . . . I got authorization to shoot . . .' See Shahar Ginossar, 'Shooting and Hitting', http://www.shovrimshtika.org/newspapers_e.asp?number=311.

64 Gideon Levy, 'The Lowest Points in Israel', in Rafi Segal and Eyal Weizman (eds.), *A Civilian Occupation, The Politics of Israeli Architecture*, London and Tel Aviv: Verso and Babel, 2004, p. 170.

65 Tamir-Tawil, *To Start*, p. 160.

66 The brochure is titled *Emanuel, A Faithful City in Israel*, Brooklyn, NY: The Emanuel Office, 1988.

67 Thomas Leitersdorf, 'Emmanuel, a New Town in Samaria', in Harlap, *Israel Builds*, p. 144.

68 Daniel Ben Simon, 'It is strange to die after the second meeting', *Ha'aretz*, 29 March 2002 [Hebrew].

69 Shiloh's construction as an archaeological workers' camp was described in Chapter 3.

70 www.shilo.co.il.

71 Esther Zandberg, 'As close as you can get', *Ha'aretz*, 3 April 2003.

Chapter 5 Checkpoints: The Split Sovereign and the One-Way Mirror

1 Gaza-Jericho Agreement, Annex I: Protocol Concerning Withdrawal of Israeli Military Forces and Security Arrangements, Article X: Passages, http://telaviv.usembassy.gov/publish/peace/gjannex1.htm. During a period which the agreement defined as 'interim', Israel was to be respon-

sible for land passages between the Palestinian Territories and Egypt and Jordan, as well as (with some adjustments) to the terminal at the Gaza seaport (which was never built) and in all Palestinian airports (the only Palestinian airport – the Dahanieh airport in Gaza – was bombed and destroyed during the early days of the Intifada in 2000).

2 Gaza-Jericho Agreement, Annex I, Article X, clause 2.b.1.

3 Israeli security would be 'separated [from passengers] by tinted glass'; Gaza-Jericho Agreement, Annex I, Article X, clause 3.d.2.

4 Gaza-Jericho Agreement, Annex I, Article X, clause 3.d.1.

5 Gaza-Jericho Agreement, Annex I, Article X, clauses 3.e, 9.c.

6 Mourid Barghouti, *I Saw Ramallah*, Ahdaf Soueif (trans.), London: Bloomsbury, 2005, pp. 12, 20.

7 Gideon Levy, 'Twilight zone: more than meets the eye', *Ha'aretz*, 3 September 1999. See also a discussion of the terminal in an excellent article about Israeli surveillance technologies in Israel and the Occupied Territories: Elia Zureik, 'Constructing Palestine through Surveillance Practices', *British Journal of Middle Eastern Studies* 28, 2001, pp 205–27.

8 The eight separate Oslo Accords are: (1) Declaration of Principles On Interim Self-Government Arrangements (13 September 1993); (2) The Paris Protocol on Economic Relations (29 April 1994); (3) Agreement on the Gaza Strip and the Jericho Area (4 May 1994); (4) Agreement on Preparatory Transfer of Powers and Responsibilities Between Israel and the PLO (29 September 1994); (5) The Israeli–Palestinian Interim Agreement on the West Bank and the Gaza Strip (also known as Oslo II) (28 September 1995); (6) Hebron Protocol (17 January 1997); (7) The Wye River Memorandum (23 October 1998); (8) The Sharm el-Sheikh Memorandum (4 September 1999).

9 The Fourth Geneva Convention (12 August 1949), Part III/Section III: Occupied Territories, http://www.yale.edu/lawweb/avalon/lawofwar/geneva07.htm.

10 Michel Foucault, *Discipline and Punish: The Birth of the Prison*, Alan Sheridan (trans.), New York: Vintage, 1977.

11 In this way these articles of the Oslo Accord were presented to the Palestinians and to foreign governments. Domestically they were obviously presented as harsh security measures.

12 Tal Arbel, 'Mobility Regimes and the King's Head: A History of Techniques for the Control of Movement in the Occupied West Bank' (presented at 'Comparative Occupations: Chechnya, Iraq, Palestine, Governing Zones of Emergency' Workshop, Middle East Institute, Harvard University, 25–26 February 2006).

13 Gorenberg, *Accidental Empire*, p. 131.

14 Shlomo Gazit, *The Carrot and the Stick: Israel's Policy in Judaea and Samaria, 1967–68*, New York: B'nai Brith, 1995, p. 204.

15 'Within the first year of the first Intifada, for example, no less than 1,600 curfews were imposed, so that by late 1988 over 60 per cent of the population had been confined to their homes for extended periods of time.' Neve Gordon, *Israel's Occupation: Sovereignty, Discipline and Control*, Berkeley, CA: California University Press, forthcoming (chapter 6).

16 Leila Farsakh, 'The Economics of Israeli Occupation: What Is Colonial about It?' (presented at 'Comparative Occupations: Chechnya, Iraq, Palestine, Governing Zones of Emergency' Workshop, Middle East Institute, Harvard University, 25–26 February 2006).

17 The Accord left to Israel the right to determine what the diameter of water pipes in the water networks connecting the archipelago of Palestinian enclaves would be when these pipes ran through Israeli-administered zones. In this way Israel could effectively control the rate of flow and the quantity of water transported between locations. See Amira Hass, 'Colonialism under the Guise of a Peace Process', *Theory and Criticism*, 24, spring 2004, p. 192.

18 In the context of the Oslo Accords, the Israeli government guaranteed the Palestinians and United States that no new settlements would be established and existing settlements would not be expanded, except for the 'natural growth' of existing settlements. Under the banner of 'natural growth', Israel has established new settlements under the guise of 'new neighbourhoods' of existing settlements. Between September 1993, on the signing of the Declaration of Principles, and September 2000, the time of the outbreak of the second Intifada, the population of the West Bank settlements (excluding East Jerusalem) grew from 100,500 to 191,600, representing a growth rate of some 90 per cent. In East Jerusalem at the same time, the population grew from 146,800 in 1993 to 176,900 in 2001, an increase of just 20 per cent. See Lein and Weizman, *Land Grab*.

19 This is the definition according to the International Organization for Standardization (ISO) – the international standard-setting body composed of representatives from national standard bodies (www.tqm.org).

[20] Yehouda Shenhav, *Manufacturing Rationality*, Oxford: Oxford University Press, 1999. See also Uri Ben-Eliezer, 'Post-Modern Armies and the Question of Peace and War: The Israeli Defense Forces in the "New Times"', *International Journal of Middle East Studies*, 36, 2004, pp. 49–70.

[21] An amendment to a 2005 Pentagon spending bill sponsored by Senator John McCain bars 'cruel, inhuman and degrading treatment' of prisoners in US custody, but still allows such treatment when the prisoners are not in US custody. This bill was rendered immediately unenforceable by a specially tailored counter amendment, the Graham-Levin Amendment that seeks to limit judicial review.

[22] A major US project to create a 'virtual border' seeks to extend American surveillance networks and compile and share vast amounts of biometric and other data so that 'terrorists' can be identified and intercepted while still nominally 'abroad'. See Eric Lichtblau and John Markoff, 'Accenture Is Awarded U.S. Contract for Borders', *New York Times*, 2 June 2004.

[23] Ariella Azoulay and Adi Ophir, 'The Monster's Tail', in Michael Sorkin (ed.) *Against the Wall*, New York: The New Press, 2005, pp. 3–4.

[24] Gilles Deleuze, 'Postscript on the Societies of Control', *October,* 59, Winter 1992. 3–7.

[25] OCHA, West Bank, 'Closure Count and Analysis,' September 2006. In the year between the evacuation of Gaza in August 2005 and September 2006 these restrictions increased 39 per cent. See www.ochaonline.un.org. According to a position paper by B'Tselem, *Freedom of Movement – Siege,* there are 457 mounds of earth, 95 concrete blocks and 56 ditches. See the full report at www.btselem.org.

[26] According to the conservative estimates of the World Bank, per capita gross domestic product (GDP) in the West Bank and Gaza dipped by about 30 per cent between 1999 and 2005. In 2005, unemployment in the Palestinian Authority was 40 per cent in Gaza and 29 per cent in the West Bank, with 56 per cent of the residents of Gaza currently below the poverty line (75 per cent are estimated to be below this line in 2007), more than double the rate before the second Intifada (22 per cent). some 70 per cent of the population of Gaza are now unable to meet their families' daily food needs without assistance. According to the World Bank, the main reason is restrictions on the movement of people and goods. See World Bank, 'West Bank and Gaza Economic Update and Potential Outlook', http://www.worldbank.org/we. A recent report by the United Nations Relief and Work Agency (UNRWA) warns of a lack of basic food supplies due to frequent closures of the border crossings that prevent goods from reaching Gaza from Egypt. See http://www.un.org/unrwa/news/index.html.

[27] Amira Hass, 'Israeli restrictions create isolated enclaves in West Bank', *Ha'aretz,* 24 March 2006.

[28] Alice Rothchild, 'Pitching in for health on the West Bank', *Boston Globe*, 6 March 2004. Quoted in Gordon, *Israel's Occupation* (chapter 6).

[29] Zygmunt Bauman, *Society Under Siege*, London: Polity, 2002.

[30] Raviv Drucker and Ofer Shelah, *Boomerang, The Israeli Leadership Failures during the Second Intifadah*, Jerusalem: Keter Books, 2005, p. 330.

[31] www.machsomwatch.org.

[32] Azmi Bishara, *Checkpoints: Fragments of a Story*, Tel Aviv: Babel Press, 2006 [Hebrew], p. 10.

[33] Ibid., p. 17.

[34] Eyal Weizman, 'The Subversion of Jerusalem's Sacred Vernaculars', in Michael Sorkin, *The New Jerusalem*, New York: Monacelli, 2003, pp. 120–45.

[35] Bishara, *Checkpoints*, p. 231.

[36] Amos Harel and Avi Isacharoff, *The Seventh War*, Tel Aviv: Miskal – Yedioth Aharonoth Books and Chemed Books, 2004, p. 343.

[37] Baruch Spiegel, 'Issues of the Wall, presentation at the Van Leer Institute, Jerusalem', 17 February 2006. The plan was published in English as it was meant to placate, amongst other things, the American administration, and be officially adopted by the government.

[38] Ministry of Defence Press Release: 'Defence Minister Mofaz appoints Brig.-Gen. (Res.) Baruch Spiegel to head team dealing with civilian and humanitarian issues vis-a-vis security fence', 27 January 2004, http://www.israel-mfa.gov.il/MFA/Government/Communiques/2004; Druker and Shelah, *Boomerang*, p. 331.

[39] Glenn Kessler, 'US aid to Palestinians goes to checkpoints, Zionist organization', *Washington Post*, 5 May 2005.

[40] http://www.securityfence.mod.gov.il/Pages/ENG/Humanitarian.htm.

[41] Ministry of Defence Press Release: statement, 15 January 2006, http://www.mod.gov.il/WordFiles/n32301062.doc.

[42] Baruch Spiegel, 'Balancing Rights – The Security Fence and the Palestinian Civilian Population',

presentation transcript, 18 March 2006, the Jerusalem Centre for Public Affairs, http://www.ngo monitor.org/issues/Balancing%20RightsTheSecurityFenceandthePalestinianCivilianPopulationText.htm.

43 OCHA, 'Closure Count', footnote 27.

44 Arbel, *The Kings Head*. See also Machsom Watch, *A Counterview, Checkpoints 2004*, www.machsom watch.org.

45 Machsom Watch, *Checkpoints 2004*.

46 Amira Hass, 'The humanitarian lie,' 28 December 2005, www.counterpunch.org.

47 Aluf Benn, Arnon Regular and Akiva Eldar, 'Rice: Israel and PA Clinch Deal on Gaza-Egypt Border Crossing', *Ha'aretz*, 15 November 2005; Jamie Chosak, 'Opening Gaza to the Wider World: The Israeli–Palestinian Agreement on Movement and Access', Washington: The Washington Institute, 30 November 2005, http://www.washingtoninstitute.org/templateC05.php?CID=2412.

48 The principles for Rafah Crossing are outlined in the 'Agreement on Movement and Access', http://www.usembassy.it/viewer/article.asp?article=/file2005_11/alia/a5111510.htm.

49 Israel controls the observers' access to the crossing: the European (currently Italian) observers live in Israel. In order to get to work, they have to pass through a military crossing, which Israel often closes on the grounds that it has received information of planned terrorist attacks. Without the observers the Rafah border crossing is closed. Source B'tselem to Defence Minister: 'Stop using Rafah Crossing to pressure Gaza civilians', www. btselem.org, 30 August 2006.

50 Through the permit system Israel continues to control the population registry in the West Bank and Gaza. Almost every change in the registry made by the Palestinian Authority requires the prior approval of Israel. By controlling the population registry, Israel can determine who is a 'Palestinian resident' and who is a 'foreigner'. Only 'residents' are allowed to enter via the Rafah and the Allenby crossings.

51 See the way this policy has been dealt with in Jerusalem in Chapter 1, p. 47–52.

52 The Law of Citizenship and Entrance into Israel, 2003/544 – this law forbids the spouses of Israeli citizens from Gaza or the West Bank to gain the status of Israeli residency.

53 For an in-depth analysis, see Eyal Benvenisti, *The International Law of Occupation*, Princeton: NJ Princeton University Press, 1993, pp. 7–25 and pp. 107–48. Although the position of Israeli governments since 1967 has been to reject the applicability of the Geneva Convention to the West Bank and Gaza (claiming that no internationally recognized sovereignty existed there prior to the occupation), it has however taken upon itself to abide by what it called the 'humanitarian' clauses of the convention.

54 James Ron, *Frontiers and Ghettos: State Violence in Serbia and Israel*, Berkeley, CA: University of California Press, 2003, p. 262. See the review of this book in Neve Gordon, 'Theorizing Israel's Occupation', *HAGAR, Studies in Culture, Polity and Identities*, 6 (2) 2006, pp. 115–35.

55 'Sharon Defends pro-peace Stance', *New York Times*, 28 May 2003.

56 Leila Farsakh, 'The Economics of Israeli Occupation'. After Oslo, Israel started replacing its low-wage Palestinian labor force with guest workers mainly from Africa and southeast Europe.

57 Real GDP in the West Bank and Gaza Strip grew by 2.3 per cent per annum between 1994 and 1999, implying a decline in per capita income, in view of the population growth rate of 4 per cent. GDP per capita in the West Bank and Gaza Strip fell by 18 per cent between 1995 and 1996, which were years of frequent border closures. It fell a further 35 per cent between 2000 and 2005. During the thirty-two months when the Labor Party was in government (September 1993–June 1996), Israel's real GDP per capita grew at an annual average rate of about 3.4 per cent, compared to only about 1.3 per cent annually previously. Between 1995 and 2000, Israel's GDP rose from 270 billion shekels to 470 billion (in 2004 prices). From an annual level of $14.8 billion in 1993, exports increased to about $20 billion in 1996, about 11 per cent growth rate per year since Oslo, which is higher than the 7 per cent rate of growth in exports during the comparable pre-Oslo years. Leila Farsakh, 'The Economics of Israeli Occupation'. Also Sara Roy, 'Decline and Disfigurement: The Palestinian Economy after Oslo', in Carey, *The New Intifada*, London and NY: Verso, 2001, pp. 91–110.

58 OCHA, 'Closure Count'.

59 The World Bank, the IMF and the Ad Hoc Liaison Committee (AHLC) have acquired oversight of the Palestinian Finance Ministry, helping it to manage economic policy. The World Bank has effectively become the manager of the donors' funds.

60 A demonstration of Israel's control over humanitarian action was provided in April 2006 when local Palestinian employees of UNRWA dealing with food and health aid refrained from coordinating with Hamas officials because they feared being blacklisted by Israel and the United States. This lack of cooperation has been mentioned as one of the likely reasons for the rapid spread of

avian flu in Gaza in the spring of 2006. Akiva Eldar, 'Coming Soon: Kosovo in Gaza? Aid Organizations in Gaza Paralyzed Fearing Ties with Hamas-led Government', *Ha'aretz*, 4 April 2006.

61 This situation is at the heart of what Rony Brauman, David Rieff and others called the 'humanitarian paradox', the dilemma faced by humanitarian organizations and NGOs operating in war zones. It implies that while operating on a purely humanitarian level (the humanitarian hopes to gain better access to places of crisis by presenting the humanitarian space as an apolitical, neutral one), they will not be able to avoid political instrumentalization and thus may play into the hands of power itself. Furthermore, by attempting to pull out from situations where they may be instrumentalized and by acting as 'witnesses' (Brauman's position), humanitarians are in danger of themselves politicizing relief work (Rieff). See Rony Brauman, 'From Philanthropy to Humanitarianism', *South Atlantic Quarterly*, 2/3, Spring 2004, pp. 397–417; and David Rieff, *A Bed for the Night: Humanitarianism in Crisis* (New York: Simon and Schuster, 2002). David Shearer, head of OCHA, claims that the situation in Gaza is becoming similar and will demand similar measures to those undertaken following the Kosovo crisis in 1999; that is, an international UN mandate on the area. OCHA, *Gaza Strip Situation Report,* 29 March 2006, http://www.humanitarianinfo.org/opt/docs/UN/OCHA/ochaSR_Gaza290306.pdf.

62 Ariella Azoulay, 'Hunger in Palestine: The Event That Never Was', in Anselm Franke, Rafi Segal and Eyal Weizman (eds), *Territories, Islands, Camps and Other States of Utopia*, Cologne: Walter Koening, 2003, pp. 154–7. According to chief of military intelligence Amos Gilead, 'hunger is when people walk around with a swollen belly, collapse and die. There is no hunger in Palestinian territories.' Druker and Shelah, *Boomerang*, p. 329. Azoulay, *Hunger*, pp. 154–7. Since Hamas was elected to power in January 2006, Israel has used the weapon of economic strangulation as a means of political pressure by withholding all Palestinian tax monies – about $60 million a month – which it is legally obligated to transfer to the Palestinian Authority. Israel has also mobilized the international community to suspend aid until Hamas recognizes 'Israel's right to exist' and enters into a political process. However, the international boycott of Gaza residents to pressure the Hamas government has been counter-productive, with both Israel and donor countries desperately seeking for a way out. The poverty created in Gaza is more threatening.

63 Elia Zureik, 'Surveillance Practices', p. 227.

64 Barghouti, *I Saw Ramallah*, p. 10.

Chapter 6 The Wall: Barrier Archipelagos and the Impossible Politics of Separation

1 Nadav Sharagai, 'Same Sharon, same Temple Mount, same potential for explosion,' *Ha'aretz*, 28 May 2003.

2 All quotes in this paragraph are from Dana Gilerman, 'Trying to make the Wall transparent,' *Ha'aretz*, 1 April 2004, and Esther Zandberg, 'The Israeli Architectural Association does not want to face reality,' *Ha'aretz*, 18 November 2003.

3 The barrier is composed of a sequence of fortifications measuring between 35 and 100 metres in width. The main component of the barrier is a touch-sensitive, 'smart', three-metre-high electronic fence, placed on a 150-centimetre-deep concrete foundation (to prevent digging under it) and topped with barbed wire (to prevent climbing over it). It also has day/night-vision video cameras and small radars. About 60 kilometres of solid wall have been built or planned through or around Palestinian cities.

4 In June 2002 a survey of the Israeli public by *Ma'ariv* and 'Market Watch' identified 60 per cent support for the Wall with 25 per cent against. At the end of 2004, according to the 'Peace Index' survey, 83 per cent of the Israeli public supported the Wall.

5 Raviv Drucker and Ofer Shelah, *Boomerang, The Israeli Leadership Failures during the Second Intifadah*, Jerusalem: Keter Books, 2005, pp. 255–66.

6 For the H plan see p. 80–2.

7 In order to decide what kind of sovereignty could possibly be granted to the Palestinians on the isolated territorial shards allocated to them, the IDF (not the government) has set up a special team within the International Law unit of the Military Advocate General's Office to examine existing models of limited or 'soft' sovereign forms. Case studies researched include examples from present-day Puerto Rico to Germany under the occupation forces in the decade after World War II.

8 The Ariel loop is a particularly intrusive fold that stretches deep into the heart of the West Bank

in order to incorporate the settlement-city of Ariel (population 17,000). This loop was announced in July 2003 and faced immediate international diplomatic outrage. The region of Ariel has the densest settler population. In this area rather wealthy suburban settlements are crowded in close proximity to impoverished Palestinian villages and towns. With an Israeli per-capita GDP twenty times larger than that of Palestinian GDP, the economic disparity between the neighbouring communities (concretized by the proposed path of the Wall) is one of the highest between any two other neighbouring populations worldwide.

9 Danny Tirza, 'The Strategic Logic of Israel's Security Barrier', *The Jerusalem Institute for Contemporary Affairs*, 5, (18), 8 March 2006, http://www.jcpa.org/brief/brief005–18.htm.

10 This practice was explicitly forbidden by the Israeli High Court of Justice only in January 2006, after a petition exposed it. See HCJ 143/06.

11 Yehezkel Lein, *Behind the Barrier, Human Rights Violations as a Result of Israel's Separation Barrier*, Jerusalem: B'Tselem, April 2003, www.btselem.org.

12 'Under the Guise of Security: Routing the Separation Barrier to Enable Israeli Settlement Expansion in the West Bank', joint report by Bimkom, Planners for Planning Rights, and B'Tselem, December 2005. See http://www.btselem.org/english/Publications/summaries/200512_Under_the_Guise_of_Security.asp.

13 The main entrepreneurs involved in the expansion of several settlements along the path of the Wall, amongst them Tzufin and Modi'in Illit, is Lev Leviev, originally a diamond tycoon and one of Israel's most powerful and connected businessmen. (He has also functioned as a go-between between Ariel Sharon and the presidents of Kazakhstan and Uzbekistan.) One of the developments built on the land robbed from the poor Palestinian farmers of Bil'in is a massive $230 million project, with 5,800 apartments planned. See Gadi Algazi, 'Offshore Zionism', *New Left Review*, 40, July–August 2006, pp. 31–3.

14 Arik Meirovski, 'The Separation Fence reduced the price of flats in the Occupied Territories by 10 to 15 per cent', *Ha'aretz* 28 March 2006.

15 Algazi, 'Offshore Zionism', p. 30.

16 Minutes of the hearing of the Tel Aviv Magistrate's Court, held on 20 November 2002. Quoted in Yehezkel Lein, *Behind the Barrier, Human Rights Violations As a Result of Israel's Separation Barrier*, Jerusalem: B'Tselem, April 2003 http://www.btselem.org.

17 The Palestinian Authority claims that the current path of the barrier annexes to Israel 466 archaeological sites of major importance, mainly around East Jerusalem. According to Palestinian researchers Mohammad Jaradat and Jamal Barghouth, the total number is 1,084 sites. See Mohammad Jaradat and Jamal Barghouth, *Review of Culture and Heritage; Multi-sector Review of East Jerusalem*, at www.multi-sector.org/review/culture/; Mazal Mualem, 'Route Restraints cause Movement of Fence based on Past Communities', *Ha'aretz*, 17 October 2003.

18 Tirza: 'Due to weather conditions, there are seventy days a year when aircraft flying in and out of Israel must fly above the West Bank. We wanted to build a double fence in the area near the airport in order to secure it from missiles, but there are 19,000 Palestinians living in this area [and] Secretary of State Condoleezza Rice said Israel could not leave people to live in enclaves.' See Tirza, 'The Strategic Logic'.

19 http://isala.judysenglish.co.il/paper.htm (no longer available online).

20 More than 200 people were injured in the violent dispersal of the joint Israeli–Palestinian demonstrations in Bil'in, and many were arrested. Algazi, 'Offshore Zionism', pp. 30–1.

21 There is a multi-perspective problem regarding the semantics of the project: Israelis prefer to use the term 'fence', as in 'separation fence' or 'antiterrorist fence', hoping to minimize the barrier's apparent scale and make it appear benign and almost domestic – along the lines of 'good fences make good neighbours'. The Israeli and Palestinian opposition prefer the term 'Wall', emphasizing the urban areas where the barrier is a wall. Their campaign hopes to equate it in the Western imagination with the Berlin Wall, a barrier that was similarly composed throughout most of its route as a fencing system. When talking to former Palestinian President Mahmoud Abbas, President George W. Bush called the barrier 'a wall', but when talking with Sharon, 'a fence'. The International Court of Justice accepted the term 'Wall' as a general term regardless of materiality of the section in question.

22 Lindsay Bremner, 'Border/Skin', in Michael Sorkin (ed.), *Against the Wall; Israel's Barrier to Peace*, New York: The New Press, 2005, pp. 122–37.

23 HCJ 2056/04, *Beit Sourik Village Council vs. The Government of Israel, Commander of the IDF Forces in the West Bank*, 30 June 2004.

[24] The first time that the government decided to make changes to already constructed sections of the route, and publicly announced its intention to do so, was in February 2004, in advance of the wall debate in the International Court of Justice in the Hague. The Ministry of Defence began to change the Wall's route in the northern area where it completely enveloped the area of Baqa al-Sharqiya.

[25] Data updated routinely on the site of B'Tselem. www.btselem.org.

[26] www.securitybarrier.mfa.gov.il. This echoes the way the German Democratic Republic (East Germany) referred to the Berlin Wall – 'The Anti Fascist Security Rampart'. See Ines Weizman, 'Talking Walls', in Kyong Park (ed.), *Urban Ecologies,* Hong Kong: Map Publishers, 2005, pp. 97–9.

[27] On this issue of temporariness see Chapter 3, especially pp. 103–5.

[28] Adi Ophir, 'A Time of Occupation', in Roane Carey and Jonathan Shainin (eds), *The Other Israel*, New York: The New Press, 2003, p. 60. See also Ariella Azoulay and Adi Ophir, *Bad Days*, Tel Aviv: Resling, 2002 [Hebrew].

[29] The practice of security operates, as AbdouMaliq Simon has remarked, in similar terms to the logic of stock-derivatives. The price of derivatives is driven by market volatility. High volatility implies potential for high profits. Similarly, security agencies speculate on future risks based on information regarding present positions. It is therefore not surprising to see that security forces tend to produce volatility. AbdouMaliq Simon, 'Assembling Douala', in Alev Cinar and Thomas Bender (eds), *Urban Imaginaries: Locating the Modern City*, Minneapolis: University of Minnesota Press, 2007.

[30] Shlomo Swirski, *The Price of Occupation,* Tel Aviv: Mapa Publishers, 2005, p. 93 [Hebrew].

[31] Aeyal M. Gross, 'The Construction of a Wall between The Hague and Jerusalem: The Enforcement and Limits of Humanitarian Law and the Structure of Occupation', forthcoming in *Leiden Journal of International Law*.

[32] Alan Dershowitz, 'Israel follows its own law, not bigoted Hague decision', *Jerusalem Post*, 11 July 2004. The ICJ rejected out of hand the Israeli government's claim for 'tactical necessity' in routing the barrier around settlements. In their ruling, the international judges noted that: 'The infringement of Palestinian human rights cannot be justified by military exigencies or by the requirements of national security or public order', because the Palestinian lands over which Israel constructed the barrier were expropriated in order to secure settlements which were themselves illegal according to international law. The judges have called on the Israeli government to stop the construction, tear down the sections of the barrier already built, and compensate the Palestinians directly affected. With a majority of 13 to 2, they furthermore advised the UN Security Council to consider its options for 'further action' – diplomatic code for a variety of possible sanctions – to enforce this. See ICJ website on: http://www.icj-cij.org/icjwww/idocket /imwp/imwpframe.htm. Following the ruling, the United Nations General Assembly adopted a resolution condemning the Wall. One hundred and fifty nations voted in favour of the draft, ten abstained, and six – including the United States, Micronesia, the Marshall Islands and Australia – opposed it.

[33] David Kennedy, *The Dark Side of Virtue: Reassessing International Humanitarianism*, Princeton, NJ; Princeton University Press, 2004, pp. 235–323 (see, in particular, the chapter 'Humanitarianism and Force', especially p. 295). See also the discussion of this issue and of Kennedy's ideas in an article by his former student Aeyal M. Gross, 'The Construction of a Wall'.

[34] Akiva Eldar, 'Because of Route Change: Israel lost 700 million shekels', *Ha'aretz*, 21 December 2006.

[35] Tirza, 'The Strategic Logic'. Under the category of 'Humanitarian Concerns' the Ministry of Defence website reads: 'Israel's government realizes that the construction of the Security Fence can introduce hardship into the lives of innocent Palestinians and regrets those hardships. All attempts to minimize such problems have been and will continue to be made. The matrix of civilian bonds and ties – economic, educational, medical etc, between Palestinian villages and cities has been thoroughly examined as well as the way they were affected by the construction of the Security Fence.' http://www.securityfence.mod.gov.il/Pages/ENG/Humanitarian.htm.

[36] Nadav Shragai, 'Settlers plan mass court petitions over revised fence route', *Ha'aretz*, 26 August 2004.

[37] Aluf Benn, 'New fence route to be presented to U.S. first, then cabinet', *Ha'aretz*, 7 September 2004.

[38] In January 2004 I was asked by Yehezkel Lein from B'Tselem to provide an 'expert opinion' on a case study related to this issue. Contrary to claims by the Ministry of Defence, the military

logic of drawing the route of the barrier according to topography tends to be compromised when the state aims to include areas earmarked for the future expansion of settlements. In the case of the settlement of Tzufin, north of Qalqilya, the route was drawn 2 kilometres east of the settlement's built-up area, with the purpose of encompassing some tracts of land in the settlement's jurisdiction area. As a result, Palestinian residents of Jayyous were separated from their vineyards. In other words, the path of the barrier has compromised military logic by supporting the interests of the settlement council and those of real estate developers who want to invest in developing this land.

[39] After pressure from settlement councils, the IDF has so far approved seventeen 'special security zones' (referred to by the IDF spokesperson as 'depth-' or 'mini-barriers') and has already constructed three of them in the northern part of the West Bank. See Nadav Shragai and Nathan Guttman, 'IDF proposes 400–metre security zone around Settlements', *Ha'aretz*, 3 October 2003.

[40] Palestinians have only restricted access to more than 700 kilometres of West Bank roadways on forty-one 'sterile' roads reserved for the use of Jews only. Yehezkel Lein, *Forbidden Roads: The Discriminatory West Bank Road Regime*, Jerusalem: B'Tselem, August 2004. www.btselem.org.

[41] Prime Minister Olmert's unilateral 'realignment plan', if ever implemented, does not aim to alter the principles of the West Bank's geography of archipelagos. The plan calls for the evacuation of only about twenty isolated settlements and for the consolidation of others into larger settlement blocks.

[42] This was President Bush's 'reward' for Sharon's announcement of his plan to unilaterally evacuate the settlements and military bases of Gaza, unwittingly tying the evacuation of Gaza with annexation plans in the West Bank: 'it is unrealistic to expect that the outcome of final status negotiations will be full and complete return to the armistice lines of 1949, and all previous efforts to negotiate a two-state solution have reached the same conclusion.' See US International Information Programs at usinfo.state.gov/mena/archive/2004/apr/14–125421.html.

[43] The Ministry of Defence provides some details on its website: more than 10 million square metres of earth were relocated and 3,000 kilometres of barbed wire laid out. The barrier has an estimated per-kilometre construction cost of \$2 million and is the largest national infrastructure project (in terms of both size and price) ever undertaken in Israel. See http://www.securityfence.mod.gov.il/Pages/ENG/execution.htm.

[44] Aluf Benn, 'PM says would allow contiguous Palestinian territory in W. Bank', *Ha'aretz*, 5 December 2002.

[45] Meron Benvenisti, 'An Engineering Wonder', *Ha'aretz*, 5 June 1996. This editorial later appeared in French in *Pre/occupations d'espace/ Jerusalem au Pluriel*, Marseille: Image En Manoeuvres Editions, 2001, pp. 171–3.

[46] At the end of 2006, the southern continuation of the 'Tunnel Road' was extended into two parallel levels, the original ground-level road leads to the refugee camp of El-Arub while the upper-level road, supported over the lower one on columns, is an exclusively Jewish road leading to the Etzion settlement block.

[47] OCHA, 'Closure Count and Analysis', January 2006. See www.ochaonline.un.org.

[48] The unnamed Israeli official quoted in the following article is Danny Tirza: Amira Hass, 'Israel asks PA donors to fund new, upgraded West Bank roads,' *Ha'aretz*, 5 September 2004.

[49] Ibid.

[50] Similarly, the new railway connection between Tel Aviv and Jerusalem will run through tunnels when it passes through the West Bank.

[51] Eyal Shahar, 'Bi-national road', *Ma'ariv*, 19 March 2005.

[52] One of the earliest examples of such partition of sovereignty was proposed just prior to the outbreak of World War II. In March 1939 the Nazi Foreign Minister Joachim von Ribbentrop demanded that the Polish government return Danzig to the Reich and proposed the creation of an extraterritorial highway to connect Germany with its enclave city. The German highway would, however, divide Polish territory. A solution to this problem was to be achieved by building several bridges that would span the highway and on which there would be Polish sovereignty. On 26 March 1939, the Polish government rejected any such course of action. See Deborah Dwork and Robert Jan van Pelt, *Auschwitz*, New York: Norton, 2002, p. 109.

[53] Eyal Weizman, 'The Politics of Verticality', at http://www.opendemocracy.net/debates/article.jsp?id=2&debateId=45&articleId=801 first published on 24 March 2002.

Chapter 7 Urban Warfare: Walking Through Walls

[1] Walter Benjamin, *One-Way Street and Other Writings*, trans. Edmund Jephcott and Kingsley Shorter, London and New York: Verso, 1979, p. 295.

[2] Georges Perec, *Species of Space and Other Pieces*, ed. and trans. John Sturrock, London: Penguin Books, 1999.

[3] Nuha Khoury, 'One Fine Curfew Day', Jerusalem: Miftah (www.miftah.org).

[4] I have witnessed some of these conferences. In January 2003 Stephen Graham passed on to me half of his ticket worth £1,000, to attend the second day of the Annual 'Urban Warfare Conference' organized by a security institute called SMI in London. This was a surreal event where military personnel, arms dealers and academics from NATO, the UK, the United States and Israel as well as representatives of the RAND corporation, exchanged practical and theoretical views on urban military operations and essential equipment within the conference hall and over dinner. On another such military conference organized in 2002 by the Faculty of Geography at Haifa University, see Stephen Graham, 'Remember Falluja: Demonizing Place, Constructing Atrocity', *Society and Space*, 2005, 23, pp. 1–10, and Stephen Graham, 'Cities and the "War on Terror"', *International Journal of Urban and Regional Research*, 30,2 June 2006, pp. 255–76.

[5] Simon Marvin, 'Military Urban Research Programs: Normalising the Remote Control of Cities', paper delivered to the conference, *Cities as Strategic Sites: Militarisation Anti-Globalization & Warfare*, Centre for Sustainable Urban and Regional Futures, Manchester, November 2002.

[6] One of the reading lists of the Operational Theory Research Institute, included the following titles: Christopher Alexander, *The Endless Way of Building: Patterns of Events, Patterns of Space, Patterns of Language*; Gregory Bateson, *Steps to An Ecology of Mind* and *Mind and Nature: A Necessary Unity*; Beatriz Colomina (guest editor), *Architecture Production*; Gilles Deleuze and Felix Guattari, *A Thousand Plateaus* and *What is Philosophy*; Clifford Geertz, *After the Fact – Two Countries, Four Decades, One Anthropologist*; Catherine Ingraham, *Architecture and the Burdens of Linearity*; Rob Krier, *Architectural Composition*; J.F. Lyotard, *The Post-Modern Condition: A Report on Knowledge*; Marshall McLuhan and Quentin Fiore, *The Medium is the Massage: An Inventory of Effects*; W.J. Mitchell, *The Logic of Architecture*; Lewis Mumford, *The Myth of the Machine*; Gordon Pask, *Cybernetics of Human Learning*; Ilya Prigogine, *Is Future Given? The End of Certainty* and *Exploring Complexity*; John Rajchman, *The Deleuze Connections*; Bernard Tschumi, *Questions on Space*, *Architecture and Disjunction* and *Event-Cities 2*; and Paul Virilio, *The Lost Dimension*.

[7] Quotes are from Caroline Glick, 'Halutz's Stalinist moment: Why were Dovik Tamari and Shimon Naveh Fired?,' *Jerusalem Post*, 17 June 2006.

[8] 'U.S. Marines uses Israeli Tactics in Falluja Baghdad', *Middle East Newsline*, 6 (418), 10 November 2004; Justin Huggler, 'Israelis trained US troops in Jenin-style urban warfare,' *The Independent*, 29 March 2003; Yagil Henkin, 'The Best Way Into Baghdad', *New York Times*, 3 April 2003.

[9] Interviews with Shimon Naveh were conducted on 15 September 2005 (telephone), 7 March 2006 (telephone), 11 April 2006 and 22–23 May 2006 (at an intelligence military base in Glilot, near Tel Aviv). All transcripts and translations into English of the interviews were sent to Naveh for confirmation of content. All future references to the interview refer to those above unless stated otherwise.

[10] Non-linear and network terminology has had its origins in military discourse since the end of World War II and has been instrumental in the conception in 1982 of the US military doctrine of 'Airland Battle', which emphasized inter-service cooperation and the targeting of the enemy at its systematic bottle necks – bridges, headquarters and supply lines – in attempts to throw it off balance. It was conceived to check the Soviet invasion of Central Europe and was first applied in the Gulf War of 1991. The advance of this strand led to the 'Network Centric Doctrine' in the context of the Revolution in Military Affairs (RMA) after the end of the Cold War.

[11] John Arquilla and David Ronfeldt (eds), *Networks and Netwars: The Future of Terror, Crime, and Militancy*, Santa Monica, CA: RAND, 2001, p. 15; see also David Ronfeldt, John Arquilla, Graham Fuller and Melissa Fuller, *The Zapatista 'Social Netwar' in Mexico*, Santa Monica, CA: RAND, 1998. In the latter book the authors explain that swarming was historically employed in the warfare of nomadic tribes and is currently undertaken by different organizations across the spectrum of social-political conflict – terrorists and guerrilla organizations, mafia criminals as well as non-violent social activists.

[12] Eric Bonabeau, Marco Dorigo and Guy Theraulaz, *Swarm Intelligence: From Natural to Artificial Systems*, Oxford: Oxford University Press, 1999; Sean J. A. Edwards, *Swarming on the Battlefield: Past, Present and Future*, Santa Monica, CA: RAND, 2000; Arquilla and Ronfeldt, *Networks and Netwars*.

[13] Friction refers to uncertainties, errors, accidents, technical difficulties, the unforeseen, and their effects on decision, morale and actions. See Peter Paret, 'Clausewitz', in Peter Paret, *Makers of Modern Strategy, From Machiavelli to the Nuclear Age*, Oxford: Oxford University Press, 1986, pp. 197, 202. Clausewitz: 'The tremendous friction, which cannot, as in mechanics, be reduced to a few points, is everywhere in contact with chance, and brings about effects that cannot be measured . . . action in war is like movement in resistant element . . . it is difficult for normal efforts to achieve even moderate results.' See Carl von Clausewitz, *On War*, ed. and trans. Michael Howard and Peter Paret, Princeton, NJ: Princeton University Press, 1976 [1832], pp. 119–21. The tendency for diffusing command in battle was already apparent in Clausewitz's account of the wars of the Napoleonic era. Napoleonic command was based on the assumption that even the best operational plan could never anticipate the vicissitudes of war and that commanders must be encouraged to make tactical decisions on the spot. This was made a central tenet with the nineteenth-century Prussian General Moltke, in his *Auftragstaktik* or 'mission oriented tactics'. Moltke refrained from issuing any but the most essential orders: 'an order shall contain everything that a commander cannot do by himself, but nothing else.' See Hajo Holborn, 'The Prusso-German School: Moltke and the Rise of the General Staff', in Paret, *Makers of Modern Strategy*, pp. 281–95, esp. p. 291. According to Manuel De Landa, this encouragement of local initiative and diffused command is what allows a dynamic battle to self-organize to some extent. 'Manoeuvre warfare', as developed by several military theorists in the period between the two World Wars and practised by the Wehrmacht as well as the Allies in European battles of World War II, is based on principles such as increased autonomy and initiative. Manuel De Landa, *War in the Age of Intelligent Machines*, New York: Zone Books, 1991, pp. 71, 78–9.

[14] See Chapter 2.

[15] 'The Generalship of Ariel Sharon', a round table discussion at the Operational Theory Research Institute (OTRI) of the IDF's Academy of Staff and Command. 24–25 May 2006.

[16] Stephen Graham, 'Constructing Urbicide by Bulldozer in the Occupied Territories', in Stephen Graham (ed.), *Cities, War and Terrorism*, Oxford: Blackwell, 2004, p. 332.

[17] Tacitus, *The Agricola and The Germania*, London: Penguin Classics, 1971.

[18] Raviv Druker and Ofer Shelah, *Boomerang*, Jerusalem: Keter, 2005, pp. 197, 218.

[19] Quoted in Shimon Naveh, 'Between the Striated and the Smooth: Urban Enclaves and Fractal Maneuvers', *Cabinet Magazine*, July 2006, pp. 81–8.

[20] At least 80 Palestinians were killed in Nablus between 29 March and 22 April 2002. Four Israeli soldiers were killed; see www.amnesty.org.

[21] Amnesty International, *Shielded from Scrutiny: IDF Violations in Jenin and Nablus*, 4 November 2002; B'tselem, *Operation Defensive Shield: Soldiers' Testimonies, Palestinian Testimonies*, September 2002.

[22] Adania Shibli, 'Faint Hints of Tranquility', Anton Shammas (trans), *Al-Adaab Magazine*, May–June 2002.

[23] Sune Segal, 'What Lies Beneath: Excerpts from an Invasion', *Palestine Monitor*, November 2002; www.palestinemonitor.org.

[24] Eyal Weizman interview with Gil Fishbein, Tel Aviv, 4 September 2002.

[25] Ofer Segal-Az K'ariel, *Fighting in Jenin 2002*, Tel Aviv: Ma'arachot Publications, Ministry of Defence, 2006, p. 45 [Hebrew].

[26] Quoted in Henkin, 'The Best Way Into Baghdad'.

[27] In the survey, Nurhan Abujidi found that 19.6 per cent of buildings affected by forced routes had only one opening, 16.5 per cent had two, 10 per cent had three, 4.1 per cent had four, 2.1 per cent had five and 1.0 per cent had eight. See Nurhan Abujidi, 'Forced To Forget: Cultural Identity and Collective Memory/Urbicide. The Case of the Palestinian Territories, During Israeli Invasions to Nablus Historic Center 2002–2005', paper presented to the workshop 'Urbicide: The Killing of Cities?', Durham University, November 2005.

[28] In an interview for the popular Israeli daily *Ma'ariv* at the beginning of 2003, Kochavi mused about the biblical beauty of the city visible from the windows of his headquarters: 'Look! Nablus is the prettiest City in the West Bank . . . especially pretty is the Kasbah that resembles the old city of Jerusalem, sometimes even prettier than it.' Following a long colonial, and certainly an Israeli tradition of military officers displaying curiosity about the culture of the colonized, Kochavi consulted Dr Itzik Magen, the IDF's Civil Administration Chief of Archaeology, before the attack, regarding the historical value of some of the buildings that happened to stand in his planned zone of manoeuvre. While acknowledging a certain list of 'must not destroy' (which he did not always adhere to), 'simple' homes were accepted as 'legitimate targets'. Amir Rapaport, 'City Without a

Break', *Ma'ariv* Saturday supplement 10 January 2003; Eyal Weizman and Mira Asseo, in interview with Itzik Magen, 21 June 2002.

29 Amir Oren, 'The Big Fire Ahead', *Ha'aretz*, 25 March 2004.
30 Druker and Shelah, *Boomerang*, p. 213.
31 Both quotes above are from ibid., pp. 213–14, 220.
32 Killing operations conducted by 'Arabized' (soldiers disguised as Arabs) or uniformed soldiers now take place almost daily in the West Bank. The most common legal basis for killings during these raids is that the victim 'violently attempted to resist arrest' (no such option even exists when killings are conducted remotely from the air). According to figures released by B'Tselem, between the beginning of 2004 and May 2006 alone Israeli security forces killed 157 persons during attacks referred to as 'arrest operations'. See 'Take No Prisoners: The Fatal Shooting of Palestinians by Israeli Security Forces during "Arrest Operations"', B'Tselem, May, 2005. www.btselem.org; Al-Haq (Palestinian human rights organization), 'Indiscriminate and Excessive Use of Force: Four Palestinians Killed During Arrest Raid,' 24 May 2006, www.alhaq.org.
33 Quoted in Sergio Catignani, 'The Strategic Impasse in Low-Intensity-Conflicts: The Gap Between Israeli Counter-Insurgency Strategy and Tactics During the Al-Aqsa Intifada', *Journal of Strategic Studies*, 28, 2005, p. 65.
34 Druker and Shelah, *Boomerang*, p. 218.
35 Aviv Kochavi captured the attention of the media in February 2006 when the Chief Legal Adviser to the IDF recommended that he not make a planned trip to a UK-based military academy for fear he could be prosecuted for war crimes in Britain; for an earlier statement implicating Kochavi in war crimes, see Neve Gordon, 'Aviv Kochavi, How Did You Become a War Criminal?', www.counterpunch.org/nevegordon1.html.
36 Chen Kotes-Bar, 'Bekichuvo' [Starring Him], *Ma'ariv*, 22 April 2005 [Hebrew].
37 Eyal Weizman and Nadav Harel interview with Aviv Kochavi, 24 September 2004, at an Israeli military base near Tel Aviv [Hebrew]; video documentation by Nadav Harel and Zohar Kaniel.
38 Bernard Tschumi, *Architecture and Disjunction*, Cambridge, MA.: MIT Press, 1997. Naveh has recently completed the translation into Hebrew of some of the chapters in Tschumi's book.
39 Terminology mainly from Gilles Deleuze and Félix Guattari, *A Thousand Plateaus, Capitalism and Schizophrenia*, Brian Masumi (trans.) New York and London: Continuum, 2004, and Gilles Deleuze, *Difference and Repetition,* New York: Columbia University Press, 1995, among other works.
40 'Sedentary space is striated by walls, enclosures and roads between enclosures, while nomadic space is smooth, marked only by "traits" that are effaced and displaced with the trajectory.' Gilles Deleuze and Félix Guattari, *A Thousand Plateaus,* p. 420. On the rhizome see Introduction, pp. 3–28, on the war machine see pp. 387–467: on the smooth and the striated see pp. 523–51. Deleuze and Guattari were aware that states or their agents may transform themselves into war machines, and that, similarly, the conception of 'smooth space' may help form tools of domination.
41 Amos Harel and Avi Isacharoff, *The Seventh War,* Tel Aviv: Miskal – Yedioth Aharonoth Books and Chemed Books, 2004, pp. 254–5.
42 Interview with Gil Fishbein.
43 Tsadok Yeheskeli, 'I Made Them a Stadium in the Middle of the Camp' '*Yedioth Aharonoth*' 31 May 2002, access also on: http://gush-shalom.org/archives/kurdi_eng.html.
44 Three hundred and fifty buildings, mostly homes, were destroyed, a further 1,500 were damaged and about 4,000 people left homeless. Twenty-three Israeli soldiers were killed. Amnesty International, *Shielded from Scrutiny: IDF Violations in Jenin and Nablus*, 4 November 2002; and Stephen Graham, 'Constructing Urbicide by Bulldozer'.
45 The following information is largely based on filmed research that Nadav Harel, Anselm Franke and I undertook during the rebuilding of the camp on August 2004.
46 Nadav Harel, Eyal Weizman and Anselm Franke, filmed interview, Jenin, August 2004.
47 A popular committee is a form of political representation that emerged during the first Intifada. It is based on the participatory democracy that developed within the occupied villages, refugee camps and cities under occupation. In most places, political parties from the main factions in the PLO, as well as Hamas and Islamic Jihad, appointed representatives'.
48 Gideon Levy, 'Tank lanes built between new Jenin homes', *Ha'aretz*, 10 May 2004.
49 'We got blamed for doing it this way but we made the roads wider for cars and ambulances – it would be silly not to. We just wanted to make a normal living area . . . we see it from a technical aspect, not in terms of war; the Israelis will come in regardless.' See Justin McGuirk, 'Jenin', *Icon*

Magazine, no. 24, June 2005, http://www.icon-magazine.co.uk/issues/024/jenin_text.htm. Members of the popular committee believed, however, that the decision to widen the roads was undertaken consciously by UNRWA in order to protect the new homes and were related to conditions imposed by an insurance policy.

[50] Moreover, about a hundred families in the camp managed to obtain financial aid from Saddam Hussein, some months before he was overthrown: each family which had lost its home received $25,000, which was generally used to refurbish interiors and add furniture and electrical equipment. Levy, 'Tank Lanes', Harel, Weizman and Franke, filmed interviews.

[51] Quoted in Levy, 'Tank Lanes'. This is not always typical of the position of other refugees who were delighted with their new homes.

[52] Quoted in Hannan Greenberg, 'The Limited Conflict, This is How you Trick Terrorists', *Yedioth Aharonoth*, www.ynet.co.il.

[53] Zuri Dar and Oded Hermoni, 'Israeli Start-Up Develops Technology to See Through Walls', *Ha'aretz*, 1 July 2004; Amir Golan, 'The Components of the Ability to Fight in Urban Areas', *Ma'arachot*, 384, July 2002, p. 97; The American Defense Advanced Research Projects Agency (DARPA) launched the *VisiBuilding* programme to promote the development of sensor technologies to scan structures from a distance and create detailed views of their interiors. Ross Stapleton-Gray, 'Mobile mapping: Looking through Walls for On-site Reconnaissance', *Journal for Net Centric Warfare* C4ISR, 11 September 2006.

[54] Brian Hatton, 'The Problem of our Walls', *The Journal of Architecture*, Volume 4, Spring 1999, p. 71. Krzysztof Wodiczko, *Public Address,* Walker Art Centre, Minneapolis, 1991, published in conjunction with an exhibition held at the Walker Art Center, Minneapolis, 11 Oct. 1992–3 Jan. 1993 and the Contemporary Arts Museum, Houston, May 22–Aug. 22, 1993.

[55] Pamela M. Lee, *Object to Be Destroyed: The Work of Gordon Matta-Clark*, Cambridge, MA: The MIT Press, 2001.

[56] Robin Evans, 'The Rights of Retreat and the Rights of Exclusion: Notes Towards the Definition of the Wall', in *Translations from Drawing to Building and Other Essays*, London: Architectural Association, 1997, esp. p. 38; Brian Hatton, 'The Problem of Our Walls', *Journal of Architecture* 4 (71), Spring 1999, pp. 66–67.

[57] Hannah Arendt, *The Human Condition*, Chicago: University of Chicago Press, 1998, pp. 63–4.

[58] Giorgio Agamben, *Homo Sacer: Sovereign Power and Bare Life*, Stanford, CA: Stanford University Press, 1998, p. 187.

[59] Robert McNamara is of particular interest in this context, because under JFK's administration of the so-called 'best and the brightest', a number of academics and business directors were promoted to executive power. With McNamara as secretary of defence, technocratic management theory became the ubiquitous language for all military matters in the Pentagon during the 1960s. Guided by theoretical 'models', systems analysis, operational research, 'game theory' and numbers-driven management, McNamara's group of 'whizz kids' believed war was a rational business of projected costs, benefits and kill-ratios, and that if only these could be maximized, war could be won. Although the Pentagon under McNamara put much effort into modelling, and then fighting, according to these models, the Vietnamese guerrillas refused to act as 'efficient consumers' in the Pentagon's market economy, or as the 'rational opponents' in the 'game theories' of RAND – indeed, opinion has it that this approach led to the unnecessary prolongation of the Vietnam war. Paul Hendrickson, *The Living and the Dead*, New York, Vintage Books, 1997; Yehouda Shenhav, *Manufacturing Rationality*, Oxford: Oxford University Press, 1999.

[60] 'With the growing integration of industrial society, these categories are losing their critical connotation, and tend to become descriptive, deceptive, or operational terms . . . Confronted with the total character of the achievements of advanced industrial society, critical theory is left without the rationale for transcending this society. The vacuum empties the theoretical structure itself, because the categories of a critical social theory were developed during the period in which the need for refusal and subversion was embodied in the action of effective social forces.' Herbert Marcuse, *One-Dimensional Man, Studies in the Ideology of Advanced Industrial Society*, Boston, MA: Beacon, 1991 [1964].

[61] Alistair Horne, *A Savage War of Peace: Algeria 1954–1962*, New York: Viking, 1978.

[62] Marshal Thomas Bugeaud, *La Guerre des Rues et des Maisons*, Paris: J.-P. Rocher, 1997. The manuscript was written in 1849 at Bugeaud's estate in the Dordogne, after his failure to suppress quickly the events of 1848. He did not manage to find a publisher for the book, but distrib-

uted a small edition among colleagues. In the text, Bugeaud suggested widening Parisian streets and removing corner buildings at strategic crossroads to allow a wider field of vision. These and other suggestions were implemented by Haussmann several years later; see Sharon Rotbard, *White City, Black City*, Tel Aviv: Babel, 2005, p. 181. [Hebrew] See also Thomas Bugeaud, *The War of Streets and Houses*, Chapter 3: 'Offensive Against The Riot' on http://www. cabinemagazine. org/issues/22/ bugeaud.php.

[63] Auguste Blanqui, *Instructions pour une Prise d'Armes,* Paris: Société encyclopédique française, 1972; see www.marxists.org/francais/blanqui/1866/instructions.htm.

[64] Rotbard, *White City, Black City,* p. 178.

[65] Benjamin Runkle, 'Jaffa, 1948, Urban Combat in the Israeli War of Independence', in Col. John Antal and Maj. Bradley Gericke (eds), *City Fights*, New York: Ballantine Books, 2003, p. 297.

[66] On this, see Ryan Bishop, 'The Vertical Order Has Come to an End: The Insignia of the Military C3I and Urbanism in Global Networks', in Ryan Bishop, John Phillips and Wei-Wei Yeo (eds), *Beyond Description: Space Historicity Singapore*, Architext Series, London and New York: Routledge, 2004, pp. 60–78.

[67] Hannan Greenberg, 'The Commander of the Gaza Division: The Palestinians are in shock', *Ynet*, 7 July 2006, www.ynet.co.il.

[68] Ofer Shelah and Yoav Limor, *Captives in Lebanon*, Tel Aviv: Yedioth Aharonoth Books, 2007, p. 197 [Hebrew].

[69] Amir Rapaport, 'Dan Halutz is a Bluff, Interview with Shimon Naveh', *Ma'ariv*, Yom Kippur Supplement, 1 October 2006.

[70] 'Networks are generally nested in hierarchies, nomads stick to riding camels and raiding, and war machines run on coal and petrol'. Paul Hirst, *Space and Power: Politics, War and Architecture*, London: Polity, 2005, p. 4.

[71] Naveh explained it with a metaphor from the world of Jewish theology: it is an 'institutional conflict between Hassidim and Mitnagdim . . .' Mitnagdim, Hebrew for 'opponents', is a term used to refer to Ashkenazi Orthodox Jews who opposed, from the late eighteenth century, the new religious practices of Hassidic Judaism. The term is commonly used to refer to inner institutional conflicts within a Jewish context between innovators and conservatives.

[72] The state comptroller requested explanations for the fact that Naveh also worked part time at Tel Aviv University, and for the high pay that researchers received for extra hours. An investigation by the deputy commander of human resources at the IDF later cleared OTRI of such suspicions, but the General Staff leaked information about the investigation to the press. See Caroline Glick, 'Halutz's Stalinist moment: Why were Dovik Tamari and Shimon Naveh Fired?', *Jerusalem Post*, 17 June 2006 and Rapaport, 'Dan Halutz is a Bluff'. Currently Naveh is employed by US Marine Corps Development Command as senior mentor (sage) for their operational experiment 'Expeditionary Warrior'.

[73] Yaakov Amidror, 'There is no Remote Control Wars,' *Ha'aretz*, 4 July 2006.

[74] Yaakov Amidror, 'Catastophe to Military Thought', Makor Rishon, www.makorrishon.co.il; http://www.makorrishon.co.il/show.asp?id=13186.

[75] Rapaport, 'Dan Halutz is a Bluff'.

[76] In a press conference on the Hebron Accord, former Prime Minister Benjamin Netanyahu was quoted as saying 'Hot pursuit is a sub-issue. It's a specific instance of a generic issue, and the generic issue is the freedom of action of Israel to protect its citizens wherever they are. And against whatever threats emanate from anywhere.' Ministry of Foreign Affairs, www.mfa.gov.il.

Chapter 8 Evacuations: Decolonizing Architecture

[1] The information on which this chapter is based has been gathered mostly first hand in the process of my involvement with planners from the Palestinian Ministry of Planning in preparation for the evacuation, and in debates and plans regarding possible reuse of the settlements in case they were left intact by Israeli forces. I was invited by the ministry to take part in this project and did so during several meetings from April to August 2005, when it became clear that the settlements were to be destroyed. Some of the conversation and the quotes are taken

from other meetings, including a round table discussion at Shaml, the Palestinian Diaspora and Refugee Centre, on 6 November 2004.

[2] Esther Zandbreg, 'A pile of garbage with a view to Gaza's beach', *Ha'aretz*, 1 September 2005.

[3] Ibid.

[4] Natan Gutman and Shlomo Shamir, 'Rice: there is no place for the wholesale destruction of settlers' homes in the Gaza Strip during evacuation', *Ha'aretz*, 7 April 2005; Erica Silverman, 'Getting closer, Settlers gone, Gazans look forward to the Withdrawal of Israeli military forces', Al-Ahram, 1–7 September 2005.

[5] Yuval Yoaz and Aluf Ben, 'Sharon: Ideally I would have left the homes standing', *Ha'aretz*, 3 May 2005.

[6] 'Arab Billionaire Offers to Buy Evacuated Gaza Settlements', *Ha'aretz*, 18 February 2005.

[7] Quoted in Greg Myre, 'Homes of Israeli Settlers Pose a New Set of Anxieties', *The New York Times*, 23 January 2005.

[8] Ibid.

[9] Anthony Vidler, *The Architectural Uncanny*, Cambridge, MA: MIT Press, pp. 3–62.

[10] Myre, 'Homes'.

[11] A draft text attached to the planning document that I was showed read 'The colony blocs on the sand dune areas in the north and south shall not be used for urban development and must be cleared of all colony elements . . . these are the finest landscapes; areas of rare and exceptional landscape and nature values.'

[12] Abbas signed a government decree that the land reverts to the Palestinian government, but the decision met resistance. Some Palestinian landowners demonstrated that they owned some of the land prior to the construction of the settlements; some of them have secured the backing of local militia gangs to enforce their claim. Before elected to the government Hamas claimed a portion of the land as recompense for having chased the Israelis out of Gaza.

[13] Aluf Ben, 'Pullout Still Poses Rubble Trouble', *Ha'aretz* 13 July 2005.

[14] The Foundation for Middle East Peace, 'Settlement Database and Suitability Assessment', http://www.fmep.org/settlement_info/settlement_database.html or http://asp.fmep.org/app/settlement/ShowSettlementTablePage.aspx; Palestinian Ministry of Planning, 'Regional Plan of the Southern Governorates 2005– 2015', http://withdraw.sis.gov.ps/english/RP.html.

[15] This in itself could explain why there are 12,000 people registered as residents in refugee camps such as Daheisha in the West Bank, but only 8,000 actually living there.

[16] See this discussion in the specific context of the reconstruction of the Jenin refugee camp in Chapter 7, pp. 204–5.

[17] Marxist revolutionaries of the nineteenth century were the first to employ this strategy. They believed that the pace of change could be accelerated by acts of indiscriminate violence designed to provoke the ruling power to throw off the mask of legality and reveal itself to the peasants and workers in all its brutality. The 'politique du pire' was also apparent throughout the process of decolonization and revolution from Vietnam to Algeria and South America, where guerrillas often prevented living conditions to improve and sometimes even destroyed the structures and services on which the population depends. This was rather successful in politicizing the population who blamed the ruling power whose duty it is to provide those structures and services. See Michael Ignatieff, *The Lesser Evil*, Princeton, NJ: Princeton University Press, 2004, pp. 61, 67–8, 102.

[18] Norma Masriyeh Hazboun, 'Israeli Resettlement Schemes for Palestinian Refugees in the West Bank and Gaza Strip since 1967', Shaml, the Palestinian Diaspora and Refugee Centre, http://www.shaml.org/publications/monos/mono4.htm#Introduction. See official UNRWA figures on the issue of rehousing refugees in: *UNRWA 1950–1990, Serving Palestine Refugees*, Vienna: UNRWA, Public Information Office, 1990. Also United Nations, *Annual Report of the Commissioner General of the UNRWA*, Official Records of the dates: 1 July 1973–30 June 1974; 1 July 1975–30 June 1976; 1 July 1980– 30 June 1981; 1 July 1982–30 June 1983; 1 July 1985–30 June 1986; and Israel's Ministry of Defence, *Judea- Samaria and the Gaza District: A Sixteen-Year Survey (1967–1983)*, Jerusalem: Ministry of Defence Publishing, 1983.

[19] Knesset Minutes, 4–6 December 1967 [Hebrew].

[20] See Chapter 2, pp. 58–9.

[21] Joseph Weitz, *My Diary and Letters to the Children*, Ramat Gan: Masadah Press, 1973, p. 292 [Hebrew]; Rana'an Weitz, *An Overview of the History of the Settlement in Israel*, Jerusalem, 2003, pp. 95–8 [Hebrew]; Yigal Allon, *In Search of Peace*, Tel Aviv: Hakibutz Hameuhad, 1989, p. 16 [Hebrew].

[22] Yemima Rosenthal (ed.), 'Levy Eshkol, the third Israeli Prime Minister, Jerusalem: State Archive, the series for the commemoration of Israel's presidents and Prime Ministers', Jerusalem, 2002, p. 582.

23 See Chapter 2 pp. 68–70.

24 Sharon, *Warrior*, p. 259.

25 Quoted in Hazboun, 'Resettlement Schemes'.

26 Sharon, *Warrior,* p. 258–60.

27 Quoted in Hazboun, 'Resettlement Schemes'.

28 In 1977 when Likud came to power the size of plots was reduced to 125 square metres. The reduction was argued as a response to a shortage of suitable land, but must also be understood against the background of the increased demand for land for the expansion of Jewish settlements in the Gaza Strip.

29 The policy was boosted again in 1976, during Rabin's government, when then Minister of Defence Shimon Peres attempted to solicit international sponsorship for building homes for Gaza refugees. Understanding the political sensitivity of overt funding for this purpose, he set up the clandestine 'Trust Fund for the Economic Development and Rehabilitation of Refugees', which operated with funds received from private donors abroad, and continued to provide plots for refugees. Hazboun, 'Resettlement Schemes'.

30 The housing projects established for refugees in Gaza: the Canada project, 1972 – 891 families (5,370 people) in 488 houses; the Shuqairi project in Khan Younis, 1973 – 135 families (848 people) in 128 houses; the Brazilian project in Khan Younis, 1973 – 436 families (2,820 people) in 422 houses; the Sheikh Radwan project in Gaza City, 1974 – 790 families (5,029 people) in 809 houses; al-Amal project in Khan Younis, 1979 – 802 families (4,853 people) in 842 houses. Sites where plots of lands and financial assistance were provided included: Nasr site in Gaza town, 1974 – 36 houses were constructed on 36 plots of land, with 36 families (186 people); the Sheikh Radwan project, July 1976, where 1,000 plots of land were allocated, accommodating 1,186 families (7,190 people); Beit Lahia project in Jebalia, October 1977 – 472 houses constructed, with 832 families (5,280 people); Tal al-Sultan project in Rafah, April 1978 – 943 houses, 1,041 families (6,399 people); Al-Amal project in Khan Younis, July 1979 – 184 houses, 343 families (2,084 people); Rafah Brazilian project, July 1979 – 109 houses, 161 families (1,038 people); Nazleh site in Gaza town, April 1981 – 168 houses, 163 families (1,195 people). These figures are from UNRWA, Accommodation Office, Gaza, June 1989, 1991, quoted in Hazboun, 'Resettlement Schemes'.

31 According to Hazboun, 95.6 per cent of relocated refugees in the Sheikh Radwan resettlement scheme, believe that their conception of and contribution to the national struggle is as strong now as it was prior to relocation. See Hazboun, 'Resettlement Schemes'.

32 Frantz Fanon, *The Wretched of the Earth*, London: Penguin, 2003, p. 27.

33 One such, Al-Muqata in Ramallah, was originally constructed by the British as a police headquarters, then used as a base and prison by the Jordanian Army between 1948 and 1967, and in the same capacity by the IDF after 1967. In 1993 it became Arafat's compound-headquarters until its almost complete destruction by the Israeli military in spring 2002.

34 Sharon, *Warrior.* p. 400.

35 Daily press briefing by The Offices of the UN, Spokesman for the Secretary-General and the Spokesperson for the General Assembly President, http://www.un.org/News/briefings/docs/2005/db051222.doc.htm; Aluf Benn, 'Debris from Gaza homes razed in pullout may be sent to Sinai', *Ha'aretz*, 14 July 2005.

Chapter 9 Targeted Assassinations: The Airborne Occupation

1 These attacks have been referred to as: 'targeted killing', 'assassinations', 'targeted assassinations', 'liquidations', 'extra-judicial executions' and 'focused prevention'. The choice of terminology has implications to those arguing for or against the legality of the act. I have chosen to use the term 'targeted assassination' as it combines an operational logic with the designation of an illegal act.

2 Yedidia Ya'ari and Haim Assa, *Diffused Warfare: War in the 21ˢᵗ Century*, Tel Aviv: Miskal–Yediot Aharonot Books and Chemed Books, 2005 [Hebrew], pp. 9–13. The book summarizes the positions developed within the 'Alternative Team' and under the influence of OTRI. Yedidia Ya'ari, the former commander of the Israeli Navy, and Haim Asa, a former member of a comparable Air Force think-tank, directed the team. Affiliated to it were Air Force pilot Dror Ben David, Brig. General Gadi Eisenkott and Brig. General Aviv Kochavi. General Benni Gantz was assigned to implement this study within the IDF. The 'Alternative Team' was operating in cooperation with

the US 'Transformation' group under US Secretary of Defense Donald Rumsfeld. In 2006 Chief of Staff Dan Halutz dismantled the 'Alternative Team'. There was also a large number of parallel and smaller teams with similar aims, for example the Military Research Centre for the Study of the Tactical Environment directed by Gabrial Siboni. On the latter, see Gabrial Siboni, 'The Importance of Activity', *Bamahane* [In the Camp: IDF's official journal], 31 December 2004, pp. 14–18 [Hebrew].

3 The last of the terms was coined in a joint programme between former fighter squadron commander Dror Ben David and researchers at OTRI. See Chapter 7, p. 217.

4 Halutz constantly defended the technology behind his airborne assassinations, even when it regularly took the lives of many bystanders. When asked for his reaction to the death of many civilians in an operation of targeted assassination, he famously retorted, 'if you want to know what I feel when I release a bomb, I will tell you: I feel a light bump to the plane as a result of the bomb's release. A second later it's gone, and that's all. That is what I feel.' See Vered Levy-Barzilai, 'Halutz: the high and the mighty', *Ha'aretz*, 21 August 2002.

5 Israel Harel, 'The IDF protects itself', *Ha'aretz*, 29 August 2006. On another occasion, while he was still chief of the Air Force, Halutz reportedly mentioned 'Why do you need to endanger infantry soldiers . . . I can resolve the entire Lebanon [situation] from the air in 3 to 5 days a week maximum.' See Amir Rapaport, 'Dan Halutz is a bluff, interview with Shimon Naveh', *Ma'ariv*, Yom Kippur Supplement, 1 October 2006.

6 Interview with Ephraim Segoli, Tel Aviv, 22 May 2006.

7 These assassinations have been undertaken either for revenge (as in the assassinations of those involved in the Munich Olympic massacre), in attempt to prevent attacks (such as the killing in 1996 of the main Palestinian bomb maker, Yehiya Ayash, in Gaza) or to 'decapitate' enemy organizations. Khalil Al-Wazir (or Abu-Jihad) PLO deputy-commander was killed in for this reason in Tunis in 1988; Hezbollah Secretary General Sheikh Abbas Mussawi was killed by an Israeli aerial attack in 1992, the head of the Islamic Jihad, Fathi Shakaki, was killed by Mossad agents in Malta in 1995. Yassir Arafat has reportedly escaped more than half a dozen assassination attempts.

8 B'Tselem: '683 people killed in the conflict in 2006', 28 December 2006, http://www.btselem.org/english/Press_Releases/20061228.asp.

9 Sven Linqvist, *A History of Bombing*, Linda Haverty Rugg (trans.), New York: The New Press, 2000, entry 101.

10 Philip Anthony Towle, *Pilots and Rebels: The Use of Aircraft in Unconventional Warfare, 1918–1988*, London: Brassey's, Defence Publishers, 1989, p. 17; David Willard Parsons, 'British air control: a model for the application of air power in low-intensity conflict?', *Airpower Journal*, Summer 1994, on http://www.airpower.maxwell.af.mil/airchronicles/apj/apj94/parsons.html.

11 Quoted in Lt. Colonel David J. Dean, USAF, 'Air power in small wars: the British air control experience', *Air University Review*, 34 (5), July–August 1985.

12 Ibid.; David Omissi, *Air Power and Colonial Control: The Royal Air Force 1919–1939*, Manchester: Manchester University Press, 1990; David MacIsaac, 'Voices from the Central Blue, the Air Power Theorists', in Peter Paret (ed.), *Makers of Modern Strategy, From Machiavelli to the Nuclear Age*, Oxford: Oxford University Press, 1986, pp. 624–47, especially p. 633.

13 Linqvist, *A History of Bombing*, entry 102.

14 Darryl Li, 'Gaza Consultancy – Research Findings, 20 to 27 August 2006' [draft submitted to B'Tselem], 10 September 2006. Testimony number 3287. Unpublished.

15 Orna Ben-Naftali and Keren Michaeli, '"We must not make a scarecrow of the Law": a legal analysis of the Israeli policy of targeted killings', *Cornell International Law Journal*, Spring 2003, p. 234, footnote 22.

16 The quote is from Segoli in an interview. In November 2002 a car travelling in a remote part of Yemen was destroyed by a missile fired from an unmanned Predator drone, killing six suspected members of al-Qaeda. While the US administration did not publicly acknowledge responsibility for the attack, officials let it be known that the CIA had carried it out. The killing of Abu Musab al-Zarqawi in June 2006 and the attempt to kill Ayman al-Zawahiri in January 2006 were undertaken from the air. Previous strikes killed Mohammed Atef, al-Qaeda's military chief, and Hamza Rabia, a senior operative in Pakistan. Currently, the US military plans to double the number of Predator and Global Hawk drones used for surveillance and targeting. See Anthony Dworkin, 'The Yemen Strike: the war on terrorism goes global', Crimes of War Project, 14 November 2002, available at http://www.crimesofwar.org/onnews/news-yemen.html; Chris Downes, '"Targeted killing" in an age of terror: the legality of the Yemen Strike', *Journal of Conflict and Security Law*, 9 (2), 2004, pp. 277–9.

[17] Segoli in interview.

[18] Aharon Yoffe, 'Focus preemption, chances and dangers', *Nativ*, 109 (2), March 2006 [Hebrew]. See also Ya'ari and Assa, *Diffused Warfare*, p. 37.

[19] Interview with an Israeli Air Force pilot, 10 April 2006.

[20] David A. Fulghum and Robert Wall, 'Israel starts reexamining military missions and technology', *Aviation Week*, 20 August 2006.

[21] Interview with former member of Unit 504, May 2006.

[22] Ariel Meyerstein, 'Case Study: The Israeli strike against Hamas leader Salah Shehadeh', Crimes of War Project, http://www.crimesofwar.org/onnews/news-shehadeh.html 19 September 2002.

[23] Ludwig von Bertalanffy defines a system as a complex of interacting elements. Thus a system's problems, according to Bertalanffy, are problems of the interrelations of great numbers of variables, which occur in the fields of politics, economics, industry, commerce and military conduct. See Ludwig von Bertalanffy, *General System Theory: Foundations, Development, Applications*, New York: George Braziller, 1976.

[24] This logic was reflected in a presentation to US security personnel at the Washington DC Brookings Institute in March 2006 by Avi Dichter, the former chief of Israel's General Security Service (GSS). Dichter, the driving force behind the tactical success and frequent application of targeted assassinations, observed that 'by eliminating . . . generators of terror through arrests (the preferred method) or by targeted killings (if absolutely necessary), a state can greatly disrupt the operations of terrorist organizations'. See Avi Dichter and Daniel Byman, *Israel's Lessons for Fighting Terrorists and Their Implications for the United States* (Analysis Paper Number 8), March 2006, Saban Centre for Middle East Policy at the Brookings Institute, Washington, DC.

[25] Interviews with Shimon Naveh were conducted on 15 September 2005 (telephone), 7 March 2006 (telephone), 11 April 2006 and 22–23 May 2006 (at an Intelligence military base in Glilot, near Tel Aviv). All interview transcripts and translations into English were sent to Naveh for confirmation of content. All future references to the interview refer to those above unless otherwise indicated.

[26] B'Tselem, 'IDF helicopter missile-fire kills four Palestinian civilians and wounds dozens', August 2002, http://www.btselem.org/English/Testimonies/20020831_Tubas_Killing_Witness_Aref_Daraghmeh.asp.

[27] Neve Gordon, 'Rationalizing extra-judicial executions: the Israeli press and the legitimization of abuse', *International Journal of Human Rights*, 8 (3), Autumn 2004, p. 305. In 2005, *Ha'aretz*, Israel's liberal daily newspaper, began publishing the names of Palestinians killed as a matter of policy.

[28] Indeed, during the 1991 Gulf War, the public was fed images of 'kamikaze bombs' as proof of the technological superiority and surgical skills of the US military. Harun Farocki, 'War from a distance', lecture delivered at the Academy of Fine Arts, Vienna, 13 January 2005.

[29] *Ma'ariv* Gallup poll of 10 August 2001 revealed that 76 per cent of the public polled supported assassinations. In later years, and in particular as a result of the killing of many bystanders, public support had dropped considerably. In June 2003, at the start of the campaign to assassinate the leaders of Hamas, an opinion poll carried out by the daily newspaper *Yedioth Ahronoth* found that 58 per cent of Israelis polled said the military should at least temporarily discontinue targeted killings. See Raviv Druker and Ofer Shelah, *Boomerang*, Jerusalem: Keter Press, 2005, p. 216.

[30] This argument was introduced after Siham Thabet, the wife of the assassinated secretary of the Fatah Movement in Tulkarm, Thabet Thabet, filed in January 2001 the first of several petitions to the HCJ, asking the court to outlaw the use of extra-judicial executions. Thabet Thabet was killed by Israeli snipers on the last day of 2000. See Ben-Naftali and Michaeli, '"We must not make a scarecrow of the law"'.

[31] David Kretzmer, 'Targeted killing of suspected terrorists: extra-judicial executions or legitimate means of defense?', *The European Journal of International Law*, 16 (2), 2005, pp. 196, 207.

[32] Press briefing by Colonel Daniel Reisner, director of the International Law Department of the IDF Legal Division, Israeli Ministry of Foreign Affairs, www.mfa.gov.il, 15 November 2000.

[33] The Israeli legal scholar, Eyal Benvenisti, claimed that the proper measure to judge whether Israel continues to be bound by the obligations of an occupying power are facts on the ground: 'If there were areas under Palestinian control, they were not subject to Israeli occupation.' Eyal Benvenisti, 'Israel and the Palestinians: what laws were broken', Crimes of War Project http:// www.crimesofwar.org/expert/me-intro.html. Charles Shamas, a Ramallah-based legal expert, claims that since Israel still exercises effective control over movement between localities, over supply of goods and over access to natural resources, it has in effect authority over the enactment of Palestinian legislation, and therefore continues to be bound by the duties of an occupying power.

34 Indeed, since the evacuation of Gaza, the IDF has become even more willing to employ violence against the Palestinians. In 2006 alone, Israeli forces killed 405 Palestinians in Gaza, half of them civilians, including 88 minors. B'Tselem, '683 people killed in the conflict in 2006'. In June 2006, Israel bombed the electric grid in Gaza, cutting off the electricity supply to 700,000 people. During 2006, Israel killed 22 Palestinians in targeted assassinations.

35 See Chapter 2, pp. 63–4.

36 Druker and Shelah, *Boomerang*, p. 161.

37 'The IDF published a list of seven "assassination candidates"', *Ha'aretz*, 6 July 2001.

38 In his article 'Necropolitics', Achilles Mbembe follows Michel Foucault and argues that the sovereignty of political power is not only located within the institutions of the geographically defined nation state, nor as post-modern thinkers suggest, within the operational networks of supranational institutions, but in the capacity of power to make decisions regarding life and death (even if this may take place outside the traditional boundaries of the state's jurisdiction). According to Michel Foucault, the other side of politics that engages with the management of life (bio-politics) is the administration of death (thanato-politics). Michel Foucault, *Society Must Be Defended: Lectures at the Collège de France, 1975–1976*, New York: Picador, 2003, p. 25; Achille Mbembe, 'Necropolitics', *Public Culture*, 15 (1), Winter 2003, pp. 11–40.

39 In this context IDF operational planners draw on the principles of game theory – a branch of applied mathematics conceived to provide the tools to model environments in which various rational players interact. Game theory was developed after World War II as a strategic logic by Thomas Schelling and others at the US Air Force think-tank RAND Corporation in order to evaluate alternative nuclear strategies, and was later used to 'manage' the Vietnam War. John von Neumann and Oskar Morgenstern, *Theory of Games and Economic Behavior* (commemorative edn), Princeton, NJ: Princeton University Press, 2004 [1944]; Thomas Schelling, *The Strategy of Conflict*, Cambridge, MA: Harvard University Press, 2006 [1960]. In the context of the low-intensity environment, 'game theory' is sometimes used for modelling the behaviour of guerrilla and terror organizations, of the governments that support them, as well as of the international community. Its influence on Israeli military strategy stems from the fact that, since the 1960s, the mathematics faculty at Jerusalem's Hebrew University has become one of game theory's leading centres worldwide. Robert Aumann was awarded the 2005 Nobel Prize in Economic Sciences together with Thomas Schelling for his contribution to 'game theory'.

40 Quoted in Amos Harel and Arnon Regular, 'IAF probe: civilians spotted too late to divert missiles in Gaza strike', *Ha'aretz*, 7 March 2006. See also Soha Abdelaty, 'Intifada timeline', *Al-Ahram*, 30 September–6 October, 2004, http://weekly.ahram.org.eg/2004/710/fo5.htm; Vincent Cannistraro, 'Assassination is wrong – and dumb', *The Washington Post*, 30 August 2001.

41 Ya'ari and Assa, *Diffused Warfare*, p. 147. According to a statement by then Chief of Staff Ya'alon in June 2003, targeted assassinations have replaced politics altogether. 'Liquidations', he claimed 'gave the political levels a tool to create a change of direction.' Druker and Shelah, *Boomerang*, p. 162 and note 96.

42 For many years, Yassir Arafat remained at the top of Israel's most wanted list. The *dibbuk* haunting Israeli security services, Arafat's 'irrational character' was blamed for almost every political stalemate or outbreak of violence. Chief of Military Intelligence Amos Gilead, who developed a personal obsession with him, described Arafat as 'in the best psychological condition in a state of conflict, flames, suffering and blood'. Only an explicit promise extracted from Sharon by Bush prevented the IDF from doing what it really wanted to do. Gil Eyal, *The Disenchantment of the Orient: Expertise in Arab Affairs and the Israeli State*, Palo Alto, CA: Stanford University Press, 2006, p. 189.

43 Ibid., p. 183.

44 A few examples: the assassination on 31 July 2001 in Nablus led to the Hamas suicide bombing on 9 August in a Jerusalem pizzeria. The suicide bombing on 4 August was in response to the Israeli assassination of Salah Shehada on 23 July 2002. On 10 June 2003, Israel's attempted assassination of the senior Hamas political leader in Gaza, Abd al-Aziz Rantissi, which wounded him and killed four Palestinian civilians, led to the bus bombing in Jerusalem on 11 June that killed sixteen Israelis.

45 B'Tselem, 'Palestinians killed by the Israeli security forces during the course of an assassination'; http://www.btselem.org/English/Statistics/Palestinians_killed_during_the_course_of_an_assasination.asp.

46 Eight people were killed in July 2005 in assassinations, six of them the intended targets. In the ten months prior to the evacuation of the Gaza Strip in August 2005, Israeli forces killed 563

Palestinians there, while during the previous ten-month period, 264 were killed. B'Tselem: 'Palestinians killed by the Israeli security forces during the course of an assasination'.

47 Ibid.

48 Amos Harel and Arnon Regular, 'IAF probe: Civilians spotted too late to divert missiles in Gaza strike', *Ha'aretz*, 7 March 2006.

49 Harel, 'Nothing "surgical"'. B'Tselem figures are on http://www.btselem.org/English/Statistics/Casualties.asp.

50 Chris McGreal, 'We're Air Force pilots, not mafia. We don't take revenge', *Guardian*, 3 December 2003.

51 Interview with an Israeli Air Force operator of unmanned drones, April 2005.

52 Quoted in: Meron Rapoport, 'Italian TV: Israel used new weapon prototype in Gaza Strip', *Ha'aretz*, 12 October 2006. All signs led an independent Italian investigative team to believe that this munitions were 'Dense Inert Metal Explosives' or DIME. These comprise a carbon-fibre casing filled with tungsten powder – a metal capable of conducting very high temperatures. Upon detonation, the tungsten particles are propelled outward in a relatively small (about 4 metres) but very deadly cloud, causing severe burns, loss of limbs and internal burns. Air Force Research Laboratory, 2005 Accomplishment, http://www.afrl.af.mil/accomprpt/may05/accompmay05.asp.

53 HCJ 769/02. *The Public Committee against Torture in Israel* v. *The Government of Israel*. Previous petitions to the High Court of Justice against targeted assassinations (for example HCJ 5872/2002, *M.K. Muhammed Barake* v. *Prime Minister and Minister of Defence*) were dismissed.

54 'Evil' in this context is best understood, following Adi Ophir, as a category displaced from the realm of the divine or diabolical, and relocated in a social order in which suffering and pain could have been, but was not, prevented. See Adi Ophir, *The Order of Evils: Toward an Ontology of Morals*, Rela Mazali and Havi Care (trans.), New York: Zone Books, 2005, chapter 7.100: 'Evils can only be justified by appealing to more grave hypothetical evils that could have been caused if the prevention or disengagement actions would have taken place (3.432). The justification displaces the discussion from one order of exchange, in which the one harmed tries to create a link between damage or suffering and compensation, to another order of exchange, in which the defendant tries to create a link between evils that occurred to possible evils that might have occurred'.

55 Michael Ignatieff, *The Lesser Evil: Political Ethics in an Age of Terror*, Princeton, NJ: Princeton University Press, 2004.

56 These conditions include: '[they are] applied to the smallest number of people, used as a last resort, and kept under the adversarial scrutiny of an open democratic system . . .' Furthermore, 'assassination can be justified only if . . . less violent alternatives, like arrest and capture, endanger . . . personnel or civilians . . . [are not possible, and] where all reasonable precautions are taken to minimize collateral damage and civilian harm.' Ignatieff, *The Lesser Evil*, pp. 8, 129–33.

57 Quoted in Amos Harel and Avi Isacharoff, *The Seventh War*, Tel Aviv: Miskal–Yedioth Aharonoth Books and Chemed Books, 2004, p. 343.

58 Ophir, *The Order of Evils*, chapter 7.100.

59 B'Tselem, 'A death foretold: firing of "rubber" bullets to disperse demonstrations in the Occupied Territories', November 1998. http://www.btselem.org/english/publications/summaries/199805_a_death_ foretold.asp.

60 Harel, '"Nothing 'surgical"'.

61 B'tselem: 683 people killed in the conflict in 2006, www.btselem.org, 27 December 2006.

62 At the moment this gap closes between the *possible* and the *actual* application of force, war is no longer a language, violence is stripped of semiotics and simply aims to make the enemy disappear as a subject. 'Total wars' – marking the other limit of the conceptual spectrum, beyond their meaning in the total mobilization of society – are those wars that no longer allow any communication to take place. Colonial wars have often been total wars, because the 'natives' were not perceived to share the same 'humanity' as the colonizers and thus could not be considered a party capable of rational behaviour and discourse. Terror is 'total' as well, because, most often, it places no legal or moral limits to violence, no distinction between innocence and guilt. Moreover, it acts to attack the very possibility of discourse. Degree and distinctions are precisely what makes war less than total.

63 On Israeli militarism see Uri Ben-Eliezer, 'Post-modern armies and the question of peace and war: the Israeli Defense Forces in the "New Times"', *International Journal of Middle East Studies*, 36, 2004, pp. 49–70, at p. 50. See also Ben-Eliezer, *Making of Israeli Militarism*, Bloomington, IN: Indiana University Press, 1998, pp. 1–18; Baruch Kimmerling, *Invention and Decline of Israeliness: Society, Culture*

and the Military, Berkeley, CA: University of California Press, 2001, p. 209. Further on the concept of militarism, see Michael Mann, 'The roots and contradictions of modern militarism', *New Left Review*, I-162, 1987.

64 Halutz quotes are taken from Amir Oren, 'The tenth round', *Ha'aretz* weekend supplement, 14 January 2006; Dayan's quote is from Foundation for Middle East Peace, 'Sharon's Enduring Agenda: Consolidate Territorial Control, Manage the Conflict', *Settlement Report*, 14 (1), January–February 2004, http://www.fmep.org/reports/vol14/no1/01-sharons_enduring_agenda.html.

65 Stephen Graham, 'Vertical geopolitics: Baghdad and after', *Antipode*, 36, pp. 12–23, esp. p. 18; Shaul Shai, 'Subteranean warfare', *Ma'arachot*, 389, May 2003, pp. 36–43 [Hebrew].

66 Although thirteenth-century English common law extended property rights from the depths of the earth to the height of the sky ('Cujus est solum, ejus est usque ad coelum et ad inferos'), air travel over private properties led to a reduction in the vertical limit of land ownership. Paul Fauchille, a French legal scholar, suggested the concept of 'freedom of the skies'. Paul Fauchille, 'Le domaine aérien et le régime juridique des aérostats', *Revue Générale de Droit International Public*, 8, 1901, see http://www.ppl.nl/100years/topics/airandspacelaw/ (12 January 2005). However, the analogy with Hugo Grotius' 'freedom of the seas' was rejected following the 1919 Versailles Peace Conference after World War I had revealed the devastating potential of air power. During World War II, the 1944 Chicago Convention on International Civil Aviation confirmed the sovereignty of states over the airspace above their territories. National sovereign space thereafter incorporated an aerial dimension defined by the vertical extension of state borders in a conic shape (whose converging point is the centre of the earth) capped by the as yet undefined and highly contested legal boundary between national airspace and free outer space. As one frequently cited example demonstrates, this extrusion of sovereignty means that commercial flights are forbidden to serve alcohol when traversing Saudi airspace. See David Pascoe, *Airspaces*, London: Reaktion Books, 2001, p. 9; on sovereignty in airspace see P.P.C. Haanappel, 'The Transformation of Sovereignty in the Air', in Chia-Jui Cheng (ed.), *The Use of Air and Outer Space, Cooperation and Competition*, The Hague: Kluer Law International, 1998, p. 13. In clauses concerning the security of airspace, the first Oslo Accord of 1993 states that 'all aviation activity or usage of airspace . . . shall require the prior approval of Israel'. Gaza-Jericho Agreement Articles [Oslo I], Article XII, Security of the Airspace.

67 Gilead Sher, *Just Beyond Reach, The Israeli-Palestinian Peace Negotiation 1999–2001*, Tel Aviv: Miskal–Yediot Aharonot Books and Chemed Books, 2001, p. 424 [Hebrew]. Overriding control was sought over the electromagnetic spectrum as well. Because the territorialization of the electromagnetic spectrum is not spatial but functional, proposals for 'territorial compromise' were manifesting themselves in the allocation of energies and wavelengths. During the years of the Oslo process, Israel allocated radio frequencies to the Palestinian Authority but these were usually 'leftover frequencies' of poor quality, somewhat mirroring the fragmentation of the terrain. However, unable to use these frequencies efficiently, Palestinian broadcasters routinely trespassed into Israeli ones. That situation promptly inaugurated a new 'war of the airwaves' that saw raiding, temporary occupations and control of 'wave-territories', and with it, the complete breakdown of public (or bilateral) order across the spectrum.

68 According to Avraham Shay: 'it is impossible to divide the airspace [over Israel and Palestine] because it is simply too small considering the speed of objects that pass through it . . . for that reason the airspace over the region has to be functionally united and centrally regulated'. Avraham Shay in interview with Eyal Weizman and Mira Asseo, 21 November 2002.

69 Israeli military use of outer space has been reinforced by the launch, in 2002, of the Ofek-5 earth-observation spy satellite and the further development of three advanced military satellites for intelligence-gathering purposes. See Amnon Barzilai, 'Israel successfully sends Ofek 5 spy satellite into orbit', *Ha'aretz*, 28 May 2002.

70 In accordance with this strategy of aerial domination, the Israeli pullout from Gaza did not include the Air Force's redeployment from its airspace. Before the evacuation, the government declared that, following the evacuation, 'the state of Israel will monitor and supervise the outer envelope of land, will have exclusive control of the Gaza airspace, and will continue its military activity along the Gaza Strip's coastline'. Quoted in: 'Prime Minister Ariel Sharon's four-stage disengagement plan', *Ha'aretz*, 28 May 2004; Arnon Regular, 'PA: Gaza will remain occupied territory', *Ha'aretz*, 10 December 2004.

71 A tunnel could also be sold for several tens of thousands of dollars depending on length and quality. Human Rights Watch, 'Razing Rafah: mass home demolitions in the Gaza Strip', October

2004. After the IDF exposed a number of tunnels in 2004 the price of a single AK47 7.62 mm bullet sky-rocketed to US$7.

[72] According to an IDF spokesperson, similar attacks took place on 29 September 2002, 17 December 2003 and 25 June 2004.

[73] B'Tselem, 'Destruction of houses and property on the Rafah-Egyptian border', http://www.btselem.org/english/Razing/Rafah_Egyptian_Border.asp.

[74] Human Rights Watch, 'Razing Rafah'. Israeli Ministry of Foreign Affairs, 'Weapon smuggling tunnels in Rafah – Operation Rainbow', 17 May 2004.

[75] In order to make tunnels collapse, the IDF employs random high-explosive blasts to destabilize the hollowed-out ground, and at one point even thought of cutting a deep canal along Gaza's borders, and filling it with seawater or raw sewage. This idea was only dropped when geologists warned that it would contaminate the remaining coastal aquifer waters and may prompt international demands that Israel supply more water to Gaza. Conal Urquhart and Ewen MacAskill, 'Two-mile Gaza moat to foil tunnels to Egypt', *Guardian*, 18 June, 2004.

[76] Arel Segal, 'Subteranean Corps', *Ma'arachot*, 389, May 2003, pp. 34–45 [Hebrew].

Postscript

[1] Upon its first showing at MoMa/NYC in 1964, the exhibition 'Architecture without Architects' became one of the most influential references on a generation of architects who were looking to inspire modern architecture. Bernard Rudofsky, *Architecture Without Architects: A Short Introduction to Non-Pedigreed Architecture*, Albuquerque, NM: University of New Mexico Press, 1987 [1964]. The architectural theorist Felicity Scott showed how, by concentrating on the formal dimension of vernacular architecture, Rudofsky displayed a romantic (and sometimes orientalist) attitude that erased more complex processes of politics and history of some of the people whose architecture was celebrated. See Felicity Scott, 'Bernard Rudofsky: allegories of nomadism and dwelling', in Sarah Goldhagen and Réjean Legault (eds), *Anxious Modernisms: Experimentation in Postwar Architectural Culture*, Cambridge, MA: MIT Press and Montreal: Canadian Center for Architecture, 2000, pp. 215–37; Felicity Scott, 'Underneath aesthetics and utility: the untransposable fetish of Bernard Rudofsky,' *Assemblage*, 38 (April) 1999, 58–89; Felicity Scott, 'Revisiting Architecture without Architects', *Harvard Design Magazine*, Fall, 1998, p. 69–72.

[2] Robert Venturi, Denise Scott Brown and Steven Izenour, *Learning from Las Vegas: The Forgotten Symbolism of Architectural Form*, Cambridge, MA: MIT Press, 1977.

[3] http://www.arij.org/back_/back-index.htm.

[4] http://www.bimkom.org/aboutEng.asp.

[5] This issue has been developed in various chapters in this book. In Chapter 3, it has been expressed in the Pyrrhic victory of Palestinians in appealing to the Israeli High Court of Justice against the requisition of their lands. In Chapter 5, it was demonstrated in the apparent complicity between humanitarians and the military in improving the checkpoint system throughout the West Bank (pp. 149–53). In Chapter 7, it has been demonstrated in the logic of the reconstruction of the Jenin Refuge Camp (pp. 201–5).

[6] This is one of the reasons Giorgio Agamben observed that humanitarians 'maintain a secret solidarity with the powers they ought to fight'. For him, both concentrate on the 'human' rather than on the 'political' aspect of being. Agamben further warned that 'there are no humanitarian solutions to humanitarian problems'. See Giorgio Agamben, *Homo Sacer: Sovereign Power and Bare Life*, Stanford, CA: Stanford University Press, 1998, p. 133 (for the quote above).

[7] 'In carrying out humanitarian assistance . . . MSF acts as a witness and will speak out, either in private or in public about the plight of populations in danger for whom MSF works.' See www.msf.org 'About MSF'. There are different modes of humanitarian intervention in the Occupied Palestinian Territories: neutral intervention (International Committee of Red Cross, UNRWA), humanitarian action combining intervention with acting as a witness (MSF, Oxfam), and the new form of popular activism for the protection of the population under occupation (civil missions, the International Solidarity Movement (ISM), Ta'ayush). In the context of its work in Palestinian areas, MSF has surprisingly adopted a stand of neutrality rather than that of being witnesses. See Sari Hanafi and Linda Tabar, 'The Intifada and the aid industry: the

impact of the new liberal agenda on the Palestinian NGOs', *Comparative Studies of South Asia, Africa and the Middle East*, 23 (1–2), 2003, pp. 205–14.

[8] Furthermore, the humanitarian must allow for the possibility that he/she may need to withdraw from participating in a situation when the consequences of complicity with power may become counter-productive. There are no rules by which to define when complicity may turn against the interest of the victims; a degree of complicity with power is almost always inevitable, and must be defined in each situation anew. In any case, as Brauman insisted, it is by 'remaining in a relation of tension to power' that one can limit the danger of political instrumentalization. Rony Brauman, 'From philanthropy to humanitarianism', *South Atlantic Quarterly*, 2/3, Spring 2004, pp. 397–417, especially pp. 399, 406.

[9] The Israeli Committee Against House Demolition (ICAHD) is a non-violent, direct-action group originally established to oppose and resist Israeli demolition of Palestinian houses in the Occupied Territories. ICAHD's activities now comprise several interrelated spheres: resistance and protest actions in the Occupied Territories; rebuilding destroyed Palestinian homes (rebuilding is seen as an act of resistance), efforts to bring the reality of the occupation to Israeli society; and mobilizing the international community for a just peace. See www.icahd.org/eng/.

[10] 'ICAHD aids Palestinians in filing police claims, in dealing with the Israeli authorities, in arranging and subsidizing legal assistance . . . In this way we learn about the internal workings of the Occupation, which we then convey to the broader public . . .' See www.icahd.org/eng/about.asp?menu=2&submenu=1.

[11] The military conceives of some of its own 'practice' as forms of research. Shimon Naveh claimed that since very little 'intelligence' can be produced about guerrilla and terror groups before military operations actually take place (often it is hard, if not impossible, for the military to penetrate these organizations), one of the only ways to gain knowledge regarding its organizational logic is to attack it. The assumption is that attacking the enemy in an unpredictable manner, randomly prodding it, will induce it to surface, reveal itself and assume shape, and when its shape becomes visible, it can be further attacked with more precision. This mode of action is what philosopher Brian Massumi recently defined as *incitatory* operation: militaries consciously contributing to the actual emergence of the threat they are purportedly there to pre-empt. Brian Massumi, *Potential Politics and the Primacy of Preemption* (forthcoming). According to Naveh, 'Raids are a tool of research . . . they provoke the enemy to reveal its organization . . . most relevant intelligence is not gathered as the basis upon which attacks are conducted, but attacks become themselves modes of producing knowledge about the enemy's system.'

[12] On the map we marked the built fabric of the settlements and of the Palestinian communities, the municipal boundaries of the settlements and the extent of Israeli annexed 'state land', which was now incorporated into the settlements' regional councils to serve as reserves for their future development and expansion. A further analysis of the map attempted to resolve the territorial paradox that asked how, with a built fabric of less than 2 per cent of the total land of the West Bank, had settlements managed to achieve such a degree of control and to induce such territorial fragmentation.

[13] For the map see Eyal Weizman and B'Tselem, *West Bank Settlement Map*, Jerusalem: B'Tselem, 2002. Published online at www.btselem.orgwww.btselem.org/Downloads/settlements_map_eng.pdf. For the report see Yehezkel Lein and Eyal Weizman, *Land Grab: Israel's Settlement Policy in the West Bank*, Jerusalem: B'Tselem, 2002. Published online at www.btselem.org.

[14] The research and the map were produced as evidence by the Palestinian legal team at the International Court of Justice in the Hague in its ruling on the Wall in the winter of 2003. Although they gained the status of 'evidence in action' against the government, Lein and I were later alarmed to learn that Israeli Ministry of Defence planners had themselves made use of it for their own purposes.

[15] www.btselem.org/Downloads/separation_barrier_map_eng.pdf. This map is updated every few months.

[16] '. . . [the Palestinians] had no detailed maps of their own at Oslo; nor, unbelievably, were there any individuals on the negotiating team familiar enough with the geography of the Occupied Territories to contest decisions or to provide alternative plans.' The lack of attention given to geography was reflected, according to Said, by the fact that 'none of the many dozens of news reports published or broadcast since the present crisis began has a map been provided to help explain why the conflict has reached such a pitch'. Edward Said, 'Palestinians under Siege', *London Review of Books*, p. 22; www.lrb.co.uk, 24 December 2000.

17 At the beginning of 2005 the Israel Association of Architects decided to react to the continuing debate around *A Civilian Occupation* by dedicating its annual conference to the relation between architecture and politics. They invited Deputy Prime Minister Shimon Peres and the Minister of Education Shimon Shitrit to each inaugurate a day within the two-day conference entitled *Archi-Politics* to which they invited the contributors to the collection. At the end of the conference, the new head of the IAUA, Yitzhak Lir, publicly retracted the banning and apologized for it. The retraction has had a strong effect on the Israeli architectural community, and caused a new set of further debates. The catalogue was published in 2003. See Rafi Segal and Eyal Weizman, *A Civilian Occupation: The Politics of Israeli Architecture,* Tel Aviv and London: Babel Press and Verso Books, 2003.

18 http://roundtable.kein.org/node/146.

19 Eyal Weizman, 'The Politics of Verticality', www.opendemocracy.net 24 March 2002.

20 The London Consortium is an academic collaboration between four institutions: the Architectural Association; Birkbeck, University of London; the Institute of Contemporary Arts; and Tate Galleries.

21 Zvi Efrat was the curator of the exhibition 'The Israeli Project', which opened at the Tel Aviv Museum on October 2000. It was the first critical analysis of the spatiality of Israel's founding years and the state project underpinning it. For the catalogue see Zvi Efrat, *The Israeli Project, Building and Architecture 1948–1973,* Tel Aviv: Tel Aviv Museum, 2005. See also Zvi Efrat, 'The Plan,' in Segal and Weizman (eds), *A Civilian Occupation,* pp. 59–78.

22 Sharon Rotbard has inaugurated the series 'Architectures' at Babel (Tel Aviv), and contributed to it the volume *White City, Black City* – a path-breaking critical investigation of the history of Tel Aviv and Jaffa. The book undoes much of the constructed Zionist mythology of Tel Aviv as a White City built out of the tabula-rasa of its beach sands. Sharon Rotbard, *White City, Black City,* Tel Aviv: Babel Publishers, 2005. See also Sharon Rotbard, 'Wall and Tower: the Mould of Israeli Architecture', in Segal and Weizman (eds), *A Civilian Occupation,* pp. 39–58.

Index

Ramallah, city of 18, 99, 133, 182, 188, 248
Ramon, Minister of Internal Affairs Haim 164
RAND Corporation 14, 190, 305n
Rantissi, Abd al-Aziz 247–8
Red Crescent 204
Red Cross, International Committee for *see* ICRC
refugee camps *see* individual place names
Reisner, Colonel Daniel 245
rendition, extraordinary 144
Revolution in Military Affairs *see* RMA
Rice, Secretary of State Condoleezza 152, 226
RMA 190
Rockefeller Museum 41
Ronel, Ayala 169
Ronfeldt, David 190–192
Rotbard, Sharon 4, 212
Rubenstein, Attorney General Elyakim 277n
Rumsfeld, Donald 215

Sabra, refugee camp of 231
Sadat, President Anwar 61, 75, 90
Sagiv, Tuvia 54
Said, Edward 262
Salah Shehadeh *see* Hamas
Salim, Jamal 247
Saraya al-Quds 190
Sayert Matkal 246
Sebastia, Palestinian village of 88
Security and Foreign Relations Committee *see* Knesset
Segal, Rafi 261, 263, 264
Segoli, Ephraim 238, 241
Separation Wall, West Bank *see* West Bank Wall

settlements *see* individual place names
sewage problems 20–22, 273n
Shakedy, Chief of Israeli Air Force Eliezer 249, 252
Shalev, Arie 89
Shamir, Prime Minister Yitzhak 142
Shanhav, Yehouda 143
Sharm el-Sheikh, Egyptian town 58, 233
Sharon, Prime Mimister Ariel 3, 54, 61–68, 70, 73–74, 78, 80–82, 84, 87, 88, 90–91, 94, 97, 98, 100, 113, 121, 149, 156, 163–168, 177, 178, 179, 192–196, 230–231, 233, 246, 249, 286n
Sharon-Wachman plan 80–82, 281n
Shati, refugee camp of 70, 230
Shatila, refugee camp of 231
Shawer, Mahmoud 248
Shay, Avraham 254
Shazly, Lieutenant-General Sa'ad El 61, 71
Sher, Gilead 55
Shevah, Gershon 221
Shhunot 8
Shibli, Adania 194
Shiloh, settlement of 135
Sinjel, village of 133
Solana, Javier 228
Sosonovsky, Silvina 115
Spiegel, Baruch 149
Storrs, military governor Colonel Ronald 27, 28–30, 33, 43

Taibeh, town of 150
Tal, Israel 62
Tamari, Dov 75, 187, 215
Tanzim al-Fatah 190, 248
Technion Institute of Technology 80
Tel Rumeida, settlement of 275n

Temple Mount *see* Haram al-Sharif
Tirza, Danny 161, 162, 166, 169, 174–175, 181
Town Planning Ordinance (1936) 30
towns *see* individual place names
TRADOC 76
Tschumi, Bernard 200, 210
Tubas, village of 243
Tulkarm, refugee camp of 188
tunnels, on Israeli-Palestinian border 254–258, 307n
Tzufin, settlement of 294n

UNDP 234
Union of Palestinian Medical Relief Committees 147
Unit 63–64, 68, 246, 242
United Nations
  Development Program *see* UNDP
  Office for the Coordination of Humanitarian Affairs *see* OCHA
  Relief and Works Agency *see* UNRWA
  Special Committee on Palestine *see* UNSCOP
UNRWA 204–205, 231, 291, 308n
UNSCOP 14, 271n

Vikton, Justice of Israeli High Court 99–100, 106, 132
villages *see* individual place names

Wachman, Avraham 80, 281n, *see also* Sharon-Wachman plan

Wall *see* West Bank Wall
walls, military techniques for moving through 211–214
War (1948) 18, 31, 60
War of Attrition (1968 to 1970) 60, 68, 72
War, Six Day (1967) 9, 17, 31, 38, 57, 59, 64, 69, 211
War, Yom Kippur (1973) 62, 71–77, 79
Warsaw Pact 76
Weiss, Daniella 88
Weizman, Ezer 17, 90, 105
Weizmann, Chaim 38, 114
Werbert, Gilbert 115
West Bank Wall 7, 13, 20, 153, 161–184, 293n, 294n
Willenbacher, Berthold 205
Wolfensohn, James 228
Wolfowitz, Paul 228
World Bank 14, 291
World Zionist Organization *see* WZO
WZO 114, 124, 125, 126

Ya'alon, Chief of Staff Moshe 216, 238, 246, 251
Yadin, Chief of Staff Yigal 276n
Yamit, town of 233
Yaski, Avraham 46
Yassin, Sheikh 247
Yeshuvim 8

Ze'evi, Rehavam 94
Zevi, Bruno 37
Zureik, Elia 159